New Mentalities of Government in China

China continues to transform apace, flowing from the forces of deregulation, privatization, and globalization unleashed by economic reforms which began in late 1978. The dramatic scope of economic change in China is often counterposed to the apparent lack of political change as demonstrated by continued Chinese Communist Party (CCP) rule. However, the ongoing dominance of the CCP belies the fact that much has also changed in relation to practices of government, including how authorities and citizens interact in the management of daily life.

New Mentalities of Government in China examines how the privatization and professionalization of 'public' service provision is transforming the nature of government and everyday life in the People's Republic of China (PRC). The book addresses key theoretical questions on the nature of government in China and documents the emergence of a range of 'new mentalities of government' in China. Its chapters focus on areas such as clinical trials, conceptualizing government, consumer activity, elite philanthropy, lifestyle and beauty advice, public health, social work, volunteering, and urban and rural planning.

Offering a topical examination of shifting modes of governance in contemporary China, this book will appeal to scholars in the fields of anthropology, history, politics, and sociology.

David Bray is Senior Lecturer in Sociology and Social Policy at the University of Sydney, Australia. He is the author of *Social Space and Governance in Urban China: The Danwei System from Origins to Reform* (2005).

Elaine Jeffreys is Associate Professor, School of International Studies, University of Technology Sydney, Australia. Her recent publications include *Prostitution Scandals in China: Policing, Media and Society* (Routledge, 2012).

Routledge Studies on China in Transition
Series Editor: David S.G. Goodman

1 **The Democratisation of China**
Baogang He

2 **Beyond Beijing**
Dali Yang

3 **China's Enterprise Reform**
Changing state/society relations after Mao
You Ji

4 **Industrial Change in China**
Economic restructuring and conflicting interests
Kate Hannan

5 **The Entrepreneurial State in China**
Real estate and commerce departments in reform era Tianjin
Jane Duckett

6 **Tourism and Modernity in China**
Tim Oakes

7 **Cities in Post Mao China**
Recipes for economic development in the reform era
Jae Ho Chung

8 **China's Spatial Economic Development**
Regional transformation in the Lower Yangzi Delta
Andrew M. Marton

9 **Regional Development in China**
States, globalization and inequality
Yehua Dennis Wei

10 **Grassroots Charisma**
Four local leaders in China
Stephan Feuchtwang and Wang Mingming

11 **The Chinese Legal System**
Globalization and local legal culture
Pitman B. Potter

12 **Transforming Rural China**
How local institutions shape property rights in China
Chi-Jou Jay Chen

13 **Negotiating Ethnicity in China**
Citizenship as a response to the state
Chih-yu Shih

14 **Manager Empowerment in China**
Political implications of rural industrialisation in the reform era
Ray Yep

15 **Cultural Nationalism in Contemporary China**
The search for national identity under reform
Yingjie Guo

16 **Elite Dualism and Leadership Selection in China**
Xiaowei Zang

17 **Chinese Intellectuals Between State and Market**
Edward Gu and Merle Goldman

18 **China, Sex and Prostitution**
Elaine Jeffreys

19 **The Development of China's Stockmarket, 1984–2002**
Equity politics and market institutions
Stephen Green

20 **China's Rational Entrepreneurs**
The development of the new private business sector
Barbara Krug

21 **China's Scientific Elite**
Cong Cao

22 **Locating China**
Jing Wang

23 **State and Laid-Off Workers in Reform China**
The silence and collective action of the retrenched
Yongshun Cai

24 **Translocal China**
Linkages, identities and the reimagining of space
Tim Oakes and Louisa Schein

25 **International Aid and China's Environment**
Taming the yellow dragon
Katherine Morton

26 **Sex and Sexuality in China**
Edited by Elaine Jeffreys

27 **China's Reforms and International Political Economy**
Edited by David Zweig and Chen Zhimin

28 **Ethnicity and Urban Life in China**
A comparative study of Hui Muslims and Han Chinese
Xiaowei Zang

29 **China's Urban Space**
Development under market socialism
T.G. McGee, George C.S. Lin, Mark Y.L. Wang, Andrew M. Marton and Jiaping Wu

30 **China's Embedded Activism**
Opportunities and constraints of a social movement
Edited by Richard Louis Edmonds and Peter Ho

31 **Marketization and Democracy in China**
Jianjun Zhang

32 **The Chinese State in Transition**
Processes and contests in local China
Edited by Linda Chelan Li

33 **China's Governmentalities**
Governing change, changing government
Edited by Elaine Jeffreys

34 **China's Cotton Industry**
Economic transformation and state capacity
Björn Alpermann

35 **Serious Crime in China**
Policing and politics
Susan Trevaskes

36 **The Chinese State's Retreat from Health**
Policy and the politics of retrenchment
Jane Duckett

37 **China's Changing Welfare Mix**
Local perspectives
Edited by Beatriz Carrillo and Jane Duckett

38 **Small Town China**
Rural labour and social inclusion
Beatriz Carrillo

39 **Tiger Girls**
Women and enterprise in the People's Republic of China
Minglu Chen

40 **China's Thought Management**
Edited by Anne-Marie Brady

41 **Rural Tax Reform in China**
Policy processes and institutional change
Linda Chelan Li

42 **Young Chinese in Urban China**
Alex Cockain

43 **Prostitution Scandals in China**
Policing, media and society
Elaine Jeffreys

44 **Unequal China**
The political economy and cultural politics of inequality
Edited by Wanning Sun and Yingjie Guo

45 **Elites and Governance in China**
Edited by Xiaowei Zang and Chien-Wen Kou

46 **Choosing China's Leaders**
Edited by Chien-Wen Kou and Xiaowei Zang

47 **Rural Policy Implementation in Contemporary China**
New socialist countryside
Anna L. Ahlers

48 **NGO Governance and Management in China**
Edited by Reza Hasmath and Jennifer Y.J. Hsu

49 **Dams, Migration and Authoritarianism in China**
The local state in Yunnan
Sabrina Habich

50 **New Mentalities of Government in China**
Edited by David Bray and Elaine Jeffreys

New Mentalities of Government in China

Edited by David Bray and Elaine Jeffreys

Routledge
Taylor & Francis Group
LONDON AND NEW YORK

First published 2016 by Routledge

2 Park Square, Milton Park, Abingdon, Oxfordshire OX14 4RN
711 Third Avenue, New York, NY 10017

Routledge is an imprint of the Taylor & Francis Group, an informa business

First issued in paperback 2018

British Library Cataloguing in Publication Data
A catalogue record for this book is available from the British Library

Library of Congress Cataloging in Publication Data
Names: Bray, David, 1965– editor. | Jeffreys, Elaine, 1960– editor.
Title: New mentalities of government in China / edited by David Bray and Elaine Jeffreys.
Description: New York, NY : Routledge, 2016. | Series: Routledge studies on China in transition ; 50 | Includes bibliographical references and index.
Identifiers: LCCN 2015031293| ISBN 9781138917750 (hardback) | ISBN 9781315688848 (ebook)
Subjects: LCSH: Public administration–China. | Government accountability–China. | Economic development–Political aspects–China. | Social change–Political aspects–China. | China–Politics and government–2002–
Classification: LCC JQ1510 .N495 2016 | DDC 320.951–dc23
LC record available at http://lccn.loc.gov/2015031293

ISBN: 978-1-138-91775-0 (hbk)
ISBN: 978-1-138-35148-6 (pbk)

Typeset in Times New Roman
by Wearset Ltd, Boldon, Tyne and Wear

For Barry Hindess and Michael Dutton, whose rethinking of the nature of government and government in China inspired this book.

Contents

Illustrations

Figures

Table

Contributors

David Bray is Senior Lecturer in Sociology and Social Policy at the University of Sydney. His current research charts the socio-technical assemblages that constitute China's rapidly changing built environments. He is the author of *Social Space and Governance in Urban China: The Danwei System from Origins to Reform* (2005, Stanford University Press).

Carolyn Cartier is Professor of Human Geography and China Studies at the University of Technology Sydney and Adjunct Research Director for China Urban at the Australian Centre for China in the World. Her new research focuses on urbanization and the Party-state in China.

Melinda Cooper is Associate Professor in the Department of Sociology and Social Policy at the University of Sydney. She is the author of *Life as Surplus: Biotechnology and Capitalism in the Neoliberal Era* (2008, University of Washington Press); and, with Catherine Waldby, *Clinical Labor: Tissue Donors and Research Subjects in the Global Bioeconomy* (2014, Duke University Press).

Michael Dutton is Professor of Politics at Goldsmiths, University of London. He is the author of: *Policing Chinese Politics* (2005, Duke University Press), for which he won the AAS Levenson Prize in 2007; *Streetlife China* (1998, Cambridge University Press); *Policing and Punishment in China* (1992, Cambridge University Press); and co-author of *Beijing Time* (2005, Harvard University Press). Publishing in journals such as *Public Culture*, *Social Text*, *positions*, and *Boundary 2*, Dutton's work is characterized by a strong interest in China and theory.

Barry Hindess is Emeritus Professor of Politics at the Australian National University. He has published widely in the areas of social and political theory. His publications include: *Corruption and Democracy in Australia* (2004, Australian National University); *Us and Them: Anti-elitism in Australia*, with Marian Sawer (2004, API Network, Australia Research Institute, Curtin University of Technology); *Governing Australia: Studies in Contemporary Rationalities of Government*, with Mitchell Dean (1998, Cambridge University Press); *Discourses of Power: From Hobbes to Foucault* (1996, Wiley); and numerous papers on democracy, liberalism, and empire and neo-liberalism.

Lisa Hoffman is Associate Professor of Urban Studies at the University of Washington (UW) Tacoma and a member of the China faculty at the Henry M. Jackson School of International Studies, UW Seattle. Her research focuses on contemporary governmental and subject formations in China, with attention to urban processes and spatialities. Previous projects have examined the emergence of urban professionals, rural urbanization, and discourses of green urbanisms. She is author of *Patriotic Professionalism in Urban China: Fostering Talent* (2010, Temple University Press) and co-editor with Heather Merrill of *Spaces of Danger: Culture and Power in the Everyday* (2015, University of Georgia Press).

Elaine Jeffreys is Associate Professor in the School of International Studies, Faculty of Arts and Social Sciences, at the University of Technology Sydney. Elaine is the author of *Sex in China*, with Haiqing Yu (2015, Polity); *Prostitution Scandals in China: Policing, Media and Society* (2012, Routledge); and *China, Sex and Prostitution* (2012 [2004], Routledge). She is the editor of *Celebrity Philanthropy*, with Paul Allatson (2015, Intellect); *China's Governmentalities: Governing Change, Changing Government* (2011 [2009], Routledge); *Celebrity in China*, with Louise Edwards (2010, Hong Kong University Press); and *Sex and Sexuality in China* (2009 [2006], Routledge).

Gary Sigley is Professor in Asian and Chinese Studies at the University of Western Australia. His current research focuses on the politics of cultural heritage in southwest China, with a particular interest in the 'Ancient Tea Horse Road'.

T.E. Woronov is Senior Lecturer in the Department of Anthropology at the University of Sydney. Her work has focused on the politics of children, youth, and education in the PRC, and she has published widely on topics including Chinese children's nationalism, education for quality (*suzhi jiaoyu*), and governmentality. Her book *Class Work: Vocational Schools and China's Urban Youth* (2016, Stanford University Press) is an ethnographic study of working-class youth culture and new class formations in urban China.

Su Xuezhong is a doctoral candidate at the University of Technology Sydney. His research is on the development of philanthropy education for children and youth in the People's Republic of China.

Haiqing Yu is Senior Lecturer in contemporary Chinese media and culture at the University of New South Wales. Haiqing is the author of *Sex in China*, with Elaine Jeffreys (2015, Polity); and *Media and Cultural Transformation in China* (2009, Routledge). Her research covers two broad disciplines: media studies and cultural/sociological studies, focusing on the political economy of digital media and communication in China, contemporary Chinese youth culture and sexuality, and social movements. Haiqing has published widely in these areas in refereed academic journals.

Acknowledgements

The editors would like to acknowledge funding support from the following institutions (in alphabetical order):

- Academy of the Social Sciences in Australia (ASSA) (ASSA Workshop Programme 2012–2013);
- Australian Centre on China in the World (CIW), Australia National University (CIW Resources for Chinese Studies 2012);
- Australian Research Council Future Fellowship FT100100238 (Future Fellow Jeffreys); and
- Faculty of Arts and Social Sciences, University of Technology Sydney.

Funding and support resulted in an international workshop, 'New Mentalities of Government in China: Emerging Professions, Vocations and Associations', University of Technology Sydney, 6–7 December 2012, which contributed to the formation of this book.

Every effort has been made to contact copyright holders for their permission to reprint material in this book. The publishers would be grateful to hear from any copyright holder who is not here acknowledged and will undertake to rectify any errors or omissions in future editions of this book.

David Bray and Elaine Jeffreys
August 2015

Note on Chinese names

Names in Chinese are usually presented as family name followed by personal name. There are two exceptions: the first is when someone with a Chinese family name has a non-Chinese personal name; the second is when someone with a Chinese name has indicated through publication that they wish to be known by their personal name followed by their family name.

1 New mentalities of government in China

An introduction

David Bray and Elaine Jeffreys

New Mentalities of Government in China looks at recent transformations in the nature of government and the governance of everyday life in the People's Republic of China (PRC). China continues to transform apace, flowing from the forces of deregulation, privatization, and globalization unleashed by economic reforms which began in late 1978. The dramatic scope of economic change in China is often counterposed to the apparent lack of political change as demonstrated by continued Chinese Communist Party (CCP) rule. However, the ongoing dominance of the CCP belies the fact that much has also changed in relation to practices of government, including how authorities and citizens interact in the management of everyday life – for example, through the roles played by professionals, volunteers and 'everyday experts' in public affairs. This book addresses key theoretical questions on the nature of government in China and documents the emergence of a range of new mentalities of government in (and about) China via chapters on clinical trials, conceptualizing government, consumer activity, elite philanthropy, lifestyle and beauty advice, public health, social work, volunteering, and urban and rural planning.

This chapter introduces the key concepts, themes, and contents of the book as follows. We first introduce the concept of 'government', defined as guiding the changing imbrication of 'people' and 'things', and outline the hybrid processes wherein new mentalities of government can emerge. We then explore these themes in relation to specific fields of public life by summarizing the subject matter and arguments of the other ten chapters that comprise the book.

Key concepts and themes: government, governmentality, and hybridity

New Mentalities of Government in China extends Michel Foucault's work on 'governmentality' to consider questions of government in present-day China (Foucault 1991 [1978]). Defined as 'the conduct of conduct', the concept of governmentality is concerned with the 'how' of governing – how we govern, how we are governed – and the relationship between the state, the government of others, and the government of ourselves – or any more less calculated means of directing how we behave and act (Dean 1999: 2). As Foucault (2007: 193) explains, the word 'conduct' refers to both the activity of conducting others or things, and the ways in which one conducts oneself, 'lets oneself be conducted', 'is conducted', and the manner in which one behaves 'as an effect of a form of conduct'.

The concept of governmentality reconfigures conventional understandings of the nexus between government and power by decentring 'the problem of the State' – the tendency to reduce the operation of political power to the actions of a nation-state, understood as a relatively coherent and calculating political subject. Rather than defining political rule in terms of a state that extends its sway throughout society by means of an apparatus of control, it draws attention to the diversity of forces and knowledges involved in efforts to regulate the lives of individuals, and the conditions within national territories, in pursuit of various goals. In doing so, it suggests that government is neither operationalized nor exercised strictly through prohibitions and controls. On the contrary, the government of society is achieved through the administering and fostering of life itself ('biopolitics') – for example, attending to the processes of fertility, birth, health, disease, sexuality and lifespan, and their relationship to particular lifestyles (Foucault 1991).

Although studies of biopolitics generally focus on physical and biological existence, Foucault's definition of government refers to a complex of 'people' and 'things' that encompasses the non-human, the natural and the artificial, and the corporeal and the ethical. As Thomas Lemke (2015: 5) points out, Foucault never explicitly addressed 'the problem of human and non-human relations' or 'the nature of technoscientific practices and their profoundly productive effects on human bodies, as well as the ways in which these practices are deeply implicated in what constitutes the human'. However, Foucault (1991: 93, 95) provides the theoretical space for such discussions by also describing governmentality as: 'the right disposition of things, arranged so as to lead to a convenient end [...] for each of the things that are to be governed'. Government thus defined is about how to conduct the imbrication of people and things, that is, the relations of people to territory, wealth, resources and means of subsistence (which includes variables such as climate, soil, water, flora, fauna), and other 'things' such as customs, habits, and ways of thinking and acting.

We therefore use the phrase 'mentalities of government' to draw attention to the ways in which fields of knowledge and domains of expertise give rise to new ways of thinking about how to guide the shifting interactions between people and things. As economic, social, cultural, and political contexts transform, new discourses emerge through attempts to redefine the range of problems that government should address and to formulate strategic interventions for their solution. This ongoing work of making government 'thinkable' is undertaken by a vast range of officials, professionals, and other kinds of experts, whose training and status (authorized or self-proclaimed) empowers them to establish norms of behaviour and enact measures for the realization of those norms (Miller and Rose 1990). Norms are established not only through laws, regulations, and ethical directives, but also through spatial, technical, and scientific practices, creating material frameworks that structure and direct behaviour in particular ways.

The emergence of new cohorts of expertise and modes of citizen engagement reflects the changing roles and goals of government in China and is shaping new forms of governance. Government in Mao-era China (1949–1976) operated almost entirely through official organs and agencies in a hierarchical and highly regulated system of formal authority. This system administered and mobilized the population through state-run urban work units (*danwei* 单位) and rural collectives to participate in the governing of everyday life. In the post-1978 era of market-based economic reform, the old 'mass-line' mode of government has been progressively replaced, but not entirely supplanted, by more complex and diffuse forms of governance, which increasingly rely on expertise and service provision from a host of new professions and professionals, and vocationally oriented organizations and people, focusing on new social problems and citizenries, and using new or reconfigured practices and technologies.

The chapters in this book highlight the critical roles played by a range of experts in transforming diverse fields of government in present-day China. These include: urban planners seeking to brand China's cities and modernize the countryside; social workers striving to ameliorate growing socio-economic divides; government and community workers promoting philanthropy and volunteering; hospital managers concerned with financing public medicine; public health agencies dealing with the spread of the human immunodeficiency virus (HIV); and online lifestyle gurus who aim to guide 'ordinary' citizens through a labyrinth of consumer choices. Some contributors explore the emergence of new areas of expertise in fields such as philanthropy, social work, and lifestyle advice. Others chart the ways in which existing cohorts of expertise, for example in areas of urban planning, city management, hospital administration and public health, have been reconfigured to address new problems, often by adapting transnational 'best' professional, scientific, and technical practices.

Taken as a whole, the different chapters that comprise this book demonstrate the complex realities of government in contemporary China by revealing how new governing mentalities have emerged to solve new problems of government, while illustrating how Mao-era legacies influence the possibilities of the present. The solutions to such problems often draw on western neoliberal frameworks regarding 'appropriate' professional practice, but these solutions are variously enabled, compromised, or even transformed through their interaction with older practices of government in China. Thus, Melinda Cooper shows how the structural legacies of the Mao-era hospital (centralized management, specialized departments and large numbers of patients) have facilitated the integration of China's urban hospitals into global networks of contract clinical research. Gary Sigley argues that the community outreach and capacity-building potential of Chinese social workers as new professionals has been constrained by a continued socialist-style tradition of administrative domination. Lisa Hoffman reveals that volunteers in government-promoted community programmes in Chinese cities view their experiences as being informed by a fusion of universal values, practices associated with the United Nations' Millennium Development Goals, Mao-era collectivism and traditional Chinese virtues. As these examples suggest, efforts to characterize China's changing modes of governance in terms of either neoliberal or Mao-era governmentalities, or as a predictable combination of both, are doomed to failure. Government in contemporary China involves dynamic, hybrid forms.

Chapter outline: towards a Chinese governmentality

Michael Dutton and Barry Hindess explore the utility of analysing contemporary China through the conceptual framework of governmentality in Chapter 2. Dutton and Hindess begin by drawing attention to a historical coincidence: 'governmentality' emerged in Europe as a critique of a '(Marxist) theory of the State' in the same year that China adopted economic reforms, which generated dramatic institutional and social changes. They initially posit that both phenomena can be ascribed to simultaneous 'crises of Marxism': the former resulting from a collapse in European left-wing academic consensus on the nature of the capitalist state; the latter deriving from a reinterpretation of the process of socialist transition as Chinese reformers rejected Mao Zedong's emphasis on politics in favour of prioritizing economic development.

However, as Dutton and Hindess note, the 'crises of Marxism' explanation fails to account for important factors on both sides of the Euro-Asian landmass. On the one hand, the concept of governmentality was taken up by a group of influential scholars who, through a range of grounded case studies, pushed the analytic in new directions far removed from Marxist debates over theories of state (see Burchell *et al.* 1991; Barry *et al.* 1996). On the other hand, China's economic reforms began to take on a dynamic of their own, as a new logic of economic efficiency started to usurp the old rationale of socialist transition, leading not only to a proliferation of new domains of economic activity, but also to the emergence of many new realms of knowledge and professional expertise. Hence, the expansion of Foucault's conceptual framework into a wider-ranging field of governmentality studies was paralleled by the fracturing of China's unified Party-state into a myriad of dispersed regimes of governmentality.

Dutton and Hindess conclude that a governmentality approach is appropriate for understanding contemporary China, not because China is the same as Europe or because it is belatedly adopting European developments in government practice, but rather because Maoism has left China with a legacy which places an emphasis on the government of conduct that is similar to that which can be found in the European tradition. Western-style neoliberalism developed from a particular view of good government as 'frugal government', or the least possible government, which assumed that the development of economic processes and society would be hindered by too much government intervention (Foucault 2008: 27–47). This understanding transformed the flow of power in western liberal societies by dispersing it away from 'the State' into various semi-autonomous regimes of care. Frugal government developed in China through Maoism and concepts of self-reliance, producing an experimental mass-line mode of government policy and practice that mobilized the population to transform the state of things, while using the least possible material resources.

This experimental approach continues to influence governance in contemporary China, merging in ad hoc, unexpected and sometimes productive ways with new modes of operationalizing government and encouraging citizen engagement. Hence, understanding China's changing governing rationalities requires an examination of the different histories and genealogies of politics that combine legacies from the Mao era with features of neoliberal politics that have emerged during the reform era. The remaining chapters consequently address a range of areas in which new concerns of government merge with existing and new cohorts of expertise and modes of citizen engagement, and new social, scientific, and technical forms of reasoning and practices.

In Chapter 3, Elaine Jeffreys and Su Xuezhong demonstrate China's changing and hybrid mentalities of government by examining the revival of Lei Feng (雷锋) – a Mao-era socialist role model – as the 'celebrity face' of a 2012–2013 government advertising campaign to promote civic behaviours. Lei Feng was a peace-time soldier with the People's Liberation Army who died in an accident in 1962. He became famous in 1963 when his life-story, encapsulated in a diary that celebrates Mao Zedong Thought and the 'socialist' values of altruism, thrift, and working hard for public goals, was promoted through a national mobilization campaign as a model of socialist citizenship. Media statements by Chairman Mao and Premier Zhou Enlai urged the Chinese populace to 'Learn from Comrade Lei Feng' and to 'Learn the Correct Class Stance and How to Practice the Revolutionary, Proletarian-communist Spirit of Selflessness from Comrade Lei Feng' ('Zhongguo qingnian chuban' 1963). Exposure through public education and subsequent commemorative events have ensured that most people in China are familiar with the Lei Feng 'spirit' of selfless public service. That spirit is sometimes caricatured as 'old-fashioned' through spoofs and the sale of retro-revolutionary fashion and kitsch (Steen 2014), and even ridiculed for its 'brainless simplicity' (Humphrey 2005: 41). However, in 2012 Lei Feng became the symbol of a two-year-long government campaign encouraging China's citizens to adopt 'good' civic behaviours.

Jeffreys and Su show how 1960s socialist imagery and values have been variously recast by Party-state organs, through an interplay with the media and popular culture, to promote different understandings of state–society relations, while attempting to keep alive the notion that the PRC's revolutionary history and the CCP matters. 'Learning from Lei Feng' initially entailed helping others to demonstrate and forge class solidarity, and working hard to promote socialism in the context of limited resources. After a brief association with Red Guard activism and revolutionary Maoism, the Lei Feng spirit was refashioned as a means of cultivating people with the civic virtues required to modernize reform-era China. Lei Feng is now linked to philanthropy and volunteering, which are usually viewed in the context of state withdrawal from providing comprehensive social welfare as a 'quintessentially neoliberal dynamic' (Hemment 2012: 523).

The linkage between philanthropy and the Lei Feng tradition of helping others, a historical tradition unique to the PRC and the CCP, reinforces the CCP's self-proclaimed role as the guarantor of the common good, while advancing new models of Chinese citizenship. In Mao-era China, private wealth was nationalized and philanthropy was viewed in Marxist terms as a means by which the propertied classes attempted to placate the labouring classes (Zhou and Zeng 2006: 368). Learning from Lei Feng now means encouraging super-rich entrepreneurs and 'ordinary' volunteers alike to contribute to the task of building a modern, prosperous and stable China, by supplementing the government provision of welfare services.

Governing people and space

Chapters by David Bray and Carolyn Cartier look at the transformation of everyday life in urban and rural China through governing practices centred on economic development and spatial planning.

In Chapter 4, Carolyn Cartier contends that one of the PRC's key government strategies – developing domestic services and consumption as the foundation of the national economy – makes the city the pivotal site of China's economic future, and for the formation of new professions and lifestyles. But entry into the 'global' capitalist economy is not the only factor governing urban consumer-citizen activity in China today, as demonstrated by Party-led efforts to open up spaces for economic activity *and* guide citizens' participation in new consumer landscapes. In the mid-2000s, amid unprecedented growth in urban incomes, some consumer activity emerged in the form of large-scale participatory events associated with neoliberal-style strategies of urban boosterism (the act of promoting a city, town, or organization, with the goal of improving public perception of it). However, the forms and aesthetics of those activities were reminiscent of Mao-era 'passions' for mass activity and political excess (Dutton 2005).

Cartier examines urban landscapes of surplus capital and the simultaneity of consumer activity with 'Maoist characteristics' with reference to the National Civilized City Programme, an initiative of the Central Office of Spiritual Civilization, under the Central Guidance Commission for Building Spiritual Civilization, of the CCP. Established in 2005, the Civilized City programme is not a distinct government policy. However, it seeks to standardize urban governance and strengthen urban economies by promoting civilized cities and citizens (Spiritual Civilization Committee 2011). Different jurisdictions apply and compete for the honorary title of a National Civilized City by meeting certain assessment criteria. The criteria include evidence of non-corrupt government and a fair, legal trading environment, and a living environment that is healthy, comfortable, socially stable and ecologically sustainable, and supports healthy adolescent development and effective rural–urban policy implementation.

While promoting local urban development, the Civilized City programme revives Mao-era ways of thinking about model (socialist) structures and citizen participation, and reorients them to meet contemporary social management goals. It has encouraged local government promotion of large-scale consumer-oriented, but volunteer-serviced, activities to market and brand particular cities. These include mega-events such as the 2010 Shanghai Expo and the 2013

Xiamen International Marathon, which were staffed by organized volunteers, and associated with public service campaigns to encourage civic pride, and civil practices such as 'no spitting and littering', and orderly queuing for public transport. Cartier concludes that continuous efforts to attain and retain the National Civilized City title are transforming the national landscape and everyday life, by making cities and their citizens responsible for adopting benchmark urban quality standards, reflected in architecture, services, employment, consumption practices, and civic behaviours.

In Chapter 5, David Bray examines one strategy to spread 'civilization' beyond the cities into China's rural hinterlands through the relocation of villagers into urban-style residential compounds (*xiaoqu* 小区). This initiative, part of a much larger national programme to 'Build a New Socialist Countryside', is underpinned by the expansion of urban planning into the countryside. In 2007, the 1990 Urban Planning Law was revised and reissued as the Urban and Rural Planning Law (*Zhonghua renmin gongheguo chengshi guihua fa* 1990; *Zhonghua renmin gongheguo chengxiang guihua fa* 2007). Through mandating a regime of coordinated long-term 'master planning' for all territorial jurisdictions right down to the administrative village, the new law ensures that professional urban planners enjoy a vastly enhanced role in the ongoing reconstruction of China's built environments.

In recent years, urban planners have played a particularly significant role in rethinking forms of residential design and, in collaboration with government planning agencies, have created a new standardized national model for residential development known as the *xiaoqu* (micro-district). The standardization of the *xiaoqu* as a design model was first codified in 1994 for application in urban housing projects (*Zhonghua renmin gongheguo jianshebu* 1994). However, the recent extension of urban planning into the countryside has seen the *xiaoqu* model transposed into rural settings as part of an explicit policy objective to 'urbanize' and 'civilize' rural communities.

Bray describes the relocation of a Jiangsu village community into a new master-planned *xiaoqu*, focusing on the social implications of the new technologies and spatial forms that are built into the *xiaoqu*. He argues that everyday life has been radically reinscribed through the mediation of technologies such as plumbing, piped cooking gas and broadband communication, and by encoding *xiaoqu* space according to an urban logic that literally eliminates the space for traditional village activities, such as growing vegetables and raising productive animals. Like many similar projects throughout China, this intervention is justified by authorities as part of a grander national strategy to bring about urban–rural integration and to provide the conditions for rural people to achieve a moderately affluent standard of living. It also encourages a particular style of life and citizenship within each *xiaoqu* and links the multitude of *xiaoqu* together through technological networks that foster a unified national practice of modern citizenship.

Governing wealth and need

The next three chapters examine government responses to new demands for social services and the emergence of private wealth in reform-era China, focusing on the development of social work, elite philanthropy, and volunteering.

In Chapter 6, Gary Sigley examines the development since the 1990s of social work as a new profession in the PRC. In western societies, the history of social work as a profession is marked by debate over its role as a technology of government, being viewed as both a negative and intrusive form of 'social policing' and a positive promoter of self-governing citizens through 'self-help' practices (Camilleri 1996; Chambon *et al.* 1999). Following the PRC's founding in 1949, nascent social work practices 'disappeared' from mainland Chinese cities as the new CCP-led regime, and its ranks of politicized cadres, began to allocate employment and welfare services through the socialist work unit system, and as non-Marxist disciplines such as sociology and psychology fell into disrepute (Bray 2005).

The post-1978 opening of China's labour markets and the gradual demise of the state-run work unit system led to rapid economic growth and urbanization, creating a range of 'social problems' that require new government responses. This situation encouraged the re-establishment of social work as a discipline for study at tertiary-level educational institutions; the formation of professional associations for social workers; and the creation of specific jobs for social workers within local government organizations. The expansion of social work has been further promoted by the government emphasis on 'community building' (*shequ jianshe* 社区建设), which has opened the space for both professional innovations and broader citizen participation in community-level governance (Bray 2009).

Sigley concludes that the role and scope of social work, especially its potential to generate grass-roots participation in community governance, has been enabled and constrained by the PRC Government's policy emphasis on building a 'harmonious society' (*hexie shehui* 和谐社会). The harmonious society discourse has encouraged the expansion of community-based social work to address new social problems, especially those associated with socio-economic inequality. But the corollary emphasis of the harmonious society discourse on 'maintaining social stability', combined with the top-down administrative legacies of the Mao era, has also constrained the development of social work as a profession. Local government authorities are reluctant to cede their historical control over and reconfigured responsibility for 'social management' to social workers whose professional training could encourage a shift towards participatory, rather than top-down and paternalistic, patterns of community governance.

In Chapter 7, Elaine Jeffreys places elite philanthropy in international perspective by exploring the divergent paths, and related controversies, of elite philanthropy in the PRC – a new site for philanthropy – and the United States – the traditional home of capitalism and 'big-money' philanthropy. Throughout the Mao era, curtailment of the monetary economy, combined with state ownership and distribution of public resources, prevented private enterprise and the accumulation of significant private wealth, and also eliminated the spaces for organized, 'private' philanthropy. Until the 1990s, the necessities of everyday life – food, employment, housing, education, health care, and other social services, were provided to urban residents through the socialist work unit, with additional forms of direct state assistance being provided to people without family support, work or livelihood.

The recent development of philanthropy in the PRC is highlighted in a 1994 article in the *People's Daily* about the establishment of a government-supported charity federation; it states that readers were probably seeing the Chinese characters for charity and philanthropy (*cishan* 慈善) for the first time (Sun Yuemu 1994: 4). Although organized philanthropy has expanded since then, the 2008 Sichuan earthquake is widely viewed as putting philanthropy 'on the map' in China. It not only led to a major increase in charitable giving (public donations in 2008 exceeded the documented amount for the preceding decade), but also prompted widespread debate about the philanthropic responsibilities of the newly rich (Jeffreys 2011; Wang Zhuoqiong 2008).

Jeffreys demonstrates that government-sponsored moves to professionalize philanthropy in China have combined with strong media and public supervision of charitable activities to regulate the activities of wealthy elites in a manner that does not have an obvious parallel in western countries. In the United States, a history of religious conviction, social mobility, and tax incentives has ensured that elite philanthropy is construed as a voluntary moral responsibility of elites who deserve their wealth. In the PRC, elite philanthropy is a discipline imposed on the newly rich to assist the PRC Government in realizing what President Xi Jinping has described as 'the great renaissance of the Chinese nation' and 'the Chinese dream' of ever-higher living standards ('China's new president' 2013).

In Chapter 8, Lisa Hoffman examines the shift from state-directed welfare provisioning to government-supported ways of addressing social problems in urban communities that include non-governmental or social organizations, and citizen volunteering. The inability of the urban work unit system to satisfy public demand for services, and to reach people who were not associated with a work unit, became apparent as early as the mid-1980s. It became obvious in the 1990s as 'non-profitable' state-owned enterprises closed down or restructured, resulting in growing numbers of unemployed and laid-off workers (nearly 12 million people by 1997) (Cai 2006: 16), and as millions of rural migrants entered China's cities to work in the burgeoning construction and service industries (an estimated 52 million people by 1999, rising to over 102 million by 2004) (World Bank 2009: 41). The need to develop cost-effective and sustainable 'non-work-based social provisions' that would also support national policies to build a harmonious society, by developing community governance and strengthening social management, has resulted in a raft of often experimental regulations designed to promote volunteer organizations and volunteering.

Hoffman draws on anthropological fieldwork conducted in Dalian City to reveal that participants view government-supported experiments with volunteering/charitable giving as both 'Chinese' and 'new' (and western), and as existing in intermediary spaces between the state and society. Interviewees explained their participation with reference to Confucian and Taoist conceptions of benevolence and reciprocity. They also noted the 'newness' and 'foreign' nature of organized volunteering when compared to Mao-era forms as expressing a broad concept of human compassion rather than class-based solidarity, and being an individual (private/voluntary) response to human suffering rather than a state-enforced (public) duty. At the same time, participants referred to Mao-era ethics of selflessness and model citizenship, and contemporary ideals of patriotism and civic responsibility, as reasons for participating in government-organized mass-volunteering activities, whether providing support to local community residents on National Volunteers Day, or participating in mega-events such as the Beijing Olympics. These mixed references to Chinese tradition, Maoist values, and new/foreign ideas highlight the emergence of culturally specific forms of volunteering practices, even though their development is linked to the global expansion of private giving and volunteerism, as advocated by the United Nations (see unv.org).

Governing bodies and selves

The final three chapters examine the ways in which the body and 'the self' have been reconfigured as objects of governance in contemporary China through biomedical innovations and activism, and discourses of human quality and self-improvement.

In Chapter 9, Melinda Cooper examines health care as a site of experiment in reform-era China, focusing on the urban Chinese hospital and efforts to partially subsidize public health care through sales of clinical data to international and domestic pharmaceutical industries. During the Mao era, Chinese traditional medicine and western biomedicine were fused through state-run services and mass mobilization campaigns to provide rudimentary health care and eradicate infectious diseases. After 1978, the responsibility for health care provision was relocated from central to provincial and local authorities, creating an uneven geographical distribution of (quality) medical services. In the 1990s, the state-funded urban (work unit) hospital system was also replaced by a commercial system in which hospitals were largely funded by client fees for drugs and services.

The often-catastrophic effects of trading state-funded for profit-oriented health care attracted public and government attention in the 2000s amid media reports of hospital overcrowding, and families bankrupted by inflated drug costs, medical negligence and corruption (Office of the World Health Organization Representative in China and Social Development Department of China State Council Development Research Center 2005). In response, and at the behest of central government, the urban hospital has refashioned itself as an experimental export zone and knowledge park, financing its health care operations through the sale of data from clinical trials to the multinational pharmaceutical industry.

Cooper shows how government authorities have sought to leverage existing scientific expertise and a huge patient base to turn the hospital system into a source of indigenous biomedical experimentation and innovation. Such experimentation is facilitated by the hybrid, postsocialist status of the urban Chinese hospital system. Unlike in the United States, where clinical trials are typically outsourced to private clinics, clinical trials in China usually take place in large, urban-based government hospitals with affiliated medical schools. This is because the Chinese hospital system retains many of the features of the hospital as a work unit: namely, a professionally qualified work force, centralized management, massive caseloads, and highly specialized departments. Unlike the stereotypical profit-oriented private hospital in western countries, the proceeds from Chinese clinical trials are also partly being used to expand affordable public health services, as well as to provide new professional training in pharmacological and clinical research, and build international research centres. Operating within the legitimating principle of improving access to health care, the urban Chinese hospital has become a hybrid institution that encourages physicians to act as health care providers *and* clinical investigators, while patient bodies are leveraged as clients of health services *and* experimental assets assisting the PRC's expressed goal of becoming a world-leading innovator in research and development by 2020 (State Council 2006).

In Chapter 10, Yu Haiqing examines the dividing practices that structure China's response to the governance of HIV and acquired immune deficiency syndrome (AIDS). Until the mid-1990s, AIDS was viewed in the PRC as an 'outsiders' disease, controlled by restrictions on entry visas and the importation of blood products, or else as a 'distant' problem associated with drug use among ethnic minorities living in China's border regions (Jeffreys and Yu 2015: 123–4). Then, in the mid-1990s, HIV infection was discovered among large numbers of poor rural people in China's central provinces who had sold blood, and subsequently within blood-selling families and communities. Since 2001, the spread of HIV in China has become linked to sexual transmission, resulting in a new focus on the behaviours and practices of members of so-called bridge populations, especially intravenous drug users, former commercial blood donors, sex workers, and men who have sex with men (Jeffreys and Yu 2015: 125–9).

Although the governance of AIDS in China appears to have aligned with global norms, Yu argues that its decentralized structure, the contradictory impetus of related policies, and the ongoing media stigmatization of people living with HIV and AIDS, have exacerbated rather than overcome the tendency for government interventions to 'distance' people living with HIV and members of the population categorized as 'at risk'. When combined with Chinese discourses of *suzhi* (human quality 素质) and the rhetoric of crisis, this has encouraged both biased responses and extraordinary policing measures. AIDS orphans as 'innocent victims' often receive better treatment than their perceived 'non-innocent' counterparts – those who are infected through 'greed' (poor rural people) or 'immoral' and 'irresponsible' behaviours (sex workers and drug addicts). Health interventions targeting marginalized people designated as 'most at-risk', such as sex workers and men who have sex with men, contribute to their new social stigmatization as 'carriers of disease'. People who knowingly sell or buy sex while infected with serious sexually transmissible infections face detention and potential jail sentences of up to five years, according to Article 360 of the Criminal Law of the PRC (1997).

Yu concludes that new forms of social activism and political subjectivities are being forged in turn around the deleterious effect of exclusion on ailing bodies and those marked by the potentiality of HIV infection. People living with HIV and their supporters are engaging in various forms of biopolitical activism or struggling 'against the processes implemented for conducting others' (Foucault 2007: 201), by offering visible and concrete displays of support for people affected by AIDS. Chinese 'non-normative' sexual groups are also using digital media, business and social networks, securing funding from AIDS-related international organizations, and mobilizing the discourse of 'pride' to contest their marginal status, critique China's HIV governance, and foster a culture of tolerance in Chinese society. In short, such groups are promoting different forms of collective action and aspirations.

In Chapter 11, T.E. Woronov examines the emerging phenomenon of '*daren*' (达人 beauty and lifestyle bloggers), who use new media technologies to advise consumers on how to navigate their way through the seemingly limitless choice of beauty, fashion, and lifestyle products now available from China's retail market. While the *daren* mostly do not have professional credentials, they can be understood as a Chinese example of 'everyday experts' – a growing global cohort of amateurs who provide lifestyle advice through magazines, television reality and makeover shows, and the internet. These 'experts' operate in the realm of the mundane, rather than the technical, and specialize in guiding individuals to make appropriate market-based consumer choices in order to construct the 'best' possible self.

The emergence of the *daren* in China has been enabled by the rapid simultaneous growth of the beauty industry, the internet, and a middle class, flowing from deeper transformations in the structure of China's economy and in discourses of gender, consumption, and identity. The state-promoted expansion of consumer markets for domestic consumption has been accompanied by the expansion of an affluent middle class and the emergence of new discourses valorizing consumption. At the same time, transformations in gender discourse, which posit *beauty* as essential to female identity, has privileged women as consummate *consumers* and resulted in the development of a strong market in China for cosmetics and related beauty products. As well as covering fashion and beauty, popular *daren* blogs also offer advice on a range of other products targeted at middle-class female consumers, including travel, healthy food, weight loss and exercise programmes and accessories.

Woronov concludes that the *daren* help their followers as aspirational consumer-citizens understand how to put together all aspects of their lives for beautiful results. During the Mao era, the state-controlled media presented images of model workers in state-defined production regimes as exemplary models for members of the Chinese public to emulate. The *daren* as online 'entrepreneurs of the self' present a similarly pedagogical but different model of exemplary citizenship. They show visitors to their social media sites how to make the right consumer choices, that is, how to purchase and wear the fashions and cosmetics necessary to be middle-class urban beauties.

Conclusion

The chapters in this book draw upon a wide variety of examples to demonstrate some of the complex and hybrid ways through which new mentalities of government have emerged in contemporary China. Strategies to govern people in China have multiplied and morphed to deal with the appearance of a diverse range of new subjectivities including consumers, philanthropists, people living with HIV and AIDS, social workers, volunteers, and urbanized villagers. At the same time, the dynamic forces of economic reform and globalization have brought a wealth of new consumer products, built environments, technologies, pharmaceuticals, and other 'new things' into the everyday material lives of Chinese citizens. In documenting these complex new assemblages of 'people' and 'things', contributors underscore the extent to which contemporary practices of government in China cannot be reduced to a simple binary relationship between the state and the individual citizen. On the contrary, they highlight the crucial roles played by a range of intermediary actors – professionals, officials, volunteers, and everyday experts – in making day-to-day government both 'thinkable' and possible.

References

Barry, A., Osborne, T., and Rose, N. (eds) (1996) *Foucault and Political Reason: Liberalism, Neo-Liberalism, and Rationalities of Government*, Chicago: University of Chicago Press.

Bray, D. (2005) *Social Space and Governance in Urban China: The Danwei System from Origins to Reform*, Stanford: Stanford University Press.

Bray, D. (2009) 'Building "community": new strategies of governance in urban China', in E. Jeffreys (ed.), *China's Governmentalities: Governing Change, Changing Government*, Abingdon: Routledge, pp. 88–106.

Burchell, G., Gordon, C., and Miller, P. (eds) (1991) *The Foucault Effect: Studies in Governmentality*, Chicago: University of Chicago Press.

Cai, Y. (2006) *State and Laid-Off Workers in Reform China*, Abingdon: Routledge.

Camilleri, P.J. (1996) *(Re)constructing Social Work: Exploring Social Work Through Text and Talk*, Aldershot: Avebury.

Chambon, A.S., Irving, A., and Epstein, L. (eds) (1999) *Reading Foucault for Social Work*, New York: Columbia University Press.

'China's new president Xi Jinping calls for "great renaissance"' (2013) *News.com.au*, 17 March. Online. Available: www.news.com.au/world-news/chinas-new-president-xi-jinping-calls-for-great-renaissance/story-fndir2ev-1226599385204 (accessed 2 July 2014).

Criminal Law of the People's Republic of China (1997) Adopted by the Second Session of the Fifth National People's Congress on 1 July 1979; revised at the Fifth Session of the Eighth National People's Congress on 14 March 1997 and promulgated by Order No. 83 of the President of the People's Republic of China on 14 March 1997. Online. Available: www.asianlii.org/cn/legis/cen/laws/clotproc361 (accessed 2 July 2015).

Dean, M. (1999) *Governmentality: Power and Rule in Modern Society*, London: Sage Publications.

Dutton, M.R. (2005) *Policing Chinese Politics: A History*, Durham: Duke University Press.

Foucault, M. (1991 [1978]) 'Governmentality' (Lecture at the Collège de France, 1 February 1978), in G. Burchell, C. Gordon, and P. Miller (eds), *The Foucault Effect: Studies in Governmentality*, Chicago: University of Chicago Press, pp. 87–104.

Foucault, M. (2007) *Security, Territory, Population: Lectures at the Collège de France 1977–1978*, Houndsmills: Palgrave Macmillan.

Foucault, M. (2008) *The Birth of Biopolitics: Lectures at the Collège de France 1978–1979*, New York: Palgrave Macmillan.

Hemment, J. (2012) 'Redefining need, reconfiguring expectations: the rise of state-run youth voluntarism programs in Russia', *Anthropological Quarterly*, 85, 2: 519–54.

Humphrey, C. (2005 [1997]) 'Exemplars and rules: aspects of the discourse of moralities in Mongolia', in S. Howell (ed.) *The Ethnography of Moralities*, London: Routledge, pp. 25–48.

Jeffreys, E. (2011) 'Zhang Ziyi and China's celebrity philanthropy scandals', *PORTAL Journal of Multidisciplinary International Studies*, 8, 1: 1–21. Online. Available: http://epress.lib.uts.edu.au/journals/index.php/portal/article/view/1627/2292 (accessed 16 June 2015).

Jeffreys, E. and Yu, H.-Q. (2015) *Sex in China*, Cambridge: Polity Press.

Lemke, T. (2015) 'New materialisms: Foucault and the "government of things" ', *Theory, Culture & Society*, 32, 4: 3–25.

Miller, P. and Rose, N. (1990) 'Governing economic life', *Economy and Society*, 19, 1: 1–31.

Office of the World Health Organization Representative in China and Social Development Department of China State Council Development Research Center (2005) *China: Health, Poverty and Economic Development*, Beijing, December. Online. Available: www.who.int/macrohealth/action/CMH_China.pdf (accessed 2 July 2015).

Spiritual Civilization Committee (2011) '*Quanguo wenming chengshi ceping tixi* (2011)' [National civilized city evaluation system (2011)]. Online. Available: http://gdzh.wenming.cn/cpzh/201310/t20131010_850736.html (accessed 2 July 2015).

State Council of the People's Republic of China (2006) 'Guojia zhongchangqi kexue he jishu fazhan guihua gangyao (2006–2020)' [Medium-to-Long Term Program of National Science and Technology Development 2006–2020], 9 February 2006. Online. Available: www.gov.cn/jrzg/2006-02/09/content_183787.htm; http://sydney.edu.au/global-health/international-networks/National_Outline_for_Medium_and_Long_Term_ST_Development1.doc (accessed 11 May 2015).

Steen, A. (2014) ' "To live is to serve the people": the spirit of model soldier Lei Feng in postmodernity', in A. Hume (ed.) *The Changing Landscape of China's Consumerism*, Oxford: Chandos Publishing, pp. 151–76.

Sun Yuemu (1994) 'Wei cishan zhengming' [Rehabilitating charity], *Renmin Ribao*, 24 February, p. 4.

Wang Zhuoqiong (2008) 'Quake triggers donation deluge', *China Daily*, 5 December. Online. Available: www.chinadaily.com.cn/china/2008-12/05/content_7273896.htm (accessed 2 July 2015).

World Bank (2009) *From Poor Areas to Poor People: China's Evolving Poverty Reduction Agenda: An Assessment of Poverty and Inequality in China*, Poverty Reduction and Economic Management Department, East Asia and Pacific Region, March. Online.

Available: www-wds.worldbank.org/external/default/WDSContentServer/WDSP/IB/2009/04/14/000333038_20090414011802/Rendered/PDF/480580v10Revised0Box338876B01Public10.pdf (accessed 2 July 2015).

'Zhongguo qingnian chuban xuexi Lei Feng zhuanji Maozhuxi tici xiang Lei Feng tongzhi xuexi, Zhou Enlai, Dong Biwu, deng tongzhi, de tici he shi wen tongshi fabiao' [China Youth Magazine publishes a collection on learning from Lei Feng. It includes Chairman Mao Zedong's calligraphic inscription to 'Learn From Comrade Lei Feng', and inscriptions by senior leaders such as Zhou Enlai and Dong Biwu] (1963) *Renmin Ribao*, 5 March, p. 1.

Zhonghua renmin gongheguo chengshi guihua fa (1990) [Urban Planning Law of the People's Republic of China]. Online. Available: www.jincao.com/fa/law19.09.htm (accessed 2 July 2015).

Zhonghua renmin gongheguo chengxiang guihua fa (2007) [Urban and Rural Planning Law of the People's Republic of China]. Online. Available: www.china.com.cn/policy/txt/2007-10/29/content_9139260.htm (accessed 2 July 2015).

Zhonghua renmin gongheguo jianshebu [Ministry of Construction of the People's Republic of China] (1994) *Chengshi juzhu qu guihua sheji guifan* [Planning and Design Standards for Urban Residential Areas], Beijing: Zhongguo Jianzhu Gongye Chubanshe.

Zhou Qiuguang and Zeng Guilin (2006) *Zhongguo Cishan Jianshi* [A Brief History of Charity in China], Beijing: Renmin Chubanshe.

2 Governmentality studies and China

Towards a 'Chinese' governmentality

Michael Dutton and Barry Hindess

Is a governmentality approach useful for the analysis of government in contemporary China and is there something that might be described as a 'Chinese' form of governmentality? This chapter addresses these questions in three stages. We first note how governmentality emerged as an object of study coincident with what has been called a 'crisis of Marxism' both in Western Europe and in the People's Republic of China (PRC). We explain how the shift of focus to new mentalities of government in Europe took place at the same moment as China was undergoing a radical reconfiguration of its notion of government and everyday life. We then detail how these shifts occasioned different conceptualizations of 'frugal government'. In the western context, it led to an art of 'the least possible government', while in China it would grow out of a Maoist notion of self-reliance.

The 'splintering' (in theory and practice) of the Marxist state

Governmentality as a field of academic study emerged in some respects out of a theoretical crisis within western Marxism. This crisis arguably arose in the late 1970s when, to use the words of Louis Althusser (1978: 215), 'something snapped'.[1] That something was the 'Marxist theory of the State'.

It is tempting, although somewhat incorrect, to suggest that Chinese governmentality was born of this same crisis because something also 'snapped' in Chinese Marxism in the late 1970s. Having rejected the Cultural Revolution, dismissed class struggle as the primary mechanism of change and abandoned the idea of an 'all-round dictatorship of the proletariat',[2] Chinese Marxism embarked on a road that appeared to return it to the materialism of Karl Marx's 1859 'Preface' to *A Contribution to the Critique of Political Economy*:

> In the social production of their existence, men inevitably enter into definite relations, which are independent of their will, namely relations of production appropriate to a given stage in the development of their material forces of production.... At a certain stage of development, the material productive forces of society come into conflict with the existing relations of

> production.... Then begins an era of social revolution. The changes in the economic foundation lead sooner or later to the transformation of the whole immense superstructure.
>
> (Marx 1971 [1859]: 20–1)

With its emphasis on developing the productive forces, this approach seems to offer a different programme for transition to a socialist society – promote capitalist relations of production to generate economic development and thereby create the material conditions for the transition to socialism. In China, it led to the valorizing of a type of market regime that, by 1978, had led the Chinese Communist Party (CCP) to move beyond the classic Marxist formula to announce a radical economic reform programme that slowly and unevenly pushed China towards the embrace of a fully blown (socialist) market economy.

What distinguishes the Chinese case from that of Western Europe is that this was not just a theoretical question; the rethinking of Chinese Marxism has generated major institutional and societal change, and transformed the Chinese state. What had once been, to use the Chinese expression, an 'all-round' or comprehensive dictatorship gave way to a splintering of the state question into a series of debates about iron-clad economic laws, key areas of modernization, developments in specialized knowledge regimes and increasing productivity through markets. The economy became a privileged domain in all affairs of state. Development would no longer be driven by political intensity born of sacrifice and passionate commitment. Instead, politics and the state were turned into a rational, protective shell surrounding an economic machine driven by market-based incentives (Dutton 2005: 163).

Market-based initiatives require legal protection and that required the development of a full legal code.[3] Thus law, like the state, was no longer regarded as a class tool, but increasingly came to be regarded as an arbiter of truth that, in the last instance, was also an instrument to protect the market.[4] Increasingly, the Party slogan, 'Seeking Truth From Facts' (*shishiqiushi* 实事求是), which on the surface does not seem very different from the neoliberal obsession with evidence-based policy, meant seeking market veridiction.

Alongside legal reform, histories had to be retold,[5] philosophy rewritten,[6] and when marketization led to an increasing degree of affluence in large parts of China's eastern seaboard, a culture industry developed. All of these changes, and more, took place as the Chinese state increasingly divested itself of the spaces it had once totally colonized. Large parts of what had formally been the responsibility of the state were gradually privatized, and the profit motive, and new specialisms and professions necessary for the smooth functioning of the market economy, were introduced and developed.

The development of the market economy became the new basis upon which the Party sought to legitimize its rule following the failed Maoist attempts to develop a radical socialist alternative built around political intensity. The machinery of state that had once been used to channel and harness political intensity was gradually dismantled, rebuilt, realigned, and reverse-engineered to enable it to adapt to the central space allocated to market veridiction. This was necessary because market veridiction operates in quite a different fashion from regimes of political veridiction.

Like market veridiction, political veridiction operates through harnessing and channelling affective flows, but with a different rhythm, focus, and set of truth claims, it constitutes a quite different language game.[7] Where the Maoist political promised a socialist modernity based on the state's colonization of everything, economic reform as an overarching mentality of government has gradually dispersed everything through the use of market forces. Where the Maoist control of the state employed centralized planning and the machinery of political intensification to deploy its forces economically, the economic reform programme uses market mechanisms and the individual profit motive. Unlike Maoism, market-based modernization programmes run through, between and sometimes away from the state, rather than being generated out of it. As market forces took hold, the dictatorial, total and repressive Marxist state apparatus splintered into questions of investment, economy, profit and the law. It was because of these sorts of concrete changes in China that a number of western scholars of China found a useful toolbox in Michel Foucault's work on mentalities of government (Foucault 1991 [1978]; see Bray 2005; Dutton 2005; Greenhalgh and Winckler 2005; Hoffman 2010; Jeffreys 2011).

Thus, at around the same time, at either end of the globe, in different realms of knowledge production and for radically different reasons, a series of theoretical questions emerged out of Marxist debates about the state. In rethinking the approach to take in relation to these questions of the state, the European 'crisis' provided the conceptual tools to understand the importance of changing mentalities of government. In China, the transformation from Maoism to the market demonstrated concretely a changing mentality of government.

From a theory of the state to theorizing government

'We have to be frank about it, there does not really exist any "Marxist theory of the State"', said Louis Althusser in 1978 (Althusser 1978: 219). That same year Michel Foucault offered a radical redrafting of the question of 'the State' around the arts and concerns of government, which he termed governmentality. This approach, therefore, appeared at a crucial juncture. It appeared at the moment the Marxist theory of the State was crumbling as a theoretical concept, not through violent struggles, revolutions, or concrete political actions – events which would take place 11 years later, when the Berlin Wall came down – but rather by a turn in theory.

In western Marxist intellectual circles in the 1970s, the concept of the State began to crumble under the crippling weight of a theory of the State that was little more than a formal and institutional elaboration of the dictatorial consequences of class struggle. Class struggle itself was little more than a class specification of the friend and enemy distinction that underpins Carl Schmitt's concept of the political (Schmitt 1996). The state as a tool for the condensation and intensification of the political struggle against the enemy was, almost by definition, always functioning as a total state. Class struggle framed a binary understanding of the political that, as a concrete tool, took the form of a dictatorial state.

The concept of a dictatorship of the proletariat hardened the Marxist approach to the State, turning it into a 'special apparatus', to use Lenin's words. This special apparatus was necessarily repressive because of the nature of the enemy it faced. Rendered thus, the Marxist theory of the State posited a formation that was both totalizing and repressive. Yet, as Althusser (1971: 134–6) notes, it was descriptive rather than theoretical.

Althusser (1978) responded to the emergence of post-structuralist critiques that challenged the unities upon which this Marxist theory of the State rested by conceding points, while simultaneously endeavouring to incorporate aspects of the new approach into Marxist theory as a supplement. Althusser (1978) conceded that there was a positivism present in Marx's overly arithmetic and calculable conceptualization of surplus value in *Capital* (Volume 1).[8] The arithmetic formula that rendered the presence of surplus value visible to reason only came to the fore by reducing labour power to a commodity form, thus raising the temptation 'for this (arithmetical) presentation of surplus value [to] be taken for a complete theory of exploitation', Althusser claimed.[9] On the theory of the State, he acknowledged that Marxism drew a 'negative demarcation line and definition'[10] and therefore lacked the type of 'positivity' he would bring to the question by employing the psychoanalytic theory of interpolation. This, then, enabled class fluidities to be explained within the template of the existing Marxist theory of the State (Althusser 1971). More radically, perhaps, the Althusserian-inspired theorist, Nicos Poulantzas (1978), attempted to incorporate post-structuralist elements into a new Marxist theory of the State by building on Foucault's notion of power as fluid to theoretically redefine the state as a condensation of class relations.

All of these attempts at salvaging a Marxist theory of the State were to no avail because, ultimately, the concept of class struggle always intervened to produce the simply binary of friend and enemy, which inevitably led to 'the enemy' and 'the State' being rendered as repressive and total. It was precisely this repressive rendition of a total state that attracted one of Foucault's earliest critiques. In response to Marxist conceptions of the state, Foucault said:

> [O]ne of the first things that has to be understood is that power isn't localized in the State apparatus and that nothing in society will be changed if the mechanisms of power that function outside, below, and alongside the State apparatuses, on a much more minute and everyday level, are not also changed.
>
> (Foucault 1980: 60)

By 1978, questions of 'the State' had given way to broader concerns about security, population and government, and understandings of the flow of power as not built around the state, but rather running through it, flowing into and out of its cracks, welling up around different issues and transforming its function while giving it life.

In his February 1978 lecture on 'Governmentality', Foucault (1991) showed how a different concept of government, built around a changing mentality, extended questions beyond, through, and away from the concerns of state and led towards thoughts that privileged the government of the economy and the regime of market veridiction that flowed from that privileging.[11] In Europe, he argued, this could all be traced back historically to the moment of Sovereignty and the Prince (Foucault 1991: 91). Just as it was under the watchful eye of Louis XIV that disciplinary power emerged,[12] so too it was under the watchful eye of the Prince that the word 'economy' gained its modern meaning (Foucault 1991: 91–2; for a different account see Walter 2011). The significance of this in terms of the modern regime of market veridiction lies in the fact that this new understanding of the word gradually, unevenly, and in disparate and often disconnected ways, brought on a new regime of truth. It is a regime of truth that gained theoretical expression and formulation in political economy and when that was tied to the *raison d'état*, it formed the basis of a new art of government which, as Foucault (2008: 27–9) pointed out, was the art of the least possible government, or what he called 'frugal government'.

Frugal government transformed the flow of power by dispersing it into various semi-autonomous regimes of care, which, within technologies of economic profit, found political expression in liberalism – the political form the word 'economy' took as the regime of market veridiction took hold.[13] Frugality in western contexts was subsequently not confined to an economic jurisdiction; it spread throughout society through the market. Critically, this notion of frugality, tied as it was to economy, swelled into a more general economy of power. Governmentality thus plots the theoretical path away from a focus on grand questions of sovereignty, the state and other such abstractions, towards studies of the micro-physics of power expressed in institutional forms.

Chinese governmentality was different; frugality came to government in contemporary China through Maoism. It was not frugal government, but frugalness within government and this took the name self-reliance. Self-reliance was an inherently political creed – it had once saved the CCP and as a result was a part of the Party's lexicon. Frugality had, by necessity, become a way of life for Chinese communists forced to flee the cities for the bandit-ridden and remote wilderness of Jinggangshan after the massacre of communists in Shanghai in 1927. Frugality involved making do and in Jinggangshan that meant an investment in indigenous, telluric ways and knowledge forms.

The Maoist creed of self-reliance that emerged from this first encounter with rural China spread across the Party and, much later, into the concerns of government, producing a mode of government policy and practice that involved continual experimentation and an ability to make ad-hoc adjustments. While not producing an 'art of the least possible government', it was an art of government that demanded the use of the least possible material resources. Frugality within government then spread to cover all facets of life because government policy was anything but frugal in the life space it colonized.

For Maoism, frugality rendered as self-reliance was an important part of a political programme to enable communists to be one with the people in thought and deed. This creed is still one of the theoretical bedrocks of the CCP. However, with the introduction of economic reforms, it increasingly moved from being a moral pillar to becoming an abstraction. With self-reliance rendered abstract, the concrete form that frugality took in the economic reform period was efficiency.

With the Chinese economic reform, frugality was tied back to the word economy and, as that transition occurred, it moved from informing a political creed into something that reinforced the privileging of the regime of market veridiction. '[T]he market must be that which reveals something like a truth', says Foucault (2008: 32). In reform-era China, truth would be revealed in the iron-clad 'economic laws' that were underpinned by a strong streak of positivism running through the discipline of political economy (Reglar 1985).

Frugalness as efficiency opened onto marketized spaces and new knowledge regimes. As the other chapters in this book show, changes in economics, history, law and philosophy accompanied policy changes in health care (Cooper; Yu), spatiality (Bray; Cartier), and morality campaigns (Jeffreys and Su). They have also led to the formation of new disciplines (Sigley), new questions (elite philanthropy and volunteering, Jeffreys; Hoffman) and new concerns such as the biopolitics of beauty and the internet (Woronov).

In short, the singularity of political focus that had once dominated the Maoist period has been shattered into an array of different domains as the logic of the market spread into more and more domains. However, even as this new system of market veridiction gradually superseded the old unified political system, there was still, often in de-politicized forms, an echo of Maoism. That echo is a continuing style of thought.

Sebastian Heilmann and Elizabeth Perry (2011: 7) note this continuing attachment to a Maoist style of thought in what they call the 'guerrilla-style policy making' system that prevails in contemporary Chinese government. It is a mentality not a policy formulation. It involves controlling the commanding heights of the economy, a fundamental belief in public property rights, and an acceptance of pervasive administrative interference and Party supervision of senior managers. In policy terms, it means ceaseless change, tension management, continual experimentation, and ad-hoc adjustments (Heilmann and Perry 2011: 1–29).

Although the politics of Mao has long gone, aspects of this style of thought remain and have spread from government into business (Cheng and Liu 2003) and from business into a new style of management (Li Kaicheng 2010; see also Cooper in this book). This is because in China, Maoism is more a forethought than an afterthought. That is to say, it constitutes the ground upon which the new strategies of reform have been concretely and theoretically built, sometimes as simple continuations but more often as a mix of continuation at one level and turning away at others. The break-up and scattering of the old political unities produced by a Maoist technology geared to the production of political intensity has not stopped a continuation of certain aspects of a style of Maoist thought, but rather tied that style into a new notion of the economy. The other chapters in this book examine elements of this new economy and the new concerns and professions it is producing in detail, with many chapters tracing the links between these new elements and older styles of thought.

Thus far, we have suggested that Chinese governmentality appeared in the western context as a viable object of study as a result of the coincidental development of two very different crises of Marxism at the western and eastern sides of the Euro-Asian landmass[14] – one generating governmentality theory and the other producing developments in Chinese practices of government that could be read through the lens of 'governmentality'. However, we noted at the outset that this point of connection misrepresents a far more complex, diverse and concrete set of political questions. In Europe, the real crisis facing Western European Communist Parties was not the lack of a theory of the state; it was lack of popular support for the various communist parties in national elections. In China, economic reform was not a response to a theoretical debate about the nature of the Marxist theory of the State; it stemmed from the gradual introduction of market mechanisms designed to help develop the productive forces. These changes produced their own dynamics, just as the new notion of market veridiction created new demands.

'A crisis of theory' explanation therefore does not really capture the complexity of what was happening either in Europe or in China at the time. Our implicit suggestion that the crisis of Marxism created a space in which the Foucauldian notion of governmentality could emerge is also something of an oversimplification. We noted Foucault's reactions, in lectures delivered in France, to Marxism's focus on the repressive character of the state. Yet reading these against Althusser's 'crisis of Marxism' does not explain how the concept of governmentality was taken up and turned into a research programme or a 'School', mostly in England but with connections in Australasia and Canada. That owed much to the coming together in and around London of a small group of individuals who, on top of their individual contributions, also edited in various combinations, the short-lived but influential journal *Ideology and Consciousness* and two important books, *The Foucault Effect* and *Foucault and Political Reason* (Burchell *et al.* 1991; Barry *et al.* 1996).[15]

In China, there is the historic coincidence that the last of the radical Maoist campaigns before Mao's death was a campaign to study an all-round dictatorship of the proletariat, which was followed by the death of Mao and the arrest of the radicals. The ensuing political arrests and purges of the left encouraged a new reading of Marxism that pushed the focus back on economics and away from class struggle. However, these events had little to do with the crisis of Marxism on the other side of Euro-Asia. Hence, while it is tempting to use the crisis of Marxism as a framing device for the emergence of a Chinese governmentality, this shorthand is too neat to be true.

Nevertheless, we are left with a useful coincidence of timing in which the development on one side of the world produce a novel approach to the analysis of governmental practices on the other. That is to say, at the time Foucault's 'Governmentality' lecture was being written, the Chinese state was opening itself up to new questions of government. Given that governmentality is an approach to the analysis of government developed in Europe, and initially in relation to European conditions, this begs the question whether a governmentality approach can be used for the analysis of government in China.

Theorizing government in contemporary China

We began this chapter by suggesting that the emergence of Chinese governmentality as an object of study could be seen as resulting from simultaneous crises of Marxist theory on the western and eastern sides of the Euro-Asian landmass. We went on to argue that neat rhetorical formula was substantially indefensible, that both crises of Marxist theory should be more properly described in different terms. In the western context, the crisis that we, following Althusser (1978), had originally identified as one of Marxist theory should be seen as a crisis in the ability of communist parties in Western Europe to both attract and retain popular support. In China, what we called a crisis was a matter of the death of Mao Zedong, closely followed by the CCP abandoning Maoist forms of popular struggle and shifting its focus from one pole of Marxist theory, class and related forms of popular struggle, to Marxist theory's other great pole, economic change. Of course, these poles are not unconnected – Karl Marx's 1859 'Preface' argues that when the forces and relations of production come into conflict, 'then begins an era of social revolution' – but it makes a huge difference to the conduct of a ruling party on which of the two it focuses its energies (Marx 1971 [1859]: 20–1). One prioritizes popular struggle – Mao's focus in his later years – and the other prioritizes expansion of the productive forces.

However, while our tale of Western and Eastern crises of Marxist theory offers a useful, if not entirely reliable, frame in which to locate case studies of Chinese governmentality, it does not address the basic question of what exactly governmentality analysis has to offer our understanding of conditions in non-western societies, and China in particular. What do we have to assume in order to transfer governmentality analysis to China?

Three possibilities are worth considering here. The least illuminating, and one that requires little further comment, is that, just as 'the west' has picked up many Chinese inventions and practices over the centuries, China may well have picked up recent governmental practices from 'the west', and it might be interesting to see how they worked out in this alien context.[16] At its best, this view is likely to illuminate some of what is happening in China, but there is always the risk of it, first, sliding into one of the two views we consider below and, second, obscuring anything that cannot easily be read as borrowing or adaptation.

As a non-academic illustration of this last point, we might recall that much recent English-language reporting of popular protest in China has stressed the importance of social media – Facebook, Twitter, and less expensive local alternatives – and thus of American innovation, in a manner that was already familiar from earlier western reporting of the Arab and East-European Springs – only the names of people, locations, and security organizations seemed to change. This left sceptical readers wondering what had happened to indigenous, Chinese or Arab, forms of social organization: had they been rendered helpless by police or were they simply displaced by the electronic toys and the new techniques imported from 'the west' that these toys made possible?

Two other possibilities are worth considering: one is that governmentality has spread to the east following its early outbreaks in Europe and North America; and the other that reflection on the government of others and even of oneself, in something like Foucault's sense, might be a human universal and therefore that governmentality happens in China as it does in other places. While the first image of governmentality as a plague spreading across the world like the Black Death but in the opposite direction does have a certain appeal, it is perhaps more appropriate to think of this as a minor variation on what Dipesh Chakrabarty (2002: 6) calls 'historicism' – that is, of the view that history happens 'first in the West and then elsewhere' but without the strange pretence of European superiority that Chakrabarty identifies. Although it has often been disputed (Chakrabarty 2002; Dussel 1995, 1996; Fabian 1983; Scott 2004; Thornton 2001), this familiar and destructive historicism remains far too influential in the contemporary social sciences, suggesting that the rest of the world, and therefore China, is always somewhere behind 'the west', even if a few parts appear to be catching up rapidly. In practice, we suspect that, once they were aware of its character, no serious exponent of the governmentality approach would wish to be associated with this view, but it might be easy to slip into it without noticing.

What, then, of the idea that government, and reflection upon it, might be a human universal? The difficulty here is that, while, sometimes in interviews, Foucault does discuss government in general terms, specifically in relation to power and domination, his key discussions of government and governmentality focus resolutely on European materials. In his 'Governmentality' lecture and related publications we find him referring to early eighteenth-century European (mostly French) discussions of the government of a wife, household, estate, or parish, and even of a community, usages that were once familiar but have now been abandoned in the western context and all of which share a concern with how the conduct of individuals or of groups might be directed (Foucault 1991). Yet, along with this focus on individuals and groups, we also find Foucault (1991: 91) insisting that one form of government was seen as 'special and precise', namely, 'the particular form of governing which can be applied to the state as a whole'. 'Governmentality' as a mode of analysis has been particularly concerned to understand how this form of governing has been understood (that is, to understand its rationalities) and how other forms of government (the government, that is, of the conduct of individuals and groups) have been brought within its remit.

What is not so clear from the text of Foucault's 'Governmentality' lecture are the ways in which his discussion draws on Aristotle's treatment of government in *The Politics* (Aristotle 1998). Like Foucault, Aristotle discusses various forms of government – of a wife and children, a household and of slaves – but he also accords the government of the state a special place in his broader discussion (Hindess 2005). Thus, assuming that there is more to Chinese governmentality than adapting a few practices and habits of thought gathered from 'the west', what grounds might we have for assuming that governmentality, in something like Foucault's sense, can reasonably be applied to China?

Rather than seek a Chinese tradition of thinking about politics that corresponds to the Aristotelian tradition that has been so influential in the western context and in Foucault's own discussion of governmentality, we have suggested that governmentality in China can be seen as the outcome of a history that is radically different from the one that Foucault has traced in the western context. Governmentality, with Chinese characteristics, belongs to the legacy of Maoism. It is part of what remains after Mao's grand projects were abandoned and the CCP directed its attention towards the economy. Our point, of course, is not that Mao was the Chinese Aristotle, but rather that, in limited but important respects, Mao's focus on channelling the energies of individuals, groups, and collectivities towards a particular end had similar concerns to those produced through the Aristotelian focus on the government of conduct. Maoism, in being centrally concerned with the transformation of everyday life, that is, with the wives and children, households, and (former) 'slaves' of the now 'liberated' China, made the government of these domains central to its mode of rule.

More than institutional forms, Maoism produced mentalities of government that clustered around ideas not just about rulership, but also about revolutionary change. One of the key ideas was that the state and government were crucial tools that could help produce social transformation. Clearly, Maoism failed in its aim of producing such total social transformation. But in its endless attempts to induce such change – employing everything from art to education, from political campaigning to the reorganization of everyday life – it produced a particular and quite resilient style of thought. It was a style of thought that would survive even after its all-consuming focus on the political had been repressed. It would survive but realign itself to face the market.

It is this style of thought that still shadows contemporary China, largely because it continues to inform the so-called guerrilla-style public policy of government, the new management techniques that employ Maoist principles, the red tourist industry, and even the critical and sometimes ironic redeployment of Maoism in art and in kitsch (see also Cartier; Cooper; Jeffreys and Su in this book). It is a style of thought that manifests in certain ways of doing. This style may even register in domains that no longer directly fall within the purview of government because it is a style that transcends political boundaries. How this legacy has been interpolated, expelled, repressed, transformed or redirected into a positivity within limits now imposed by the market, how it has insinuated itself into contemporary discourses, how it has splintered or been realigned to form new configurations under conditions of market veridiction, all point to something other than the reemergence of radical Maoism, nostalgia, or the lingering remnants of past forms that will vanish as soon as economic reform gains the upper hand. It is important to note, however, that while this Maoist style of thought is not without a certain politics, it is nevertheless a style rather than a political viewpoint.

This book helps to unpack that style of thought in a number of ways and in a number of key areas of contemporary Chinese life. While showing the transformation of certain domains under the influence of market reform or the emergence of new domains with new problems, collectively these chapters still flag the fact that this style of thought has persisted. Neither remnant in form nor nostalgic in outlook, this Maoist mentality, when faced with a regime of market veridiction, has resulted in a series of hybridic, uneven, and sometimes contradictory forces being brought into play. Governmentality, as a method of focusing on styles of thought in the government of various domains, offers a novel and productive way of addressing such hybridity.

Notes

1 In hindsight, Althusser's story seems highly implausible. What or where was the Marxist theory of the State? Even Althusser admits that Lenin laid down only the foundations of a theory. At this time, Althusser's was but one of the Marxist theories of the state that made their way into English language. Althusser's problem was that the European communist parties were all losing support and, apart from Eurocommunism, there were few strategies as to how to lure back intellectuals who had deserted the communist parties. Althusser's 'Ideological State Apparatus', while being one attempt to develop a theory of the State, was not widely supported. In effect, what had 'snapped' was the idea that the labour movement and Marxist theory could be brought together under the leadership of a communist party (Althusser 1978: 215).

2 The idea of an all-round dictatorship of the proletariat (*quanmian wuchanjieji zhuanzheng* 全面无产阶级专政) emerged in the PRC in 1975, when a political campaign to study the Marxist theory of the State took place.

3 It is often said that the PRC 'lacked' law or rule of law in the conventional western sense before the introduction of economic reforms. There are reasons why Maoist guerrilla-style politics when wed to socialism had no need for the law. But once the market influences grew, a more conventional western reading proffered the idea of law governing everything, including the state. The PRC's first criminal code came into effect in 1980 and by the end of the 1980s the PRC had a massively developing legal infrastructure.

4 In the early 1980s a series of debates opened up on the question of law as a class tool (see Zhou Fengju 1980).

5 Chinese debates in the 1980s within historiography, which announced its own crisis, centred on a reappraisal of the idea that the masses are the makers of history and all history is the history of class struggle (Su Shuangbi 1982).

6 Debates within the field of philosophy would take place throughout the 1980s in the pages of the then seminal philosophy journal *Philosophical Questions* (*Zhexue Yanjiu* 哲学研究).

7 As Boris Groys (2009) notes, economics and markets do not lie at the heart of all regimes. In his words, the former Soviet Union was 'the project of subordinating the

economy to politics to allow politics to act freely and sovereignly. The economy functions in the medium of money. It operates with numbers. Politics functions in the medium of language' (Groys 2009: xv).

8 That, according to Althusser (1978: 219), was 'defined by the difference (in value) between the value produced by labour power on the one hand, and the value of the commodities necessary for the reproduction of this same labour power (wages) on the other'.

9 Althusser (1978: 219) would go on to imply that this was a misunderstanding produced by Marx's own order of exposition rather than a fundamental problem of theory. That is to say, Marx covered these hidden elements but not in his explanation of surplus value. Thus the temptation.

10 Marx and Lenin, says Althusser (1978: 219), often repeated warnings to avoid all the bourgeois conceptions of the state, therefore a negative demarcation line and definition.

11 The centrality of market veridiction becomes apparent when governmentality is read as a history of the present and alongside *The Birth of Biopolitics: Lectures at the Collège de France 1978–1979* (Foucault 2008: 27–47).

12 Speaking of a medallion showing Louis XIV before a parade of his troops, Foucault (1978: 189) would comment: 'Let us take this medal as evidence of the moment when, paradoxically but significantly, the most brilliant figure of sovereign power is joined to the emergence of the rituals proper to disciplinary power'.

13 Foucault (2008: 31–2) says:

> The importance of economic theory – I mean the theory constructed in the discourse of the *économistes* and formed in their brains – the importance of the theory of the price–value relationship is due precisely to the fact that it enables economic theory to pick out something that will become fundamental: that the market must be that which reveals something like a truth. This does not mean that prices are, in the strict sense, true, and that there are true prices and false prices. But what is discovered at this moment, at once in governmental practice and in reflection on this governmental practice, is that inasmuch as prices are determined in accordance with the natural mechanisms of the market they constitute a standard of truth which enables us to discern which governmental practices are correct and which are erroneous. In other words, it is the natural mechanism of the market and the formation of a natural price that enables us to falsify and verify governmental practice.

14 We refer to the sides of a single Euro-Asian landmass in order to avoid any reference to two separate continents. As J.G.A. Pocock (2002) argues, Europe and Asia are not two distinct continents in the conventional geo-physical sense of the term – that is, they are not distinct land masses separated by water or joined by no more than a narrow strip of land, as North and South America are joined by the relatively narrow strip of land now called Central America. To label Europe and Asia as distinct continents is a geopolitical move in which the boundaries (a) are always open to contestation and (b) carry unpleasant connotations that have no place in our argument.

15 On the idea of a governmentality school, see Mitchell Dean (1999) and William Walters (2012). See also Colin Gordon's sceptical observations in an interview with Jacques Donzelot (Donzelot and Gordon 2008: 51–2).

16 See, for example, Peter Larmour's illuminating study of institutional reform by Pacific Island governments (Larmour 2005).

References

Althusser, L. (1971) *Lenin and Philosophy and Other Essays*, London: Monthly Review Press.

Althusser, L. (1978) 'The crisis of Marxism', *Marxism Today*, July: 215–27.

Aristotle (1998) *The Politics*, Indianapolis: Hackett Publishing.

Barry, A., Osborne, T., and Rose, N. (eds) (1996) *Foucault and Political Reason: Liberalism, Neo-Liberalism, and Rationalities of Government*, Chicago: University of Chicago Press.

Bray, D. (2005) *Social Space and Governance in Urban China: The Danwei System From Origins to Reform*, Stanford: Stanford University Press.

Burchell, G., Gordon, C., and Miller, P. (eds) (1991) *The Foucault Effect: Studies in Governmentality*, Chicago: University of Chicago Press.

Chakrabarty, D. (2002) *Habitations of Modernity: Essays in the Wake of Subaltern Studies*, Chicago: University of Chicago Press.

Cheng Dongsheng and Liu Lili (2003) *Huawei Zhengxiang* [The Truth about Huawei], Beijing: Xiandai Zhongguo Chubanshe.

Dean, M. (1999) *Governmentality: Power and Rule in Modern Society*, London: Sage.

Donzelot, J. and Gordon, C. (2008) 'Governing liberal societies: the Foucault effect in the English-speaking world', *Foucault Studies*, 5: 48–62.

Dussel, E. (1995) *The Invention of the Americas: Eclipse of 'the Other' and the Myth of Modernity*, New York: Continuum Publishing.

Dussel, E. (1996) *The Underside of Modernity: Apel, Ricoeur, Rorty, Taylor and the Philosophy of Liberation*, New York: Humanities Press.

Dutton, M. (2005) *Policing Chinese Politics: A History*, Durham: Duke University Press.

Fabian, J. (1983) *Time and the Other: How Anthropology Makes Its Object*, New York: Columbia University Press.

Foucault, M. (1978) *Discipline and Punish: The Birth of the Prison*, London: Penguin Books.

Foucault, M. (1980) 'Body/power', in C. Gordon (ed.), *Power/Knowledge: Selected Interviews and Other Essays 1972–1977*, New York: Harvester Wheatsheaf, pp. 55–62.

Foucault, M. (1991 [1978]) 'Governmentality' (Lecture at the Collège de France, 1 February 1978), in G. Burchell, C. Gordon, and P. Miller (eds), *The Foucault Effect: Studies in Governmentality*, Chicago: University of Chicago Press, pp. 87–104.

Foucault, M. (2008) *The Birth of Biopolitics: Lectures at the Collège de France 1978–1979*, New York: Palgrave Macmillan.

Greenhalgh, S. and Winckler, E.A. (2005) *Governing China's Population: From Leninist to Neoliberal Biopolitics*, Stanford: Stanford University Press.

Groys, B. (2009) *The Communist Postscript*, London: Verso.

Heilmann, S. and Perry, E. (2011) *Mao's Invisible Hand: The Political Foundations of Adaptive Governance in China*, Boston: Harvard University Press.

Hindess, B. (2005) 'Politics as government: Michel Foucault's analysis of political reason', *Alternatives*, 30: 389–414.

Hoffman, L. (2010) *Patriotic Professionalism in Urban China: Fostering Talent*, Philadelphia: Temple University Press.

Jeffreys, E. (ed.) (2011 [2009]) *China's Governmentalities: Governing Change, Changing Government*, Abingdon: Routledge.

Larmour, P. (2005) *Foreign Flowers: Institutional Transfer and Good Governance in the Pacific Islands*, Honolulu: University of Hawaii Press.

Li Kaicheng (2010) *Xiang Mao Zedong Xue Guanli* [Learning Management from Mao Zedong], Beijing: Xiandai Zhongguo Chubanshe.
Marx, K. (1971 [1859]) *A Contribution to the Critique of Political Economy*, London: Lawrence and Wishart.
Pocock, J.G.A. (2002) 'Some Europes in their history', in A. Pagden (ed.), *The Idea of Europe: From Antiquity to the European Union*, Washington and Cambridge: Woodrow Wilson Center and Cambridge University Press, pp. 55–71.
Poulantzas, N. (1978) *State, Power, Socialism*, London: Verso.
Reglar, S. (1985) 'The law of value debate: a tribute to the late Sun Yefang', in B. Brugger (ed.), *Chinese Marxism in Flux, 1978–1984*, London: Croom Helm, pp. 171–203.
Schmitt, C. (1996) *The Concept of the Political*, Chicago: University of Chicago Press.
Scott, D. (2004) *Conscripts of Modernity: The Tragedy of Colonial Enlightenment*, Durham: Duke University Press.
Su Shuangbi (1982) *Jiejidouzheng yu Lishikexue* [Class Struggle and the Science of History], Shanghai: Shanghai Renmin Chubanshe.
Thornton, A. (2001) 'The developmental paradigm, reading history sideways, and family change', *Demography*, 38, 4: 449–65.
Walter, R. (2011) *A Critical History of the Economy: On the Birth of the National and International Economies*, Abingdon: Routledge.
Walters, W. (2012) *Governmentality: Critical Encounters*, Abingdon: Routledge.
Zhou Fengju (1980) 'Fa danchun shi jiejidouzheng de gongju ma?' [Is law purely a tool of class struggle], *Faxue Yanjiu*, 1: 1–10.

3 Governing through Lei Feng

A Mao-era role model in reform-era China

Elaine Jeffreys and Su Xuezhong

This chapter demonstrates China's changing and hybrid mentalities of government by examining the revival of Lei Feng (雷锋) – a 1960s socialist role model – as the public face of a 2012–2013 government advertising campaign to promote civic behaviours, especially volunteering. Lei Feng, depicted in Figure 3.1, was a peace-time soldier with the People's Liberation Army (PLA), who died in an accident in 1962. He became famous in 1963 when his life-story, encapsulated in a diary that celebrates Mao Zedong Thought and the 'socialist'

Figure 3.1 Comrade Lei Feng reading *Mao Zedong's Selected Works* (source: photograph by Elaine Jeffreys, Hunan Lei Feng Memorial Hall, 2013).

values of altruism, thrift, and working hard for public goals, was promoted through a national mobilization campaign as a model of socialist citizenship. Media statements by Chairman Mao and Premier Zhou Enlai urged the Chinese populace to 'Learn from Comrade Lei Feng' and to 'Learn the Correct Class Stance and How to Practice the Revolutionary, Proletarian-communist Spirit of Selflessness from Comrade Lei Feng' ('Zhongguo qingnian chuban' 1963). Subsequent commemorative events have ensured that most people in China are familiar with the Lei Feng 'spirit' of selfless public service. That spirit is sometimes caricatured as 'old-fashioned' through spoofs and the sale of retro-revolutionary fashion and kitsch (Steen 2014), and even ridiculed for its 'brainless simplicity' (Humphrey 2005: 41). However, in 2012, Lei Feng became the 'celebrity face' of a two-year-long government communication campaign encouraging China's citizens to adopt 'good' civic behaviours.

Lei Feng's official media presence in 2012 was greater than at any other point in the history of the People's Republic of China (PRC), based on the number of occurrences of the keyword 'Lei Feng' in the online database for the media voice of the Chinese Communist Party (CCP) – the *People's Daily* – between 1960 and 2013 (Renmin Ribao Dianziban 1946–present). As Figure 3.2 shows, Lei Feng became a major focus of national media attention in 1963 (around 260 hits). Apart from commemorative publicity each decade since then, media publicity about Lei Feng increased in 1966, 1977 and 1981 (around 300 hits, respectively), temporarily peaked in 1990 (525 hits), climaxing in 2012 (579 hits). These dates correlate with specific government campaigns: (1) Mao's 1963 call to 'Learn from Comrade Lei Feng'; (2) the 'official' start of the Great Proletarian Cultural Revolution in 1966; (3) the 1977 campaign to 'smash the Gang of Four' after Mao's death in 1976 – the 'Gang' (Jiang Qing, Wang Hongwen, Yao

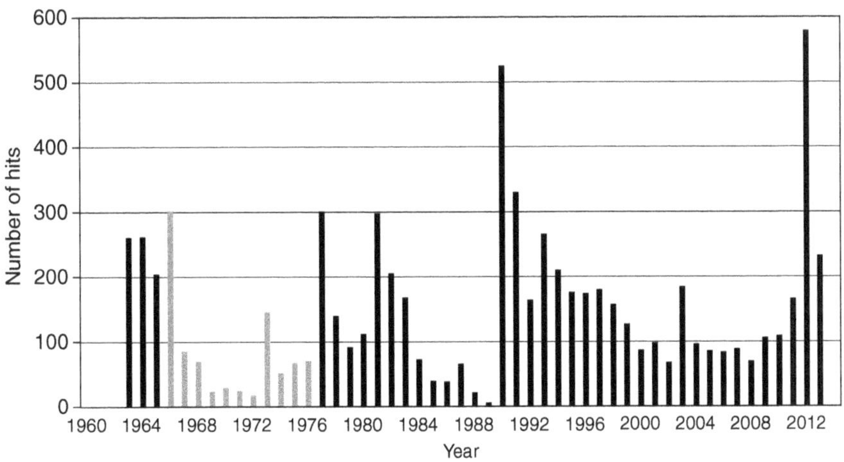

Figure 3.2 Number of hits for 'Lei Feng' in the *People's Daily* (1960–2013) (source: Renmin Ribao Dianziban (1946–present) OriProbe Information Services, Windsor, Canada).

Wenyuan, and Zhang Chunqiao) were officially blamed for the 'ten-year-disaster' of the Cultural Revolution; (4) the trial of the Gang for 'crimes against the people' in 1981; (5) the launch in 1990 of youth education campaigns after the 1989 crackdown on protesters in Tiananmen Square; and (6) the 2012–2013 campaign to promote civic behaviours and volunteering, which also commemorated the fiftieth anniversary of Lei's death and Mao's call to 'Learn from Lei Feng'.

Foreign correspondents dismissed the government-led revival of Lei Feng as anachronistic. A report by Andrew Jacobs (2012) in the *New York Times* describes it as 'old school propaganda' by a 'ruling party that is struggling to cultivate a sense of legitimacy', but lacks comprehension of contemporary values. According to Jacobs, Lei Feng is a 'joke' because he only 'follows marching orders'. In a report for the *New Yorker*, Evan Osnos (2013) similarly calls Lei Feng his favourite 'Chinese anachronism'. Noting that government-sponsored films about Lei Feng had bombed at the box office, he concludes that 'Chinese people, today, have learned that getting ahead requires relentless self-definition', unlike the collectivist-minded 'late, great icon of Socialist dedication' (Osnos 2013).

Such criticisms present Lei Feng as frozen in time, rather than acknowledging the evolving nature and political uses of his fame in both the Maoist and reform era. Portrayals of Lei Feng do indeed exhibit a sense of continuity through history. But that continuity resides less in his identification with Mao-era ideals of unrelenting hard work and self-sacrifice in pursuit of revolutionary goals, than in his embodiment of the less grandiose ethical imperative of displaying kindness to others. Criticisms of Lei Feng as a 'brainless' anachronism have little to offer in the way of explanation either for the CCP's continued (and intensive) use of Lei Feng, or for the changing ways in which his persona has been utilized and represented.

An alternative way of making sense of Lei Feng's contemporary presence is to consider him as a postsocialist celebrity. Arif Dirlik (2005: 229–50) coined the term 'postsocialism' to highlight the hybridity of reform-era China as being a reaction and response to revolutionary Maoism *and* global capitalism, and therefore as both 'postsocialist' and 'postcapitalist' by adopting market mechanisms to correct the entrenched poverty of Mao-era socialism, and inserting a self-proclaimed socialist country into global capitalism. It may seem unusual to characterize Lei Feng as a 'celebrity', since at face value a dead socialist role model shares little in common with a contemporary film or pop star. But on a conceptual level, celebrity can be understood as an industry-coordinated 'media process' and 'the celebrity' may be theorized as a commodity, text, or sign that is 'productively consumed by audiences and fans' (Turner 2004: 20). As we demonstrate below, Lei Feng can be conceptualized as a postsocialist celebrity in the sense that he is presented through contemporary commercial and media processes as being both a 'dead famous' but 'obsolete' creation of Mao-era propaganda, *and* a 'living text' imprinted with different, and changing, visions (both official and popular) of what past, present, and future Chinese citizenship signifies.

We use Michel Foucault's definition of government as 'the conduct of conduct' to demonstrate Lei Feng's significance as the historical and contemporary face of government efforts to guide citizen behaviours, a referent for 'counter-conduct' or resistances to such efforts, and a means by which individuals may debate the conduct of others and modify their own conduct (Foucault 2007: 191–226). First, we outline the history of Lei Feng and his creation, via state-controlled media, as a socialist role model. Second, we trace how Lei Feng was dislodged from his original Mao-era incarnation as a new proletarian citizen in the wake of the PRC's post-1978 rejection of radical socialism and adoption of market-based economic reforms. Third, we explore the reform-era commercialization of Lei Feng and his infiltration, via satire, parody, and advertising, into the world of contemporary popular culture. Fourth, we examine the recent revived and modified use of Lei Feng by the PRC Government to promote civic behaviours. Finally, we consider two domains in which this revived use of Lei Feng has been prominent: the endorsement of philanthropic activities by entrepreneurs through the ascription or appropriation of the title 'living Lei Feng'; and the perception of Lei Feng-linked volunteering and charitable activities by Chinese students. In the latter case, we present the results of an online multiple-choice survey of Chinese university students, conducted in late 2013, to shed light on how Lei Feng is conceptualized by contemporary youth in a period of revived use by government. We conclude that 1960s socialist imagery and values have been recast by Party-state organs, through an interplay with the media and popular culture, to promote new understandings of state–society relations, while attempting to keep alive the notion that the PRC's revolutionary history and the CCP matters.

Proletarian role model

The original Lei Feng was linked to technologies for governing the conduct of others and the self that were based on three fundamental principles of Maoist politics. The first was the 'friend–enemy' opposition of class struggle (Dutton 2005). The second was a mass-line asceticism that aimed to incentivize people living in a poor nation forged after decades of war to work hard collectively with minimal resources to create a modern, socialist China. The third was the revolutionary creed of 'serving the people' (see also Dutton and Hindess, in this book).

The friend–enemy opposition framed daily life in Mao-era China (1949–1976) and was embedded in life-stories presented for public emulation in the state-controlled media, such as that of Lei Feng. Lei Feng became a focus of national media attention on 5 May 1961, when the *People's Daily* featured an origin story about him titled 'A Suffering Child Becomes an Outstanding People's Soldier' (Jun Fen 1961).[1] The page-four article tells of a poor peasant boy being saved by the CCP and becoming an active socialist citizen. It claims that Lei Feng was born in Hunan Province around 1940 and was orphaned at the age of six. His father died after being tortured by the invading Japanese Army; subsequent reports say he was previously beaten by members of the Nationalist Party Army

(Zhang Huixin 2009: 5–8). The CCP defeated these armies to establish the PRC. Lei's mother committed suicide after she was raped by the son of a local landowner (Jun Fen 1961). His older brother died slowly following a machinery accident and his younger brother starved to death. The family-less Lei Feng roamed the countryside foraging for food until his village was liberated by the PLA. After participating in a class-struggle session, where the landlord responsible for his mother's death and other crimes was executed, Lei Feng was placed under the care of local Party organizations and went to school. This narrative presents the CCP by implication as a 'friend' in the struggle of Lei Feng and the Chinese people against their enemies and to realize a better life.

The article concludes that Lei Feng, and by extension other citizen-friends of 'New China', naturally wanted to follow in the footsteps of those who had sacrificed their lives fighting to establish the PRC by contributing to nation construction (Jun Fen 1961). After graduating from secondary school, Lei Feng responded to Party calls for volunteers to accelerate agricultural production, being honoured as a 'labour model' for his outstanding service. In 1958, he learnt to drive a tractor and later participated in projects to dam a river in Hunan Province, and accelerate mining and steel production in Liaoning Province. In 1960, he joined the PLA and then the CCP. As a peace-time soldier, Lei Feng committed his life to alleviating the hardships experienced by the Chinese people. Anecdotes about him indicate that he worked hard, lived frugally and, apart from buying and reading Mao's publications, gave his earnings to local Party projects and helped people in need. In the words attributed to Lei Feng: 'The Party is my family, the people are my family' (Jun Fen 1961).

Following a second article on 25 January 1963, which stated that Lei Feng had died in an accident on 15 August 1962, aged 22 ('Guofangbu pizhuan' 1963), Lei Feng became the feature of a six-page edition of the *People's Daily* on 7 February 1963. The front-page editorial enjoins its readers to 'Be Clear About What to Love and What to Hate' by joining a movement to commemorate Lei Feng, which was gathering pace in military areas of Liaoning by people who knew him or had heard about him ('Ai zeng fenming' 1963). Other reports add that Lei Feng's revolutionary spirit, as exemplified by many small acts of kindness to others, will live forever in people's hearts. They encourage readers to be like Lei Feng – 'a rustless screw' devoted to serving the people and the socialist cause, and constantly heightening one's proletarian class consciousness through the diligent study of Marxism–Leninism–Maoism ('Weida de putong yi bing' 1963).

Diary excerpts attributed to Lei Feng state that: 'After studying the four volumes of *Mao Zedong's Selected Works*, I now truly understand what kind of a man I should be and what I am living for: I live to improve the lives of others.' Another entry says: 'I live to serve the people wholeheartedly, that is, to struggle for the liberation of humankind/communism' (Zhen *et al.* 1963: 2). Yet another famous entry highlights the dual nature of Lei Feng as a model of how to behave towards friends and enemies. It enjoins people to 'treat comrades like the breeze in spring, treat work with enthusiasm like hot summer sunshine, treat individualism like the autumn breeze sweeping away withered leaves, and treat the enemy as ruthlessly as the cold winter' (Liaoning ribao 1963).

The next front-page article about Lei Feng in the *People's Daily* is dated 5 March 1963; 5 March is now known in China as Lei Feng Day, with 1963 being cited retrospectively as the first year of a more than 50-year tradition ('Zhongguo qingnian chuban' 1963). It notes that the *China Youth Magazine* had issued an album on learning from Lei Feng, containing calligraphic inscriptions about Lei Feng by Chairman Mao and other CCP leaders, and an excerpted *Diary of Lei Feng*. The article concluded that Mao's inscription, 'Learn from Comrade Lei Feng', would undoubtedly attract an enthusiastic response.

Mao's call to 'Learn from Comrade Lei Feng' became what the *CPC Encyclopedia* (1995–2014) describes as 'an atomic bomb in everyone's brain', as PRC citizens were mobilized to participate in a nationwide campaign to become 'living Lei Fengs'. On 8 March 1963, the China Federation of Trade Unions issued a notice calling for workplaces to implement activities for workers and their families to learn from Lei Feng how to behave towards others ('Quanguo zonggonghui' 1963). The PLA Literature and Arts Publishing House published a document to assist with this process in April, called *The Diary of Lei Feng 1959–1962* (*Lei Feng Riji 1959–1962* 1963). Lei Feng was the subject of two songs composed in 1963: 'Learn from Lei Feng, the Good Role Model' and 'Take Up Lei Feng's Gun' (Ren and Ren 1990; 'Jieguo Lei Feng de qiang' 2009). The August First Film Studio released a feature film, *Lei Feng*, in March 1965 (dir. Dong Zhaoqi 1964). Commemorative Lei Feng Memorial Halls were built in Liaoning Province in 1964 and Hunan Province in 1968 (Lei Feng Memorial Hall of Hunan China n.d.; 'Shenyang junqu' 2009).

Thus, by the start of the Cultural Revolution (1966–1976), Lei Feng had been presented via mass media and mobilization activities as the epitome of socialist personhood – altruistic, diligent, thrifty, self-effacing, and motivated by love of the CCP, the PRC, and the Chinese people, as demonstrated by his thoughts and deeds as represented in his diary. Lei's self-enforced austerity and willingness to help others is illustrated in diary entries recording how he gave money and food to a fellow soldier when he heard that his colleague's mother was ill, but he had no money to return home or to buy her food (Qi and Xu 2006: 115), and in entries recording his willingness to darn his colleagues' socks and tattered clothing. An entry dated 15 October 1961 presents this 'selfless' revolutionary ethos as heroic:

> Sunday today. I didn't go out; instead I washed 5 mattresses for the comrades in my squad, repaired Gao Kuiyun's bedcover, assisted the cooks to wash more than 600 catties of cabbage, swept inside and outside the room, and other things.... In all, I've done what I should have done. I'm tired but happy.... It's glorious to be a nameless hero.
>
> (Qi and Xu 2006: 150)

This representation of Lei Feng was altered by the Cultural Revolution and subsequently by the CCP's negation of revolutionary Maoism in 1981.

From revolutionary to civic-minded citizen

In 1966, Lei Feng symbolized devotion to Mao Zedong and continuous revolution, an obvious contrast with early depictions of him as a model of revolutionary class unity and more recent depictions of him as simply a civic-minded citizen. A front-page article in the *People's Daily* dated 5 December describes how 2.5 million Red Guards had come to Beijing to see Chairman Mao ('Jiefangjun zhanshi' 1966). The Red Guards refer to a youth paramilitary social movement formed after Mao called on Chinese youth in mid-1966 to take the revolution to a new stage, by opposing those persons within the Party in positions of bureaucratic authority who were compromising the revolution by taking 'the capitalist road', or 'enemies' masquerading as 'friends'. The article provides stories about the Red Guards' acts of public service and praises them as reliable revolutionary successors, citing their familiarity with Mao Zedong's ideas and Lei Feng's deeds, and love of everything associated with the word 'public' (proletarian) (公), and opposition to the word 'private' (capitalism) (私) ('Jiefangjun zhanshi' 1966). Front-page stories in the *People's Daily* on 5 March in 1970 and 1973 similarly call on young people in urban workplaces and agricultural collectives to learn from Lei Feng how to distinguish between the correct (Maoist) class line of continuous revolution and the revisionist line of capitalist restoration ('Ba Maozhuxi' 1970; 'Relie xiangying weida' 1973).

Publicity about Lei Feng then diminished until after Mao's death, when Lei Feng became a part of the 1977 campaign to promote the PRC's new leader, Hua Guofeng, and to condemn the main proponents of continuous revolution – the Gang of Four – as counter-revolutionaries. A front-page article in the *People's Daily* on 5 March presents a calligraphic inscription by Hua Guofeng urging Chinese youth to 'Learn from Lei Feng', adding that his spirit of modest altruism offered a powerful critique of the publicity-grabbing and power-hungry Gang (Renmin Ribao, Hongqi Zazhi 1977). Another article dated 12 November accuses the Gang of 'killing' Lei Feng (Liaoningsheng junqu zhengzhi pipanzu 1977). It explains that Deng Xiaoping (PRC leader after Hua Guofeng) had overheard an old man declaring that Lei was dead when he saw soldiers sitting on a public bus while women and children were standing. The article attributes this lack of civility to the Gang's control over the media and promotion of antagonistic class struggle to obtain power. It also accuses the Gang of falsely denouncing veteran leaders and slandering them as Lei Feng-style 'empty-headed screws'. It concludes that after the Gang's arrest, people had seen new examples of 'living Lei Fengs' on the streets and were joyfully declaring that 'Uncle Lei Feng is back!' Lei Feng is used in this context to epitomize friendship and civility against the enmity generated by the Gang of Four.

Lei Feng's image was therefore revived along with the CCP's negation of the Cultural Revolution, which was associated with the Gang of Four, and dissociated (to some extent) from Mao, in an attempt to reclaim some of the CCP's earlier standing as *the* vanguard party. Maoist concepts of continuous revolution and capitalist roaders directly undermined the Party's legitimacy by challenging understandings of the vanguard party as automatically taking the revolution forward towards socialism and serving the interests of the people. The practical indeterminacy of these concepts also meant that the Cultural Revolution quickly descended into factional-fighting. As 'citizen-friends' sought to identify their 'enemies', amorphously defined as people without a correct proletarian class consciousness, the allocation of class identity became a matter of political and social rivalries (Blecher 1986: 143). A large proportion of Party members were accused of following the capitalist road at one stage or another; many people were accused of being capitalist roaders because other people wanted their jobs or state-allocated homes; and even the Red Guards fought each other to prove that one group or another had a better understanding of Mao Zedong Thought. In short, the praxis of the Cultural Revolution exposed the unstable nature of Marxist–Leninist–Maoist concepts of class as a definitional category and basis for collective social action.

Lei Feng was further dissociated from radical Maoism along with the PRC's post-1978 adoption of market-based economic reforms, also known as 'socialism with Chinese characteristics' (Deng Xiaoping 1983). In February 1981, shortly after the Gang were sentenced to life-imprisonment, the *People's Daily* ran a front-page article stating that the Communist Youth League was encouraging widespread publicity of Lei Feng activities to promote 'socialist spiritual civilization' ('Changdao gongchan zhuyi' 1981). This concept, first articulated by Deng Xiaoping in 1979, refers to the goal of upholding core socialist values, while developing a market economy, and is associated with government efforts to promote political stability and ethical-cultural development in the context of rapid social change (Deng Xiaoping 1979; see also Cartier in this book).

The penultimate peak in official Lei Feng publicity occurred in 1990, following the suppression of student-worker protests in China, and the collapse of the Berlin Wall (and ultimately the collapse of communism in Eastern Europe), in mid-to-late 1989. On 5 March 1990, the *People's Daily* ran a front-page article calling on the nation to learn from Lei Feng how to build socialism with Chinese characteristics ('Zhongyang haozhao' 1990). This was preceded by a January 'Notice' from the Communist Youth League calling on Party and youth organizations to promote a nationwide campaign for young people to learn from Lei Feng, persist with the socialist road and combat 'bourgeois liberalization/spiritual pollution' ('Gongqingtuanzhongyang' 1990). The latter terms referred to combating the perceived negative consequences of China's initial opening up to the rest of the world, including new social problems such as crime and calls for political democratization.

On 5 March 1993, the *People's Daily* ran another front-page article about Lei Feng stating that Hu Jintao (then president of the CCP Central Party School, subsequently PRC President 2003–2013) had given a speech commemorating the thirtieth anniversary of Mao's call to 'Learn from Comrade Lei Feng' ('Zai jinian Mao Zedong' 1993). Hu declared that every citizen who wished to contribute to China's rejuvenation could do so by learning from Lei Feng – an ordinary yet extraordinary 'anybody'. He added that a supportive public environment and incentive mechanisms (awards) were required to foster a new generation of Lei Fengs – people with the patriotic socialist habits of austerity, hard work and ardent 'rustless-screw-style' innovation.

Hu's invocation of the first Lei Feng Day gestured towards historical continuity, while highlighting a more delimited use of Lei Feng as a civic-minded citizen that retained a connection with the Maoist past in terms of generic core values, but was dissociated from revolutionary class politics. 'Learning from Lei Feng' was no longer about helping others to demonstrate and forge class solidarity. Rather, it had been remoulded as a means of cultivating people with the civic virtues required to modernize new 'New China'. These virtues – patriotism, altruism, frugality, hard work, and innovation – derive from the Mao-era experimental (mass-line) mode of government policy and practice that mobilized the Chinese people to transform the state of things, while using the least possible material resources. However, both the substance of those virtues and who embodies them have been transformed in the reform period.

Commercialization and entry into popular culture

Along with the PRC's development of a consumer society, Lei Feng entered the realm of popular culture, a transition initially shepherded by reform-era Party publicity machinery focused on historical-patriotic education. The *Diary of Lei Feng* has been reprinted in more than 200 editions, many of which are collector's items (Zhang Jun 2007). The Lei Feng Memorial Halls are now revolutionary tourism sites. To mark the PRC's sixtieth anniversary in 2009, the 1960s *Lei Feng* film was rereleased as a DVD and repackaged as part of a collection of 'red cinema classics' ('Lei Feng (DVD)' n.d.). An animation series, called *The Story of Lei Feng*, went to air on 1 June 2009 on China's Network Television to coincide with International Children's Day ('Lei Feng de gushi' n.d.). A television series called *Lei Feng* also aired in 2009, casting Olympic diver Tian Liang as Lei Feng. This casting choice attracted controversy, with many people, including some of Lei Feng's 'former military colleagues' reportedly considering Tian an inappropriate stand-in for the 'real' Lei Feng because he is a 'womanizing big spender' ('70 wei Lei Feng zhanyou' 2009; 'Jilü cha feiwen' 2009). Such debate highlights the continued investment of the Party-state and/or certain sectors of the Chinese populace in authorizing public understandings of an authentic Lei Feng.

Lei Feng is the subject of an official Lei Feng website (www.chinaleifeng.com), which went live in May 2012 to mark the fiftieth anniversary of his death. The website provides up-to-date 'news' about Lei Feng and Lei Feng activities, and has interactive forums such as blogs, telephone hotlines, and bulletin boards. Lei Feng has even been reinvented by Party publicists as an award-winning cartoon superhero, 'Lei Feng Knight', who helps others and gives out Christmas presents (Pan and Qu 2014; see Figure 3.3).

Today, Lei Feng hats, T-shirts, bags, badges, and posters can be bought at markets and tourist sites across China, and through multiple online stores; many

Figure 3.3 Lei Feng Knight as Father Christmas (source: photograph by Su Xuezhong, Hunan Lei Feng Memorial Hall, 2013; reproduced courtesy of He Wenlong).

of these products display Mao-era political slogans that have ongoing relevance in the present, whether celebratory or satirical. Such items often display an image of Lei Feng above a slogan in red Chinese characters which says: 'Serve the People'. That slogan was used during the Mao era to underscore the goal of the revolution and was used by President Hu Jintao to describe one of the 'eight rules of conduct' of contemporary Party officials. The other rules reiterate the Lei Feng–Maoist ethos – love China, be diligent, be honest, live plainly, and help others, although 'follow Mao' has been replaced with 'be law-abiding' and 'follow science' ('New moral yardstick' 2006).

One enterprising Chinese condom manufacturer has used Lei Feng iconography to sell packs of condoms (Mitchell 2006). The boxed sets contain a classic image of Lei Feng and the textual injunction to 'Learn from Lei Feng'. When asked about the logic of using Lei Feng's visage to sell condoms, the manufacturer replied: 'Lei Feng would have supported safe sexual conduct and responsible family planning, I believe. And his condoms are stronger than his socks. He would not need to repair them' (cited in Mitchell 2006).

Multiple versions of Lei Feng are celebrated and parodied in other commercial forms. Singer Xue Cun (2013) became famous briefly in the early 2000s for a folk-pop song circulated online with humorous animation called 'All North-Eastern Chinese are Living Lei Fengs'. Designer Zhang Liang has created a commercially successful series of cuddly 'red dolls' composed of a 'little Lei Feng' and his fictitious 'family members' (Li Muyang 2012). Artist Dai Xiang (2012) has created a microblog called the 'New Story of Lei Feng', which contains photoshopped pictures of a doll of Lei Feng in contemporary settings: removing graffiti, reading Mao's works in McDonald's, and appearing in commercial advertisements. In interview, Dai stated that his creation of a 'living Lei Feng' aimed to encourage people to reflect on what Lei Feng meant to them personally. In his words: 'Most people know about Lei from political propaganda. However, independent thinking allows us to decide what Lei means to us now' (Dai Xiang 2012).

Such independent thinking has included making Lei Feng a part of China's 'spoof' culture – a largely youth-based subculture of user-generated media production, which typically involves the remixing and parodying of established works, especially photoshopping and circulating comical images. One such poster satirizes the reform-era slogan 'Let Some People Get Rich First' by photoshopping a 1960s image of Lei Feng washing an army truck, removing the truck and substituting a Ferrari ('Dangdai Lei Feng de biaozhun' n.d.). The Chinese words beneath the image translate as: 'Today's Lei Feng: The Most Glorious Thing in the World is to be Rich and the Most Glorious People are Rich People'. The use of Lei Feng's image here can be read ambiguously as supporting or criticizing the 'affluent materialism' of contemporary Chinese consumers, when compared to Lei Feng's famed frugality and the egalitarian poverty of the Mao era.

In 2012, Hu Xijin, the editor of the *Global Times*, reposted a spoof image on his Twitter-like Weibo microblog of two contemporary political icons photoshopped into Lei Feng images – the artist Ai Weiwei, known for his criticisms of the PRC Government's stance on democracy and human rights, and academic Kong Qingdong, known for his anti-western, anti-capitalist, and anti-economic reform views. While claiming to be saddened by the use of Lei Feng iconography in this context, Hu concluded that: 'The louder the volume of the government campaign to study Lei Feng, the more such spoofs will be enthusiastically circulated online' (cited in Goldkorn 2012).

The popularity of such spoofs contradicts the internet witticism that: 'Early generations of PRC citizens learnt from Lei Feng, subsequent generations (1989ers) revolted against him, and people born in and after the 1990s have forgotten him' (see Mattis 2012). China's internet users – the largest online population in the world – are predominantly young and educated (China Internet Network Information Center 2014). While netizens sometimes present their spoofs as active acts of resistance to the Party-state, many are simply having 'fun'. Irrespective of whether they are intended as critique or entertainment, Lei Feng spoofs contribute to the flow of mutating imagery and narratives about Lei Feng, amplifying the repetitive force of associated government advertising aimed at generating support for generic nation-unifying tasks (developing the economy, promoting national pride through commemorative and celebratory events, and building community and civic behaviours).

In short, the images and life-stories associated with the figure of Lei Feng have become part of contemporary popular and consumer culture, whereby texts from multiple media collectively create a public profile of a 'living Lei Feng' that is no longer under the exclusive control of any individual or institution, including the PRC Government. Although Lei Feng came to fame through the Party-state propaganda machinery, commercial media processes have turned him into a celebrity by providing the means to recreate and circulate multiple new stories about him. As Lei Feng gradually became objectified and imprinted with new interpretations, it also became possible for the Party-state publicity machinery to adapt him to serve new social functions. The flexible nature of Lei Feng's postsocialist celebrity is underscored by the recent government use of Lei Feng as the 'face' of a national campaign to promote contemporary civic behaviours, especially volunteering.

Philanthropy 'poster-boy'

Lei Feng's revival as the celebrity face of a government campaign to promote volunteering in 2012–2013 aimed to draw large groups of young people into planning for the PRC's future, while commemorating its history. Volunteering – defined by the PRC Government as the not-for-profit giving of time, intellect, strength, and skills to support public benefit activities and promote social harmony – has been a growing focus of Chinese public policy since the late 1980s (Ministry of Civil Affairs of the PRC 2013). In 1987, the Ministry of Civil Affairs advocated organizing community-based volunteer services for disadvantaged urban residents (Li Maoping 2012: 28). In 1994, the national China Young Volunteers Association was established under the Chinese Communist Youth League's leadership to promote volunteering and provide services for people in need. The PRC's Ninth Five-Year Plan for National Economic and Social Development (1996–2000) and Summary of the 2010 Long-term Objectives proposed expanding community-based volunteering ('Zhonghua renmin gongheguo' 1996). By 2013, China had an estimated 40 million registered volunteers, mobilized in part as a result of natural disasters and mega-events such as the 2008 Sichuan Earthquake and Beijing Olympics ('Yao Ming huo guoji zhiyuanzhe' 2014; see also Cartier and Hoffman in this book).

The newfound importance ascribed by the government to volunteering is confirmed by the 'China Social Services Volunteer Team Building Guidelines for 2013–2020', which advocate that registered volunteers should comprise 10 per cent of China's population by 2020 (Ministry of Civil Affairs of the PRC 2013). Registered volunteer organizations are organized and mobilized by government departments and Communist Party committees, including the Communist Youth League Committees and Young Volunteer Associations, through coordination with community, non-profit and business organizations (United Nations Development Programme 2011). The expansion of volunteering in the PRC thus aims to incentivize individuals and community and non-profit organizations to work with the state, rather than independently of it, to develop a regulated philanthropic sector that will complement government-provided welfare services by 2020 (Guowuyuan 2014).

Lei Feng was first enlisted in a high-profile fashion as the face of government efforts to promote a philanthropic culture in 2000, when the Central Committee of the Communist Youth League and the Young Volunteers Association renamed Lei Feng Day 'China Youth Volunteer Service Day' ('Zhongguo qingnian zhiyuan fuwuri' 2012). This action linked Lei to the UN International Volunteer Day and Millennium Development Goals, which include eradicating extreme poverty, combating AIDS and malaria, and ensuring environmental sustainability. Thus, it connected Lei Feng to new programmes of domestic and international governance.

In March 2012, the CCP Central Committee Office released a document called 'Suggestions on Enhancing Efforts to Learn from Lei Feng', stating that local communities and residents should be encouraged to provide volunteer services following Lei Feng's example of helping others, reflecting 'traditional Chinese virtues' and based on love of the CCP, China, socialism, and the Chinese people ('Zhonggong zhongyang bangongting yinfa' 2012). The document urged Party organizations and local and provincial-level governments to organize diverse Lei Feng activities using multiple media forms. Examples included: biannual awards to recognize outstanding community service; prizes for volunteer-themed student essays, theatre, and exhibitions; promoting the Lei Feng Memorial Halls; using art, film, television, literature, the internet, and mobile phones to spread the 'Lei Feng Spirit'; and promoting Lei Feng activities in workplaces, shopping malls, and transport hubs, etc. As a result, images of Lei Feng and endorsements to 'Learn from Lei Feng' could be observed throughout the PRC in 2012–2013.

Government advertising for the campaign drew on Lei Feng iconography and symbolism, but also encouraged China's citizens to express universal love and empower themselves as 'global' self-governing individuals, rather than to demonstrate revolutionary solidarity through individual sacrifice. For example, the PRC's Publicity and Information Department, the State Administration for Industry and Commerce, the State Administration of Radio, Film and Television, and the General Administration of Press and Publication, issued a series of 12 poster-style public service advertisements (PSAs) titled 'Be Civic-Minded and Create a New Trend' (*jiangwenming shuxinfeng* 讲文明树新风). The first poster celebrates the 50 years since Lei Feng's death with the slogan 'Lei Feng Will Always Be With Us (1962–2012)', ascribing a ubiquitous aspect to the Lei Feng spirit (*Lei Feng yizhi zai women shenbian* 雷锋一直在我们身边 1962–2012). It juxtaposes a classic 1960s image of Lei Feng with images of contemporary doctors and nurses giving elderly people free health checks at Community Lei Feng Service Sites ('Renmin ribao kandeng de' 2012).

Other posters in the series link Lei Feng to environmental concerns and concepts of compassion presented as a Chinese and universal human attribute. One poster displays an image of university-student volunteers against a leafy backdrop conducting water quality tests and planting a tree. A slogan emblazoned in large characters at the top of the poster says: 'Caring for Nature Requires Everyone's Help'. Beneath this message, in smaller characters, is the slogan 'Learn from Lei Feng, Contribute to the Lives of Others, Improve Yourself' (*Xuexi Lei Feng: Fengxian taren tisheng ziji* 学习雷锋 奉献他人 提升自己). Yet another poster shows an image of two hands holding a heart-shaped photograph of contemporary volunteers – a visual symbol of compassion and philanthropy – against a blue and green backdrop signifying an environmentally clean and beautiful China. The slogan 'Learn from Lei Feng: Contribute to the Lives of Others; Improve Yourself' is placed beneath the image. Other posters produced by local governments used similar slogans and used modern, stylized representations of Lei Feng, or evoked him by name and through visual metonymy, such as in brightly coloured prints of young, happy people wearing Lei Feng hats ('Guangzhou xuyao qianwan ge Lei Feng' 2013).

The posters reveal an effort to reshape and update the figure of Lei Feng to encourage Chinese citizens to volunteer to meet new social imperatives. While appealing to Mao-era traditions of altruistic public service, they introduce a focus on self-improvement and self-fulfilment that differs from the socialist ethos of the original Lei Feng campaign. The message of the original campaign was about working selflessly for the good of society and even abolishing the self from civil acts. When the diary version of Lei Feng revels in the glory of being a 'nameless hero', he does so in the spirit of a hard-nosed form of socialism in which the individual is literally irrelevant – only the good of society matters. In contrast, the message of the new publicity materials is that one can help others and help oneself at the same time. The materials encourage people to contribute voluntarily to public welfare in the context of a more open and complex society, one where the Party-state has reduced capacity to compel individuals to pursue its goals through mass mobilization activities, and consequently has to use new governing strategies to encourage responsible citizenship.

The 'carrot' for volunteering is self-enhancement in the sense of 'feeling good' about helping others, and in the practical sense of 'self-entrepreneurialism' – that is, acquiring experiences and skills that may enhance one's career opportunities in a competitive job market ('Daxuesheng wei qiuzhi er zuo zhiyuanzhe' 2013). These inducements reiterate the standard rationales for youth volunteering in western societies, which is to meet people, have fun and improve their career prospects (Case Foundation 2006: 6). While arguably introducing neoliberal forms of governance, the government-led promotion of such rationales also turns on the general impetus of reform-era education, which is for young people to become 'good (socialist) citizens' by improving their personal capacities or qualities (*suzhi* 素质) (see Woronov and Yu in this book).

Figure 3.4 shows one of a series of posters posted on residential noticeboards in Chaoyang District, Beijing, urging young people to 'improve themselves' during the summer holidays by following Lei Feng's example *and* promoting the 'Beijing Spirit', that is, by practising 'traditional-socialist' Chinese virtues (helping others) and fostering patriotic, innovative, inclusive, and ethical 'new' trends (civic behaviours and volunteerism) ('Guanyu shujia qijian kaizhan' 2012). One of two images portrays a girl helping to maintain a clean and ecologically friendly urban living environment; she is described as a 'Youth

Figure 3.4 Be an ethical person; learn from Lei Feng how to be a young emissary for community civilization (source: photograph by Elaine Jeffreys, Chaoyang District, Beijing, 2012).

Environmental Protection Guard'. In the other image, the same girl is portrayed standing at the entrance of a block of residential apartments; she is described as a '[Residential] Community Building Doorkeeper', meaning she is watching the neighbourhood and ready to provide assistance when needed. A slogan below the images urges young people to 'Be Ethical People and Learn from Lei Feng; Be a Young Emissary for Community Civilization'. To the right of the slogan is a badge-like circle which displays an image of Lei Feng shining like a rising sun above two children to guide them. Local schools were encouraged to submit stories about exceptional 'Emissaries' to the District Spiritual Civilization Office for awards ('Guanyu shujia qijian kaizhan' 2012).

As the preceding discussion suggests, Lei Feng's image and persona has been released from the burdens of political-ideological consistency with Maoist tenets, turning him into a heterogeneous symbol of social action. The use of Lei Feng in the 2012–2013 government communication campaign legitimizes efforts to promote philanthropy by linking volunteerism to a historical tradition unique to the PRC and the CCP, when charity was once viewed in Marxist terms as means by which the propertied classes attempted to placate the labouring classes (Zhou and Zeng 2006: 368). The government advertising also appeals to diverse Chinese cultural forms (traditional, socialist, and reform-era concepts of *suzhi*) and elements of 'neoliberal' governing discourses (civic pride, self-empowerment and autonomous, participatory citizenship). This coupling of 'socialist' and 'neoliberal' rationales for volunteering is not necessarily experienced by targeted audiences as incongruous, because volunteerism and 'doing good' involve people and affect. They refer to heterogeneous spaces for social action and self-making, rather than self-evident actions (see also Hoffman in this book).

The use of Lei Feng in this context therefore denotes a sense of cultural continuity with forms of citizenship that are claimed to already exist but which in fact are actually being created. Two examples that illustrate this point are the new links forged between Lei Feng and entrepreneurs; and university students' reflections on Lei Feng-related volunteering activities and the contemporary value and use of Lei Feng.

Entrepreneurs and philanthropy

The heterogeneous spaces for social action and self-making brought into play by the revived governmental use of Lei Feng are underscored by the new links forged between Lei Feng and entrepreneurs. The title of a 'living Lei Feng' was first used in 1963 to refer to PLA soldiers who assisted with agricultural production ('Jiefangjun dali zhiyuan' 1963). It was subsequently used as a positive appellation to refer to members of the revolutionary classes – workers, cadres, peasants, and soldiers – who worked to help each other as 'citizen-friends' of socialist China.

The title of a 'living Lei Feng' was not associated with entrepreneurs historically because private wealth was a target of active political hostility in the PRC until Deng Xiaoping's advocacy of the slogan 'Let One Segment of the Population Get Rich First and Guide Others Along the Way', and Jiang Zemin's advocacy of the 'Three Represents' theory, which welcomes entrepreneurs into the ranks of the CCP. According to Jiang Zemin (PRC president 1993–2003), the Three Represents is about 'blazing new trails for the development of Marxist theory': it means uniting with the innovative, advanced productive forces to make China strong and the Chinese people rich (Jiang Zemin 2002). Members of this group include: freelance professionals, private entrepreneurs, managerial and technical staff employed by non-public and overseas-funded enterprises, and CEOs of state-owned enterprises. Jiang concluded that 'the people' should unite with entrepreneurs because 'it is improper to judge whether people are politically progressive or backward simply by whether they own property or how much property they own'. Instead of equating personal wealth with political incorrectness, Jiang (2002) suggested that the Chinese public should judge the newly rich based on how their work contributes to the goal of building socialism with Chinese characteristics.

The official endorsement of entrepreneurship has been followed by a more recent equation of philanthropy with socialist construction, demonstrated by the creation of Lei Feng titles and awards to CEOs to recognize their public service. On 27 February 2013, a ceremony attended by senior government and military officials was held in Beijing to commemorate the fiftieth anniversary of Mao's call to 'Learn from Lei Feng', and acknowledge the outstanding public service of 50 people, by presenting them with the PRC's first national 'Lei Feng Awards' (Li Haixiu 2013). The ceremony was part of a symposium on 'Normalizing Learning from Lei Feng Activities', launched through collaborations between government- and corporate-funded foundations, and supported by state-run media.

President Xi Jinping described Lei Feng and two award winners (Luo Yang and Guo Mingyi) as 'the backbone of China' during one of his incoming speeches to the National People's Congress in 2013, stating that more 'Lei Fengs' were needed to achieve the 'China Dream' of rejuvenating China and achieving ever-higher living standards ('Xi Jinping: Lei Feng' 2013). Luo Yang, CEO of the state-run Shenyang Aircraft Corporation Logistics Equipment Company, received a posthumous award for innovating military aviation technology. Guo Mingyi, a miner, was awarded for a history of starting work early, donating blood and donating to good causes despite his low income (Li Haixiu 2013).

While these awardees belong to the 'friend' tradition of good cadres and workers, Cao Dewang, a rags-to-riches private entrepreneur and philanthropist, also received a national Lei Feng award. Chief Executive of Fuyao Glass, Cao Dewang has an estimated net worth of USD1.2 billion (Zeveloff 2012). He has received numerous awards for donating USD800 million to philanthropic causes since 1983, including 'China's Best Corporate Citizen' in 2005 and China's 'Top Philanthropist' in 2011 ('Cao Dewang jianli' n.d.). He has also been called a 'new-era living Lei Feng' by China's media (Tian 2011).

Other members of China's newly rich elite have claimed the aura of a 'living Lei Feng' for themselves. Real-estate magnate and philanthropist Pan Shiyi (2012) describes China's first generation of super-rich entrepreneurs as 'living Lei Fengs' for working hard to drive the Chinese economy and providing everybody with the opportunity for private wealth creation. In 2012, billionaire philanthropist Chen Guangbiao attracted controversy for posting photographs of himself dressed as Lei Feng on his microblog ('Chen Guangbiao toudai' 2012).

These representations of CEOs as 'living Lei Fengs' arguably embody the neoliberal imperative that individual competition for wealth and influence, rather than collective class struggle and selfless devotion to others, is the key to improving oneself and the commonweal.

However, public discussions of Chen Guangbiao's 'Lei Feng photo-shoot' demonstrate that contemporary presentations of Lei Feng provide opportunities for individuals to debate the conduct of others and to modify their own conduct. Chen told reporters that when he agreed to do a photo-shoot with artist Shu Yong, he had no idea that Shu wished him to pose as Lei Feng; he had agreed to the request because he admired and tried to practise Lei's spirit of dedication to the Chinese people ('Chen Guangbiao toudai' 2012). Shu Yong claimed that the photographs aimed to parody neither Chen nor Lei, but rather to promote public discussions of contemporary understandings of the 'spirit of Lei Feng'. In responses to the photographs, which were widely circulated on the Chinese internet precisely because they were viewed as 'funny', some netizens described Chen Guangbiao as a 'living Lei Feng'. Others condemned him as 'a rich show-off'. Yet others argued that Chen Guangbiao is a publicity-seeking narcissist, but one whose activities may nevertheless help to counter the perceived 'uncaring' individualism of contemporary China by encouraging people to help other people ('Chen Guangbiao "Lei Feng zhao"' 2012; Lei Juanli 2012).

In short, Party and government organizations have proved keen to raise the public profile of entrepreneurs as 'friends of the people', and some CEOs have proved equally keen to label themselves as 'living Lei Fengs', whether to promote their philanthropy or justify their right to be rich first. Such actions aim to counter the legacy of Mao-era class politics, which linger on in counter-claims that CEOs cannot be 'living Lei Fengs' because their wealth is derived from corruption rather than hard work (Wu Zhifeng 2012). However, such claims are unlikely to be translated into calls for collective class action because of the perceived 'failure' of Maoist politics and growing acceptance of new ideas about how to promote the common good, as demonstrated by student survey responses.

Student reflections on volunteering and Lei Feng

In late 2013 we conducted an online multiple-choice survey of Chinese university students with a view to understanding the extent of student participation in Lei Feng-related volunteering activities and to shed light on the function and public reception of Lei Feng.[2] The survey was not undertaken with the aim of providing a definitive or scientific account of Lei Feng's audience reception. The 415 respondents to the survey came from three Chinese universities: a top-tier university in Beijing; and technology and teacher-training universities in Hebei and Yunnan Province. Students majored in a range of subjects: 60 per cent in science or engineering; 25 per cent in humanities (mainly languages); 12 per cent in administration or commerce. Nearly 96 per cent were under 30 years of age and hence in the age group that might be expected to have 'forgotten Lei Feng'.

The survey responses indicate that volunteering is a common experience for young people in China, largely in the context of Lei Feng activities organized by schools and universities. Most respondents (86 per cent) had participated in volunteering activities, with most of these activities being linked to Lei Feng. Moreover, nearly 80 per cent of respondents said their volunteering experiences had been organized by a school or university.

However, it appears that volunteering around Lei Feng Day is not compulsory, even for school children. Around one-quarter of the total sample had not engaged in Lei Feng activities. While around one-fifth of survey respondents indicated that they regularly participated in Lei Feng Day activities, two-thirds said they rarely participated in Lei Feng activities. Only 2 per cent indicated that they had never participated in Lei Feng Day activities, but only 4 per cent stated that they engaged in Lei Feng Day activities because they had no choice other than to participate.

The survey results provide insight into how respondents conceive of Lei Feng and view the utility of volunteering and philanthropy. They suggest that educated young people do not associate Lei Feng with revolutionary politics; nor do they believe that exclusive government-sponsored welfare is a viable option in China today.

Unsurprisingly, given government communication, the responses indicate that young educated people have a basic knowledge of the Lei Feng narrative, and at least one aspect of Lei's persona – his legendary willingness to help others – has remained stable. Students were asked to identify the year of Lei Feng's death, with options ranging from 1920 to 1990. The majority of respondents (68 per cent) correctly knew that Lei Feng died in 1962. The main facts of his life were well known: 96 per cent selected the option that he died in an accident and 83 per cent thought he was a member of the PLA. Around 10 per cent thought that Lei was a factory worker, but no one thought that he was a poet or a free thinker. Most respondents reported that Lei Feng's key characteristic was a willingness to help others (90 per cent) followed by a love of socialism (just over 7 per cent).

More than half of the survey respondents did not see Lei Feng as having a class identity, while another 10 per cent saw class as irrelevant. Only 15 per cent thought they shared a class identity with Lei Feng for a reason other than that they were Chinese, while 38 per cent thought they shared no such identity in any sense, did not know, or thought that the idea was irrelevant.

Nearly three-quarters of respondents chose to answer the question 'Lei Feng is…' by picking the option that Lei Feng is a role model for people today. Only 13 per cent chose to answer that Lei Feng was a role model for people in the past; and less than 5 per cent thought that he was either a fictional character or an invention of Party propaganda. None of the survey respondents selected the option that Lei Feng was 'nothing special' or 'not relevant to today's China'. When asked how they would describe a 'living Lei Feng', the majority of students answered that a living Lei Feng is someone who helps others (72 per cent) or who works voluntarily for the Chinese people (24 per cent).

Despite a poor track record of active volunteering, most of the respondents (89 per cent) indicated that there should be more philanthropy in China; only 2 per cent thought that philanthropy is unnecessary because the government should be responsible for providing social welfare. While 31 per cent thought that helping others and strangers should be voluntary, 57 per cent again thought that helping others helped themselves. Putting the figures together, the majority of the respondents (98 per cent) believe that helping others is either a form of self-help, or a voluntary and natural activity.

The survey results suggest that the government use of Lei Feng to promote civic behaviours and volunteering has been effective in some respects. Respondents were familiar with the life-story of Lei Feng, who they largely appear to view as a good role model for contemporary civic engagement. Consistent with the redrafted official narrative, Lei Feng no longer appears to be tied by respondents to the Maoist revolutionary politics of class struggle and egalitarianism; he is tied to ideas which suggest that people should help each other and look after each other, and that helping others helps oneself. As a result, Lei Feng's image and persona can be associated with seemingly neoliberal conceptions of a reduced role for government in the provision of social welfare, and an enhanced role for individual citizens, without any inherent incongruence in the eyes of the respondents to this particular survey, at least.

Conclusions

Lei Feng epitomizes the changing and hybrid nature of rationalities for governing the conduct of others and the self in contemporary China. Lei Feng originally was a symbol of revolutionary class unity, being promoted by the Party-state as a 'friend' of the people, whose life and deeds demonstrated love of the CCP, the PRC, socialism and the Chinese people, and opposition to a common, albeit vanquished, group of 'enemies' – the exploitative propertied classes. At the start of the Cultural Revolution, he symbolized devotion to Maoism and continuous revolution; by the end, he symbolized opposition to the incitement of class struggle within the internal ranks of the people and the Party. Lei Feng has since become a retro-revolutionary kitsch commodity *and* a postsocialist celebrity who can be promoted and reconfigured by the PRC Government, and supporters and critics of that regime alike. In his latest official incarnation, Lei Feng has been employed in the service of a conception of government that almost evokes neo-liberal ideas of 'small government' and an individualist notion of citizenship. This shift is underscored by his various uses as an incentive device for corporate philanthropists and the 'face' of a national campaign to promote volunteering.

The breadth and flexibility of contemporary government and popular uses of Lei Feng undermines claims by foreign correspondents that the state-led promotion of Lei Feng to encourage philanthropy represents a return to the use of a rigid 'old-school propaganda' that is destined to fail in the more open, fluid and individualistic environment of the reform period. Lei Feng is currently used popularly to ambiguously satirize the unequal 'richness' and individualistic materialism of contemporary China. He has been deployed by the non-state sector to provide a simultaneous critique of Mao-era egalitarian poverty and reform-era inequalities of wealth, while also being used in state-sponsored volunteering campaigns aimed at addressing the insufficiencies of China's current socio-economic system, and creating a 'better' future.

Repackaging Lei Feng enables the CCP to emphasize a core continuity of the socialist modernization project in the form of ethical citizen behaviours, even as understandings of modernizing China and Chinese citizenship have changed. While a symbol of revolutionary continuity, Lei Feng is now used officially to naturalize or domesticate inequality through philanthropy, rather than reinvoking the conditions that the revolution set out to overcome. Such dual communication seeks to legitimize one-party rule by keeping alive the notion that the PRC's history and the CCP matters. But it does so by metonymically linking Lei Feng with the less antagonistic, and hence potentially more persuasive, conceptions of state–society relations that are embedded in government advertising promoting national pride and civic behaviours. The irony of Lei Feng's celebrity is that the original Lei Feng supposedly desired nothing more than to help others and be erased from history.

Notes

This research was supported under the Australian Research Council's Future Fellowship funding scheme (FT100100238).

1 Excerpts from a diary by an individual called Lei Feng were first published between 30 August 1959 and 15 November 1960 in a Shenyang military newspaper, for internal use only (Ji Xiaoli 2004).

2 The survey methodology and questions are available from Elaine.jeffreys@uts.edu.au.

References

'70 wei Lei Feng zhanyou lianming dizhi Tian Liang tuiju Wang Baoqiang yan Lei Feng' [70 of Lei Feng's military comrades boycott Tian Liang, they want Wang Baoqiang to play Lei Feng] (2009) *Zhongguowang*, 3 April. Online. Available: www.china.com.cn/culture/txt/2009-04/03/content_17546738.htm (accessed 17 July 2015).

'Ai zeng fenming lichang jianding hao bu liji zhuanmen li ren; xiang Lei Feng nayang zhongyu geming shiye; Liaoning guangda qingnian relie xuexi Lei Feng shiji shoudao shenke jiaoyu' [Be clear about what to love and what to hate; be selfless and altruistic; be loyal to the revolution like Lei Feng; Liaoning youth enthusiastically learn from Lei Feng] (1963) *Renmin Ribao*, 7 February, p. 1.

'Ba Maozhuxi dangzuo "liangshi, wuqi, fangxiangpan"; Lei Feng gongshe pinxia zhongnong renzhen xuexi Lei Feng buduan tigao jieji douzheng he liangtiao luxian douzhen juewu cujin le sixiang geminghua' [Make the works of Chairman Mao our food, weapons and guide; people in a poor rural commune earnestly study Lei Feng to improve their ideological awareness of class struggle and the two-line struggle, and revolutionize their thoughts] (1970) *Renmin Ribao*, 5 March, p. 1.

Blecher, M.J. (1986) *China, Politics, Economics, and Society: Iconoclasm and Innovation in a Revolutionary Socialist Country*, London: F. Pinter.

'Cao Dewang jianli' [Cao Dewang's resume] (n.d.) *Mingren Jianli*. Online. Available: www.gerenjianli.com/Mingren/02/ndok301enikisea.html (accessed 21 July 2015).

Case Foundation (2006) *Citizens at the Center: A New Approach to Civic Engagement*. Online. Available: http://casefoundation.org/wp-content/uploads/2014/11/CitizensAt-TheCenter.pdf (accessed 10 April 2015).

'Changdao gongchan zhuyi daode shuli wenming limao xinfeng, tuanzhongyang haozhao jinyibu kaizhan xue Lei Feng huodong' [Promote communist morality, develop a new trend: the Central Committee of the Communist Youth League call for a campaign to learn from Lei Feng] (1981) *Renmin Ribao*, 12 February, p. 1.

'Chen Guangbiao "Lei Feng zhao" wangshang re zhenyi cheng zao liao dao hui bei zhiyi' [Chen Guangbiao's 'Lei Feng photo' naturally provokes online controversy] (2012) *Renminwang*, 6 March. Online. Available: http://culture.people.com.cn/GB/22219/17302599.html (accessed 21 July 2015).

'Chen Guangbiao toudai Lei Feng mao shouchi gangqiang ban Lei Feng' [Chen Guangbiao poses as Lei Feng, wearing a Lei Feng cap and holding a rifle] (2012) *Renmin Dianshi*, 5 March. Online. Available: http://tv.people.com.cn/GB/150716/156855/233970/17290417.html (accessed 21 July 2015).

China Internet Network Information Center (2014) 'Statistical report on internet development in China', July 2014. Online. Available: www1.cnnic.cn/IDR/ReportDownloads/201411/P020141102574314897888.pdf (accessed 1 May 2015).

CPC Encyclopedia (1995–2014) 'Half century evolution of "Lei Feng Spirit"'. Online. Available: http://cpcchina.chinadaily.com.cn/2012-02/21/content_14661089.htm (accessed 21 July 2015).

Dai Xiang (2012) 'Xin Lei Feng gushi' [The new story of Lei Feng], *Fengniao.com*, 13 February. Online. Available: http://image.fengniao.com/hot/pic_show_2672_1.html#img (accessed 21 July 2015).

'Dangdai Lei Feng de biaozhun: shijieshang zui guangrong de shi – zheng' [Contemporary Lei Feng criteria: the world's most glorious thing – making money] (n.d.) Aitupian.com. Online. Available: www.aitupian.com/weibopic/468117.html (accessed 27 July 2015).

'Daxuesheng wei qiuzhi er zuo zhiyuanzhe qiye: geng kanzhong zhiyuan jingshen' [College students volunteer for seeking jobs and enterprises attach greater importance to volunteerism] (2013) *Sohuwang*, 8 May. Online. Available: http://learning.sohu.com/20130508/n375245969.shtml (accessed 21 July 2015).

Deng Xiaoping (1979) 'Speech greeting the Fourth Congress of Chinese writers and artists', 30 October. Online. Available: https://dengxiaopingworks.wordpress.com/2013/02/25/speech-greeting-the-fourth-congress-of-chinese-writers-and-artists (accessed 30 July 2015).

Deng Xiaoping (1983) 'Our work in all fields should contribute to the building of socialism with Chinese characteristics', 12 January, *Selected Works of Deng Xiaoping Volume 3 (1982–1992)*. Online. Available: www.china.org.cn/english/features/dengxiaoping/103381.htm (accessed 29 July 2015).

Dirlik, A. (2005) *Marxism in the Chinese Revolution*, Lanham: Rowman and Littlefield.

Dong Zhaoqi (dir.) (1964) *Lei Feng* (feature film), Beijing: Bayi Dianying Zhipianchang.

Dutton, M.R. (2005) *Policing Chinese Politics: A History*, Durham: Duke University Press.

Foucault, M. (2007) *Security, Territory, Population: Lectures at the Collège de France 1977–1978*, Houndsmills: Palgrave Macmillan.

Goldkorn, J. (2012) 'Lei Feng in the age of the microblog', *Danwei*, 5 March. Online. Available: www.danwei.com/lei-feng-in-the-age-of-the-microblog (accessed 21 July 2015).

'Gongqingtuanzhongyang guanyu jinyibu kaizhan xue Lei Feng jingshen zuo "si you" qingnian huodong de tongzhi (1990 nian 1 yue 9 ri)' [Notice of the Central Committee of the Communist Youth League on furthering the spirit of learning from Lei Feng and becoming youth with the 'four haves', 9 January 1990] (1990) *Leifeng.org*. Online. Available: www.leifeng.org.cn/5007.asp?NewsID=765 (accessed 22 July 2015).

'Guangzhou xuyao qianwan ge Lei Feng' [Guangzhou wants millions of Lei Fengs] (2013) *Dayangwang*, 21 March. Online. Available: http://m.dayoo.com/126722/126727/126735/201303/21/126735_29632478.htm (accessed 23 April 2015).

'Guanyu shujia qijian kaizhan "Jianxing Beijing jingshen: zhengdang xue Lei Feng shequ wenming xiaoshizhe" zhuti jiaoyu shijian huodong de tongzhi' [Notice on Practicing the 'Beijing Spirit' during the summer break: 'Learn from Lei Feng', be an emissary for civic life] (2012) *Zhongguo Wenmingwang*, 10 August. Online. Available: http://bj.wenming.cn/chy/zlzx/201208/t20120816_810253.html (accessed 3 February 2015).

'Guofangbu pizhuan shouyu Shenyang budui gongchengbing mou bu siban guangrong chenghao "Lei Feng Ban" – Shenyang budui lingdao jiguang longzhong juxing mingming dahui [Department of Defence grants the glorious title of 'Lei Feng Unit' to the Fourth Unit of the Shenyang Army Engineering Soldiers: Shenyang military leaders hold a naming ceremony] (1963) *Renmin Ribao*, 25 January, p. 2.

Guowuyuan [State Council of the PRC] (2014) Guowuyuan guanyu cujin cishan shiye jiankang fazhan de zhidao yijian [Guidance from the State Council on promoting the healthy development of philanthropy], 24 November. Online. Available: www.gov.cn/zhengce/content/2014-12/18/content_9306.htm (accessed 10 June 2015).

Humphrey, C. (2005 [1997]) 'Exemplars and rules: aspects of the discourse of moralities in Mongolia', in S. Howell (ed.) *The Ethnography of Moralities*, London: Routledge, pp. 25–48.

Jacobs, A. (2012) 'Chinese heroism effort is met with cynicism', *New York Times*, 6 March, p. A7.

Ji Xiaoli (2004) 'Lei Feng zhe yi dianxing shi ruhe shuli qilai de' [How Lei Feng was set up as a model], *Zhonghua Xinwenbao*, 5 March, p. T00.

Jiang Zemin (2002) 'Full text of Jiang Zemin's report at 16th Party Congress', *People's Daily*, 18 November. Online. Available: http://english.people.com.cn/200211/18/eng20021118_106985.shtml (accessed 21 July 2015).

'Jiefangjun dali zhiyuan gongshe zhengqu nongye zengchan' [The People's Liberation Army strongly supports commune agricultural production] (1963) *Renmin Ribao*, 29 July, p. 1.

'Jiefangjun zhanshi he hongweibing xiaojiang' [PLA soldiers and Red Guards] (1966) *Renmin Ribao*, 5 December, p. 1.

'Jieguo Lei Feng de qiang' [Take up Lei Feng's gun] (2009) *Xinba Yuepu*, 18 December. Online. Available: http://pu.sinbam.com/score/2009/12181003.html (accessed 21 July 2015).

'Jilü cha feiwen duo jian paichang Tian Liang yan Lei Feng wangshang zhengyi da' [Sex scandals and lack of self-discipline: Tian Liang's role as Lei Feng triggers online controversy] (2009) *Renminwang*, 30 March. Online. Available: http://ent.people.com.cn/GB/9047781.html (accessed 21 July 2015).

Jun Fen (1961) 'Ku haizi chengzhang wei youxiu renmin zhanshi' [A suffering child becomes an outstanding people's soldier], *Renmin Ribao*, 5 May, p. 5.

'Lei Feng de gushi' [Lei Feng' story] (n.d.) Zhongguowangluodianshitai dongmantai chupin [China Network Television Animation Production]. Online. Available: http://donghua.cntv.cn/program/leifezhuanti/shouye/index.shtml (accessed 21 July 2015).

'Lei Feng (DVD)' (n.d.) *Jingdong*. Online. Available: http://item.jd.com/20002571.html (accessed 23 July 2015).

Lei Feng Memorial Hall of Hunan China (n.d.) Online. Available: http://hnleifeng.org.cn (accessed 30 July 2015).

Lei Feng Riji 1959–1962 [The Diary of Lei Feng 1959–1962] (1963) Beijing: Jiefangjun Wenyi Chubanshe.

Lei Juanli (2012) 'Chen Guangbiao ban Lei Feng yin reyi zicheng shensheng gan chongying quanshen' [Chen Guangbiao's pose as the 'sacred' Lei Feng attracts controversy], *Beijing Chenbao*, 5 March. Online. Available: http://news.163.com/12/0305/02/7RQ3H8IV00014AED.html (accessed 21 July 2015).

Li Haixiu (2013) '50wei xue Leifeng xianjinrenwu xihuo "Leifeng Jiang"' [50 advanced people in 'Learning from Lei Feng activities' are given 'Lei Feng Awards'], *Guangming Ribao*, 28 February, p. 1. Online. Available: http://epaper.gmw.cn/gmrb/html/2013-02/28/nw.D110000gmrb_20130228_5-01.htm?div=-1 (accessed 21 July 2015).

Li Maoping (2012) 'Zhiyuan fuwu yu shehuizhuyi hexin jiazhi tixi dazhonghua' [The popularization of volunteer services and socialist core values], *Shehuizhuyi Yanjiu*, 4: 27–30.

Li Muyang (2012) 'Balinghou nühai sheji "mengban" Lei Feng gongzai shou zhuipeng' [The 'cute' Lei Feng doll designed by a post-1980s girl is popular], *Duoweixinwen*, 5 March. Online. Available: http://life.dwnews.com/news/2012-03-05/58636189.html (accessed 22 July 2015).

Liaoning ribao (1963) 'Lei Feng riji zhaichao' [Excerpts from Lei Feng's diary], *Renmin Ribao*, 7 February, p. 3.

Liaoningsheng junqu zhengzhi pipanzu [Liaoning Provincial Military District Political Criticism and Study Group] (1977) 'Cong "Lei Feng shushu buzaile" tanqi' [Let's talk about the "death of Uncle Lei Feng"], *Renmin Ribao*, 12 November, p. 3.

Mattis, P. (2012) 'Another Lei Feng revival: making Maoism safe for China', *China Brief*, 12, 5, 2 March. Online. Available: www.jamestown.org/single/?tx_ttnews%5Btt_news%5D=39091&no_cache=1#.VaSFr40w9jo (accessed 14 July 2015).

Ministry of Civil Affairs of the PRC (2013) Zhongguo shehui fuwu zhiyuanzhe duiwu jianshe zhidao gangyao (2013–2020 nian) de tongzhi [China Social Services Volunteer Team Building Guidelines 2013–2020], 1 June. Online. Available: www.mca.gov.cn/article/zwgk/fvfg/shgz/201401/20140100573025.shtml (accessed 1 May 2015).

Mitchell, J. (2006) 'Comrade condom', *Asia Sentinel*, 8 November. Online. Available: www.asiasentinel.com/society/comrade-condom (accessed 20 July 2015).

'New moral yardstick: "8 honors, 8 disgraces"' (2006) *Gov.cn*, 5 April. Online. Available: www.gov.cn/english/2006-04/05/content_245361.htm (accessed 20 July 2015).

Osnos, E. (2013) 'Ignoring Lei Feng: China's failed revolutionary biopics', *The New Yorker*, 13 March. Online. Available: www.newyorker.com/online/blogs/evanosnos/2013/03/lei-feng-communist-china-failed-films.html (accessed 1 September 2014).

Pan Shiyi (2012) 'Pan Shiyi: Wang Shi deng shi diyidai qiyejia wo shi dierdai [Pan Shiyi: Wang Shi and others are the first generation of private entrepreneurs; I am part of the second generation], *Fenghuangwang*, 28 November. Online. Available: http://finance.ifeng.com/news/people/20121228/7495750.shtml (accessed 21 July 2015).

Pan Xiaodong and Qu Xiaoqu (2014) 'Xingsha dansheng guochan chaoren "Lei Feng xia"' [Xingsha has produced a home-grown national superman 'Lei Feng Knight'], *Tianxia*

Hunan, 19 March. Online. Available: www.txhn.net/hnwhrd/201403/t20140319_332944.htm (accessed 30 July 2015).
Qi Zengmei and Xu Bo (2006) *Lei Feng*, Harbin: Harbin Chubanshe.
'Quanguo zonggonghui xiang geji gonghui zuzhi fa chu tongzhi haozhao guangda zhigong xiang Lei Feng xuexi' [The China Federation of Trade Unions issues a notice to all trade union organizations, calls for workers to learn from Lei Feng] (1963) *Renmin Ribao*, 8 March, p. 3.
'Relie xiangying weida lingxiu Maozhuxi de haozhao Beijing guangda qingshaonian shenru kaizhan xue Lei Feng huodong tamen xuexi Lei Feng ai zeng fenming de wuchan jieji lichang shenru pipan Liu Shaoqi yilei pianzi de xiuzhengzhuyi luxian' [Enthusiastic response to Chairman Mao's call: Beijing youth develop activities to learn from Lei Feng how to develop the proletarian stance of knowing what to love and hate, and to criticize the revisionist line represented by the swindler Liu Shaoqi] (1973) *Renmin Ribao*, 5 March, p. 1.
Ren Zhiping and Ren Yongzhong (1990) 'Yi shou zansong zhongcheng he fengxian de ge: fang "xuexi Lei Feng hao bangyang" geci zuozhe Hong Yuan' [A song praising loyalty and dedication: interview with Hong Yuan, the composer of 'Learn From Lei Feng, the Good Role Model'], *Renmin Ribao*, 4 March, p. 8.
Renmin Ribao Dianziban (1946–present) OriProbe Information Services, Windsor, Canada.
Renmin Ribao, Hongqi Zazhi, Jiefangjun Bao (1977) 'Xiang Lei Feng tongzhi xuexi' [Learn from Comrade Lei Feng], *Renmin Ribao*, 5 March, p. 1.
'Renmin ribao kandeng de "jiang wenming shu xinfeng" gongyi guanggao' [The People's Daily publishes 'Be civic-minded and create a new trend' public service announcements] (2012) *Renminwang*, 17 September. Online. Available: http://media.people.com.cn/GB/22114/349264 (accessed 22 July 2015).
'Shenyang junqu Lei Feng jinianguan' (2009) [Lei Feng Memorial Hall of the Shenyang Military Region] (2009) *Liaoning Xinwen*, 23 April. Online. Available: www.lnd.com.cn/htm/2009-04/23/content_640581.htm (accessed 22 July 2015).
Steen, A. (2014) '"To live is to serve the people": the spirit of model soldier Lei Feng in postmodernity', in A. Hume (ed.), *The Changing Landscape of China's Consumerism*, Oxford: Chandos Publishing, pp. 151–76.
Tian Lei (2011) 'Lei Feng jingshen yong buguo shibu guoshi' [The timeless Lei Feng spirit], *Huanghe Chenbao*, 2 March. Online. Available: http://epaper.sxycrb.com/hgyx/cb/content/20110302/Articel03005AH.htm (accessed 21 July 2015).
Turner, G. (2004) *Understanding Celebrity*, London, Thousand Oaks: Sage.
United Nations Development Programme (2011) *State of Volunteerism in China: Engaging People through Ideas, Innovation and Inspiration*. Online. Available: www.unv.org/fileadmin/docdb/pdf/2011/corporate/China%20Volunteer%20Report%202011_English.pdf (accessed 23 July 2015).
'Weida de putong yi bing' [A great ordinary soldier] (1963) *Renmin Ribao*, 7 February, p. 2.
Wu Zhifeng (2012) 'Rang guoqi laozong xue Lei Feng hui you yong ma?' [Is there any point in asking CEO's of state-owned enterprises to learn from Lei Feng?], *Wodesohu*, 6 March. Online. Available: http://8521wu.blog.sohu.com/206233273.html (accessed 21 July 2015).
'Xi Jinping: Lei Feng, Guo Mingyi, Luo Yang dou shi women "minzu de jiliang"' [Xi Jinping: Lei Feng, Guo Mingyi, and Luo Yang, are the 'backbone' of China] (2013) *Chuncheng Wanbao*, 7 March. Online. Available: http://ccwb.yunnan.cn/html/2013-03/07/content_679202.htm?div=0 (accessed 17 July 2015).

Xue Cun (2013) *Sogou Yinyue*. Online. Available: http://music.sogou.com/singer/7d/detailSinger_%D1%A9%B4%E5.html (accessed 21 July 2015).

'Yao Ming huo guoji zhiyuanzhe zuzhi niandu dajiang' [Yao Ming receives award from international volunteer organization] (2014) *Xinhua*, 23 October. Online. Available: http://news.xinhuanet.com/world/2014-10/23/c_1112950913.htm (accessed 1 May 2015).

'Zai jinian Mao Zedong deng lao yi bei gemingjia wei Lei Feng tongzhi tici sanshi zhounian dahui shang Hu Jintao tongzhi de jianghua' [Comrade Hu Jintao's speech at a general meeting to celebrate the thirty year anniversary of inscriptions by Mao Zedong and other veteran revolutionaries on Lei Feng] (1993) *Renmin Ribao*, 5 March, p. 1.

Zeveloff, J. (2012) 'China's biggest philanthropist puts America's biggest philanthropist to shame', *Business Insider*, 17 May. Online. Available: www.businessinsider.com/cao-dewang-biggest-philanthropist-in-china-2012-5 (accessed 21 July 2015).

Zhang Huixin (2009) *Lei Feng de Gushi* [The Story of Lei Feng], Nanjing: Nanjing Daxue Chubanshe.

Zhang Jun (2007) 'Xianhongse lishi de zhenshi xiezhao: Lei Feng Riji de xuanzhai zhengli yu bianzhuan zhuishu' [Real revolutionary history: the editing and compilation of *Lei Feng's Diary*], *Dangshi Zongheng*, 3: 27–8.

Zhen Weimin, Tong Xiwen, and Lei Runming (1963) 'Maozhuxi de hao zhanshi: Lei Feng [Lei Feng: good soldier of Chairman Mao], *Renmin Ribao*, 7 February, p. 2.

'Zhonggong zhongyang bangongting yinfa "Guanyu shenru kaizhan xue Lei Feng huodong de yijian"' [Office of the Central Committee of the Chinese Communist Party issues the 'Suggestions on Strengthening Activities to Learn from Lei Feng'] (2012) *Zhongguo Gongchandang Xinwenwang*, 2 March. Online. Available: http://cpc.people.com.cn/GB/64114/64124/17279819.html (accessed 21 July 2015).

'Zhongguo qingnian chuban xuexi Lei Feng zhuanji Maozhuxi tici xiang Lei Feng tongzhi xuexi, Zhou Enlai, Dong Biwu, deng tongzhi, de tici he shi wen tongshi fabiao' [China Youth Magazine publishes a collection on learning from Lei Feng. It includes Chairman Mao Zedong's calligraphic inscription to 'Learn From Comrade Lei Feng', and inscriptions by senior leaders such as Zhou Enlai and Dong Biwu] (1963) *Renmin Ribao*, 5 March, p. 1.

'Zhongguo qingnian zhiyuan fuwuri "Xiang Lei Feng tongzhi xuexi"' [China Youth Volunteer Service Day 'Learn from Comrade Lei Feng'] (2012) *Beiweiwang*, 3 March. Online. Available: http://news.beiww.com/2012/0303/article_99404.html (accessed 21 July 2015).

Zhonghua renmin gongheguo guomin jingji he shehui fazhan '95' jihua he 2010 nian yuanjing mubiao gangyao [The Ninth Five-Year Plan for National Economic and Social Development and Summary of the 2010 Long-term Objectives of the People's Republic of China] (1996) National People's Congress, 7 March. Online. Available: http://cpc.people.com.cn/GB/64184/64186/66686/4494253.html (accessed 21 July 2015).

'Zhongyang haozhao quanguo jinyibu hongyang Lei Feng jingshen: Jiang Zemin, Yang Shangkun, Li Peng, Qiao Shi, Yao Yilin, Song Ping, Li Ruihuan fenbie tici' [Central Committee call for the country to further promote the spirit of Lei Feng: Jiang Zemin, Yang Shangkun, Li Peng, Qiao Shi, Yao Yilin, Song Ping, Li Ruihuan, write inscriptions] (1990) *Renmin Ribao*, 5 March, p. 1.

Zhou Qiuguang and Zeng Guilin (2006) *Zhongguo Cishan Jianshi* [A Brief History of Charity in China], Beijing: Renmin Chubanshe.

4 Governmentality and the urban economy

Consumption, excess, and the 'civilized city' in China

Carolyn Cartier

The idea of new mentalities of governance in China directs attention towards daily life in the context of rapid urban growth and widespread social change. Restructuring of the Chinese urban economy from manufacturing to service industries has established 'white', 'grey', and 'pink' collar office jobs, and generated Monday-to-Friday work routines with expectations for diversified urban services and weekend leisure lifestyles. Streetscapes in China's city centres now periodically swell with 'chuppies' (Chinese urban professionals) and leisure-time consumers with disposable incomes and evolving consumer interests. People expect to take part in the achievements of China's economic success through access to jobs and housing, and opportunities for consumption, leisure, and travel. In the midst of vast new urban consumer landscapes, it is far from obvious that the Chinese city remains the site of state policies and practices that seek to promote, guide, and monitor consumer-citizen conduct.

This chapter introduces the National Civilized City programme, an initiative of the Central Office of Spiritual Civilization, under the Central Guidance Commission for Building Spiritual Civilization, of the Chinese Communist Party (CCP). The National Civilized City programme seeks to standardize urban governance while promoting the urban economy, yet it also continues elements of Mao-era models for citizen conduct and volunteerism (Cartier 2013). For example, in the mid-2000s, cities staged large-scale participatory events to generate visitor revenue, events with forms and aesthetics reminiscent of Maoist 'passions' for mass actions (Dutton 2005). At first glance, such consumer activity with Maoist characteristics seems to suggest a kind of 'Maoism meets consumer capitalism' in the contemporary Chinese city. In fact, such mass events exemplify evolving conditions of consumer mentalities over the past decade.

To explain how the Party-state governs the city and citizens through the National Civilized City programme, I first sketch the idea of an urban governmentality in genealogical perspective, in order to frame how the National Civilized City serves as a technology of governmentality. I then introduce outsize consumer activity and mass volunteer-consumer events through the idea of excess and surplus accumulation. Finally, I interpret the apparent contradiction of 'volunteerism meets consumer capitalism' through the National Civilized City programme, which amalgamates established modes of contemporary, reform-era urban governance with an ideology of models and model volunteers rooted in the Mao era. I conclude that the civilized city system is a technology of urban governmentality to guide uniform urban development.

Towards urban governmentality

How do we conceive of rationalities and strategies for governing the space of the city in China, or something that might be called 'urban governmentality'? Cities in China are territorial areas defined by the state. They co-register the governing space of subnational territory with the jurisdictions of citizenship and the state-led economy (Cartier 2015).

Although Foucault never specified an urban governmentality, we are able to pursue the idea through a genealogy of his work, as well as through interviews that reveal his thoughts about the relationship between city and nation. As Stuart Elden (2007) notes, Foucault's 'governmentality' lecture, the fourth of 13 lectures in the 1978 course 'Security, Population, Territory', literally had a life of its own. Published as a stand-alone article, first in Italian, and then in English in the journal *Ideology and Consciousness* in 1979, it was subsequently reprinted and circulated widely in the edited collection *The Foucault Effect* (Burchell *et al.* 1991). The set of lectures from Foucault's two courses in 1978–1979 appeared in print in French only in 2004 and in English in 2007–2008. Now governmentality is chapter four, '1 February 1978', in *Security, Population, Territory* (Foucault 2007). In this volume, Foucault's articulation of governmentality assumes its originating place, after the lecture on the security apparatus and before the lecture on the origins of government in pastoral power.

In the 1979 course, *The Birth of Biopolitics*, Foucault (2008) viewed the idea of governmentality in broader, interrelated scales of social and political life. *The Birth of Biopolitics* examines the comparative development of neoliberal economy in political-economic history. It diverges from Foucault's own earlier treatment of disciplinary techniques and rationalities of government to analyse the history of neoliberalism and comparative state formation.

These stages of Foucault's work also represent different spatial contexts and scales: the scholarship of governmentality has tended to analyse discrete, context-driven regulation of the populations, whereas the dynamics of neoliberalism concern spaces of market circulation between urban, national, and global scales of activity. Yet by comparison to governmentality as the exercise of power over the populations (Barry *et al.* 1996; Burchell *et al.* 1991; Dean 1999; Miller and Rose 1990; Rose 1999; Rose *et al.* 2006), including a vibrant body of important work on governing the populations in China (Anagnost 2004; Bakken 2000; Bray 2005; Dutton 1992; Dikötter 2002; Jeffreys 2009; Kipnis 2006; Yan 2003), Foucault offers no road map to neoliberalism's spatial contexts. Foucault's historical examination of the contexts of power – the panopticon, the prison, and the asylum – depended on observing, monitoring, recording, and controlling populations in discrete spatial settings. For example, early publication of the governmentality lecture, circulating with Foucault's

(1977) work on the microphysics of power, distinguished in Michael Dutton's (1992) treatment of carceral practices in China, *Policing and Punishment in China*, attaches the governmentality literature on China to discrete spaces of state surveillance and spaces of interiority, including the body and the citizen. These spatial contexts differ from processes of spatial change that characterize the urban economy.

Nevertheless, we can find in Foucault's history of neoliberalism, *The Birth of Biopolitics*, how governing the market economy opens up to broader meso-scales of change. The political rationality of modern neoliberalism pursues markets through circulatory spaces of economic activity – cycles of investment, production, consumption, and accumulation that contribute to the production of space (Lefebvre 1991). Indeed, contemporary neoliberalism embraces the urban scale for its distinctive and contingent growth economies in 'cultural industries' of the city (Kearns and Philo 1993; Scott 2000).

With the shift to neoliberalism as a political rationality, the spatial contexts of Foucault's interests open up to levels of socio-spatial governance relevant to economic policy and social management in the urban milieu. Foucault himself writes:

> So, we have been trying out this notion of governmentality and … seeing how this grid of governmentality, which we may assume is valid for the analysis of ways of conducting the conduct of mad people, patients, delinquents, and children, may equally be valid when we are dealing with phenomena of a completely different scale, such as an economic policy, for example, or the management of a whole social body, and so on. What I wanted to do … was to see the extent to which … the analysis of micro-powers, or of procedures of governmentality, [are] not confined by definition to a precise domain determined by a sector of the scale, but should be considered … a method of decipherment which may be valued for the whole scale, whatever its size.
>
> (Foucault 2008: 186)

In this passage, the 'whole scale' points to the spatialities of governing knowledges relevant to social groups and society at large. Realization that Foucault viewed the idea of governmentality in broader, interrelated scales of social and political life invites thinking about urban governmentality.

Concern with political-economic transformation at the urban scale also emerges in Foucault's three *dispositifs* or knowledge apparatuses of the state: legal-juridical, disciplinary, and security, among which security is the prevailing contemporary *dispositif*. These form historically, sequentially and have come to exist simultaneously with increasing complexity (Foucault 2007: 8). By contrast to the disciplinary regime, which 'operates through the enclosure and circumscription of space, security requires the opening up and release of spaces, to enable circulation and passage' (Elden 2007: 565). The shift to the security apparatus entails a preponderant spatial shift from discrete spaces of the disciplinary regime to expansive spatial relations of circulatory, long-distance, and networked economic activity. In the People's Republic of China (PRC), this spatial shift is a recent event. It began decisively when the Party-state dismantled the economic basis of spatial organization in the socialist city, urban work units or *danwei* (单位) as sites of production-consumption, to generate commodity housing and intensify marketization of the urban economy.

Elsewhere Foucault gives further consideration to the interrelated conditions of historical-geographical change at the urban scale. Yet these observations are not part of his main *oeuvre* and some are reflections generated by questions in two interviews: one for *Herodote* with geographers (see Crampton and Elden 2007) and a related interview by Paul Rabinow (1984) for *The Foucault Reader*. Rabinow draws out Foucault on his statements about politics and architecture, especially in regard to the idea of a politics of architecture emerging at the end of the eighteenth century. Rabinow (1984: 239) asks, 'what is particular about the eighteenth century?' Foucault's immediate reply is 'my statement was awkward in that form'. Rabinow (1984: 240) hones in on Foucault's historical rationale and implores: 'could you tell us why?' At this juncture, Foucault's answer recognizes the city:

> Well, I think that it was linked to a number of phenomena, such as the question of the city and the idea that was clearly formulated at the beginning of the seventeenth century that the government of a large state like France should ultimately think of its territory on the model of a city. The city was no longer perceived as a place of privilege, as an exception in a territory of fields, forests, and roads. The cities were no longer islands beyond the common law. Instead, the cities, with the problems that they raised, and the particular forms that they took, served as the models for the governmental rationality that was to apply to the whole of the territory.
>
> (Foucault cited in Rabinow 1984: 241)

In this passage, Foucault observes the relationship between city and nation, including the idea that 'the model of a city' represents the governing rationality of the state or 'the whole of the territory', that is, the area over which the state holds sovereignty.

Foucault's idea of a city as a model that represents the governing rationality of the state invokes the PRC's history of 'model' (*mofan* 模范 or *dianxing* 典型) places and the continuing use of the idea of models in the contemporary National Civilized City programme (Cartier 2013). In the Mao era, the CCP propaganda apparatus systematically promoted two model places, the Daqing oilfields (*Daqing youtian* 大庆油田) and the Dazhai People's Commune (*Dazhai renmin gongshe* 大寨人民公社), to induce industrial towns and villages to competitively increase production through collective labour (Shapiro 2001). Nowadays, instead of basing a model on a particular place, such as was the case when the whole nation was exhorted to 'in industry learn from Daqing', the National Civilized City programme combines measures for social control with regulations for urban governance as a model of modernization for all cities.

In these ways, institutional and ideological, the Chinese city has not fully rebuilt its socialist past or restructured from the era of state planning. We also find the socialist landscape in old *danwei* compounds, residential areas still extant behind walls with gates or portals, often monitored by volunteer security staff. Even new private housing occupies discrete spaces surrounded by walls and fronted by gates. Their spatial characteristics represent the history of urban morphology in China in which walls, wards, and gates distinguish Chinese urban space (Bray 2005: 16–36). Looking closely at these contemporary sites yields the occasional discovery of a small bronze plaque at the entry with the Chinese characters 文明单位 (*wenming danwei*) or civilized *danwei* – an award of the National Civilized City system. This current Party-state practice of visually honouring a 'civilized' place indicates how the idea of the model environment, established in the Mao era, continues to matter in the Party-state's policy understanding of the contemporary city.

Consuming excess?

Where accounts of the contemporary Chinese city frequently document razing of the historical built environment in juxtaposition with China's newest, largest buildings, many places in China still show hybrid characteristics of the past and the present – as if hovering between the space of the socialist city and the market environment. Since the growth and transformation of the urban economy in China has been particularly rapid, such potential for hybrid conditions also characterizes the emerging consumer economy. To assess emerging consumer dynamics, and towards an assessment of governing through the National Civilized City programme, I focus in this section on hybrid conditions of the urban economy through surplus accumulation in the urban economy and its qualities of 'excess'.

The problem of excess in economic surplus is a general problem of the production–consumption relationship in China's marketizing economy. Surplus accumulation, disposed as excess, theoretically indexes values of society: excess represents the potential of choice. Foremost theorist of excess Georges Bataille (1991) formulates the idea of excess specifically as a problem of 'the accursed share' (*la part maudité*) or that part of surplus whose allocation becomes, by contemporary measures, economically irrational. His historical analysis includes societies of primary urbanization, where economic surplus first emerged. For example, the Aztec civilization built monumental temples and practised ritual sacrifice, in which the chosen victims represent the accursed share in surplus human labour. In Bataille's thought, excess is as if sacred – expressed through sacrifice, destruction, and waste.

In modern states, economic excess becomes allocated to military expenditure and by households to leisure and luxury consumption – valorized in statist or market terms yet also forms of waste. In a state system like China's, which lacks transparency and reliable measures of accountability, surplus/excess also takes the form of unreported 'grey' income and monetary and in-kind bribes. Uneven distribution of surplus, and the corollary problem of symbolic excess, expressed in visible, outsize consumption in China, makes normalizing excess and the inherent inequalities it generates, representing the possibility of instability, an object of Party-state governance.

Production of large surpluses perpetuates the problem of how to absorb them and this is evident in the built environment in China. The flow of capital from surplus accumulation supports large-scale investment in urban infrastructure, and, in the extreme, construction of commercial and residential space that sits unoccupied. For example, the New Century Global Centre in the city of Chengdu was built to accommodate international conventions, yet when corruption-related questions emerged over its capitalization, just months after its completion, the Chengdu government moved the scheduled Global Fortune 500 conference to a hotel instead: the New Century Global Centre proved itself spatially unnecessary (Moore 2013). Construction of such pre-demand infrastructure gives rise to entire 'ghost cities', largely unoccupied, which exist in many regions of China. The outstanding 'ghost' consumer space is the vacant New South China Mall, measured as the world's largest shopping mall by gross leasable area when it opened, in Dongguan in 2005 ('China's ghost mall' 2013).

Today the problem of large surpluses manifests in massive pre-demand urban infrastructure and in mass consumer activity. Here, let us consider the urban built environment in relation to gross domestic product (GDP), and household income growth and luxury or non-essential 'excess' consumption. The production of space in pre-demand infrastructure perpetuates the problem of dependence on production for economic growth. In the process of seeking to rebalance the economy from production-driven to consumption-driven, the production of consumer space in the built environment only sets the stage.

Local urban authorities throughout China appear to widely accept the developers' mantra of 'build it and they will come', but historical consumer activity has not paced general growth. Through the 1980s most households continued to prioritize savings. After slow growth in the 1990s, transfers of economic surplus to households through wages, supplemented by grey income, steadily increased in the 2000s up to the Global Financial Crisis of 2007–2009.

Figure 4.1 depicts the take-off in China of per capita GDP after the 1990s and Figure 4.2 shows sustained growth in per capita disposable income of urban residents in the 2000s, up to 2007. These figures do not include unreported quasi-legal and illegal personal income or grey income, which Chinese analysts estimated at 15 per cent of 2008 GDP (Liang 2010). Grey income is often expensed directly for real estate, luxury goods, leisure and gambling, because it typically does not enter the formal banking system.

If Bataille had extended his comparative analysis of civilizational excess to China, then he would have found entire cities dedicated to processing the excess of a nation – gambling in Macao and luxury consumption in Hong Kong. Increasing Chinese tourism has made Macao and Hong Kong repeat travel destinations for mainland Chinese, and going to Hong Kong has become a veritable shopping trip because prices on luxury and brand goods are lower and choice is greater in Hong Kong than in mainland China (Cartier 2009).

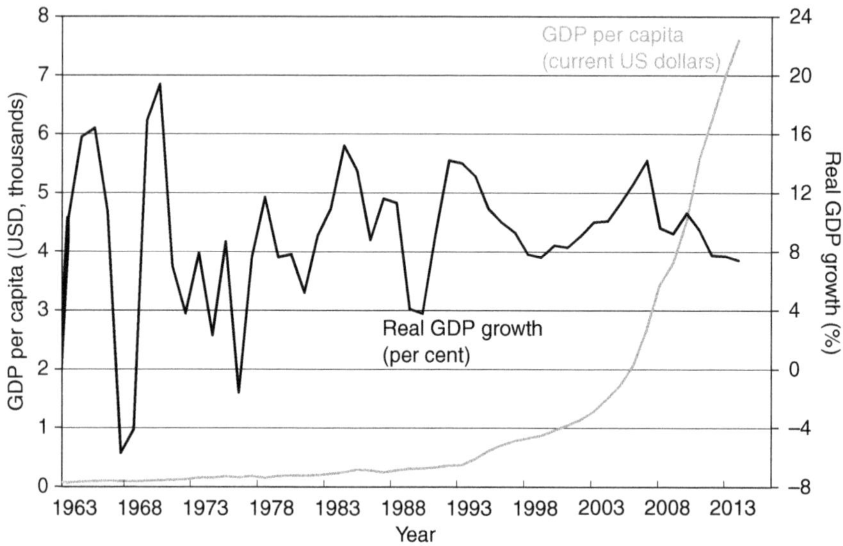

Figure 4.1 China's GDP growth and GDP per capita (source: World Bank 2015).

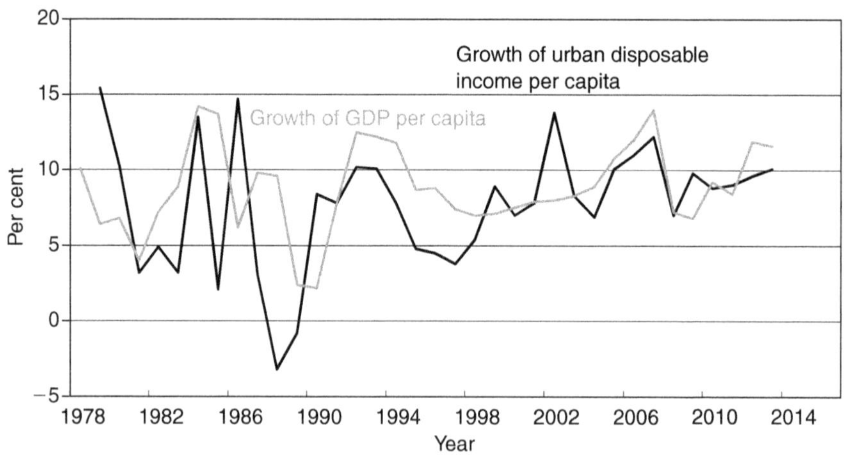

Figure 4.2 Real growth of per capita income of China's urban residents and GDP per capita (source: World Bank 2015; National Bureau of Statistics of China 2011, 2014).

Figure 4.3 shows especially high growth for Chinese luxury consumption in mainland China and Hong Kong and Macao compared to Chinese luxury consumption in other world regions.

Widespread understanding of Hong Kong as the outstanding consumer destination of the nation contributes to new mentalities of leisure consumerism

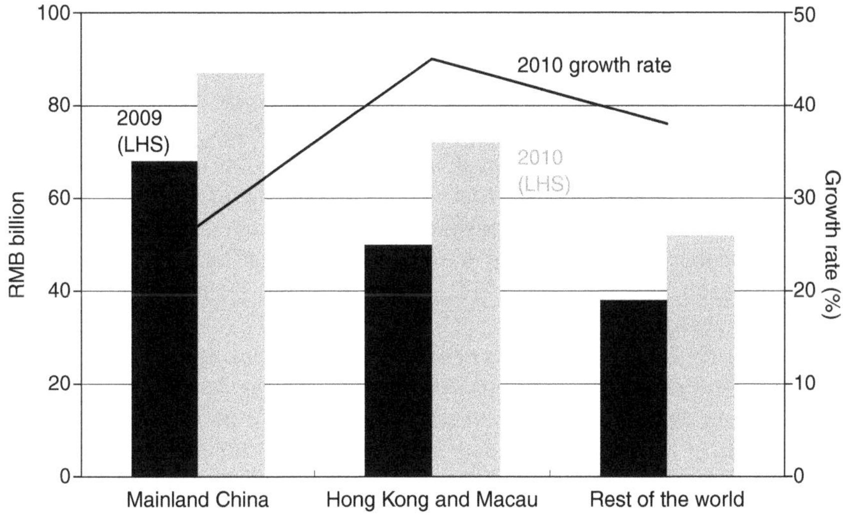

Figure 4.3 Chinese luxury consumption: mainland China vs. Hong Kong and Macau and the rest of the world (source: adapted from S&P Dow Jones Indices 2012: 12).

and their orientation to particular places. In addition to expending excess in contexts of daily life in the city, mentalities of consumer desire also become attached to travel destinations. Besides Hong Kong and Macao, Europe in general and especially France has become a major destination for luxury shopping. In Paris, Chinese tourists queue outside the Louis Vuitton (LV) flagship on Avenue des Champs-Elysées. Crushed by demand, LV limited customers to two items per entry to France, enforced by passport check, which generated an informal labour market in subcontracted shoppers (Fu 2010). Retail logistics aside, the demand for luxury goods suggests how evolving Chinese consumer mentalities prioritize positional goods that demonstrate shared social legibility. This shopper does not seek a unique item but a recognizable object owned by millions of other affluent and aspirational citizen-consumers. Desire for direct purchase in Paris also suggests how origins and quality matter: goods purchased in Europe convey greater security of authenticity even when many luxury goods firms manufacture some of their products in China.

By the mid-2000s, with sustained highs in urban household income, consumption entered a phase of exaggeration, as if celebrating the new excess, and made headlines. Some companies engaged in outsize production to generate new consumer interest. For example, a Beijing food company specializing in ice-cream mooncakes constructed, in the month of January before the Chinese New Year holiday, what was then the biggest ice-cream cake in the world ('World's biggest ice-cream cake' 2006).

Consumption of non-essential goods increased in size and quantity. A new consumer aesthetic channelled a sense of bravado achievement and wealthy consumers sought investment purchases. In Shanghai a man ordered a bouquet of 999 roses for a Valentine's Day gift (Shen 2005), while the Forbidden City in Beijing staged 'Watches and Wonders', which installed in the Qing dynasty Tai Miao (ancestral temple) watches of ten European luxury brands juxtaposed with historical timepieces. Shanghai and Hong Kong became new centres of the international auction trade in large gemstones, and Stanley Ho, the Macao casino magnate, bought and put on display in his Lisboa Casino one of the largest, flawless diamonds in the world (Cartier 2008). Purchasing in multiples or mass quantity also characterizes new consumer mentalities, from designated shopping (doing shopping for relatives and friends) to widespread enthusiasm for daily 'group bargains' (*ju huasuan* 聚划算) on Taobao.com, China's leading online shopping website.

By the early 2000s, expressions of excess in the city also emerged in the form of human multitudes in mass events associated with urban boosterism and entrepreneurialism to promote new markets – the core logic of neoliberalism. The organization of market-oriented mass activities by local officials to brand cities and raise the profile of lesser-known places coincided with the introduction of competition for world records to China. Guinness World Records is a business corporation and in 2000 it introduced a Chinese-language version of the *Guinness World Records*. (The name of the book was officially changed from *The Guinness Book of Records* and *The Guinness Book of World Records*, in the USA, to *Guinness World Records* in 2000.) The corporation established a liaison office in China to manage demand for hundreds of applications to establish or break world records (Parry 2005). From 2002 to 2007, more than 100 mass activities in China entered the Guinness World Records (Wang 2007), and by 2011 China ranked seventh on the Guinness list of most records broken by a country (Balazovic 2011).

In the 2000s, with new highs in urban income, consumer-oriented urban activity periodically surged, and mass events championed by local governments and business firms generated publicity and visitor revenue. The marketization of competitive interest in new urban economies encourages local governments to harness the social potential for mass organization and large-scale activities to brand and market their jurisdictions. For example, in 2005 the city of Shenyang organized students for a mass piano-playing event, which qualified for a world record while it also paid tribute to the city's native international star, pianist Lang Lang (Wang 2007). Such an event contributes to rebranding Shenyang, known as a city of heavy industry in China's 'rustbelt', as a city of high culture achievement.

In small and lesser known cities, urban boosterism of mass events is more challenging for local officials to profitably orchestrate while their 'official' organization makes people feel compelled to participate – the political logic of the single-party state compels assent and participation (Wang 2007). Yet the idea of using mass events to generate market activity generates contradictions: people participate on the basis of socialist-political values and institutions, inspired by history, yet find themselves faced with the neoliberal economic rationality to spend. Indeed, some events seem to orchestrate tourist spending. For example, Huludao City in Liaoning Province organized an event to set a record for the number of children playing traditional Chinese zithers. On 8 August 2007 more than 2,300 children participated in a five-minute zither performance, which qualified for a new Guinness World Record. The Guinness official record lists the organizer as the Huludao Municipal Committee of the CCP and the Huludao Municipal Government (Guinness World Records 2007). Yet the event depended on the participation of hundreds of children and their families travelling from a distance and they had to pay for their own hotel accommodation. As the head of the Qianhong Chinese Zither School in Dalian reported: 'The organizers provided nothing for us but a commemorative T-shirt. We had to pay all bills' and each participant had to pay a CNY 280 (USD35) recruiting fee (Wang 2007). Two days later, Zhoushan City, in Zhejiang province, announced that around 5,600 people took part in the 'ocean creatures costume campaign', which also earned a record for the largest gathering of people dressed as sea animals. The Guinness World Records (2015) lists the People's Government of Putuo District, Zhoushan City as the official organizer.

Historically interpreted within a Maoist political rationality, Dutton (2005: 32) explains how passions of collective activity 'exemplify the moral in action' and the political nature of excess. In Dutton's words: 'The willingness of a collectivity to go beyond its social and moral code and become excessive … constitutes, in fact, an empirical sign of the depth of their commitment to the higher moral calling of the Communist Party' (Dutton 2005: 32). This political understanding of excess emerges from the history of the revolutionary process and its fomentation of political mass events. Under reform, in this era of post-revolutionary socialism restructured for market ambitions, the history of political excess in China appears to inform passions for the market. Where mass activity was once harnessed to the political, now the Party-state seeks to promote mass consumer activity instead.

Governmentality and the 'civilized city'

Both mass events, championed by local governments and business firms, and conspicuous consumption by individuals and households buoy the new urban economy, yet they also point to the misguided market strategies of local governments and problems of inequality. The Party-state maintains abiding concern about such issues and unstintingly exhorts the people to conduct urban life with more 'civilized' characteristics. The process of civilizing is also an ongoing campaign of the Party's Spiritual Civilization Office, and over the past decade it has transformed into an approach to urban governance – the 'civilized city' (*wenming chengshi* 文明城市). But the 'civilized city' is neither a distinct government policy nor a local reform measure.

As a programme of the Central Guidance Commission for Building Spiritual Civilization, under the Publicity Department (an official rebranding of the English-language translation of the Propaganda Department), the 'civilized city' is a technology of governmentality that seeks to introduce and guide an array of standard measures of urban governance by promoting coordinated modernization among spheres of government, society, the economy, the environment and culture-as-conceived-by-the-state. It promotes replicability and seeks to entrain both officials and citizens in reproduction of state-defined urban modernity. With formal and aesthetic roots in the Mao-era political campaigns, employing model people and places to socialize results, the National Civilized City is a commercialized form of socialist mobilization linking Maoist traditions of mobilizing the masses and model strategies with contemporary urban planning.

In the landscape of the contemporary city, the 'civilized city' is conspicuously evident in large-format banners and posters, including massive advertising billboards along urban boulevards and intercity expressways. Typical slogans include: 'Be a Civilized Person, Build a Civilized City' (*Zheng zuo wenming ren, gong chuang wenming cheng* 争做文明人, 共创文明城) and 'Speak Civilly, Act Civilly, Be a Civilized Person and Build a Civilized City' (*Shuo wenming hua, ban wenming shi, zuo wenming ren, chuang wenming cheng* 说文明话, 办文明事, 做文明人, 创文明城). The slogans pair characters that relate the individual to the society, and invoke perspectives on appropriate conduct, social behaviour, and the role of the state in governing citizenship. From these perspectives, the civilized city programme continues long-running discourses about the 'quality' of a person or people and this way it can appear to be the latest effort to govern the population in the Party-state's enduring attention to 'population quality' (*renkou suzhi* 人口素质) (Anagnost 2004). As textual artefacts of propaganda, the long ribbon-lengths of red banners seem more in keeping with the Cultural Revolution than the modern city, even appearing out of context in China's new globalized built environments. Nevertheless, the signage indicates more than ongoing ideological interest to govern human conduct.

The Party promulgated a 'Resolution on Guiding Principles for Building a Socialist Society with Spiritual Civilization' in 1986, and in 1997 established a Central Guidance Commission for Building Spiritual Civilization under the supervision of the Party Publicity Department. In 2003, the Spiritual Civilization Commission established standards and selection procedures for the National Civilized Cities 'honour' (*rongyu* 荣誉) and set standards at all levels of administration: 'national civilized cities and districts'; 'civilized villages and towns'; and 'civilized [work] units'. In 2005, it established a National Civilized City Assessment System (*Quanguo wenming chengshi ceping tixi* 全国文明城市测评体系) in the form of government manuals for each administrative level and for each of the three levels of city (*shi* 市), including urban districts (*shiqu* 市区). These materials establish a policy basis for defining the civilized city.

Attaining the honorary title of National Civilized City (or district, town, or *danwei*) begins on the basis of application and screening for potential evaluation, which is carried out by a special team of the National Bureau of Statistics (Kuang 2009). Results of the first evaluation in 2005 named ten cities and three districts of provincial-level cities National Civilized Cities. Six cities have retained their status through the 2009 and 2011 evaluations: Baotou, Dalian, Ningbo, Yantai, Xiamen, and Zhangjiagang. In 2005 the programme also named 494 civilized towns and villages and 1,005 civilized work units as civilized ('Quanguo wenming chengshi, wenming danwei, xianjin danwei deng houxuan mingdan' 2005). The outcome awards honoured government institutions and companies with a bronze plaque marked 'civilized *danwei*'. Thus places gain recognition only through a process of assessment and periodic re-evaluation.

The 43-page text of the National Civilized City evaluation system for provincial-level and sub-provincial-level cities is organized around nine categories. These are: (1) non-corrupt and efficient environment for government affairs; (2) democratic and fair legal environment; (3) fair and honest market environment; (4) healthy human environment; (5) socio-cultural environment for the healthy development of adolescents; (6) comfortable and convenient living environment; (7) safe and stable social environment; (8) ecologically sustainable environment; and (9) solid and effective foundation for rural–urban policy implementation. The evaluation manuals differ by level of city – provincial-level cities, sub-provincial-level cities, prefectural-level cities, and so forth.

Together, the nine categories comprise 111 areas of evaluation in which the word *suzhi* (quality) appears only three times, within specific guidelines, and not in relation to individuals but as part of a set of goals and activities for improving urban society in general. The term *suzhi* appears in the preamble of the document as *shimin wenming suzhi* (市民文明素质) or 'quality of citizen civilization' and in three other instances relating to the quality of a civilizing activity, programme, or training (Spiritual Civilization Commission 2011: 1, 4, 16, 21). The first category of a 'non-corrupt and efficient environment for government affairs' emphasizes 'quality training' (*suzhi peixun* 素质培训) for officials. Category four, promoting a 'healthy human environment', specifies science education activities in association with implementation of the National Scientific Quality Action Plan (*Quanmin kexue suzhi xingdong jihua gangyao* 全民科学素质行动计划纲要) in which *suzhi* features only as 'scientific quality' (*kexue suzhi* 科学素质). Category five, promoting the 'healthy development of adolescents', emphasizes 'quality programmes' (*suzhi de jiemu* 素质的节目).

The first evaluation category focuses entirely on officials, education for officials, and official conduct. We might expect this category to be limited in enforcement, yet gaining and retaining civilized city status depends on self-governing officials – any rule violation or crime committed by a jurisdiction's Party secretary or mayor prevents application or nullifies civilized status. Shenzhen and Qingdao, for example, lost their status subsequent to disciplinary violations by Party secretaries (Cartier 2013). Places are disqualified from participation in the 12 months preceding evaluation in the event of any incident that represents poor governing capacity, whether official crime or corruption, environmental disaster, or food safety problems (Spiritual Civilization Commission 2011: 1). The programme requires self-governance by officials and makes the civilized city title contingent on a corruption-free officialdom. In an awarded 'civilized city', this link potentially intensifies public opprobrium of corrupt officials.

In the 2011 manual, meeting the goals of category five, 'healthy development of adolescents' is another leading programmatic precondition for civilized city application (Spiritual Civilization Commission 2011: 1). Cities seeking evaluation or re-evaluation develop programmes for youth and teenagers from 'civilized blogging' to 'healthy consumption'. In the 2012 annual civilized city evaluation index, Xiamen ranked second in the 'ideological and moral education of adolescents' (*wei chengnian ren sixiang daode jiaoyu* 未成年人思想道德教育) metric based on its implementation of 'civilized small blogs' (*wenming xiao boke* 文明小博客) in nearly 400 primary and secondary schools (Chen Guanghao 2012). Qingdao ranked first in the category for its implementation of a 'virtuous youth' (*meide shaonian* 美德少年) programme ('Guanyu kaizhan disanjie Qingdaoshi "meide shaonian" ' 2013).

The goal of category five responds to new concerns in society about consumption by youth and young adults. In 2005, the new economic excess also appeared in youth consumption of designer labels, irrespective of income, and generated consumer debt among young people for the first time ('Woguo nianqingren zhuiqiu gaoduan shechepin fuzhai xiaofei cheng shehui wenti' 2005). The issue generated national concern and subsequently many cities, including the designated civilized cities of Shenzhen and Ningbo, developed youth programmes for 'civilized consumption' (Chen Li *et al.* 2008; He Donglei 2010). In Shenzhen the local office of the National Consumer Association partnered with the city's Communist Youth League Publicity Department and the Spiritual Civilization Office to develop a poster competition depicting responsible consumption for middle-school and high-school students (Chen Li *et al.* 2008). The contest offered monetary awards, from CNY 100 to 2,000, including CNY 500 'bonus' awards for the posters with the 'best writing', 'best illustrations', and 'best topic'. Thus the city's Party offices adopted market logic to incentivize an event to discourage excess consumerism.

Category four, 'promoting a healthy human environment', is the most highly articulated set of criteria. This category particularly amalgamates both standard international urban development strategies and the political ideology of historical 'models' that originated in the Mao era: it seeks to govern both economic and political passions in the city. Featured in this category are criteria covering everything from development of cultural economy and creative industry to standards for social conduct and volunteerism (Spiritual Civilization Commission 2011: 12–19). Its evaluation standards predictably retain behavioural admonitions associated with past civilizing campaigns such as no spitting, no littering, and so on, and a section on Lei Feng-style 'moral models' (*daode mofan* 道德模范). (An ideological construction of 1960s CCP propaganda, the soldier Lei Feng was a model communist citizen and a tireless volunteer; see Jeffreys and Su in this book). It also includes two sections on volunteerism. The first volunteer guideline advocates building 'volunteer troops' (*zhiyuanzhe duiwu* 志愿者队伍), followed by a five-point section that includes developing volunteer service activities and promotion of campaigns to develop awareness of volunteerism and model activity (Spiritual Civilization Commission 2011: 18–19).

The emphasis on campaigns, models, and volunteerism continues Mao-era values and practices and repurposes them for contemporary social management goals. No matter how people regard them, these are long-established Party techniques. The evaluation guideline for volunteerism requires at least 8 per cent of the registered urban population to be signed up as volunteers (Spiritual Civilization Commission 2011: 18). These volunteers staff information stations in tourist areas and transport nodes, in addition to hospitals and various street-level functions such as gatehouses of housing compounds. The regular volunteers typically provide public assistance and policing in public places and they are usually women over 50 years of age – the retirement age for women workers (the retirement age for women civil servants is 55; the retirement age for men in China is 60, irrespective of occupation).

Cities also depend on volunteer labour to assist visitors at mega-events. Shanghai's university youth volunteers worked at the 2010 Shanghai Expo and, with their foreign-language skills, contributed to its organizational success. Overseas visitors were few in number the second time I visited the Shanghai Expo and I found myself periodically surrounded by engaging student volunteers who sought to provide directions and introduce exhibits. In 2013, more than 2,000 students from Jimei University provided volunteer services for the Xiamen International Marathon ('2,123 young volunteers poised for upcoming 2013 Xiamen Int'l Marathon' 2012). Xiamen's leading position on the National Urban Public Civilization Index likely rests on the city's higher than benchmark volunteer capacity: nearly 10 per cent or one registered volunteer for every ten people in the city (Chen Guanghao 2012).

The Civilized City programme draws on the CCP history of mobilizing the masses in order to establish and modernize volunteer labour for the contemporary city. The labour of retired women volunteers contributes directly to social reproduction, while the institutionalization of volunteer labour in society in general valorizes unpaid social work. Student volunteers are especially useful as an intermittent labour force and they are the first to be mobilized for periodic and one-off events.

Unpaid work in urban social services could be read as demonstrating extreme tendencies of neoliberalization, in which no wage is the ultimate calculation of low wage labour. Yet in China the historical record of mobilizing the masses provides a conceptual frame within which to imagine volunteerism as an honourable contribution to city and nation. The mobilization of unpaid urban volunteers arguably represents the integration of socialism and neoliberalism in China's political economy in which the Party-state entrains market rationalities from within a socialist political-aesthetic – the neoliberalizing city with Chinese characteristics.

The conjuncture of global capitalism with Party-state power in China produces political-economic contradictions in which volunteers contribute to the formation of new urban markets. Volunteers who travel to participate in record-breaking events are effectively domestic tourists whose expenditures buoy local economies. Contradiction also arguably characterizes the civilized city system's simultaneous emphasis on social control and 'correct' use of online media among urban youth and cultural industry development, which depends on competitive access to knowledge among world cities in the global economy. With attention to development of both the urban economy and the urban polity, the civilized city system continues politicized forms of social control while embracing banal consumerism.

Conclusions

The idea of an urban governmentality concerns governing the space of evolving markets and, as articulated by Foucault (2008), the exercise of political power modelled on the principles of a market economy. Modelling political power on the market economy, like the shift to the security apparatus, entails a preponderant spatial shift to the economic space of the city at large. The National Civilized City programme operates as a Party-state technology of governmentality by supporting expansion of the consumer economy, shifting from governing the populations to governing the abstract space of the urban economy.

Dutton's analysis of the changing relationship between political and economic rationalities identifies these issues: the structure of mass-line activity continues while the political mode is replaced by the economy of the contract (Dutton 2005: 272; see also Dutton and Hindess in this book). New economic mentalities, disciplined by rationalities of supply and demand, profit and loss, target and bonus, replace commitment to a political programme. In this formulation, 'excitement of the revolution' is lost as the city develops into a place of 'faux excitement of manufactured commodity desire', which 'relive[s] the past in mimicked forms rendered safe and salable for every consumer' (Dutton 2005: 315). Even consumer exuberance in China in the mid-2000s could not match the intensity of Maoist political commitments and excesses of the Cultural Revolution.

Through the civilized city programme, the work of the Party's Spiritual Civilization Commission has expanded to promote a wider domain of urban governance. With its prioritization of enhanced education for local officials and government accountability, the civilized city system challenges city governments that apply for evaluation to recognize and integrate a broad range of urban functions and development goals across multiple categories. It underscores how the Party-state's 'civilizing' project has grown beyond a set of political-linguistic techniques for socializing citizen conduct and *suzhi*. It seeks to socialize self-governance and improve government for modern urban management. It engages both citizens and officials in reproducible governing practices.

Instead of building a model on a particular place, as in the Mao era, the National Civilized City system constitutes a model for all cities. As a contemporary technology of urban governmentality, the National Civilized City programme is a political knowledge formation that serves to remodel governance on the space of the city for development of the urban economy and the production–consumption transition. With its emphasis on periodic re-evaluation, attaining and maintaining the National Civilized City 'honour' entrains cities in a continual process of striving to gain and attempt to institutionalize benchmark urban quality standards. Its ultimate outcome would theoretically produce a national landscape of uniformly civilized places, and make Foucault's passing insight about cities as 'models for the governmental rationality that was to apply to the whole of the territory' sound like a Chinese national plan.

Acknowledgements

This research was supported under the Australian Research Council's Discovery Projects funding scheme (DP120101901).

References

'2,123 young volunteers poised for upcoming 2013 Xiamen Int'l Marathon' (2012) Xiamen Municipal Government. Online. Available: http://english.xm.gov.cn/News/201301/t20130103_605722.html (accessed 16 July 2015).

Anagnost, A. (2004) 'The corporeal politics of quality (*suzhi*)', *Public Culture*, 16, 2: 189–208.

Bakken, B. (2000) *The Exemplary Society*, New York: Oxford University Press.

Balazovic, T. (2011) 'World beater', *China Daily*, 11 November. Online. Available: http://usa.chinadaily.com.cn/weekly/2011-11/11/content_14075753.htm (accessed 20 July 2015).

Barry, A., Osborne, T., and Rose, N. (eds) (1996) *Foucault and Political Reason: Liberalism, Neo-liberalism and Rationalities of Government*, London: UCL Press.

Bataille, G. (1991) *The Accursed Share: An Essay on General Economy, Volume 1: Consumption*, New York: Zone Books.

Bray, D. (2005) *Social Space and Governance in Urban China*. Stanford: Stanford University Press.

Burchell, G., Gordon, C., and Miller, P. (eds) (1991) *The Foucault Effect: Studies in Governmentality*, Chicago: University of Chicago Press.

Cartier, C. (2008) 'The Shanghai–Hong Kong connection: fine jewellery consumption and the demand for diamonds', in D.S.G. Goodman (ed.), *The New Rich in China*, Abingdon: Routledge, pp. 187–200.

Cartier, C. (2009) 'Production–consumption and the Chinese city/region: cultural political economy and the feminist diamond ring', *Urban Geography*, 30, 4: 368–90.

Cartier, C. (2013) 'The civilized city: from ideology to urban governance', in G. Barmé and J. Goldkorn (eds), *The China Story Yearbook 2013: Civilizing China*, Canberra: Australian Centre on China in the World, Australian National University, pp. 256–85.

Chen Guanghao (2012) 'Xiamen wenming chuangjian yi weimin huimin wei chufadian zhichilü da 99.8%' [Establishing Xiamen civilization: people benefitting people as the starting point for a support rate of 99.8 per cent], *Haixi Chenbao*, 5 December. Online. Available: http://news.xmhouse.com/bd/201212/t20121205_426994.htm (accessed 20 July 2015).

Chen Li, Xiong Handong, Chen Jiawen, and Wang Jiana (2008) 'Wo shi juban "aoyun yu xiaofei" banbao sheji dasai' [Shenzhen's 'Olympics and Consumption' poster design contest], *Shenzhen Wanbao*, 20 September. Online. Available: http://wb.sznews.com/html/2008-08/01/content_283018.htm (accessed 20 July 2015).

'China's ghost mall' (2013) YouTube. Online. Available: www.youtube.com/watch?v=5zPkm2SU1DM&list=TLXH2oMKzZgzw (accessed 20 July 2015).

Crampton, J. and Elden, S. (eds) (2007) *Space, Knowledge and Power: Foucault and Geography*, Aldershot: Ashgate.

Dean, M. (1999) *Governmentality: Power and Rule in Modern Society*, London: Sage.

Dikötter, F. (2002) *Crime, Punishment and the Prison in Modern China*, New York: Columbia University Press.

Dutton, M.R. (1992) *Policing and Punishment in China: From Patriarchy to 'the People'*, Cambridge: Cambridge University Press.

Dutton, M.R. (2005) *Policing Chinese Politics: A History*, Durham: Duke University Press.

Elden, S. (2007) 'Rethinking governmentality', *Political Geography*, 26, 1: 29–33.

Foucault, M. (1977) *Discipline and Punish: The Birth of the Prison*, New York: Pantheon Books.

Foucault, M. (2007) *Security, Territory, Population: Lectures at the Collège de France 1977–1978*, Houndsmills: Palgrave Macmillan.

Foucault, M. (2008) *The Birth of Biopolitics: Lectures at the Collège de France 1978–1979*, New York: Palgrave Macmillan.

Fu, J. (2010) 'France opens its arms wide to Chinese visitors', *China Daily*, 5 November. Online. Available: www.chinadaily.com.cn/world/2010-11/05/content_11504783.htm (accessed 20 July 2015).

'Guanyu kaizhan disanjie Qingdaoshi "meide shaonian" pingxuan biaozhang huodong de tongzhi' [Notice on the launch of Qingdao city's third 'virtuous youth' selection and commendation activity] (2013) *Qingdao Xuanchuanwang*, 14 March. Online. Available: www.qdxc.gov.cn/content/2013-03/14/content_9645968.htm (accessed 20 July 2015).

Guinness World Records (2007) 'Largest guzheng ensemble'. Online. Available: www.guinnessworldrecords.com/records-4000/largest-gu-zheng-ensemble (accessed 20 July 2015).

Guinness World Records (2015) 'Largest gathering of people dressed as sea animals', 10 August 2007. Online. Available: www.guinnessworldrecords.com/world-records/largest-gathering-of-people-dressed-as-sea-animals (accessed 20 July 2015).

He Donglei (2010) 'Ningbo shi gaoxinqu xiaobaowei: zhongxiaoxuesheng xiaofei zhuangkuang wenjuan diaocha baogao' [Ningbo City High-tech Zone Consumer Protection Committee: Schoolchildren Consumption Survey Report], 25 January. Online. Available: www.315cebs.com.cn/show-780-1.html (accessed 20 July 2015).

Jeffreys, E. (ed.) (2009) *China's Governmentalities: Governing Change, Changing Government*, Abingdon: Routledge.

Kearns, G. and Philo, C. (eds) (1993) *Selling Places: The City as Cultural Capital, Past and Present*, Oxford: Pergamon Press.

Kipnis, A. (2006) '*Suzhi*: a keyword approach', *The China Quarterly*, 186: 295–313.

Kuang Xinhua (2009) 'Zhongguo chengshi de zuigao rongyu' [The highest honour of the Chinese city], *Xinzhoukan*, 292. Online. Available: www.neweekly.com.cn/newsview.php?id=512 (accessed 20 July 2015).

Lefebvre, H. (1991) *The Production of Space*, Oxford: Blackwell.

Liang Fei (2010) 'Shadow incomes soar without accountability', *Global Times*, 26 August. Online. Available: http://en.people.cn/90001/90778/90862/7118376.html (accessed 20 July 2015).

Miller, P. and Rose, N. (1990) 'Governing economic life', *Economy and Society*, 19, 1: 1–31.

Moore, M. (2013) 'Corruption and the world's largest building', *Telegraph*, 13 September. Online. Available: www.telegraph.co.uk/news/worldnews/asia/china/10308029/Corruption-and-the-worlds-biggest-building.html (accessed 23 July 2015).

National Bureau of Statistics of China (2011) 'Statistical communiqué of the People's Republic of China on the 2013 National Economic and Social Development', 24 February, Online. Available: www.stats.gov.cn/english/PressRelease/201402/t20140224_515103.html (accessed 21 July 2015).

National Bureau of Statistics of China (2014) 'China's economy showed good momentum of steady growth in the year of 2013', 20 January. Online. Available: www.stats.gov.cn/english/PressRelease/201401/t20140120_502079.html (accessed 21 July 2015).

Parry, S. (2005) 'The Chinese go crazy for the Guinness Book of Records with some feats you'd never dream of', *Telegraph*, 20 February. Online. Available: www.telegraph.co.uk/news/worldnews/asia/china/1483961/The-Chinese-go-crazy-for-the-Guinness-Book-of-Records-with-some-feats-youd-never-dream-of.html (accessed 20 July 2015).

'Quanguo wenming chengshi, wenming danwei, xianjin danwei deng houxuan mingdan' [National civilized cities, civilized units and advanced units, etc., candidate shortlist] (2005) *Xinhua News Agency*, 6 September. Online. Available: www.gov.cn/jrzg/2005-09/06/content_29424.htm (accessed 20 July 2015).

Rabinow, P. (ed.) (1984) *The Foucault Reader*, New York: Pantheon Books.

Rose, N. (1999) *Powers of Freedom: Reframing Social Thought*, Cambridge: Cambridge University Press.

Rose, N., O'Malley, P., and Valverde, M. (2006) 'Governmentality', *Annual Review of Law and Social Science*, 2: 83–104.

S&P Dow Jones Indices (2012) 'Measuring the business of luxury living', McGraw-Hill, S&P Dow Jones Indices Research and Design. Online. Available: www.spindices.com/documents/research/sp-global-luxury-index-measuring-the-business-of-luxury-living-201205.pdf (accessed 20 July 2015).

Scott, A.J. (2000) *The Cultural Economy of Cities*, London: Sage.

Shapiro, J. (2001) *Mao's War Against Nature*, Cambridge: Cambridge University Press.

Shen, K. (2005) 'She'd better have a big vase', *Shanghai Daily*, 10 February, p. 1.

Spiritual Civilization Commission (2011) *Quanguo wenming chengshi ceping tixi* (2011) [National Civilized City Evaluation System (2011)]. Online. Available: www.hzwh.gov.cn/ztzl/wmcs/201103/t20110325_247842.html (accessed 16 July 2015).

Wang, K. (2007) 'China's mass Guinness record entries have darker side', *China Internet Information Center*, 28 August. Online. Available: www.china.org.cn/china/features/content_1222999.htm (accessed 20 July 2015).

'Woguo nianqingren zhuiqiu gaoduan shechipin fuzhai xiaofei cheng shehui wenti' [Chinese youth seeking high-end luxury goods, incurring consumer debt is becoming a social problem] (2005) *Zhongguo Qingnianbao*, 20 June. Online. Available: http://news.qq.com/a/20050620/000327.htm (accessed 20 July 2015).

World Bank (2015) 'World Development Indicators (1960–2014)'. Online. Available: http://data.worldbank.org/data-catalog/world-development-indicators (accessed 21 July 2015).

'World's biggest ice-cream cake' (2006) *Daily Times*, 17 January. Online. Available: http://archives.dailytimes.com.pk/infotainment/17-Jan-2006/world-s-biggest-ice-cream-cake (accessed 24 July 2015).

Yan, H. (2003) 'Neoliberal governmentality and neohumanism: organizing suzhi/value flow through labor recruitment networks', *Cultural Anthropology*, 18, 4: 493–523.

5 Rethinking and remaking China's built environments

Spatial planning and the reinscription of everyday life

David Bray

In 2009, in a quiet corner of a Jiangsu village, I came across a large, colourful sign that struck a decidedly discordant note in the otherwise rustic and peaceful scene (see Figure 5.1). It was neither a street sign nor commercial advertising. It proclaimed in bold lettering: 'Continue to liberate the mind, promote scientific development' (*jixu jiefang sixiang, tuidong kexue fazhan* 继续解放思想, 推动科学发展).

The origin of this message was also encoded in the sign; for in the background behind the slogan is an image of Tiananmen, the 'Gate of Heavenly Peace', which represents the central Chinese State. The so-called Doctrine of Scientific Development (*kexue fazhan guan* 科学发展观) was unveiled by China's recently retired 'paramount leader', Hu Jintao, in 2003, near the beginning of his decade at the apex of political power. 'Liberate the mind' was a key slogan promoted by Deng Xiaoping at the start of the reform period, to counter what he perceived to be the dogmatic application of Maoism, which had become

Figure 5.1 Village sign, Jiangsu, 2009 (source: photograph by David Bray).

dominant in the latter years of Mao Zedong's life. Although both concepts have been used in a range of contexts throughout China, their combination in a rural setting speaks to a long standing and dominant governmental discourse that posits rural China not only as under-developed economically, but more importantly, as under-developed culturally and intellectually – a repository of traditional, conservative and 'backward' (*luohou* 落后) mindsets. Hence, the ordering of clauses in the sign could seem misleading: in the case of rural China, it is not 'liberating the mind' that will lead to 'scientific development'; rather, it is the other way around. True to their technocratic training, China's authorities believe that bringing 'scientific development' to rural China will not only modernize the physical environment, but will also modernize the intellectual and cultural mindsets of the rural population. So the sign should really be understood to mean: 'Continue to liberate the mind *through* promoting scientific development.'

In fact, a particular manifestation of 'scientific development' arrived in this Jiangsu village about the same time as the sign. Just 200 metres further down the road, the vernacular village buildings make way for a brand-new, urban-style gated residential estate (*xiaoqu* 小区) built to house villagers relocated from a nearby hamlet (see Figure 5.2). It turns out that this administrative village[1] is now subject to a formal master planning process and that the new *xiaoqu* is just the first stage in a grand 20-year plan to relocate its 14 hamlets into three larger modernized rural settlements designed according to urban models of housing,

Figure 5.2 Weilong Xiaoqu, Jiangsu, 2011 (source: photograph by David Bray).

infrastructure, and service. This master plan, created by professional urban planners from the Jiangsu Bureau of Urban Planning and Design, as part of the national programme to 'Build a New Socialist Countryside' (*jianshe shehuizhuyi xin nongcun* 建设社会主义新农村), is an exemplary embodiment of the governmental discourse which posits 'scientific development' as an agent for far-reaching social transformation.

Urban planning is not, per se, a *new* mentality of government, and as a profession it has been present since the inception of the People's Republic of China (PRC) (Bray 2005). Nevertheless, the scope and influence of urban planning has increased dramatically over recent years, most notably with its extension into the countryside. Moreover, spatial planners have emerged from relative obscurity to command a leading role in governmental programmes for national development.

This chapter demonstrates how urban planners have reshaped China's built environments and thereby contributed to significant transformations in the everyday lives of ordinary citizens. The first part examines how the concept of 'planning' has been reconceived within the PRC and how this has led to a 'spatial turn', resulting in a greatly enhanced professional role for spatial planners. The second part presents a genealogical study of contemporary residential design standards, focusing on the *xiaoqu* (small district) model, in order to demonstrate the key role played by urban planners in the development of complex spatial strategies that underpin new ways to govern the population. The third part, based on a case study of a village in Jiangsu, explores the socio-technical implications of 'scientific' spatial planning, through analysing some of the ways in which the technologies associated with the new housing estate inscribe a new way of life onto its rural residents. Continuing the case study, the fourth part focuses on the spatial configuration of the new *xiaoqu* and shows how particular types of activities ubiquitous to the old village, such as the keeping of productive animals, are no longer possible because there is literally no space for such activities to occur inside the new residential area.

The first two parts adopt a governmentality approach, focusing on the rationales that underpin professional discourses of spatial planning and residential design. The third and fourth parts employ an actor–network approach in an attempt to describe how residents of the new *xiaoqu* experience the transformation in lifestyle dictated by the shift from traditional village to master-planned estate. In conclusion, I argue that these two approaches are complementary and used together can help us better understand *both* the logic *and* the implications of urban planning in contemporary China.

From *jihua* to *guihua*: the rise of coordinated spatial planning

The governmental desire to promote 'scientific development' manifests in multiple ways, but underpinning many of these programmes has been an increasing attention to spatial planning at all scales. This culminated in 2007 when the *Urban Planning Law* (*chengshi guihua fa* 城市规划法), originally issued in

1990, was revised and reissued as the *Urban and Rural Planning Law* (*chengxiang guihua fa* 城乡规划法) (*Zhonghua renmin gongheguo chengshi guihua fa* 1990; *Zhonghua renmin gongheguo chengxiang guihua fa* 2007). The new law, which came into effect at the beginning of 2008, sets out a continuum of spatial planning practice that stretches from the entire nation, at one extreme, to the individual village at the other extreme. Under this schema, the law requires that every territorial jurisdiction, from the nation, through regions, provinces, cities, counties, districts, towns, townships, and down to the administrative village, must produce a master plan to guide development over a 20-year horizon.

The first article of the *Urban and Rural Planning Law* states that its objectives are: 'to coordinate urban and rural spatial order; to improve living conditions; and to promote the fully coordinated and sustainable economic and social development of urban and rural areas' (*Zhonghua renmin gongheguo chengxiang guihua fa* 2007). This statement signals the fact that spatial planning is conceived as part of a larger strategic project for the 'coordinated planning' of national development. Indeed, four years earlier a new policy on coordinated planning was unveiled during the Third Plenum of the Sixteenth Central Committee. Known as the 'Five Types of Coordinated Planning' (*wu ge tongchou* 五个统筹), it encompassed the following domains of planning:

1 coordinated planning of urban and rural development (*tongchou chengxiang fazhan* 统筹城乡发展);
2 coordinated planning of regional development (*tongchou quyu fazhan* 统筹区域发展);
3 coordinated planning of economic and social development (*tongchou jingji shehuì fazhan* 统筹经济社会发展);
4 coordinated planning of the harmonious development of humans and nature (*tongchou ren yu ziran hexie fazhan* 统筹人与自然和谐发展);
5 coordinated planning of domestic development and the demands of opening to the outside world (*tongchou guonei fazhan he duiwai kaifang de yaoqiu* 统筹国内发展和对外开放的要求).

(Zhonggong zhongyang 2003)

The emergence of this new approach to planning was confirmed by a significant shift in official terminology when the term '*jihua*' (计划) was replaced by the term '*guihua*' (规划) within key government planning documents. The Eleventh Five-Year Plan for National Economic and Social Development was the first to be officially referred to as a '*guihua*' rather than a '*jihua*' (Zhonggong zhongyang 2005). The significance of this shift in terminology was noted in the Chinese media when leading economist Zhang Zhuoyuan[2] explained that the change reflected the transition from a socialist centrally planned economy to a socialist market economy (Li Jing 2005). While '*jihua*' and '*guihua*' both mean 'plan', according to Zhang, the former connotes a conception of direct micro management and organization of the economy, while the latter infers a more distant mode of macro management (cited in Li Jing 2005).

Beijing-based journalist Wang Jun, who has written widely on the history and politics of urban development, also notes that the shift from '*jihua*' to '*guihua*' coincides with a recognition by key economic planners within the central administration that spatial factors play an important role in contemporary economic development (Wang Jun 2008: 136–8). '*Guihua*' has always been the term used in relation to spatial planning; urban planning in Chinese, for example, is *chengshi guihua* (城市规划). The shift from '*jihua*' to '*guihua*', then, can be read as signifying a spatial turn in governmental discourse. To underscore this point, Wang quotes Xu Lin (徐林), deputy head of the Planning Department within the National Development and Reform Commission, from an interview conducted in July 2005:

> We discovered that regional and spatial factors such as transport networks, port facilities, environmental protection and spatial location had increasingly become the key issues in government planning; problems of economic and social development had to be combined with consideration of spatial issues; or to put it another way, the planning of economic and social development had to be grounded.
>
> (Wang Jun 2008: 137)

Wang's research not only uncovers the emergence of a growing spatial consciousness among economic planners in the central government, but also illustrates why the subsequently revised planning law extended the spatial planning regime in both directions; where the 1990 *Urban Planning Law* applied only to 'cities', the 2007 *Urban and Rural Planning Law* applies to national- and regional-scale spatial units, as well as to the smaller-scale units of towns, townships, and villages (*Zhonghua renmin gongheguo chengshi guihua fa* 1990; *Zhonghua renmin gongheguo chengxiang guihua fa* 2007). While governmental practices of economic management may have shifted from micro to macro modes of intervention, authorities simultaneously sought to engender increasing coordination in planning across all scales of economic and social activity. In practice this entails not only coordinating across different territorial scales, but also coordinating between different bureaucratic planning systems. Wang Jun (2008: 136–41) refers to this as the 'battle of the three kingdoms': an ongoing struggle for influence involving the National Development and Reform Commission with its 'economic and social development plans' (*jingji shehui fazhan guihua* 经济社会发展规划); the Ministry of Land and Resources with its 'land-use master plans' (*tudi liyong zongti guihua* 土地利用总体规划); and the Ministry of Housing and Urban–Rural Construction with its 'urban and rural construction master plans' (*chengxiang jianshe zongti guihua* 城乡建设总体规划).

In this light, I agree with Gary Sigley's (2006) assessment that the move from '*jihua*' to '*guihua*' should not be interpreted as a withdrawal of the state, but rather as the emergence of a different mode of governmental operation. Sigley characterizes this transition as a shift from 'government' to 'governance', defining the latter term in the following way:

> As a technical and technocratic means of understanding government, the discourse of *governance* implies a different way of looking at the target subject (whether that be an individual, community or sector). It is often likened to the notion of 'steering', that is, guiding and leading the target in a certain direction through the use of direct and indirect methods ('economic levers', 'market mechanisms', and so on).
>
> (Sigley 2006: 5–6; emphasis added)

To this list of technocratic methods we can add the repertoires of spatial planning. Far from leaving the fate of development to market mechanisms alone, the new planning law endorses strategic professional intervention for a wide range of objectives:

> improving the ecological environment; enhancing the conservation and comprehensive utilization of resources and energy; protecting farmland, natural resources as well as historical and cultural heritage; maintaining local and ethnic characteristics and traditions; preventing pollution and other public dangers; satisfying the needs of regional population development, national defence construction, disaster prevention and alleviation, public health and public safety.
>
> (*Zhonghua renmin gongheguo chengxiang guihua fa* 2007: Article 4)

In this discursive framework, spatial planning is understood as a means to promote *good* governance across a range of policy concerns. But it is probably in relation to the governance of residential communities that spatial planners have had the most significant long-term impact. For as I discuss in the following section, the dominant model for residential design in contemporary China, the *xiaoqu*, was a prototype that emerged through a deliberative bureaucratic process which brought urban planners and government officials together to solve the problem of how best to govern the urban population in a new era in which the socialist workplace (*danwei* 单位) would no longer be the dominant social and spatial unit of the city.

Reinventing the *xiaoqu*

The concept of '*xiaoqu*' (small district) is not new. As a translation of the Russian term *mikrorayon* ('microdistrict'), it came into use within China as early as 1956 (Lu 2006: 37). However, due to the dominance of the *danwei* system during the Mao era (Bray 2005), the *xiaoqu* concept remained neglected and largely forgotten until the mid-1980s when authorities began to search for a new strategy for housing development. The key rationale for change was to lift the heavy burden of housing provision from the workplace (*danwei*) in order to improve economic productivity. But if the *danwei* would no longer provide housing then who would? The long-term strategy was to encourage the emergence of a commercial property development industry and to transform housing from a welfare subsidy, a key component of the so-called 'iron rice bowl', into a commercial product. However, it turned out that authorities were not willing to simply let the market determine new models for housing development. Instead, they decided to create a new nationally unified model underpinned by comprehensive urban planning, large-scale ('super-block') development, and strict building and design codes.

The process to develop a new housing model began in 1986 when the Ministry of Construction launched its first round of *xiaoqu* trials (*di yi pi chengshi shiyan zhuzhai xiaoqu* 第一批城市试验住宅小区), which involved the design and construction of three experimental *xiaoqu* in three different cities, respectively, Tianjin, Jinan, and Wuxi. Following these trials, in 1989, the Ministry convened a review meeting in Jinan which resulted in the establishment of a National Office for Urban Residential *Xiaoqu* Trials (*quanguo chengshi zhuzhai xiaoqu shidian bangongshi* 全国城市住宅小区试点办公室). The role of this office was to undertake analysis of the trials and to further promote the development of the *xiaoqu* residential model. Between 1989 and 1994 they organized a second round of trials which included 15 'model' *xiaoqu* designed and built in various cities throughout China.

The culmination of these trials came in 1994 when the Ministry published the first edition of a new design code: *Planning and Design Standards for Urban Residential Areas* (*chengshi juzhuqu guihua sheji guifan* 城市居住区规划设计规范) (Zhonghua renmin gongheguo jianshebu 1994). This document codifies the planning of residential areas, setting out the key principles and requirements in terms of facilities and services and various technical specifications related to land-use, infrastructure, building standards, and so on. This document is the bible for residential development and is still in use today, having gone through several editions and updates.

The first principle established in the *Design Standards* is that residential areas will be planned according to an integrated three-level spatial scheme; from larger to smaller these are residential areas (*juzhuqu* 居住区), small districts (*xiaoqu* 小区), and housing clusters (*zutuan* 组团). The document explains that the three-level scheme was arrived at after extensive 'national investigation and analysis of existing urban residential areas throughout the nation', and further claims that 'it is *scientifically logical* and accords to national conditions' (Zhonghua renmin gongheguo jianshebu 1994; emphasis added). Table 5.1 shows the relative household and population range for each of the three units.

There are two key justifications for this model; first, it satisfies three different levels of basic daily needs for residents – green space, convenience shops and bicycle parking at the housing cluster level; primary school and community services at the *xiaoqu* level; and department store, health clinic and cultural activities centre at the residential district level. Second, the three-level system harmonizes with the existing structure for urban governance: the housing cluster population size of 1,000–3,000 is the same as the population scale that comes under the jurisdiction of the Residents' Committee (*juweihui* 居委会); and the population range for a residential district, at 30,000–50,000 is the same size as

Table 5.1 Control limits for levels within residential areas

	Residential area	*Microdistrict (xiaoqu)*	*Housing cluster*
Households	10,000–16,000	3,000–5,000	300–1,000
Population	30,000–50,000	10,000–15,000	1,000–3,000

Source: adapted and translated by David Bray from Zhonghua renmin gongheguo jianshebu [Ministry of Construction of the People's Republic of China] (1994) *Chengshi juzhu qu guihua sheji guifan [Planning and Design Standards for Urban Residential Areas]*, Beijing: Zhongguo Jianzhu Gongye Chubanshe. GB 50180-93, Section 1.0.3.

the population that normally comes under the jurisdiction of the Street Office (*jiedao banshichu* 街道办事处). From this explanation it is clear that in creating the new residential model, authorities not only considered the problem of public service provision, but also designed it explicitly to conform to existing structures of urban jurisdiction.

Although the original plan was that the lowest level of urban governance, the Residents' Committee, would correspond to the smallest spatial unit, the housing cluster, subsequently the scale of the Residents' Committee has been enlarged so that in most cities in China its jurisdiction now corresponds to the *xiaoqu*. For example, the original design of Enjili Xiaoqu (恩济里小区) in Beijing (one of the 15 model *xiaoqu* included in the second round of trials) included four housing clusters, each of which had its own Residents' Committee located in an office overlooking the entrance to the cluster (Lü *et al.* 2001: 241). But during fieldwork in 2010, I discovered that the original four Residents' Committees had been amalgamated into one Community Residents' Committee (*shequ jumin weiyuanhui* 社区居民委员会) which governs the entire *xiaoqu*. Article 83 of the *Beijing Municipal Master Plan*, published in 2005, further highlights the close link between spatial scales and governmental scales:

> The community is the basic unit for organizing residents' life; with the adjustment of the scale of the Residents' Committee, we will increasingly align the Street Office and the Residents' Committee with the scale of the residential area and the *xiaoqu* respectively; to enhance the role of the community in organizing residents' life and perfecting service provision.
>
> (Beijingshi chengshi guihua sheji yanjiuyuan 2005)

The evidence presented above shows that the scale of housing development in China can be understood as a manifestation of a specific rationale of government: housing is arranged on a scale designed to correspond to the lowest level of political and social organization (Bray 2008). During the Mao era, the *danwei* was the basic unit of urban society and therefore became the basic unit for housing development. In the reform era, with the demise of the *danwei*, the Residents' Committee has been revived as the basic unit of urban governance so the new housing model, based on the *xiaoqu*, has been designed and adjusted to correspond to that scale.

China's government authorities believe that the urban population can be managed more efficiently and effectively when there is a direct correspondence between the political scale and the spatial scale (see also Cartier in this book). In practical terms, this was achieved by mobilizing urban planners to invent a residential design prototype based on the population scale of the Residents' Committee. When perfected, the prototype was simply converted into a detailed set of design standards, codified and disseminated nationally through the construction industry. Wherever housing was needed the *xiaoqu* could be deployed with no need to consider the logic underlying its origins or its implications for social transformation.

The *xiaoqu* has become so ubiquitous in urban China and so synonymous with real-estate development that it is now virtually impossible to imagine any kind of alternative. In rural China, however, the *xiaoqu* is still a relatively new phenomenon, the occasional gated enclave emerging out of a sea of vernacular architecture. In this context, there is much more scope to consider the *xiaoqu* as a transformative technology. The following case study – describing the relocation of a small traditional hamlet called Wei Cun to a new residential development known as Longwei *xiaoqu* – shows how particular forms of socio-technical change are inscribed within *xiaoqu* design.

Longwei *xiaoqu*: 'a durable inscription on the landscape'

In her study of the electricity grid in the Ivory Coast, Madeleine Akrich (1992), points to the ways in which the expansion of technological networks into new territory can bring about far-reaching reorganization of spatial, legal, political and social configurations in developing nations. Such technologies make what she calls 'a durable inscription on the landscape', and through this bring about the creation of 'such new and "modern" entities as the individual citizen' (Akrich 1992: 214–15). I argue that the contemporary Chinese *xiaoqu* functions precisely in this way.

The contemporary Chinese *xiaoqu* is inscribed with an assemblage of transformative technologies which operate *both* to nurture and normalize citizenship within the discrete community circumscribed by its enclosure, *and* to link the multitude of *xiaoqu* together through technological networks which foster a unified national practice of modern citizenship. For the new residents of Longwei *xiaoqu*, the implications are both structuring and enabling: the technologies that underpin the form and the functioning of the new 'village' circumscribe their everyday lives in significant new ways – the absences (poultry, vegetable plots, and courtyards) as much as the presences (roads, lawns, plumbing, and cable TV); at the same time, their connection to these technological networks opens up new possibilities for engagement with, and mobility across, other parts of the network. Ultimately, the apparently utopian aim to integrate urban and rural China will depend on the extent to which these mundane technological networks can be effectively and durably inscribed into the rural landscape.

The master-planned housing development – the *xiaoqu* – is the preferred model for inscribing technological networks onto the social landscapes of contemporary China. As I explain above, the standardization of residential design through the *xiaoqu* archetype is underpinned by the codification of national standards for technical specifications and construction techniques. Built environment professionals in China – planners, architects, and designers – no longer give a second thought to residential design, they simply apply the standards and specifications from their textbooks to design a *xiaoqu* that fits the particular site on which they are currently working. In Bruno Latour's (1987: 1–17) terminology, the *xiaoqu* has become a 'black box': no one thinks to question its history, logic, or technical parameters, it has become the only possible solution to the problem of residential design. For processes involving a black box, only the input and the output matter: in this case, planners input data such as the size, location, population, and density; from this they generate a specific design (the output) for the particular site. But in what follows I aim to open the black box to unpack some of the key network technologies that inhabit its dark recesses.

Like every urban residential project in contemporary China, the construction of Longwei *xiaoqu* began by preparing the site and installing basic infrastructure. Known as the 'six connections' (*liu tong* 六通),[3] they connected the site to roads, water, sewers, electricity, gas, and communications (telephone/cable TV) (Qinglong 2009: QL/D3). This might seem hardly worthy of note, except for the fact that old Wei Cun had no road connections other than a rough track and was not connected to sewers, gas, or communications. The 'six connections' are significant because they transform a piece of non-descript rural farmland into a new node on the national grid of modern, networked communities: they guarantee that the new 'village' is provided with a core complement of urban services and, through this, tie villagers into the key technological networks of contemporary urban life. Not only does this transform their experience of everyday life and their relationships with each other and the surrounding built environment, it also affords greater potential for mobility through the socio-technical media of these networks.

The first connection (roads)

In the preparatory work for the construction of Longwei *xiaoqu*, it was relatively simple to connect the site to the road network: the builders only needed to lay about 50 metres of concrete to link the new *xiaoqu* with a major through-road that connects to highways in both directions. Over the last decade, China has more than doubled the length of its highway network and has expanded its freeway network more than threefold (Guojia tongjibu 2011: 150). Thus, connecting the new *xiaoqu* to the road network not only allows residents quick access to local shops and services, but also links them into local, regional, and national transport networks. The significance of the new transport links is underscored by the fact that several villagers had moved away from the old Wei Cun precisely because it was so poorly connected. But when the village relocated, many of them moved into the new *xiaoqu* (author interview, Qinglong, 26 October 2011). The road, then, links the new 'village' into a wider network of both social connections and services, and economic and employment networks: it enables local children to access new schools in the neighbouring town and it facilitates villagers commuting to employment in nearby towns and cities.

The second and third connections (water and sewers)

Households in the old Wei Cun were not connected to the reticulated water supply, so villagers had to collect water from a communal source and store it in large vats in their kitchens. Moreover, without 'self-arriving water' (to use the Chinese term for reticulated tap water, *zilaishui* 自来水), they could not install flushing toilets so continued to use traditional latrine pits. Every home in the new *xiaoqu* is fully connected into the water supply grid and has 'self-arriving water' available in kitchens, bathrooms, and toilets. Connection to the water supply brings many conveniences: it eliminates the need to collect water or to dispose of human waste. In addition, with the installation of baths, showers, and solar water heating systems, bathing can be done privately at home rather than having to visit the communal bathhouse.

However, these conveniences do not come for free: there are installation costs as well as ongoing maintenance requirements. Not only does connection to the water grid levy a monetary cost, it also brings a technological burden – the complexities of plumbing ensure that a blocked toilet, broken cistern, or leaky pipe can cause trickier problems than were ever posed by the latrine pits. Waterborne domestic hygiene demands its own set of acquired knowledge and skills, and creates a range of new household duties and responsibilities associated with using, cleaning, and maintaining the fixtures. As a result, residents of the *xiaoqu* are conscripted into a new socio-technical network that requires them to engage with mechanical installations in accordance with inscribed procedures to enact a new standardized regime of personal and domestic hygiene. In short, 'self-arriving water' and the advent of domestic plumbing replace communal forms of water supply and bathing with privatized modes of personal hygienic practice.

One of the paradoxical features of water usage in the modern home is that having employed so much technical expertise to produce a constant and reliable supply of clean water exactly where it is needed, another sophisticated technological network has to be installed to remove the used water and the waste that it carries. Polluted water presents many potential health dangers as untreated water can readily transmit disease and contagion wherever it flows. In many parts of rural China, small-scale biogas digester plants have been utilized to transform human and animal waste into reusable resources – cooking gas and organic fertilizer – with no need for a separate sewerage system to carry the waste away. However, because Longwei *xiaoqu* is an urban-style residential development, planners were required to install a septic sewerage treatment plant and a network of sewers to carry the waste there from each of the homes.

The waste water system links to the water supply system as part of the larger plumbing infrastructure; so long as it is well maintained and remains blockage-free, the residents of Longwei need barely acknowledge its existence: a combination of water, gravity, and sealed pipes does the hard work previously done by buckets, shovels, shoulder poles, and human labour. Yet the absence of effort is itself noteworthy; on the one hand it is no doubt a kind of liberation to no longer have to engage so directly and forcefully in the management of bodily wastes, but on the other hand, the intervention of modern plumbing replaces a straightforward physical process involving human actors, their waste, and a few simple tools, with a black box process. Who knows how it disappears, where it goes and what happens to it there? And, much more to the point, who knows what to do if something goes wrong?

As the technologies of everyday life become increasingly numerous and complex, as more and more everyday processes are delegated to black box technological solutions, the role of the non-specialist human actor is further circumscribed and increasingly dependent on the intervention of technical experts. The disposal of human waste has always involved a socio-technical network, but in the shift from latrine pit to flush toilet, the role of the human actor (plumbers excepted) has been diminished to a very minor part: just deposit the waste in the appropriate receptacle, push the button, clean-up, and hope for the best – everything else has been delegated to the black box technology.

The fourth connection (gas)

Every home in the new *xiaoqu* is supplied with piped cooking gas from a local biogas station which also serves the neighbouring village. Unlike the small-scale household biogas plants commonly used in much of rural China, this larger unit operates primarily on straw, chaff, and waste timber, rather than animal and human waste. Moreover, instead of simple fermentation, this plant encompasses a more complex multi-stage process: first, the organic material is mechanically shredded, then it is partially burnt inside a vacuum chamber, and finally the resultant gas is cooled, purified, pressurized, and transferred into an expandable storage tank. From the storage tank a network of underground pipes radiate out to deliver gas into every household.

While small-scale household biogas plants are used in some of the outer-lying villages, local authorities decided that the new *xiaoqu* would be served by a single biogas station rather than individual plants. In a document tendered to the provincial Bureau of Science and Technology in pursuit of funding to support the project, local authorities claim that the larger-scale straw-fired biogas plant is superior to the fermentation-based units because it is unaffected by weather conditions (Qinglong 2008: QL/Q7): fermentation-based systems simply do not work when the temperature drops below 10 degrees Celsius (Li and Ho 2006). They also suggest that it is a much better way to manage the disposal of straw and chaff that would otherwise simply be burnt in the fields. Thus, utilizing this organic material to produce biogas not only 'turns waste into treasure', it also eliminates the atmospheric pollution associated with burning the fields after harvest.

The larger-scale system has some technical and environmental advantages over the smaller-scale system. Small-scale biogas systems are operated by the householders themselves, and while they are supposed to receive some basic training, many things can go wrong and the units often fail (Li and Ho 2006). Scaling-up and professionalizing the generation system has effectively solved the problem of technical capacity. Village authorities employ three locally trained technicians to run and maintain the straw-fired unit, and since full operation commenced in mid-2009 there have been no breakdowns of equipment and no stoppages in gas supply (author interview, Qinglong, 26 October 2011).

As a result, the individual householders need no longer be concerned with the management of biogas production. Instead, they have become consumers connected to a professionally operated network and need only turn the tap and pay the bills in order to enjoy the convenience of 'self-arriving' cooking gas.

The fifth and sixth connections (electricity and communications)

Electricity is nothing new as this locality was first connected to the state electricity grid in the early 1970s (Zhang *et al.* 2008: 155). At that time, electrification was central to national programmes for promoting modernization under the socialist planned economy. In this respect, connection to the grid would have been celebrated as technological confirmation of integration into the nation-building socialist project that Party and governmental networks had already established. However, subsequently, as the Maoist revolutionary vision faded and Party prestige waned, it was those 'durable inscriptions on the landscape', like the electricity grid, that helped to hold society together through tumultuous political, economic and social change. Every home in the old Wei Cun was fully connected to the grid, with meters installed beside each front door to measure usage. Villagers, then, have had a long period of engagement with electrical technology and the regulation of its usage, so its installation in the new *xiaoqu* represents continuity rather than transformation.

But if electricity itself is not new, its potential applications are increasing, especially in relation to communication technology. As we saw with the water supply and the sewerage system, sometimes two separate networks can combine to powerful socio-technical effect. In this case, the ceaseless energy furnished through the electrical grid combines with the global reach of the new digital cable network – through the interface of information communication technologies (phone, TV, computer) – to connect the residents of Longwei *xiaoqu* to a vast world of information and entertainment. Of course, villagers formerly had some access to these networks through broadcast television and mobile telephones, the coverage and usage of which have grown rapidly through rural China over the last decade (Murphy 2010). However, the advent of broadband cable to the household increases the volume and ease of access by many magnitudes: villagers now can watch over 100 TV channels and view thousands more internet sites.

While the longer-term impact of this leap in rural access to information communication technologies cannot yet be certain, it is clear that despite the dramatic upsurge in volume, content remains closely monitored and vetted by government authorities at many levels (Brady 2007; Buckley 2011; Zhang and Zheng 2009). Thus, the information and entertainment networks that Longwei *xiaoqu* is now connected to are mediated through a range of normative filters designed to strengthen dominant discourses of national interest, cultural value, and ethical standards, and thereby shape the formation of contemporary citizenship (Kong 2010). Connection to this dual electrical-digital network, then, is less about unfolding freedom and democracy, than it is about governmental strategies to enrol rural people into informational networks of nation-building and citizen-making.

Shaping the new 'village': no space for animals

The 'six connections' that form the basic infrastructure of Longwei *xiaoqu* are an interconnected set of black boxes, each linked to technical networks at various scales; each contributing to the modernization of village life through the reinscription of everyday processes. The *xiaoqu* itself operates as a kind of meta black box on two levels: first, as the only conceivable model for contemporary residential development the logic of its formation has been hidden behind a set of technical standards; second, it contains an expanding array of technical networks, each encased by its own black box of complex operation. The *xiaoqu* has arrived in this village because of the extension of urban planning principles to the countryside; but this, in turn, reflects the emergence of a dominant new rationale of technocratic government; one that seeks to bring about urban/rural integration through rolling out a series of standardized and professionally managed technological networks.

However, the 'six connections' are only part of the *xiaoqu* meta black box; we must also consider the spatial logic of the new 'village', its architectural forms, its urban design and its exclusion of animals. Longwei *xiaoqu* is entered from the south; from there an internal road runs straight through the middle to the northern end of the compound. Two rows of two-storey villas line each side of the road, with smaller roads leaving the central road at right-angles to access the homes. There are 11 single-household villas and 16 double-household (duplex) villas; in addition, located in the northwest corner of the compound there is one four-storey apartment block containing 16 apartments (four per floor). The central road is bitumen while the side roads and paths are paved; the remaining land is landscaped; small trees line the roads while the ground between the homes is mainly lawn interspersed here and there with clusters of shrubbery and flower beds. Each of the villas has a covered porch on the ground level adjacent to the entrance, and a balcony on the second floor immediately above. There are no enclosed yards and no internal fences of any sort: the homes simply sit directly in the midst of the landscaped parkland.

The neat vision of contemporary middle-class suburbia is somewhat undermined by the realization that there is no private land within this residential development. There is certainly no sign of the vegetable plots, fruit trees, fish ponds, or chicken coops that were ubiquitous in the old village. But it is the absence of yards that is most significant. In Chinese tradition, the ideal home was enclosed within a courtyard, or *yuanzi* (院子) (Bray 2005: 25–34); and as Liu Xin (2000: 39–40) points out, the *yuanzi* not only demarcates the symbolic domain of the family, it literally constitutes its entire wealth. Ideally the *yuanzi* is fully enclosed, its entrance marked by an ornamental gate, but in practice the *yuanzi* can still be present even without physical enclosure; often it is marked simply by a cluster of structures – houses, sheds, out-buildings – where the family's possessions are stored and arranged. In old Wei Cun, some homes were enclosed and some were not; nevertheless, all of them had a *yuanzi* of some kind.

If the *yuanzi* embodies family wealth, as a spatial form it facilitates certain types of familial social interactions. Many *yuanzi* contain more than one conjugal family unit – often the parents and one or more of their married children (usually but not always sons) will have separate homes within the *yuanzi*. In this situation, the *yuanzi* provides a spatial structure to mediate and order the relationships between branches of an extended family unit. The new *xiaoqu* is not designed to accommodate these kinds of relationships, because each household is distinctly demarcated from every other within an open, transparent and geometrically ordered public space.

The *yuanzi* form also tends to blur the distinction between inside and outside, as residents move between buildings for cooking and eating, carrying out chores, feeding domestic animals and socializing with other family members. In contrast, the *xiaoqu* is inscribed with a rigid binary spatial code based on a transparent differentiation between inside and outside. Inside the home is private: a socio-technical space designed for private activities such as the hygienic care of the individual body, the domestic consumption of goods and entertainment, interface between citizens and the digitalized world of information, the reception of guests and for the discreet management of family relationships. But as soon as the resident walks outside the door they have entered the open public domain; nothing outside the home belongs to them or is under their control; although the *xiaoqu* itself is an enclosed space, its enclosure operates at the scale of the 'village' rather than the family unit, and therefore cannot be considered a *yuanzi* in the traditional sense. This is 'collective' or 'community' space, landscaped and regulated under the management of local authorities. Unlike in the old village, there is no in-between space; simply a numbered front door that marks the boundary between inside and outside and recodes it as a threshold between private and public.

The loss of the *yuanzi* is part of a spatial reconfiguration that results both from the imperative to save land and from the desire to modernize rural life. The old Wei Cun occupied 110 mu of land, while the new residential area only takes up about 40 mu. Land has been 'saved' through eliminating the *yuanzi* as well as the vegetable plots, fish ponds, orchards, and animal enclosures. Like villagers throughout China, the residents of Wei Cun previously enjoyed use-rights to three different types of land: farmland (*nongtian* 农田), housing land (*zhaijidi* 宅基地), and private plots (*ziliudi* 自留地).[4] In more densely built-up villages, the private plots are often located on land outside, but adjacent to the village. Wei Cun, however, was not densely built-up, and the private plots were interspersed among the houses, sometimes even inside an enclosed *yuanzi*. As part of the relocation process, villagers gave up all of their former *zhaijidi* and *ziliudi*. In exchange they now technically have a share of *zhaijidi* within the new *xiaoqu*, but it has come under collective management of authorities who operate and maintain the grounds and facilities. According to one local official, each household has also been given 0.2 mu (130 m^2) of land just outside the northern perimeter fence as replacement *ziliudi* (author interview, Qinglong, 26 October 2011). However, for most households this is far less 'private plot' than they formerly enjoyed and while there is room to grow some vegetables, there is no longer any space for fish ponds or orchards, and raising pigs, chickens, and ducks is strictly forbidden in the new *xiaoqu*.

Mr Shen, one of the wealthier villagers, explained these changes in the following way:

> In the old village there is more space and no walls, so you need watch dogs to protect your place; you also have plenty of space to breed ducks and chickens; but in this enclosed *xiaoqu* you don't need to worry about safety so you don't need dogs; and there is not enough space now for poultry.
>
> (Author interview, Qinglong, 26 October 2011)

Actually there is still quite a bit of open space, certainly enough to have some poultry; what Mr Shen seems to be suggesting is that there is no *appropriate* space for poultry, nowhere that they belong in the new spatial regime that underpins this urban-style *xiaoqu*. For if the homes don't have yards, then where could the poultry live?

Recent studies have noted how the rise of modernity encouraged the banishment of livestock from urban and suburban environments. Adrian Franklin (1999: 41), for example, points out that livestock were eliminated from British cities by the middle of the nineteenth century; Andrea Gaynor (2007) describes a similar outcome achieved in the Australian city of Perth around the middle of the twentieth century. However, the two scholars provide somewhat different explanations for the removal of livestock: Franklin attributes it mainly to scientific and technical innovations, especially through improvements in transportation and refrigeration and through the application of Fordist industrial processes to meat, egg, and dairy production (Franklin 1999: 36–40); Gaynor argues that it 'primarily reflected a middle-class understanding of productive animals as unruly, destructive, and therefore incompatible with their vision of suburbs as pleasant, private, and orderly places' (Gaynor 2007: 35). Thus, where Franklin presents a functionalist explanation related to the apparently inexorable rise of modern industry, Gaynor demonstrates a longer-term struggle over the elimination of productive animals where the opposing views mirrored the divergent attitudes of different socio-economic classes. Through the first half of the twentieth century, numerous suburban residents continued to raise 'productive animals' in small-scale backyard settings, long after the benefits of industrial economic efficiency should, according to Franklin, have rendered their endeavours illogical. While the industrialization of meat and egg production was certainly a precondition which made it feasible for local government to ban backyard production in the suburbs, the fact that many people resisted this shift demonstrates a weakness in explanations based on economic determinism. Relationships between humans and animals cannot be fully accounted for through a simple cost–benefit analysis.

Like Gaynor, urban geographer Chris Philo (1995) reads the progressive exclusion of productive animals from cities as the result of new attitudes associated with the rise of modernity. In Philo's analysis these attitudes are underpinned by 'discourses (medical, hygienic, organizational and moral) that have gradually coded animals such as cows, sheep and pigs as impure, polluting, disruptive and discomforting occupants of city spaces where humans are supposed to live and work' (Philo 1995: 677). The result of this coding is the emergence of a rigid binary division between urban and rural animals: productive animals belong exclusively to the rural domain, while companion animals (dogs and cats) belong primarily to the urban domain. This geographical differentiation between animal types has remained dominant in the west until recent years, when concerns with environmental sustainability and food quality, combined with a softening of government regulation, have led to the revival of small-scale backyard poultry production in some places.

It seems paradoxical that precisely at the same time they are reappearing in the suburbs of western cities, in China the exclusion of poultry and pigs is being extended from the cities to new rural residential areas. Following Philo's analysis, I suggest that the new Longwei *xiaoqu* is coded as 'urban', but that this coding operates not just through discourses (medical, hygienic, and moral) but also through the built fabric of the residential area. Not only is the presence of productive animals seen as inimical to modern lifestyles, there is literally no space for them to occupy within the *xiaoqu*. Through eliminating the *yuanzi* and coding all outside space as public, the urban planners have simply excluded the possibility for productive animals to exist in this place.

Why does it matter that the villagers of Wei Cun have had to give up their poultry and pigs in exchange for modern new homes with all the networked conveniences of twenty-first-century life? I have no way to objectively assess the value or fairness of this deal; however, I do think it is important to explore how this transformation impacts upon the everyday lives of the villagers. On one level the loss of domestic livestock results in a reduction in household chores and, therefore, a gain in time. This primarily benefits women because, as Tamara Jacka (1997: 115) has shown, the care of domestic pigs and poultry is considered to be women's work and, depending on the number of animals, can require between 30 minutes and four hours of labour per day. No doubt many rural women would be happy to be rid of this burdensome task. Yet we should also note that the removal of animals impacts the practice of everyday village life as much as the introduction of 'self-arriving' water or cable TV. This point is not based on nostalgia for 'traditional ways', but rather on the simple fact that with the animals gone, the assemblage of things – and the associated networks – which constitute village life have been necessarily refigured and rearranged.

When Bruno Latour (1992: 254) argued for the need to resurrect 'the missing masses ... in our traditional social theories', he sought to develop a methodology that could account for the multitudinous 'facts and artifacts that make up large sections of our social ties'. But as other scholars joined the discussion, further 'missing masses' were identified, in particular the animals that live among human society. As Sarah Whatmore (1999: 26) points out, this move is designed to reconfigure the conception of 'agency' in order to treat it as 'a relational achievement, involving the creative presence of organic beings, technological devices and discursive codes, as well as people, in the fabrics of everyday living'. Ongoing developments in actor–network theory have generated new ways to think about 'the complex entanglings of human–animal relations with space, place, location, environment and landscape' (Philo and Wilbert 2000: 4). Using this approach, I demonstrate how the removal of productive animals from village space has contributed to the reinscription of everyday life in rural China.

According to Franklin (1999), domesticated productive animals occupy an ambiguous position within human understandings of nature. Building on Levi-Strauss's structural analysis of food, Franklin (1999: 41) suggests that such animals 'are neither true nature nor truly humanized (as are pets), but nature worked on by humans'. However, rather than interpreting their status as ambiguous, it seems to me that in the Chinese village setting this in-between position correlates exactly to their location in the in-between space of the *yuanzi*. Neither wild nor humanized, the poultry and the pigs belong precisely in this place that is neither inside nor outside, neither private nor public. Moreover, in so far as they *belong* in the *yuanzi*, the productive animals are both a component of family wealth and constituents of the hybrid network of organic beings, technological devices, and discursive codes that form the complex fabric of village life.

The presence of the animals in the *yuanzi* shapes both human actors and technological devices in many ways: it is by no means a simple one-sided relationship of exploitation. First, the animals require care and consideration; if they are to grow and be productive they need a suitable place to roost or sleep, their quarters need to be clean and hygienic, and they need to be fed appropriate food at particular times. Second, the animals demand attentiveness; their peculiar habits must be learnt and the farmers must be on hand at the right times to let them in or out, to put them to bed, to collect the eggs, and so on. Finally, while the *yuanzi* is their home base, the chickens and ducks are generally allowed to roam 'free-range' around the village during the day; in this sense they form a kind of sub-stratum of village society, and just as villagers will watch out for each other's children, so they will keep an eye out for each other's chickens or ducks. In short, while pigs and poultry are in the end exploited for meat and eggs and their activities are largely circumscribed by human and technological intervention through yards, enclosures, and breeding regimes, they play a significant role because of this in shaping the contours of everyday household and village life.

Elimination of the pigs and the poultry relieves village women of significant labour, but also gives rise to the appearance of another black box: egg and meat production. Formerly the villagers were closely engaged with the socio-technical process of egg and meat production; they managed the various regimes of breeding, feeding, slaughtering and butchering through acquired mastery over a rudimentary set of devices, knowledges, and skills. But with the disappearance of household animal husbandry, villagers become consumers rather than producers of these products; like the urban population, they can only buy their meat and eggs from a local (super)market. In this case the black box conceals increasingly industrialized techniques employed to produce eggs and meat, as well as specific details of their place of origin. In the past villagers knew exactly where their eggs and meat came from; now they only know that these things come from larger-scale intensive farms somewhere down the road. This is yet another aspect of their everyday life that has been delegated to a new industrial-technical process – another black box to alienate a once familiar production process.

In suburban Perth the elimination of productive animals was the result of a shift in the dominant discourse that recoded productive animals as inappropriate to suburban space (Gaynor 2007). The actual place the animals formerly occupied – the backyard – remained; it was just that over time the majority of citizens and local government authorities came to believe that the backyard was not a suitable place for productive animals. Subsequently, the fact that backyards are still common has made it possible for the return of productive animals to suburban areas in response to the emergence of new discourses of sustainability.

In Longwei *xiaoqu* the elimination of productive animals seems much more difficult to reverse. Not only have governmental discourses recoded household productive animals as inimical to modern residential environments, in addition the urban planners have literally eliminated the places where animals could belong. In relocating and reconstructing the village as an urban-style *xiaoqu*, local officials have transformed village life through spatial as well as technological and discursive reinscription. However, this intervention should not be interpreted as a 'choice' made by local authorities. On the contrary, as demonstrated in this chapter, the new residential complex reproduces a standardized residential model which has become the 'obvious' and only solution to contemporary residential development in China.

The process of village relocation, then, is not about recreating the old village and its human/animal actor networks in the new place; rather, it becomes a process of remaking the village according to a new socio-technical template. This predetermined black box fix allows the local authorities to dramatically shift the terms of the game and to enforce normative technocratic control over the spatial form, the infrastructure and the codes of everyday life in the new village. While the villagers may have been liberated from the physical privations of pre-plumbing life and the onerous labours of animal husbandry, the newly configured socio-technical networks demand that they learn a new set of skills and new modes of social practice.

Conclusion

In a recent introduction to actor–network theory, John Law (2009) argues that it should be understood as an 'empirical version of poststructuralism' and that it can be likened to a scaled-down version of Michel Foucault's episteme. In the words of Law: 'Foucault asks us to attend to the productively strategic and relational character of epochal epistemes. The actor network approach asks us to explore the strategic, relational and productive character of particular, smaller-scale, heterogeneous actor networks' (Law 2009: 145). To extend the comparison, I would argue that where a governmentality approach seeks to discern processes of order-building within discourses of government, actor–network theory looks for the relational mechanisms of order-building within the mundane socio-technical networks of everyday life. In their early work in governmentality studies, Peter Miller and Nikolas Rose (1990) drew upon a network-oriented notion of 'translation' developed by Callon and Latour (1981), as well as Latour's (1987) concept of 'action at a distance', to help explain, first, how disparate groups of experts could contribute to the formation of coherent dominant discourses and, second, how these forms of knowledge could be exercised over people, places and things at distant locations. However, despite 'borrowing' some conceptual terminology from the founders of actor–network theory, Miller and Rose remained focused on the discursive realm of government and offered few hints as to how the two approaches might be more fully integrated.

My objective in this chapter has been to try to bridge the gap between these two approaches. I utilize a governmentality approach to illuminate the changing discursive parameters of spatial planning in China, in so far as they bear directly on relationships between governance and space, then shift to an actor–network approach to follow (via case study) the actual implementation of a spatial redevelopment project and thereby to examine how radical spatio-technical transformations have remade 'the social' through rupturing old actor networks and inscribing new ones. It seems to me that to understand the significance of the rapid reconfiguration of China's built environments, the governmentality approach alone is not enough; we also need to invest in strategies for describing as closely as possible the microphysics of 'government in action'.

Notes

1 Villages in China can vary enormously in size from tiny hamlets of a few households to large settlements of several thousand people. To address this problem of scale, Chinese Communist Party (CCP) authorities have developed the concept of 'administrative villages' (*xingzheng cun* 行政村), which, as the term suggests, are the basic administrative units of rural China, each governed by a 'village committee' and a CCP Party branch. A so-called administrative village may include any number of actual 'natural' villages.

2 Professor of economics and former head of the Centre for Economic Research, Chinese Academy of Social Sciences, Beijing.

3 The number of connections can vary under certain circumstances: in colder northern regions there is usually a seventh connection for central heating; while in some locations there is no gas supply so that connection is omitted. This phrase has been in

use at least since the 1950s, when there were only three connections: roads, water and electricity (Bray 2005: 143).

4 The Chinese term that is normally translated as 'private plot' can be more directly translated as 'self-retained land' and is a relic left over from the Mao-era period of collective agriculture. In that period, the vast majority of farmland was worked collectively, with individuals awarded work-points according to how much labour they contributed. However, 5–7 per cent of land was distributed to individual families to farm for their own use – usually this land was used to grow vegetables and fruit to supplement the family's diet. After decollectivization, all farmland was divided up and contracted to families; however, the concept of 'private plots' was carried over into the new system and continued to be treated as a separate category of land.

References

Akrich, M. (1992) 'The de-scription of technical objects', in W.E. Bijker and J. Law (eds), *Shaping Technology/Building Society: Studies in Sociotechnical Change*, Cambridge, MA: MIT Press, pp. 205–24.

Beijingshi chengshi guihua sheji yanjiuyuan [Beijing Institute of Urban Planning and Design] (2005) *Beijing chengshi zongti guihua (2004–2020)* [Beijing Municipal Master Plan (2004–2020)], Beijing: Zhongguo Jianzhu Gongye Chubanshe. Online. Available: www.bjpc.gov.cn/fzgh_1/csztgh/200710/t195452.htm (accessed 10 June 2015).

Brady, A.-M. (2007) *Marketing Dictatorship: Propaganda and Thought Work in Contemporary China*, Lanham: Rowman and Littlefield.

Bray, D. (2005) *Social Space and Governance in Urban China: The Danwei System from Origins to Reform*, Stanford: Stanford University Press.

Bray, D. (2008) 'Designing to govern: space and power in two Wuhan communities', *Built Environment*, 34, 4: 392–407.

Buckley, C. (2011) 'China president calls for more Internet oversight', Reuters, USA edition. Online. Available: www.reuters.com/article/2011/02/19/us-china-politics-internet-idUSTRE71I2Y720110219 (accessed 10 June 2015).

Callon, M. and Latour, B. (1981) 'Unscrewing the big leviathan: how actors macro-structure reality and how sociologists help them do so', in A. Cicourel and K. Knorr-Cecina (eds), *Advances in Social Theory and Methodology*, London: Routledge and Kegan Paul, pp. 277–303.

Franklin, A. (1999) *Animals and Modern Cultures: A Sociology of Human–Animal Relations in Modernity*, London: Sage.

Gaynor, A. (2007) 'Animal agendas: conflict over productive animals in twentieth century Australian cities', *Society and Animals*, 15: 29–42.

Guojia tongjibu [National Bureau of Statistics of China] (2011) *Zhongguo tongji zhaiyao 2011* [China Statistical Abstract: 2011], Beijing: Zhongguo Tongji Chubanshe.

Jacka, T. (1997) *Women's Work in Rural China: Change and Continuity in an Era of Reform*, Cambridge: Cambridge University Press.

Kong, S. (2010) 'Cultural propaganda in the age of economic reform: popular media and the social construction of Shanxi merchants in contemporary China', *The China Journal*, 63: 79–99.

Latour, B. (1987) *Science in Action: How to Follow Scientists and Engineers Through Society*, Cambridge, MA: Harvard University Press.

Latour, B. (1992) 'Where are the missing masses? The sociology of a few mundane artifacts', in W.E. Bijker and J. Law (eds), *Shaping Technology/Building Society: Studies in Sociotechnical Change*, Cambridge, MA: MIT Press, pp. 225–58.

Law, J. (2009) 'Actor network theory and material semiotics', in B.S. Turner (ed.), *The New Blackwell Companion to Social Theory*, Chichester: Wiley-Blackwell, pp. 141–58.

Li Jing (2005) '"Jihua" yu "guihua" yi zi zhi cha shuomingliao shenme?' [What is the significance of the one character difference between 'jihua' (plan) and 'guihua' (plan)?], *Beijing Ribao*, 31 October. Online. Available: http://theory.people.com.cn/GB/40553/3815194.html (accessed 10 June 2015).

Li, K. and Ho, M.-W. (2006) 'Biogas China: ISIS Report 02/10/06', London: ISIS (Institute of Science in Society). Online. Available: www.i-sis.org.uk/BiogasChina.php (accessed 10 June 2015).

Liu, X. (2000) *In One's Own Shadow: An Ethnographic Account of the Condition of Post-Reform Rural China*, Berkeley: University of California Press.

Lu, D. (2006) *Rethinking Urban Chinese Form: Modernity, Scarcity and Space, 1949–2005*, Abingdon: Routledge.

Lü, J., Rowe, P.G., and Zhang, J. (2001) *Modern Urban Housing in China 1840–2000*, Munich: Prestel.

Miller, P. and Rose, N. (1990) 'Governing economic life', *Economy and Society*, 19, 1: 1–31.

Murphy, R. (2010) 'The narrowing digital divide: a view from rural China', in M.K. Whyte (ed.), *One Country, Two Societies: Rural–Urban Inequality in Contemporary China*, Cambridge, MA: Harvard University Press, pp. 166–87.

Philo, C. (1995) 'Animals, geography and the city: notes on inclusions and exclusions', *Environment and Planning D: Society and Space*, 13, 6: 655–81.

Philo, C. and Wilbert, C. (2000) 'Animal spaces, beastly places: an introduction', in C. Philo and C. Wilbert (eds), *Animal Spaces, Beastly Places: New Geographies of Human–Animal Relations*, London: Routledge, pp. 1–34.

Qinglong (2008) 'Qinglong Residents' Committee digital document archive (digitally copied November 2009).

Qinglong (2009) 'Qinglong Residents' Committee digital document archive (digitally copied November 2009).

Sigley, G. (2006) 'From "jihua" to "guihua": a preliminary critique of approaches to understanding "governance" in the Chinese context', paper presented at Asia Reconstructed: 16th Biennial Conference of the Asian Studies Association of Australia, Woolongong, NSW, Australia.

Wang Jun (2008) *Caifang ben shang de chengshi* [The City in My Notebook], Beijing: Sanlian Shudian.

Whatmore, S. (1999) 'Hybrid geographies: rethinking the "human" in human geography', in D. Massey, J. Allen, and P. Sarre (eds), *Human Geography Today*, Cambridge: Polity Press, pp. 22–40.

Zhang, X. and Zheng, Y. (eds) (2009) *China's Information and Communications Technology Revolution: Social Changes and State Responses*, Abingdon: Routledge.

Zhang Yulin, Ma Daoming, and Zhu Jianfang (eds) (2008), *Chunhua jiyi* [Chunhua Record], Nanjing University, School of Sociology.

Zhonggong zhongyang [Central Committee of the Communist Party of China] (2003) 'Zhonggong zhongyang guanyu wanshan shehui zhuyi shichang jingji tizhi ruogan wenti de jueding' [Communist Party of China Central Committee Decision on Some Issues Concerning the Perfection of the Socialist Market Economy System], Xinhuawang, 21 October. Online. Available: http://news.xinhuanet.com/newscenter/2003-10/21/content_1135402.htm (accessed 10 June 2015).

Zhonggong zhongyang [Central Committee of the Communist Party of China] (2005) 'Zhonggong zhongyang guanyu zhiding "shiyiwu" guihua de jianyi' [Communist Party of China Central Committee Proposal for Formulating the 11th Five-Year Plan], 11 October. Online. Available: www.china.com.cn/chinese/zhuanti/5zqh/1002849.htm (accessed 10 June 2015).

Zhonghua renmin gongheguo chengshi guihua fa (1990) [Urban Planning Law of the People's Republic of China]. Online. Available: www.jincao.com/fa/law19.09.htm (accessed 10 June 2015).

Zhonghua renmin gongheguo chengxiang guihua fa (2007) [Urban and Rural Planning Law of the People's Republic of China]. Online. Available: www.china.com.cn/policy/txt/2007-10/29/content_9139260.htm (accessed 10 June 2015).

Zhonghua renmin gongheguo jianshebu [Ministry of Construction of the People's Republic of China] (1994) *Chengshi juzhu qu guihua sheji guifan* [Planning and Design Standards for Urban Residential Areas], Beijing: Zhongguo Jianzhu Gongye Chubanshe.

6 From socialism to social work

Social workers, professionalism, and community governance in contemporary urban China

Gary Sigley

The People's Republic of China (PRC) has witnessed the emergence and revival of numerous professions and fields of expertise since the onset of the policy of 'reform and opening up' in the late 1970s. A relative latecomer is the profession of 'social work' (*shehui gongzuo* 社会工作), which first made an appearance during the late 1980s. With the rapid development and transformation of urban China, government authorities have turned to the profession of social work in the hope that it will help to alleviate some of the many complex social challenges that now characterize urban life in a 'socialist market economy'.[1] In cities such as Beijing, Guangzhou, Shanghai, and Tianjin, the 'social worker' (*shehui gongzuozhe* 社会工作者) has become a visible component of local government at the level of the community (*shequ* 社区). The Central Government has also recently formally legitimized the profession of social work, enabling its expansion within the system of higher education and in many other urban (and rural) contexts across China. However, the development of this new profession has not been without obstacles. The adoption of what was originally a western profession developed in the context of liberal forms of governmental reasoning, and the modern welfare state, has generated heated discussion within China as to how to best adapt, and 'indigenize' (*bentuhua* 本土化), the social work profession in ways that accord with changes in how government is practised in urban China. An analysis of the development of social work and debates about it thus promises to reveal a great deal about the changing parameters and limitations of government in present-day China.

A number of scholars claim that the PRC has entered a new 'era of social policy', noting that the first period of reform, between 1978 and 1992, was focused primarily on economic and labour reform, and the second period, from 1992 to the present, has witnessed a renewed focus on social policy in the fields of health, education, and welfare (Wang Sibin 2006a, 2006b; Xu Yongxiang in Sigley 2011). Xu Yongxiang, an influential scholar and policy adviser in the area of social work and social reform in Shanghai, agrees that China has entered the era of social policy, but argues that this aspect of the reform process cannot be compared to the dramatic reform of the economy that has already taken place. Xu (2005: 23) makes a distinction between what he calls 'the reform of the economic system and the transformation of government economic function' (*jingji tizhi de gaige he zhengfu jingji zhineng de zhuanbian* 经济体制的改革和政府经济职能的转变) and 'the reform of the social system and the transformation of government social management function' (*shehui tizhi gaige he zhengfu shehui guanli zhineng de zhuanbian* 社会体制的改革和政府社会管理职能的转变). He argues that the relationship between the reform of the economic system and related government functions has been radically transformed since 1992. However, the relationship between the reform of the social system and related government functions has not been transformed, despite the urgent need to do so. Instead, Xu (2005: 24) argues that the social problems generated by economic reform continue to be dealt with chiefly by using methods associated with the planned economy and traditional (socialist) social management methods. The result is an imbalance between the pace of economic growth and the needs of social development and social reform, and tensions within the governmental apparatus over how to best overcome such shortcomings.

This chapter takes Xu's argument one step further by examining the development of social work through the grid of an emerging Chinese governmentality, as captured in the President Hu Jintao–Premier Wen Jiabao administration's (2003–2013) policy emphasis on creating a 'harmonious society' (*hexie shehui* 和谐社会). This chapter first provides a brief genealogy of the development of social work in the modern western context, and also explains why social work did not develop as a profession in China during the Maoist period (1949–1976). It then looks at the (re)emergence of social work in China of the 1980s and 1990s. Finally, it examines efforts to adapt and 'indigenize' social work in the PRC within the harmonious society framework, and with reference to examples of social work innovations in some of China's larger cities. I conclude that the potentially positive role of social reform in generating grass-roots participation in community government has been inhibited not only by the legacy and administrative mentality (*xingzhengxing* 行政性) of the planned economy, but also by the recent conflation of social management (*shehui guanli* 社会管理) with 'maintaining social stability' (*weichi shehui wending* 维持社会稳定, or *weiwen* 维稳 in abbreviated form). It is in this context of conflicted programmes at the grass-roots level that social work has developed and, in so doing, throws into light the challenges of social reform in contemporary urban China.

A brief genealogy of social work: from west to east

The internationalization of social work and the cross-cultural challenges it faces in dealing with issues of 'universalism' and 'indigenization' have attracted a great deal of discussion in recent years (Gray 2005, 2008). There is not sufficient space to review that literature in detail here, although it highlights the diversity of social work in different western contexts (Lorenz 2008; McMahon 2003). What follows is a brief genealogy of some key trends and issues in social work, in order to provide a foundation for understanding the development of social work as a profession in the contemporary Chinese context.

Social work as a modern profession first emerged in the western context around the turn of the nineteenth and twentieth centuries, a period characterized by rapid industrialization and the governmentalization of the state (Payne 2005; Reamer 1993). Beginning in the late eighteenth century and throughout the nineteenth century, large sections of the rural populations in Northern Europe migrated to cities to find work, often as a result of being forced off the land through the 'closure of the commons'. The squalor, disease, and social upheaval that followed was presented as a problem of government around the notion of how to govern the poor (Dean 1991). In the United Kingdom and other European countries a typical response was the creation of 'poor laws', which separated 'the able-bodied poor' from 'the impotent poor', based on an understanding that 'work' was the physical and moral core of 'respectable society'. Workhouses, usually run by the state, were created to house those who could not support themselves, and ultimately to transform 'idle' labouring bodies through a series of disciplinary trainings into moral working subjects (Foucault 1977). As Peter Camilleri (1996: 26) explains: 'The effect of work and labour was discipline which transformed the "problem" individual into a rational, orderly and hence "proper" individual in which "self-reflection" or the "surveillance" over self was exercised.'

Outside the confines of the state, Christian activists, especially from Protestant denominations, were often at the forefront in working among poor urban communities. These activists, working in terms of the values and objectives of charity and philanthropy, created a diverse array of benevolent societies and self-help organizations that operated in spaces 'beyond the state' and gave early modern liberalism some of its defining features as a form of governance that operates 'at a distance' (Rose and Miller 1992). It is through the complex systems of knowledge and intervention that were developed at this time that the outlines of a modern social work movement can be discerned. Towards the end of the nineteenth century, playing out differently in different social contexts but particularly in the Anglo-speaking world through the Charity Organization Society, social work began to develop and crystallize a core set of values around notions of: 'professionalism' – that is, defining what social workers are and what they do; 'social justice' – what social work is about in the broader social context; and 'self-help' – developing methods, such as case work, and forms of intervention designed to 'help others help themselves' (Camilleri 1996: 26–7).

As a modern form of biopolitics emerged, in which the attributes of the overall population were seen to depend on the attributes of each individual, a series of further governmental problematics developed around the family (Foucault 1978). The family was viewed by the nascent liberal state as the natural site for human reproduction and child rearing. At the same time, some families were viewed as incapable of being left to their own devices – for example, those that were characterized as afflicted by inebriation, mental illness, or general social dysfunction (Donzelot 1979). This created a dilemma for the emerging liberal state as it sought both to give the family autonomy and develop ways of normalizing and moralizing deviant families. Over time, that problematic evolved into the foundations of the modern welfare state, albeit played out differently within different western social contexts. The modern profession of social work arose in this context as a form of expertise capable of crossing the divide between the 'public' and 'private' realms. It was a profession that claimed to speak on behalf of the poor, marginalized, and disenfranchised, on the one hand, and to work with the liberal state, and other institutions such as the Church, to produce desirable forms of the 'citizen-subject', on the other.

The history of the development of social work as a profession ties in neatly with Michel Foucault's (1979) characterization of modern liberal governmentality as divided between the 'care of the self' (city–citizen game) and the 'care of others' (shepherd–flock game). Social work, especially as it developed in response to liberal imperatives to govern 'at a distance', emerged as a significant method of social, familial, and moral governance of what we now call 'the social' and an integral part of an emerging biopolitics (Donzelot 1979; Parton 1994). An important hallmark of social work as a profession in the western liberal context remains the bridging of the complex relationship between the state and non-state social work providers.

Social work has proved to be a controversial profession because the practice of social work blurs the boundary between the 'public' and 'private' realms, and assumed distinctions between the 'care of the self' and the 'care of others'. As a body of professional knowledge with a more than 100-year history, the profession of social work is cognisant of its own shortcomings (Parton 1994). However, social workers typically present the profession as a body of knowledge and practice that aims to 'help others to help themselves', by providing pedagogical rather than disciplinary trainings ('Definition of social work' 2012). Social workers tend to see themselves as advocates of poor, disenfranchised, and marginalized people. Hence, social work organizations, whether religious or non-religious, are often involved in the development of more inclusive forms of social policy. For instance, the International Federation of Social Work states that the social work profession:

> promotes social change, problem solving in human relationships and the empowerment and liberation of people to enhance well-being. Utilising theories of human behaviour and social systems, social work intervenes at the points where people interact with their environments. Principles of human rights and social justice are fundamental to social work.
>
> ('Definition of social work' 2012)

By contrast, Foucault has highlighted the disciplinary underpinnings of social work as a profession and interventionist strategy of the state that targets 'society' and 'the family' (Foucault cited in Chambon *et al.* 1999). From this perspective, social work is construed as a heavy-handed affair that 'polices' families and communities regarded as 'pathological' or somehow deviating from the norm – for example, by taking children away from poor families rather than providing them with means of support. More importantly, social work is seen as having an important role in the security of 'the social' itself. In a 1972 round table discussion Foucault described social work as:

> inscribed within a larger social function that has been taking on new dimensions for centuries, the function of surveillance-and-correction: to surveil individuals and to redress them, in the two meanings of the word, alternatively as punishment and pedagogy.
>
> (Foucault cited in Chambon *et al.* 1999: 92–3)

As this suggests, the profession of social work has been implicated in many negative practices that have worked to curtail rather than enhance the autonomy of individuals.

My purpose in highlighting these different understandings of social work is not to pass judgement one way or the other, but rather to note that social work emerged in western liberal democratic societies as part of a complex series of developments within the interrelated realms of government, power, and knowledge. Can social work be taken out of the western context and placed into an entirely different social and governmental context? If so, how has the profession been adapted and/or changed to suit new circumstances? These are questions that scholars of social work have begun to address in a more rigorous fashion in recent years as the profession has expanded internationally (Gray 2005).

However, there has been limited work to date on the history of the development of social work as a profession in China. Social work as we know it in the modern sense first made its appearance in China in the wake of Christian missionary activity in the late nineteenth century (Pan Yunkang 2002: 34; Peng Xiuliang 2010: 1). Christian charity and philanthropic work are important in the Chinese context, just as they are in the western context, in so far as it is through these activities that modern notions of 'social work' are first articulated and practised. This is not to suggest that prior to the arrival of social work in China there were no discernible practices of charity, philanthropy, and social–familial intervention. On the contrary, China has a long and complex history of dynastic state and patrilineal clan projects aimed at securing social, familial, and individual wellbeing (Smith 2009). Much of this is derivative of Confucian imperatives to secure the social (*sheji* 社稷) and the clan (*jiazu* 家族), although other systems of thought and practice, such as Buddhism, also made important contributions (Smith 2009).

The development of social work in China proceeded hand-in-hand with the growing influence of the modern social sciences and the establishment of new systems for knowing, measuring, and intervening (Lam 2011). The first outlines of a modern biopolitics focused on the category of 'the population' and the 'quality' of the overall population began to emerge in China during the transition from the Qing Dynasty (1644–1911) to the Republican Era (1911–1948), and especially during the first three decades of the twentieth century (Thompson 2012). Chinese scholars, drawing upon the discourse and techniques of the western social sciences, 'discovered' that China was confronted with all manner of 'social problems' (*shehui wenti* 社会问题), which required solutions. Missionary activity and social movements aimed at alleviating the conditions of the poor and disenfranchised began to develop in this context. A prominent example was the 'rural reconstruction movement', which focused on improving economic and social conditions in China's villages (Hayford 1990).

Although social work began to make its mark in China during the early twentieth century, it did not take root in any systematic way. The philosophy and methods of social work were adopted by various social organizations and institutions of higher education began to teach social work (Lin Shunli 2013: 34). However, China was fractured by war and revolution and, unsurprisingly, the political groups that dominated during this period – the Nationalist Government (1927–1948) and subsequently the Communist Party (1949–), had more pressing priorities.

With the victory of the Chinese Communist Party (CCP) and the founding of the PRC in 1949, nascent practices of social work were further nipped in the bud. Following convention in the Soviet Union, the CCP viewed the social and 'psy' sciences (such as sociology and psychology) as anti-Marxist. Moreover, the fact that many social-work-style activities in China had been closely linked to western Christian organizations, which the CCP saw as fronts for 'imperialism', further ensured that 'social work' disappeared from mainland China (Sigley 2011).[2] The newly established CCP-led government also had recourse to other means for implementing social reform than those used in western liberal states. Most notably, with the curtailment of the monetary economy and the geographical 'fixing' of labour to suit the requirements of centralized planning, the state allocated work and resources through the urban work unit system (*danwei* 单位). Work units provided all manner of welfare and services – hospitals, schools, housing, policing, shops, and entertainment – to the urban population. Moreover, they ultimately offered the only means of access to resources and rewards in China's cities (Bray 2005; Jeffreys and Sigley 2009: 6).

There was also an underlying sense of 'anti-professionalism' during the Maoist period that would most likely have impeded the development of professional social work, even if it had been approved. This 'anti-professionalism' is captured in Maoist-era slogans that emphasize the importance of being both 'red and expert' (*you hong you zhuan* 又红又专) and 'putting politics in command' (*yi zhengzhi wei gang* 以政治为纲). The principle grass-roots unit in this context was the cadre (*ganbu* 干部) – the all-purpose Party 'professional'. Any person, or profession, from outside of this system was regarded with suspicion. The cadre did take on some of the pastoral dimensions of the 'shepherd–flock game' during the Maoist period, for example, in the intervention and resolution of disputes within the family. But in comparison with the sophisticated body of knowledge and practice (including clinical practice) that had developed around 'social work' in western societies, the social role of the cadre was circumscribed within a narrow political range.

In summary, the Maoist period created a number of obstacles to the development of social work in mainland China after 1949. First, the western social sciences were more or less eliminated from mainland China during the 1950s. Given that social work is closely aligned to the social and 'psy' sciences, this manoeuvre would have made even the suggestion of 'social work' during the Maoist period seem 'reactionary' and 'bourgeois'. Second, since the network of Party cadres reached down to the lowest levels of society through the work unit system, there was no perceived need for the forms of professional intervention that social workers could provide. The 'red and expert' Party cadre was tasked with carrying out some of the surveillance and education roles that were accorded to social workers in western societies. While this situation was more or less sustainable under the Maoist planned economy, dramatic social changes brought about by the post-1978 policy of 'reform and opening up' created a myriad of new social challenges for which the old methods appeared to be wanting. The profession of social work has (re)emerged in contemporary China as a potential solution to some of those challenges.

The era of 'reform and opening up' and the emergence of new professions

During the first few years of the policy of 'reform and opening up', the CCP encouraged the reemergence and development of certain professions which it regarded as essential for the task of realizing the 'four modernizations' (*sige xiandaihua* 四个现代化) – that is, the development of agriculture, industry, national defence, and science and technology. The legal profession, all but dismantled during the Maoist period, was one of the most obvious given its importance in (re)constructing the system of socialist legality and creating conditions for the rational conduct of business and trade (Hsu 2003). The social sciences were also generally rehabilitated, resulting in a proliferating number of surveys and investigative works (Yuan Fang 1999).

The rehabilitation and development of the social sciences was a precondition for the construction of 'the social' as an object of knowledge and government in contemporary China. As in liberal western societies, China's attempts to govern 'the social' focus on a range of biopolitical themes, such as the problematization of certain individuals, families, and communities as 'pathological', and the deployment of expert fields of knowledge, often in conjunction with the juridical apparatus, to 'normalize' and 'educate' target subjects. However, in China the forms and modes of intervention can be quite different to those practised in western societies – for example, while reform-era authorities have granted significant levels of autonomy to the family, the lingering presence of Maoist rationality has enabled a greater scope of direct state intervention into the private realm – birth control being the most salient example (Sigley 1997, 2004).

During the first decade of reform, social work remained largely neglected so far as policy development was concerned. While economic reforms advanced in the 1980s set in place the conditions for subsequent rapid social change, the government of urban society remained largely unaltered. The work unit continued to be the main provider of social services in urban areas, such as housing, education, and medical care, even though its significance as the sole source of employment began to decline (Bray 2005). The pace of urbanization began to increase in the 1980s as migrants from rural areas entered developing cities to work in construction and in the emerging service sectors. However, the system of urban governance remained largely intact, with only minor innovations and adjustments being made, for example, in the field of urban policing (Dutton 2000, 2005; Sigley 2013). As Feng Xu (2009) notes, urban government systems remained geared towards controlling rural-to-urban migrants rather than encouraging and supporting them to live in cities.

The Ministry of Education first permitted the establishment of social work as an area of specialized study in 1986, but only within a small number of institutions of higher learning (such as Peking University) (Sigley 2011). The Ministry of Civil Affairs formally raised the notion of social work as a possible area of future development in 1988, but did not provide any concrete timing or plan. In 1991, the Ministry represented China in officially joining the International Federation of Social Workers and in the same year approved the establishment of the China Association of Social Workers (*Zhongguo shehui gongzuozhe xiehui* 中国社会工作者协会), which joined the ranks of the international federation in 1992. Interest in social work during the 1980s was, therefore, primarily restricted to research. In fact, social work was not formally recognized as a profession until 2004, when it first appeared in the official list of vocations accredited through the PRC's civil service examination system (Zhang Minjie 2006).

The impetus to develop social work as a profession in mainland China began after Deng Xiaoping's 'Southern Tour' of 1992. In urging the Chinese people to emancipate their minds, and accelerate the pace of economic reform and opening up to the outside world, the veteran leader laid the groundwork for the development of what is now known as the 'socialist market economy' (*shehuizhuyi shichang jingji* 社会主义市场经济) which led to double-digit economic growth and widespread social change (Zhao 1993). In this climate of rapid socio-economic transformation conditions became conducive for the (re)emergence of social work as a profession.

Social and economic change since 1992 has had a huge impact on urban China. The process of urbanization, which had restarted in the 1980s, accelerated as increasingly large numbers of rural people migrated to urban centres. In the largest population movement in world history, between 1978 and 1999 an estimated 174 million people migrated from rural to urban parts of China (Zhang and Song 2003: 390). Although the standard of living improved for large numbers of people, social polarization emerged along with widening income gaps between the rich and the poor (Sicular *et al.* 2007; see also Jeffreys in this book). Social problems such as prostitution and drug addiction, which had resurfaced in the 1980s, became more widespread (Biddulph and Xie 2011; Jeffreys 2012). A range of other social issues, such as juvenile delinquency, domestic violence, and sexual predation, started to gain popular attention through the media (Sun Liping 2003). As the status and utility of the work unit continued to erode, and the urban community became more diverse and fluid, and more difficult to police, old methods of urban government proved to be unable to manage new social challenges effectively. This opened the space for the professional development of social work (Sigley 2011).

The reemergence of social work as a profession in China during the late 1990s and early 2000s can be attributed to three related reasons. First, social work *is* a profession, and both professional qualifications and professional attributes have become desired qualities in reform-era China (Hoffman 2010). Chinese advocates of social work consistently stress the importance of professional training and the 'professionalism' of the social worker (Zhang Hongying 2003: 136–7). They present social workers as professionals who are able to enter the community equipped with skills and knowledge that are not possessed by local cadres, who are appointed through Party-state institutions and residential committee structures. In other words, social work as a profession is presented as a potential solution to the problems facing the older structures and methods of urban governance.

Second, in modelling the experiences of post-industrial developed countries such as France and Australia, China's system of higher education embarked on a process of large-scale expansion and investment (Kang 2004). Colleges and universities were amalgamated into larger institutions, while the total intake of students into the tertiary sector more than doubled over the course of several years, creating a demand for new courses and degrees. Social work was one of the new areas of study and specialization that was given support and focus. As a result, the number of tertiary institutions that provided social work training increased from only 30 institutions in 1999 to over 200 institutions in 2006 (Law and Gu 2008: 3).

While China now produces the second largest number of social work graduates in the world, after the United States (Leung *et al.* 2012: 1042), the quality of social work teaching has suffered from the rapid expansion. This is because teachers from fields such as history, philosophy, and sociology, often with no background in social work, have been recruited to do the teaching. Moreover, until social work was listed as a vocation in the PRC's civil service examinations in 2004, there was no process of official accreditation, and thus little incentive for tertiary students to train as social workers in order to be social workers (Zhang and Zhang 2002). Despite this lag in formal accreditation, the China Association of Social Work Education (*Zhongguo shehui gongzuo jiaoyu xiehui* 中国社会工作教育协会), which was established by a handful of China's leading social work experts in 1994, has played an important role in disseminating information about social work teaching and practice through its annual conferences and flagship journal *Social Work* (社会工作), also established in 1994.

Finally, in response to the social changes and the practical implications of the 'socialist market economy', China's government authorities have developed a new strategy of 'community' (*shequ* 社区) governance, which they have presented as marking a fundamental transformation in the nature of the citizen's collective affiliation. This transformation is purported to entail a shift from being a 'person of the *danwei*' (*danweiren* 单位人) to being a 'person of the social' (*shehuiren* 社会人). In turn, this strategy marks the beginnings of a new vision of 'the social' in urban China which is underpinned by two connected elements – 'governance' and 'community'.

My use of the term 'governance' highlights a general shift in governmental reasoning in contemporary China from '*jihua*' (计划) to '*guihua*' (规划) (Sigley 2006a, 2006b). Both of these terms are rendered in English as 'to plan' or 'the plan'. However, there is a subtle but important distinction between the two in Chinese. '*Jihua*' was the conventional Chinese Marxist terminology associated with the 'socialist planned economy' (*shehuizhuyi jihua jingji* 社会主义计划经济), and was used to refer to the five-year plans for national economic and social development that were implemented during the Mao era and right up until 2005. Five-year plans are still a mainstay of Chinese governmental reasoning – PRC authorities are currently working on the Thirteenth Five-Year Plan (2016–2020). However, under the auspices of the 'socialist market economy' the economy is no longer 'planned' to the degree that it once was. The role of government nowadays is defined more in terms of 'management' or 'guidance', as encapsulated in the new use of the term '*guihua*' – a different style of planning. I associate the shift from '*jihua*' to '*guihua*' with a strategic conceptual shift from 'government' to 'governance' (see also Bray in this book). Moreover, I believe that this shift opens up the social terrain to higher levels of agency, which is a development of great significance for the emerging profession of social work.

Sitting alongside the shift towards 'governance' is the policy and practice of 'community building' (*shequ jianshe* 社区建设). As David Bray (2006: 534) notes in his discussion of the emergence of 'community' as a site of government in urban China since the mid-1990s, the Party-state introduced the notion of 'community' to designate the lowest levels of administration in urban China – that is, the 'street offices' (*jiedao banshichu* 街道办事处) and 'resident committees' (*juweihui* 居委会). 'Community' is understood first and foremost as an administrative entity and not as a 'community of citizens sharing a common interest', and therefore refers to a limited form of 'community participation'. In Bray's words:

> the term 'community' was confined within a narrow and specific definition underpinned by three key characteristics: first, the nature and functions of *community* were to be determined by government; second, the *community* would perform a largely administrative role; and, finally, each *community* would have a clearly demarcated territorial space.
>
> (Bray 2006: 534)

Despite evident limitations in terms of 'genuine' participation, the new 'community' strategy has been conducive to the development of social work for three reasons. First, through guidelines designed to encourage self-management, self-reliance, and less dependence on the state sector, 'community building' has enabled the entry of new non-state organizations and entities, such as non-governmental organizations (NGOs) and non-profit organizations (NPOs), into the terrain of urban government (see also Hoffman and Jeffreys in this book). Second, it stressed developing professionalism among grass-roots community workers, as the 'amateurism' of many former volunteer community 'cadres' came under scrutiny and was found wanting. Finally, it opened up opportunities for local experiments and innovations in grass-roots governance, with some successful examples becoming models for other areas to emulate, once approved by higher levels of government (see also Heberer and Goebel 2011; Tomba 2008).

All of these changes boded well for the arrival of the social worker into the residential compounds and alleyways of urban China. However, the development of social work in practice has been complicated by the legacies of forms of government associated with socialist China, which rely on managerialism and administrative diktat, and view the object to be governed as passive. The next section therefore outlines recent efforts to 'naturalize' and 'indigenize' social work and the factors working against that move.

Finding space for social work: legitimization, indigenization, and harmonious society

The top leadership of the Chinese Party-state has advocated reforming the 'social management system' (*shehui guanli tizhi* 社会管理体制) and expanding the profession of social work since the mid-2000s. On numerous occasions President Hu Jintao has given speeches outlining the importance of social management reform. Hu Jintao declared, for instance, that:

> Our efforts to strengthen and innovate in social management is fundamentally tied to the goal of maintaining social stability, promoting social harmony, guaranteeing the people's livelihoods, and creating a favourable social environment for the party and nation. The basic tasks of social management include harmonizing social relations, standardizing social behaviour, resolving social problems, alleviating social contradictions, furthering social justice, mitigating social risks and maintaining social stability.
> ('Hu Jintao: zhazha shishi tigao shehui guanli kexuehua shuiping' 2011)

Hu Jintao also stressed the importance of the role that the non-governmental sector could play in enhancing social management. The primary objective of social management, and thus of the government and non-governmental agencies involved, is to ensure social stability at a time of rapid transformation. This is best encapsulated in the policy of 'harmonious society'.

In 2006, a great deal of rhetorical attention was paid to separating government and society in the foundation document of the Hu Jintao–Wen Jiabao administration's overarching policy – Harmonious Society (Zhonggong zhongyang 2006). Harmonious Society was a call from the Central Committee to the Party and entire nation to mobilize and concentrate efforts on alleviating the social tensions and pressures that I have outlined above (Han 2008). It was a recognition from the very top that something needed to be done urgently. Like many other policy initiatives in China, the senior leadership formulated general guidelines and strategies rather than specific directives for the construction of a harmonious society. Nevertheless, from its inception the harmonious society campaign has emphasized 'social management' and recognized that NGOs and NPOs have a significant role to play in promoting social stability. The profession of social work, for example, was given an elevated position within the 'Harmonious Society' document, which described the development of a large cohort of professional social workers as 'an urgent task for socialist construction and the development of a harmonious society' (Zhonggong zhongyang 2006).

The rationale behind the harmonious society campaign raises important questions about the appropriate role of government in the era of the 'socialist market economy'. The notion that the development of a 'socialist market economy' required the Party-state to withdraw from the economic *and* social sectors was first articulated in the mid-1980s, after three decades of highly centralized government (Cong and Tang 2002). The Central Government's push towards the 'socialization of social welfare' was articulated through the notion of 'small government, big society' (*xiaozhengfu, dashehui* 小政府, 大社会) in the mid-1980s (Jie and Walker 2013). This concept was given some attention in the 1980s, especially in the context of reform in the newly created province and special economic zone of Hainan. However, it virtually disappeared in the wake of the government crackdown on protest movements at the end of the 1980s. It seemed that the notion of 'small government' had to be recalibrated in the light of perceived threats to social stability. Subsequently, in 1992, a number of influential political scientists began to articulate a 'neo-authoritarian' argument, modelled in part on the analysis of the so-called 'tiger economies' of Singapore, Taiwan, and South Korea, which held that the development of the 'socialist market economy' required a stronger state, and not a weaker one (Xu Yuebin and Zhang Xiulan 2005).

Under Jiang Zemin, the CCP leadership came down in favour of the 'strong state' argument and this position has been continued by subsequent leadership groups. While this context limits the extent to which social work can advocate systematic social change, the concept of 'indigenization' provides space for China's social workers to prove their utility through engaging in forms of 'controlled activism' by focusing on solving specific problems at the grass-roots level (Leung 2012). This situation distinguishes the development of social work in contemporary China from the development of social work in the context of western liberal states, even though the evolution of social work in both contexts is now informed by neoliberal reasoning.

While the notion of 'small government, big society' has not been accorded a prominent position in official discourse, aspects of its logic have infiltrated into governmental practice, not least through the acceptance that social work has a significant role to play in helping to resolve the multifarious social problems that characterize contemporary urban communities. Beginning in the late 1990s the urban metropolises of Beijing, Guangzhou, Shanghai, and Tianjin were among the first places to officially, albeit at the municipal level, endorse social work, and actively encourage the participation of social workers and social work organizations in residential communities. Shanghai authorities, in particular, were extremely innovative. In 1996, Shanghai was one of the first places to officially recognize social work as a profession, and by 1998 it had established a system for testing and accrediting 'social work organizations' (*shehui gongzuo tuanti* 社会工作团体) (Zhang Yu 2004: 9). Shanghai authorities also gave full support for the construction of 'social work stations' (*shehui gongzuozhan* 社会工作站) in most residential districts (Zhang Yu 2004: 9).

Tertiary-level social work education expanded rapidly in China after the late 1990s. In 1998, the Ministry of Education for the first time listed social work in its catalogue of officially recognized professions and noted it as an area designated for future resources and development. In 2003, the Shanghai Department of Personnel and the Shanghai Department of Civil Administration issued regulations governing the accreditation of social workers, and in November of the same year over 5,000 people took the first ever social worker accreditation test (Zhang Letian and Zhang Fenxia 2002; Zhang Fenxia 2003). In 2004, the national Ministry of Labour and Social Welfare formally listed social work as a new profession along with guidelines for standardization and accreditation (Zhang Yu 2004).

In large urban centres such as Shenzhen and Guangzhou, local government authorities have recently established 'comprehensive community service centres' (*shequ zonghe fuwu zhongxin* 社区综合服务中心) and purchased social services from NGOs and other private community service providers (Huang Chuanli 2013; Leung 2012). These centres provide a 'one stop' consultation and service facility where residents can gain access to a wide variety of support. The centres are part of government efforts to become more 'service oriented', captured in the harmonious society slogan of 'take people as the key' (*yi ren wei ben* 以人为本). Most centres have personnel who are either accredited social workers or have received some level of social work training (Zhang Xiaoqin 2012).

Despite these moves to recognize and expand the profession of social work, one of the major challenges facing social workers in the PRC today is the lack of professional autonomy and social recognition. Many of the students who undertake social work degrees have little or no intention of becoming practising social workers – they view social work simply as an entry point into the tertiary education system, it being relatively easier to meet the standards for entry into a social work degree than other, more well-established professions and fields of study.[3] In addition, many social work graduates are unable to find employment as social work professionals, even in places like Shanghai where social work is becoming *de rigueur* (Law and Gu 2008; Zhang Hongying 2003).

Social workers employed in government-funded urban community settings also encounter structural obstacles, which may undermine the 'attractiveness' of social work as a career option. These problems are related to the linking of the profession of social work with national policy goals and the legacies of the Maoist period, in terms of an emphasis on top-down administration and the grass-root cadre's all-round professional role as 'red and expert'. The linking of the development of social work with the development of 'social harmony' creates tensions regarding 'who' the profession of social work serves and for what purposes. Some Chinese academics view social work as a tool to maintain stability within the confines of the current governance system without undertaking radical political or social reform (Pan Yunkang 2002: 36; Guo Jingping 2002: 184–5). Others see social work as contributing to social stability, but also slowly changing the nature of grass-roots participation in government in a profound manner because of its emphasis on 'self-help' (Wang Sibin 2006a, 2006b; Xu Yongxiang 2005).

Some local government cadres conflate the work of social work with that of the government, thinking that they are essentially one and the same (Zhang Minjie 2006: 74). This understanding constrains the opportunities for social work as a professional practice, and for providers of social work services, to operate outside of the realm and existing practices of local government (Zhang Minjie 2006: 74). Other local government cadres look upon social workers as 'outsiders' muscling in on their territory and have a limited comprehension of the goals and potential value of social work (Sigley 2011). This prejudice against social workers is quite significant, given that the government sector is potentially the largest employer of social workers. It means that social workers who are deployed in government-run organizations, such as hospitals, schools, and residential communities, are often delegated menial administrative tasks (Zhang Minjie 2006: 74). This type of role is known as 'administrative social work' (Leung 2012: 344) and indicates that while social workers are finding their way into government positions at the community level, their full set of skills and expertise often remain underutilized.

Government policies concerned with 'maintaining social stability' (*weiwen*) have reinforced the extent to which community-level government cadres view social workers with a degree of suspicion. Grass-roots cadres are especially unwilling to allocate formal responsibilities to social workers associated with 'unknown' organizations, such as NGOs and NPOs. Government concerns to ensure social stability thus reinforce existing links between state and society, rather than encouraging the separation of roles that might be expected with a shift towards the privatization of social services through social work. One of the legacies of centralized planning is that local community government tends to view its local constituents as passive targets of administrative decree. Although there has always been some level of agency at the grass-roots – even within Maoist ideology in terms of the revolutionary potential of the masses – the actual practice of government has tended to rely upon administrative diktat. As Wang Sibin (2006b: 1) notes:

> In the era of the planned economy, the government could absolutely use political and administrative methods to manage social problems. The social structure [at that time] displayed the features of a 'totalized society' (*zongtixing shehui* 总体性社会). Under these conditions there was no need for what we now refer to as 'social work', and no need to discuss the

problem of the professionalization of social work because all economic and political resources were concentrated in the hands of government. The 'social work' of that period was politicized (*bei zhengzhihua* 被政治化).

While the broader policy framework stresses the importance of separating state and society, the promotion of community participation in local governance in contemporary urban China has not led to the withdrawal of government from this realm. Xu Yongxiang (2005) goes as far as to suggest that the separation of government and society (*zheng she zhi fen* 政社之分) that was intended in the development of 'the community' has not occurred. Instead, the 'community' has become in many cases a mere extension of government. Xu (2005) describes this situation as the '*danwei*-ization' (*danweihua* 单位化) of the community, and argues that this trend has hindered the development of an autonomous 'third sector'. Instead, NGOs and community organizations are expected to help the PRC Government at all levels to realize social policy goals (Liu and Xu 2004: 45). In other words, NGOs and NPOs are understood as performing an advocacy-consultative role with local government rather than adopting an antagonistic or adversarial role (see also Hoffman and Jeffreys in this book).

While social work as a profession in the western context was partly founded on a philosophy of 'self-help' in which 'passive subjects' are encouraged to find ways to improve their condition and govern themselves, in China the space for social workers to criticize governmental practices or stand up for the 'weaker elements' of society (*ruoshi qunti* 弱势群体) is far more limited. Yet Chinese social work scholars continue to stress the notion of 'self-help' (*zhu ren zi zhu* 助人自助), even though it refers to a different 'subject' from that articulated in the standard Party-state top-down transmission of decrees, namely, an 'active' rather than 'passive' subject (Wang Sibin 2006b: 4; Zhang Hongying 2003: 137).

Terry Leung *et al.* (2012) argue that the Party-state's desire to co-opt social work for its own instrumental purposes, on the one hand, and the potential for social work to adopt a radical interpretation of the 'take people as the key' approach, on the other hand, means that social workers in China need to walk a fine line between enabling clients to help themselves while not stepping on the toes of the local authorities. There is thus a very different sense of 'the social' in this context. Although the rhetoric of community participation in self-government is now well established, the reality is that local government authorities still view 'the social' as a field of government intervention and are reticent to yield authority within that field to newcomers such as social workers, who have been trained to work according to a quite different understanding of professional advocacy.

Conclusion

Some scholars have taken the Party-state's comprehensive strategy of harmonious society as a qualitative break with the repressive practices of the past. Luigi Tomba (2009), for example, argues that:

> Although 'harmonious society' does not appear to constitute a departure from traditional paternalistic patterns of governance, as a goal of social policies, the search for 'harmony' is essentially different from the simple call for 'order': it argues for the conscious and rational removal of the causes (whether economic, social, or behavioural) of underlying conflicts, rather than for their institutionalization and repression. It is therefore accompanied by a stress on individual behaviour, self-improvement, virtues, and responsibility. As emerges in other articles in this collection, it also defines a disciplinary regime that is different from the capillary penetration of society generally associated with the institutions of authoritarian rule. This disciplinary regime increasingly adopts governmental techniques that envisage the active participation of subjects and the agency of a wide array of players in a virtuous scheme based (when possible) on self-discipline.
>
> (Tomba 2009: 594)

While there is a ring of truth to this analysis, it still falls short of the mark.

In the case of social work, the rhetoric of creating a harmonious society would appear to open the space for seemingly 'neoliberal' strategies of governing through freedom and the self. However, the development of social work in practice is challenged by the persistence of an administrative mentality. This administrative mentality has been strengthened, rather than weakened, by the governmental emphasis on 'community building', 'social management', and 'maintaining social stability' in recent years. Harmonious society as a grand strategy appears to have been captured by the imperative to maintain social stability, and just as the urban community has been *danwei*-nized, the harmonious society rhetoric of encouraging 'active participation' has been captured and neutralized through the intervention of grass-roots cadres.

Yet social work as a profession can be interpreted as a new form of activism that has the potential to generate change at the grass-roots, both in terms of community service provision and in the very mentality of local government itself, given its professed concern with 'self-help'. As Leung *et al.* (2012: 1056) argue:

> social work is a technology of change that has an indicative ideological orientation. Technology and ideology cannot be clearly separated in social work practice. To break this ideology–technology entanglement requires governing techniques that can foster self-help and mutual help, but remain immune from invoking the quest for autonomy and self-government. Such a design is, however, no easy task. The quest for indigenization to derive a social work approach with Chinese characteristics marks the beginning of such a design.
>
> (Leung *et al.* 2012: 1056)

The development of social work is therefore caught between the complex processes of systemic reform (*tizhi gaige* 体制改革) and social transformation (*shehui zhuanxing* 社会转型).

Despite facing many institutional obstacles, social work as a profession has already established a strong foundation in the PRC. The impact that social work could have on urban communities will no doubt take some time to unfold. In many urban locales, especially along the eastern seaboard, social workers are becoming more established and recognized and are beginning to operationalize a new model for governing the social. As the practice of social work extends to other urban areas and eventually into regional and rural China, practitioners will be confronted by a whole new range of contexts and problems. For these reasons, social work and social workers are likely to remain at the cutting edge of debates over how to govern at the community level. If we wish to understand the significance of these debates and how the tensions between the 'city–citizen' and 'shepherd–flock' game will be played out in China, then the emergence of social work offers a unique perspective right at the juncture where the 'city' meets the 'shepherd'.

Acknowledgements

This research was partly funded by a grant from the University of Western Australia. I would like to thank David Bray and Elaine Jeffreys for their insightful comments. My colleagues, Violet Bacon and Maria Harries, at the University of Western Australia also deserve thanks for their advice on the history of social work in the western context.

Notes

1 This chapter primarily focuses on social work in urban China. Social work in rural China is less developed and requires further attention and research.
2 The profession of social work continued to develop and prosper in Hong Kong and Taiwan, with social workers in both countries contributing to the reintroduction of social work in mainland China in the 1990s (Tsang *et al.* 2008: 73).
3 Information based on fieldwork interviews conducted between the author and social work students in Shanghai in July 2010 and in Hangzhou in early 2015.

References

Biddulph, S. and Xie, C. (2011) 'Regulating drug dependency in China', *The British Journal of Criminology*, 51: 978–96.

Bray, D. (2005) *Social Space and Governance in Urban China: The Danwei System from Origins to Reform*, Stanford: Stanford University Press.

Bray, D. (2006) '"Building community": new strategies of governance in urban China', *Economy and Society*, 35, 4: 530–49.

Camilleri, P.J. (1996) *(Re)constructing Social Work: Exploring Social Work through Text and Talk*, Aldershot: Avebury.

Chambon, A.S., Irving, A., and Epstein, L. (eds) (1999) *Reading Foucault for Social Work*, New York: Columbia University Press.

Cong Xiaofeng and Tang Bingyuan (2002) 'Shehui gongzuo kexue jianshe de ruogan wenti yanjiu' [Research on various problems in the scientific construction of social work], *Jinan Daxue Xuebao*, 12: 1–2.

Dean, M. (1991) *The Constitution of Poverty: Towards a Genealogy of Liberal Governance*, London: Routledge.
'Definition of social work' (2012) International Federation of Social Workers, 8 June. Online. Available: http://ifsw.org/policies/definition-of-social-work (accessed 30 January 2014).
Donzelot, J. (1979) *The Policing of Families*, Baltimore: John Hopkins University Press.
Dutton, M. (2000) 'The end of the (mass) line? Chinese policing in the era of the contract', *Social Justice*, 27, 2: 61–105.
Dutton, M. (2005) *Policing Chinese Politics: A History*, Durham and London: Duke University Press.
Foucault, M. (1977) *Discipline and Punish: The Birth of the Prison*, New York: Knopf Doubleday Publishing Group.
Foucault, M. (1978) *The History of Sexuality: Volume One*, London: Allen Lane.
Foucault, M. (1979) 'Omnes et singulatim: towards a criticism of political reason', lectures delivered at Stanford University, 10 and 16 October. Online. Available: http://foucault.info/documents/foucault.omnesEtSingulatim.en.html (accessed 5 November 2012).
Gray, M. (2005) 'Dilemmas of international social work: paradoxical processes in indigenisation, imperialism and universalism', *International Journal of Social Welfare*, 14: 230–7.
Gray, M. (2008) 'Postcards from the west: mapping the vicissitudes of western social work', *Australian Social Work*, 61, 1: 1–6.
Guo Jingping (2002) 'Xiandai shehui gongzuo de jiben tezheng: zhiduhua litazhuyi' [The characteristics of contemporary social work: the institutionalization of altruism], *Beijing Daxue Xuebao*, S1: 183–9.
Han, A. (2008) 'Building an harmonious society and achieving individual harmony', *Journal of Chinese Political Science*, 13, 2: 143–64.
Hayford, C. (1990) *To the People: James Yen and the Chinese Village*, New York: Columbia University Press.
Heberer, T. and Goebel, C. (2011) *The Politics of Community Building in Urban China*, Abingdon: Routledge.
Hoffman, L. (2010) *Patriotic Professionalism in Urban China: Fostering Talent*, Philadelphia: Temple University Press.
Hsu, S. (ed.) (2003) *Understanding China's Legal System*, New York: New York University Press.
'Hu Jintao: Zhazha shishi tigao shehui guanli kexuehua shuiping' (2011) *Xinhuawang*, 19 February. Online. Available: http://news.xinhuanet.com/politics/2011-02/19/c_121100198.htm (accessed 26 October 2013).
Huang Chuanli (2013) 'Zhuanye shehui gongzuo qianru shequ gonggong fuwu yanjiu' [The entry of professional social workers into community public service provision], *Sichuan Ligong Xueyuan Xuebao (Shehui Kexue)*, 2: 10–14.
Jeffreys, E. (2012) *Prostitution Scandals in China: Policing, Media and Society*, Abingdon: Routledge.
Jeffreys, E. and Sigley, G. (2009) 'Governmentality and China', in E. Jeffreys (ed.) *Chinese Governmentalities: Governing Change, Changing Government*, Abingdon: Routledge, pp. 1–25.
Jie, L. and Walker, A. (2013) 'The big society in China: a failed experiment', *Social Policy and Society*, 12, 1: 17–30.
Kang, O. (2004) 'Higher education reform in China today', *Policy Futures in Education*, 2, 1: 141–9.

Lam, T. (2011) *A Passion for Facts: Social Surveys and the Construction of the Chinese Nation-State, 1900–1949*, Berkeley: University of California Press.

Law, A. and Gu, J. (2008) 'Social work education in mainland China: development and issues', *Asian Social Work and Policy Review*, 2: 1–12.

Leung, T. (2012) 'The work sites as ground of contest: professionalisation of social work in China', *British Journal of Social Work*, 42: 335–52.

Leung, T., Yip, N., Huang, R., and Wu, Y. (2012) 'Governmentality and the politicisation of social work in China', *British Journal of Social Work*, 42: 1039–59.

Lin Shunli (2013) 'Minguo shiqi shehui gongzuo yinru he fazhan de lujing' [The adoption and development of social work during the Republican Era], *Hebei Daxue Xuebao (Zhexue Shehui Kexueban)*, 38, 3: 34–8.

Liu Xiaoxia and Xu Yongxiang (2004) 'Shehui gongzuo zhuanyehua, zhiyehua de youyi tansuo: Shanghai lequn shegong fuwushe gean fenxi' [An investigation into the professionalization of social work: the Shanghai Lequn social provider as a case study], *Huadong Ligong Daxue Xuebao (Shehui Kexue)*, 2: 41–6.

Lorenz, W. (2008) 'Towards a European model of social work', *Australian Social Work*, 61, 1: 7–24.

McMahon, A. (2003) 'Redefining the beginnings of social work', *Advances in Social Work and Welfare Education*, 5, 1: 83–94.

Pan Yunkang (2002) 'Shehui zhuanxing yu shehui gongzuo' [Social transformation and social work], *Lilun yu Xiandaihua*, 1: 32–6.

Parton, N. (1994) 'Problematics of government: postmodernity and social work', *British Journal of Social Work*, 24: 9–32.

Payne, M. (2005) *The Origins of Social Work: Continuity and Change*, New York: Palgrave Macmillan.

Peng Xiuliang (2010) *Shouwang yu kaixin: jindai zhongguo de shehui gongzuo*, [Observing and Beginning: Social Work in Modern China], Shijiazhuang: Hebei Jiaoyu Chubanshe.

Reamer, F.G. (1993) *The Philosophical Foundations of Social Work*, New York: Columbia University Press.

Rose, N. and Miller, P. (1992) 'Political power beyond the state: problematics of government', *The British Journal of Sociology*, 43, 2: 173–205.

Sicular, T., Yue, X., Gustafsson, B., and Li, S. (2007) 'The urban–rural income gap and inequality in China', *Review of Income and Wealth*, 53, 1: 92–126.

Sigley, G. (1997) 'Governing Chinese bodies: the significance of studies in governmentality for the analysis of birth control in China', in C. O'Farrell (ed.), *Foucault: The Legacy*, Brisbane: Queensland University of Technology Press.

Sigley, G. (2004) 'Liberal despotism: population planning, government and subjectivity in contemporary China', *Alternative: Global, Local, Political*, 29, 5: 557–75.

Sigley, G. (2006a) 'Chinese governmentalities: government, governance and the socialist market economy', *Economy and Society*, 35, 4: 487–508.

Sigley, G. (2006b) 'From "*jihua*" to "*guihua*": a preliminary critique of approaches to understanding "governance" in the Chinese context', in Adrian Vickers and Margaret Hanlon (eds), *Asia Reconstructed: Proceedings of the 16th Biennial Conference of the ASAA*, Wollongong, Australia. Online. Available: http://coombs.anu.edu.au/SpecialProj/ASAA/biennial-conference/2006/proceedings.html (accessed 3 July 2013).

Sigley, G. (2011) 'Social policy and social work in contemporary China: an interview with Xu Yongxiang', *China Journal of Social Work*, 4, 2: 103–13.

Sigley, G. (2013) 'From revolution to government, from contradictions to harmony: urban community policing in post-Deng China', in R. Lippert and K. Walby (eds), *Policing Cities: Urban Securitization and Regulation in a 21st Century World*, Abingdon: Routledge.
Smith, J.H. (2009) *The Art of Doing Good: Charity in Late Ming China*, Berkeley: University of California Press.
Sun Liping (2003) *Duanlie: 20 shiji 90 niandai yilai de zhongguo shehui* [Cleavage: Chinese Society since the 1990s], Beijing: Shehui Kexue Wenxian Chubanshe.
Thompson, M. (2012) 'Foucault, fields of governability, and the population–family–economy nexus in China', *History and Theory*, 51: 42–62.
Tomba, L. (2008) 'Making neighborhoods: the government of social change in China's cities', *Chinese Perspectives/Perspectives Chinoises*, 4: 48–61.
Tomba, L. (2009) 'Of quality, harmony, and community: civilization and the middle class in urban China', *Positions: East Asia Cultures Critique*, 17, 3: 591–616.
Tsang, A., Sin, R., Jia, C., and Miu, C. (2008) 'Another snapshot of social work in China: capturing multiple positioning and intersecting discourses in rapid movement', *Australian Social Work*, 61, 1: 72–87.
Wang Sibin (2006a) 'Shehui gongzuozhe shehui zhengce shidai yu zhengfu shehui zhengce nengli jianshe' [Social workers, the era of social policy and construction of government social policy capacity], *Zhongguo Shehui Kexue*, 6: 23–30.
Wang Sibin (2006b) 'Tizhi zhuanbianzhong shehui gongzuo de zhiyehua jincheng' [The professionalization of social work during the period of systemic transition], *Beijing Keji Daxue Xuebao*, 22, 1: 1–5.
Xu Yongxiang (2005) 'Xiandai shehui gongzuo zai hexie shehui zhong de jiangou gongneng' [The function of modern social work in the construction of a harmonious society], *Xuehai*, 1: 22–9.
Xu Yuebing and Zhang Xiulan (2005) 'Zhongguo zhengfu zai shehui fuli zhong jiaose chongjian' [The role of the Chinese government in rebuilding social welfare], *Zhongguo Shehui Kexue*, 5: 13–18.
Xu, F. (2009) 'Governing China's peasant migrants: building xiaokang socialism and an harmonious society', in E. Jeffreys (ed.), *Chinese Governmentalities: Governing Change, Changing Government*, Abingdon: Routledge, pp. 38–62.
Yuan Fang (1999) *Shehuixue Bainian* [One Hundred Years of Sociology], Beijing: Beijing Chubanshe.
Zhang Fenxia (2003) 'Shanghaishi shehui gongzuo zhiye zige kaoshi fenxi baogao' [A study of the Shanghai social work accreditation examination], *Shehui*, 12: 50–2.
Zhang Hongying (2003) 'Qiantan zhongguo shehui gongzuo de fazhan quxiang' [Analysis of the development of social work in China], *Zhongguo Qingnian Zhengzhi Xueyuan Xuebao*, 22, 4: 135–9.
Zhang, K.H. and Song, S. (2003) 'Rural–urban migration in China: evidence from time-series and cross-section analyses', *China Economic Review*, 14: 386–400.
Zhang Letian and Zhang Fenxia (2002) 'Shehui gongzuo zhiye xianzhuang yu duice sikao: Shanghaishi pudong xinqu shehui gongzuo zhiyehua diaocha yu fenxi' [Reflections on the status of the professionalization of social work: an analysis of social work in Shanghai Pudong], *Shehui Kexue*, 2: 61–5.
Zhang Minjie (2006) 'Zhongguo zhuanye shehui gongzuo mianlin de san da wenti' [The three major challenges confronting professional social work in China], *Zhejiang Gongshang Daxue Xuebao*, 79, 4: 73–7.

Zhang Xiaoqin (2012) 'Shequ zonghe fuwu zhongxin jianshe de lulun jichu yu xianshi kunhuo' [Comprehensive community service centres: theory and reality], *Sheke Zongheng*, 27, 1: 42–4.

Zhang Yu (2004) 'Shehuigongzuo de bentuhua fazhan: Shanghai shehuigongzuo fazhan guocheng fenxi' [Indigenizing social work: an analysis of developments in Shanghai], *Huadongligongdaxue Xuebao*, 1: 8–12.

Zhao, S.S. (1993) 'Deng Xiaoping's southern tour: elite politics in post-Tiananmen China', *Asian Survey*, 33, 8: 739–56.

Zhonggong zhongyang (2006) 'Zhonggong zhongyang guanyu goujian shehuizhuyi hexie shehui ruogan zhongda wen de jueding' [Central Committee of the Communist Party of China resolution on the building of an harmonious society], *Xinhua Wang*, 18 October. Online. Available: http://news.xinhuanet.com/politics/2006-10/18/content_5218639.htm (accessed 15 April 2013).

7 Elite philanthropy in China and America

The disciplining and self-discipline of wealth

Elaine Jeffreys

> The problem of our age is the proper administration of wealth, so that the ties of brotherhood may still bind together the rich and poor in harmonious relationship.
>
> (Carnegie 1889: 653)

Between January and March 2010, international film star and philanthropist Zhang Ziyi became a subject of public condemnation in the People's Republic of China (PRC) after she allegedly defaulted on a pledge to donate CNY 1 million to the Sichuan earthquake disaster-relief fund (Jeffreys 2011: 4). The earthquake of 12 May 2008, which killed an estimated 70,000 people and left five million homeless, is widely viewed as putting philanthropy 'on the map' in China. Philanthropic donations in 2008 amounted to a total figure of CNY 100 billion or 0.4 per cent of China's gross domestic product, exceeding the documented total for the preceding decade (Wang Zhuoqiong 2008).

Zhang Ziyi was neither the first nor only high-profile casualty of a public backlash against mediatized elite philanthropy in the aftermath of the earthquake. Major corporations were accused of 'donation-stinginess' in chain letters posted on the internet and disseminated by mobile phone networks. A range of Chinese sports and entertainment stars were also accused of 'dishonest advertising', or failing to deliver on publicized pledges to the disaster-relief efforts (Jeffreys 2011: 10–15).

The public shaming of Zhang Ziyi and other faces of elite philanthropy in China highlights mounting conflicts over wealth distribution in the context of China's transforming economy. Prior to the introduction of economic reforms in the late 1970s that gradually dismantled the apparatus of 'socialist' centralized planning, China possessed a theoretical solution to the question of the 'proper administration of wealth'. After the founding of the PRC in 1949 and throughout the Maoist period (1949–1976), curtailment of the monetary economy, combined with state ownership and redistribution of public resources, prevented private enterprise and the accumulation of significant private wealth, and also eliminated the spaces for private philanthropy. Urban residents, in particular, came to rely on the state through the work unit system for the necessities of everyday life – employment, housing, education, health care, and other social services. At the same time, the Chinese Communist Party (CCP) placed strict controls over a state-owned media which functioned as a 'mouthpiece' for Party-state ideology and policies, through the dissemination of restricted public information (propaganda), and promotion of forms of entertainment that upheld revolutionary heroes and political role models. This meant that 'entrepreneurship', 'philanthropy', and 'celebrity', in the contemporary sense of those words, did not exist in the PRC until after it adopted a policy of market-based economic reforms and opening up to the rest of the world in December 1978.

China's economic reforms have lifted an estimated 753 million people out of absolute poverty since 1981 (World Bank 2015) and generated widening income gaps (Yao and Wang 2013). Some sectors of the population have become spectacularly rich by taking advantage of the opportunities created by privatization and the erosion of constraints on rural-to-urban migration. Other sectors of the population have shifted from poverty into precarity; they work in low-paid jobs with little opportunity for advancement and face new insecurities because of limited state welfare and the cost of privatized social services. Meanwhile, generalized increases in individual income levels, a parallel growth in the variety and quality of products available for purchase, and the loosening of former controls over an increasingly commercialized media, have resulted in the development of a consumer society, commercial forms of entertainment and more open forms of commentary. An urban elite composed of private entrepreneurs and stars has emerged alongside the bureaucrat-entrepreneurs who hold prominent institutional positions in the Party-state system (Edwards and Jeffreys 2010). As these newly rich professional or quasi-professional groups have successfully entered the spaces created by the PRC's growing shift towards a market economy, questions have been raised about the nature and extent of their philanthropic responsibilities.

The development of elite philanthropy in the PRC, and related public debates, has followed a different trajectory from that in western countries, particularly the United States (USA) – the 'home' of capitalism and big-money philanthropy.[1] The USA has a long tradition of elite philanthropy born of a history of religious conviction, social mobility and tax incentives, and related conceptions of a state–society divide, which presents elite philanthropy as a matter of individual moral responsibility (Zunz 2012). Present-day supporters of American-style elite philanthropy cite the practical benefits of well-resourced individuals financing worthy causes as providing more innovative, diverse, and efficient responses than those provided by national governments (Ostrower 1995: 113–31). Opponents argue that such benefits are undermined by the tacit valorization of 'global capitalism' and its inherent inequalities, or by people giving to causes which attract them, benefit them, or give them publicity, rather than giving where the help is needed in the long term (Nickel 2012: 176).

In the PRC today, debates about the emerging phenomenon of elite philanthropy focus less on the question of its inherent benefits and disadvantages, and more on the perceived success or failure of elites to meet their societal obligations – that is, to fulfil their end of a post-Maoist 'social contract'. The nature of this 'contract' was outlined by Xie Jingrong, Vice-President of the Chinese Association of Industry and Commerce, during a speech at the PRC's first national Charity Fair in 2012, as follows:

> Our common ideal and responsibility, based on the principles of fair competition and shared responsibility, is to rejuvenate the Chinese nation by building a prosperous, strong and harmonious nation.... The development of the non-public sector of the economy is a great achievement of the reform process. The majority of private entrepreneurs know that Party leadership, state protection, and the support of the people, is responsible for their success. They also know that social responsibility (*shehui zeren* 社会责任) comes with the accumulation of wealth.
>
> (Xie Jingrong cited in Hu and Zhang 2012)

Elite philanthropy is presented as the social duty of wealthy patriots with the goal of rejuvenating China and realizing what President Xi Jinping has described as 'the Chinese dream' of ever-higher living standards ('China's new president' 2013).

This chapter places elite philanthropy in international perspective by charting the divergent genealogies, and related controversies, of elite philanthropy in the USA and the PRC. The chapter uses a genealogical approach to examine the evolution of elite philanthropy as a controversial form of social intervention that involves particular ways of thinking about the role of 'good' government, how to conduct the lives of others, and self-government (Foucault 1991 [1978]). First, it offers a brief history of the shift in western societies from charity to organized philanthropy, and selectively documents conceptual antecedents of modern arguments in favour of elite philanthropy in the USA. Second, it reviews the leftist critique of commercial and mediatized elite philanthropy, or 'new philanthropy'. Third, the chapter describes the evolution of elite philanthropy in contemporary China, exploring both the development of supportive government policies and the disciplinary effects of expectations of philanthropy for the newly rich, as illustrated by the popular demonization of Zhang Ziyi. I conclude that the logic underpinning the rise of elite philanthropy in the PRC, and the mentality of government it reveals, challenges the universality of leftist critique.

The origins of modern (elite) philanthropy

The origins of modern philanthropy are entwined with the emergence in northern Europe during the seventeenth and eighteenth centuries of a new way of thinking about the aims and objects of government, which Michel Foucault (1991) calls governmentality. Previous conceptions of government as chiefly involving the exercise of sovereign right (divine or natural) over territory were replaced by an understanding that 'government is the right disposition of things, arranged so as to lead to a convenient end' (Foucault 1991: 93). That 'end' was a strong nation state and the 'things' that had to be governed to reach it were human populations and humans' relations to resources, the environment, social customs, disease, and other variables. Hence, 'modern government' became concerned to optimize 'life' by improving the overall condition of a population (its wealth, health, capacity to engage in labour, to reproduce, and to wage war, etc.), rather than strictly maintaining sovereignty, territory, and law, resulting in the establishment of new technologies of power that targeted humans as living beings (biopolitics) (Foucault 1991: 99; 2004: 239–54). This shift was reinforced by the demographic expansion of eighteenth-century northern Europe, which was connected with expanded agricultural production and rising private wealth, and accompanied by population dispersal, colonization, and religious dissidence (Foucault 2004: 239–54).

Donna Andrew's history of charity in London suggests that modern forms of philanthropy started to replace medieval forms of charity around the same time: 'in 1650 London had few if any privately organized and financed charitable institutions, by 1800 it had dozens' (Andrew 1989: 1). Medieval charity turned on the assumption that there would always be people who were poor, poverty being an immutable part of the world made by God. Hence, charity was focused on the donor, rather than the recipient, with giving being viewed as an act of devotion that demonstrated faith in Providence (Andrew 1989: 15, 22, 197). By the start of the eighteenth century, the growth of commerce and labour meant that more people than previously were able to support themselves, and poverty was presumed to result from a lack of employment, or improvidence, idleness, and vice (Andrew 1989: 197–8; Gross 2003: 14).

Criticisms of Church corruption and new concerns over the quality of national populations ensured that older, indiscriminate forms of charity were supplanted by organized charities aimed at improving the wellbeing of the nation by addressing 'social problems' (Andrew 1989: 49; Foucault 2004: 244). Civic-minded merchants formed joint stock or associated charities that raised money for foundling hospitals, orphanages, and educational facilities, providing self-help skills and disciplinary trainings for impoverished youth, 'penitent prostitutes', and criminals (Andrew 1989). These charities targeted donors – aristocrats and other people of means – through charity balls and bazaars, charity sermons and dinners, and benefits at theatres and operas (Andrew 1989: 80–5), making charitable donations an expression of social standing, not strictly 'faith'.

Organized philanthropy subsequently became focused on the question of how to attract and retain wealthy donors for 'worthy' causes, which required the constant solicitation of donors through elite networks, and 'proof' of the 'worthiness' of such causes. That worthiness was demonstrated through transparent management and accounting practices, and by ensuring that charity recipients were seen to be 'deserving' of assistance (Andrew 1989: 83–5). These processes eventually generated a new host of professionals – social workers, foundation directors, and development officers in the non-profit sector (Gross 2003: 48). They also introduced new modes of 'policing the poor' based on a distinction between the 'deserving' and 'undeserving'. This distinction was policed largely according to the perceived willingness (or otherwise) of potential and actual recipients of charity to adhere to dominant social mores, and transform themselves into suitable labouring subjects for the industrial revolution and nascent capitalist economy.

It is therefore now often assumed that the evolution of modern philanthropy has buttressed the capitalist system and inequality, by subjecting 'the poor' to the disciplinary technologies of labour and only providing (inadequately) for them in so far as they meet that purpose (Kapoor 2013: 48–52). However, it bears noting that having 'pitilessly torn asunder the motley feudal ties that bound man to his "natural superiors"' (Marx and Engels 1848: chapter 1), the early expansion of industrial capitalism dispersed wealth in hitherto unprecedented ways. In this context, the relationship between philanthropy and the capitalist system was less clear-cut. In the USA, for example, a nation founded in the mid-eighteenth century, the growth of the national modern economy was also accompanied by the formation of philanthropic associations designed to equip young men with the knowledge required to do business independently of traditional patronage structures (Gross 2003: 38), and by efforts to outline the philanthropic responsibilities of the entrepreneurial new rich.

Andrew Carnegie (1835–1919), a Scottish-born rags-to-riches US industrialist, was an early proponent of the claim that the free-market economy offers a solution to the problem of inequality. In an essay titled 'Wealth', Carnegie (1889: 653–64) rejected socialist philosophy as idealistic, arguing instead that the 'law of competition' had demonstrably revolutionized the condition of human life. Rather than living in universal squalor, considerably more people than previously had access to vastly improved standards of living and education, albeit especially the wealthy. Thus, the task posed for modern human society was to work out how to spread the advantages of the market economy more equitably.

Carnegie's proposed solution, which he called 'The Gospel of Wealth', justified the free-market economy and prescribed a philanthropic asceticism for the entrepreneurial new rich. Carnegie (1889) believed that inequalities between the rich and the poor were temporary and could be eliminated under what we now refer to as capitalism, so long as people with the ability and energy to produce wealth assumed responsibility for the 'proper' recirculation of their money back into society. In his view, successful entrepreneurs were duty-bound to set an example of modest, unostentatious living, to provide moderately for the legitimate needs of their dependents, and to use all their surplus revenues during their lifetime in a manner best calculated to benefit the community, rather than leaving large sums of money to be squandered by heirs or ineffective charities. At the same time, Carnegie (1889) disapproved of what he saw as 'almsgiving' – charity that maintained the poor in an impoverished state and created welfare dependency. Instead, he argued that philanthropic organizations should only help those with the desire to improve themselves and therefore society as a whole, which translated in practice into support for public libraries and higher education. Underlying Carnegie's faith in the innovative spirit and philanthropic self-discipline of the entrepreneurial new rich is the implicit belief that agents 'outside' of the processes of government could correct 'the failures' of British-style bureaucratic government and Parliamentary Monarchy.

While America's wealthy have not adopted Carnegie's principles *en masse*, philanthropy is now an integral part of elite culture in the USA; it also constitutes a way of thinking about the role of philanthropy vis-à-vis government, on the part of elites, in particular, that celebrates individual initiative and market mechanisms as a means to democratize wealth (Ostrower 1995; Zunz 2012). In 1913, the US Congress ratified the Sixteenth Amendment to the US Constitution, which instituted a national income tax system and exempted philanthropies, whether 'originating in big money, mass appeals, or communities' (Zunz 2012: 4). Alongside a growth in private wealth, this system has cemented the shift from 'charity' to 'modern philanthropy' – the planned and structured giving via a non-profit business model of 'money, time, information, goods and services, voice and influence to improve the wellbeing of humanity and the community' ('Philanthropy' n.d.). It has also encouraged a culture of elite philanthropy wherein making public donations, attending charity galas, and sitting on the boards of non-profits is viewed as a 'way of being part of Society', and a way of 'giving back' to society, by people who believe that they have earned their money, and have a right to distribute their wealth as they choose (Ostrower 1995: 6, 29–49). Interviews with wealthy people in the USA indicate that their philanthropy is informed by an understanding that national governments guarantee 'the life' of the population by providing essential welfare services through taxation-derived income, whereas philanthropy improves the quality of human life through donations to heterogeneous causes (Ostrower 1995: 4, 113–31).

Billionaire philanthropist Bill Gates expands on this framework by offering 'creative capitalism' as a twenty-first-century solution to the problem of global socio-economic inequalities (Kiviat and Gates 2008). According to Gates, creative capitalism represents a new and proactive form of corporate philanthropy. Unlike the reactive response of traditional corporate philanthropy to grant requests from unrelated non-profit organizations, creative capitalism generates a virtuous cycle of philanthropy by encouraging socially responsible companies to grasp new opportunities and profits while 'serving the people who have been left out'. It also draws in consumers who want to be associated with good causes and employees who want to work for organizations that they can feel good about in both their public and private lives (Kiviat and Gates 2008). Providing an example of creative capitalism at work, Gates notes that those multinational companies which sell (RED)-branded products donate a portion of their profits to fight HIV and AIDS in Africa (Kiviat and Gates 2008). In 2010, Gates launched a Carnegian-style campaign called The Giving Pledge, which invites the world's wealthiest individuals and families to commit publicly to giving at least half of their wealth to effective philanthropic causes of their choice either during their lifetime or immediately after their death. The campaign had attracted 137 pledges by 2015 ('Current pledgers' 2015).

Entertainment and sports celebrities enter into the realm of what is sometimes also called 'new philanthropy' by contributing their public visibility, brand credibility, and personal wealth to aid philanthropic organizations and causes. In 1986, the United Nations (UN) established a special division for non-governmental organizations (NGOs), which led to a dramatic increase in the number of America-based and other international NGOs, and subsequently to a dramatic increase in the number of indigenous NGOs with World Bank funding (Zunz 2012: 282–3). While 'NGOs have proven no more immune to corruption and inefficiencies than government bureaucracies, and coordination has remained a difficult issue', the (neoliberal) operating rationale and general expectation of NGOs is that they can distribute global philanthropic resources more effectively to local communities than can national governments (Zunz 2012: 286).

Between 2000 and 2002 the UN's Department of Public Information ran two conferences for the UN's growing ranks of celebrity advocates, calling the second conference 'Celebrity Advocacy for the New Millennium' (Alleyne 2005: 177–9). The UN and other international humanitarian organizations have made celebrities the visual focus of campaigns that are designed to promote public awareness of the need to find lasting solutions to poverty and related injustice around the world, while also achieving brand awareness. Indeed, the 'Look to the Stars: The World of Celebrity Giving' website – advertised as 'the web's number one source of celebrity charity news and information' – claims that by mid-2015 there were more than 3,500 (Hollywood-branded) celebrities involved with more than 2,000 charities that aim to 'make a positive difference in the world' ('Look to the stars' 2006–2015).

Concerned commentators variously praise and condemn the involvement of celebrity CEOs and entertainment celebrities in organized philanthropic endeavours for helping to 'make the world a better place' or entrenching the inherent inequalities of 'global capitalism'. Supporters typically praise their involvement on pragmatic grounds: the use of their money and public reputation promotes philanthropic objectives, irrespective of their individual motivations, which may be altruistic, self-interested, or a combination of both. As development economist and philanthropist Jeffrey Sachs puts it:

> In the very noisy and complicated world that we have, people that reach large numbers of people, like Madonna does, have an extraordinarily important role to play. When they're devoting their time, their money, their name, a lot of effort, a lot of organization skill to all of this, it makes a huge difference.
>
> (Sachs cited in Luscombe 2006)

Conversely, the involvement of western celebrity CEOs and entertainment celebrities in philanthropic causes has attracted criticism for embodying a 'capitalist philanthromentality' that allows individuals 'to exploit persons, environs and knowledges in the pursuit of wealth, and *only thereby accumulate a duty* to redistribute' that wealth (Nickel 2012: 176; emphasis in original). These criticisms are most forcibly expressed in neo-Marxist critiques of elite philanthropy, which present neoliberal capitalism and elite philanthropy as the transhistorical source and expression of inequality, respectively.

The leftist critique

In an article titled 'The Liberal Communists of Porto Davos', Slavoj Žižek (2006) argues that Bill Gates, George Soros, and other prominent entrepreneur-philanthropists are 'the enemy of every true progressive struggle today'. This is because while they endorse the 'anti-capitalist causes' of social responsibility – solving world hunger, protecting the environment, and so forth – they promote the free market as the solution to these problems, rather than seeing it as the cause of such problems. In doing so, Žižek (2006) argues that Gates and Soros are following in the footsteps of Andrew Carnegie, who was as famous for exploiting his workers as he was renowned for his philanthropy. Gates and Soros are similarly 'ethically problematic' public figures because they attempt to hide their pursuit of profit, and 'complicity in and co-responsibility for the miserable situation of the undeveloped', behind the 'humanitarian mask of charity' (Žižek 2006).

Žižek's addition of elite philanthropy to neo-Marxist critiques of global capital is not new, having antecedents in Karl Marx and Friedrich Engels' 1848 classic, *The Manifesto of the Communist Party*. In chapter 3 of that text, Marx and Engels denounce proponents of 'conservative/bourgeois socialism' as elite members of society who want to maintain the advantages of modern social conditions, rather than promote class struggle and genuine political reform. In their view, conservative socialists attempt to redress social grievances, but only by promoting improvements in the material, and not the political, conditions of the proletariat, in order to maintain the status quo. Identifiable members of this group include: 'economists, philanthropists, humanitarians, improvers of the condition of the working class, organisers of charity, members of societies for the prevention of cruelty to animals, temperance fanatics, [and] hole-and-corner reformers of every imaginable kind' (Marx and Engels 1848).

Marx and Engels' disdain for philanthropist-humanitarians resonates today with proponents of the contemporary leftist critique of new philanthropy, which includes corporate social responsibility initiatives and celebrity humanitarianism. Ilan Kapoor (2013: 4) argues that the problem with new philanthropy is that it depoliticizes the inherently political problem of socio-economic inequality, tackling 'the symptoms rather than the cause'. Following Žižek, he calls for a 'revolutionary overthrow of the neoliberal capitalist order' as the only genuine solution to inequality (Kapoor 2013: 124).

Critics contend that new philanthropy is apolitical because it undermines the perceived historical ethos of the discourse of humanitarian assistance – its promotion of the need for positive social change. New corporate philanthropy is seen to support the economic system that creates the need for philanthropy in the first place by relying on the mechanisms of the modern capitalist economy, for example, by incorporating philanthropic initiatives into marketing strategies to encourage investment or consumption (Nickel and Eikenberry 2009). Viewed from this perspective, new philanthropy refers to a false or bastardized form of philanthropy in that it promotes consumption, profit, and media celebration as the best means to demonstrate care for humanity. Such marketized philanthropy celebrates a continued culture of global capitalism, and disguises the exploitative nature of big business, by advancing the notion of 'giving back' through increased consumption – buying celebrity-endorsed products from which a portion of the profits are donated to humanitarian organizations – without acknowledging that it means giving back that which has already been taken away (Kapoor 2013: 114–27; Nickel and Eikenberry 2009: 980). It is not a discourse of social change, but rather a celebration by the privileged of the status quo.

Celebrity philanthropy as a major medium of new philanthropy is further decried for turning global citizenship into 'show business' (Alleyne 2005: 176; de Waal 2008). For critics, the aims of international aid organizations are potentially compromised by their growing reliance on celebrities, and thus the 'practices and predilections of the global media' (Cottle and Nolan 2007: 862, 865). This convergence is accused of leading to shallow and questionable media coverage of important social issues (Cottle and Nolan 2007: 869, 874), diverting resources away from the work of aid, distorting agenda-setting through a focus on 'safe' international issues while indulging 'a more palatable liberalism that operates at a safe remove from controversial issues at home' (Magubane 2008: 19), and guiding fans towards ill-conceived solutions to complex problems (Cooper 2007: 11–13; Littler 2008: 242). Celebrity philanthropy is therefore condemned for exacerbating existing regional inequalities between developed western nations and 'the rest of the world' by promoting wealthy western celebrities and first-world hegemony, and eliding the faces and voices of indigenous aid workers and the non-western poor as sources of knowledge and experience (Cottle and Nolan 2007: 870; Kapoor 2013: 38–42; Littler 2008: 246).

Celebrities are also tarred with the taint of false consciousness or even blatant hypocrisy because their philanthropic activism acts as a kind of brand extension, and is a part of the process of consolidating celebrity (Kapoor 2013: 19–25). Celebrity philanthropists not only get to 'stay in the news even when they have no new movie or CD to promote' (West 2007: 5), but also get to pull their personas out of the crude zone of narcissism and extravagant consumption and into the quasi-religious and heroic realm of altruism, compassion, and caring (de Waal 2008: 44; Littler 2008: 239, 241). Critics consequently present celebrity philanthropy as a contradiction in terms. Stars cannot be true philanthropists because of their vested interests as stakeholders in the capitalist system, which is seen to promote and depend on inequality. They can only 'play' at being the saviours of the disadvantaged because of their advantaged status as the personalized embodiment of wealth and privilege gained from the systematic exploitation of the poor (on celebrity philanthropy debates, see Jeffreys and Allatson 2015).

Critics conclude that new philanthropy has transformed the perceived traditional emphasis of philanthropy on compassionate benevolence and social change into a racist form of humanitarian voyeurism and individualistic commercialism (de Waal 2008: 54; Nickel and Eikenberry 2009). Far from creating active global citizens, it (re)creates a privileged class of western consumers who believe that they can deliver salvation to the rest of the world and be 'heroes-for-a-day' by consuming the 'right product' (Kapoor 2013: 80; Magubane 2008: 13). Modern philanthropy allegedly is no longer focused on the sufferers and their plight, but rather on the personal philanthropic experiences of celebrities and donors (Nickel 2012: 165). New philanthropy consequently is condemned as symptomatic of the individualistic, overly commercialized, and unequal nature of modern (western) societies.

While the leftist critique provides no *explicit* alternatives to commercial and celebritized elite philanthropy other than radical wealth distribution (an implied solution is the creation of an idealized version of the welfare state), there is a tacit notion that some philanthropic acts may be immune to critique. Kapoor (2013: 4), for example, claims that his purpose in arguing against corporate and celebrity humanitarianism is not to say that 'we should refrain from helping "poor" or marginalized people, or abstain from "rescuing" those affected by natural disasters. Of course we should come to their assistance!' This claim creates a distinction between elite philanthropy, which is 'contaminated' by its connection to money, power, and privilege, and hence considerations of self-interest, and the humanitarian or philanthropic impulse *per se*, which is theoretically free of this taint.

The moral correctness of the 'pure' philanthropic impulse and its exemption from critique appears, at least implicitly, to be grounded in an ethos of compassion. Yet as Lauren Berlant (2004) has shown, while conventionally evoking notions of 'selfless concern for others', the emotion 'compassion' implies in practice an 'interested' and 'unequal' social relation, with the emphasis being placed on what the privileged spectator feels and does for the suffering 'other'. There is always an inequity of exchange, which can produce tensions.

The modern association of philanthropy with individual choice and the exercise of privilege is indicated by the draft inclusion in the OED Online in 2002 of a new term, 'compassion fatigue' – 'apathy or indifference towards the suffering of others or to charitable causes acting on their behalf' ('Compassion, n.' 2000–). This may especially arise when there is little identification between the sources of charity and those who 'receive' the charity, and hence there is 'little payoff' for giving. The lack of an 'equitable' form of compassion undermines the notion of a pure, disinterested philanthropic urge that can be recuperated along with the eradication of capitalism. Indeed, the difficulty of incentivizing 'the not-destitute' to cultivate and exercise 'obligation' and 'benevolence' in a constant fashion towards 'those who need' explains why the development of professional philanthropy has been so closely entwined with the growth of business models and media advertising techniques of modern capitalism.

The leftist critique of (new) philanthropy is, therefore, vulnerable to several criticisms. It moralizes about the self-interested incentives of philanthropists in place of considering the practical and varied effects of philanthropy in different contexts, and idealizes an imagined pure humanitarian motive for philanthropy by default. It consequently homogenizes elite groups, and the assumed motivations and effects of elite philanthropy within the overarching narrative that all forms of elite philanthropy uphold an oppressive 'global governing regime' and suppress 'exploration of more radical alternatives' (Kapoor 2013: 120; Nickel 2012: 165). This conclusion is premised on the assumption that radical wealth redistribution is a practical and liberating option (Kapoor 2013: 124–7). But such an assumption is challenged by the example of the PRC – a nation with a history of radical wealth redistribution, and where private wealth and philanthropy are recent phenomena.

The example of China

Elite philanthropy and philanthropy more generally are new phenomena in the PRC, involving new social actors and new forms of social action that are developing largely as a result of government calls to develop a philanthropic culture in China. This is different to western accounts of philanthropy as the 'third sector', or part of 'civil society', in which citizen activity is assumed to have developed either independently of or ideally outside of the operation of government. Elite philanthropy in contemporary China primarily functions to support government social welfare objectives; it does not possess an established history of simultaneously serving to discipline the poor, and it is framed primarily as a patriotic social duty rather than a matter of individual conscience.

The recent nature of organized philanthropy in China is highlighted by a 1994 article in the *People's Daily* (*Renmin ribao* 人民日报) – the official media voice of the Communist Party. The article outlines the reasoning behind the establishment of the Liaoning Provincial Charity Federation, stating that its readers were probably seeing the Chinese-language term '*cishan* 慈善', which translates into English as both 'charity' and 'philanthropy', for the first time (Sun Yuemu 1994: 4). The article explains that the term '*cishan*' has a long and venerable history in China and refers to the act of showing kindness and compassion to others.[2] Hence, the Federation's mission was to encourage the establishment of domestic and international charities to assist the PRC Government in providing welfare services for 'the most pitiable' members of society, that is, impoverished, aged, and disabled people, who were unable to support themselves and had no family members to support them.

The article further explains that the concept and practice of charity/philanthropy had fallen into disrepute after the PRC's founding (Sun Yuemu 1994: 4). Although the article does not elaborate, this is because many traditional and Republican-era charities were associated with elite groups that became the target of revolutionary hostility – landowning gentry, entrepreneurs, and religious leaders, as well as foreign missionaries and 'imperialists' (Zhou and Zeng 2006: 4). Along with the political suppression of these groups, the Mao-era system of allocation ensured that rudimentary social services were provided for all Chinese citizens in theory through the urban work unit system and rural agricultural collectives (Wong 1994: 311–12). Additional services were provided for serving soldiers, the families of soldiers who had died fighting for the revolution, people affected by natural disasters, and households experiencing extreme hardship (Wong 1998: 141). These forms of state-provided welfare were not described as charity/philanthropy (*cishan*), but rather as services (*fuwu* 服务) relating to care (*guanhuai/zhaogu* 关怀/照顾), welfare (*fuli* 福利), relief (*jiuji* 救济), and allowances (*buzhu* 补助) (see also Hoffman in this book).

In fact, the article claims that during the height of the Maoist period – the now reviled Great Proletarian Cultural Revolution (1966–1976) – charity was denounced as the 'sugar-coated bullet' (*tangyi paodan* 糖衣炮弹) of the bourgeoisie (Sun Yuemu 1994: 4). In other words, organized charity which no longer existed in the PRC allegedly was condemned in Marxist terms as the means by which elite groups attempted to prevent class struggle (the revolution) by placating the labouring classes. The article concludes that the 'good name' of 'charity' had been rehabilitated in reform-era China to assist (not to replace) the state in meeting new social needs (Sun Yuemu 1994: 4).

The development of western-style conceptions of organized philanthropy in the PRC can thus be dated from the mid-1990s. This conclusion is confirmed by a search in the electronic database of the *People's Daily* for the keyword '*cishan*' between 1 October 1949 and 31 December 2014. The search obtained around 5,000 hits, with nearly 93 per cent occurring after 1978 (slightly fewer than 4,800 hits), and around 78 per cent in the 2000s (just over 4,000 hits) (*People's Daily* 1946–). As these figures suggest, in the aftermath of policies that decentralized economic management, and raised overall living standards at the expense of widening inequality, a space was created for philanthropies and private service providers to supplement the state's role in social welfare provision and diminish the potential for social unrest.

China today is a very unequal country. An often-cited measure of income inequality is the Gini coefficient, which ranges from 0 (perfect equality) to 1, with the 0.4 mark being understood by many analysts as a predictor for future social unrest (Yao and Wang 2013). In 1978, China had a Gini coefficient of 0.22, making it one of the most egalitarian nations in the world: everyone was poor. Figures released by the PRC's National Bureau of Statistics in 2013 indicate that the country's Gini coefficient had peaked at 0.491 in 2008, but still stood at 0.474 in 2012, making the PRC one of the most unequal nations in the world (Yao and Wang 2013). This high ranking demonstrates the partial success of the reform-era policy of rejecting Mao-era concepts of egalitarianism and allowing some people and areas 'to get rich first' in order to accelerate economic growth, and enable other people and regions to gradually achieve common prosperity (Deng Xiaoping 1983). But it also points to the emergence of new social problems as the sources of poverty and disadvantage in China have changed. Growing demands for mobile labour, and the corollary dismantling of the rural collectives and the urban work units, which operated on the basis of a sedentary population, meant that the state could no longer supply the highly variable range of services to employees and retirees that had been the norm (see also Cooper, Hoffman, and Sigley, in this book). The perception that something needed to be done about improving public service provision in this context meant that China faced the costly option of building a social welfare system. In other words, it had to create a range of standardized services that would be linked to the government's budget and made available to all citizens through government, community, and private service providers, such as unemployment and retirement benefits, and health care, aged care, disability services, education, and affordable housing (Watson 2012: 265; Wong 1994: 311–23).

Since the early 2000s, the PRC Government has attempted to enhance social service provision in part by encouraging the expansion of organized philanthropy through national policy. The Tenth Five-Year Plan for National Economic and Social Development from 2001 to 2005 proposed developing philanthropies in the context of an ageing population to strengthen the country's inadequate social security system (Zhonghua renmin gongheguo 2001: section 3, chapter 8). The Eleventh Five-Year Plan from 2006 to 2010 was more expansive, flowing from its overarching policy goal, under the leadership of the President Hu Jintao–Premier Wen Jiabao administration (2003–2013), of creating a 'harmonious socialist society' by addressing rising social inequality and promoting sustainable growth. It advocated expanding the non-profit sector, especially organizations supporting education and homeless youth (Zhonghua renmin gongheguo 2006: section 4, chapter 28). The Twelfth Five-Year Plan from 2011 to 2015 proposed using tax incentives to create a comprehensive system of registered private industry, trade, and professional associations, and urban and rural community organizations to provide services for orphaned, elderly, disabled, and disadvantaged people (Zhonghua renmin gongheguo 2011: section 1, chapter 39). Confirming the new-found importance of philanthropy in China, the State Council issued a document 'On Promoting the Healthy Development of Philanthropy' in November 2014, which urges all levels of government to introduce tax incentives to develop a comprehensive and legally registered philanthropic/volunteering sector that will complement government welfare services by 2020 (Guowuyuan 2014).

Such policies may be broadly compared to the longstanding tax incentives supporting organized philanthropy in the USA. However, as detailed below, the scale and aggression of these publicly assisted moves towards professionalization suggests that the installation of philanthropy as an explicit technique of government in the PRC does not have an obvious parallel in the USA. It also points to a radical reconfiguring of the perceived 'social contract' in China, with the responsibility for wealth redistribution and social justice being redefined as the responsibility of the beneficiaries of wealth creation, rather than solely the Party-state.

To facilitate this agenda, the PRC Government has altered the regulatory framework governing the operation of philanthropy in China. These changes aim to develop an indigenous non-profit sector by supporting demonstrably local organizations while continuing to restrict the role of foreign donors and actors, in order to moderate the sector's growth 'until the government can see how it evolves and how it develops' (Saich 2015; see also Fitzgerald 2012: 75–8). In 2004, the State Council issued regulations permitting the registration of two different types of foundations: (1) those that can raise funds from the public and generally refer to government-organized NGOs ('public fundraising foundations', *gongmu jijinhui* 公募基金会); and (2) those that must rely on private funding from wealthy individuals because they are not permitted to raise funds from the public ('non-public fundraising foundations', *feigongmu jijinhui* 非公募基金会) (State Council 2004). This has encouraged the rapid development of a foundation sector that is not ostensibly organized by government departments, even though most non-public foundations support government social welfare objectives (Feng 2013). In 2004, there were fewer than 900 public foundations and no non-public foundations in China; by mid-2015, there were more than 4,400 foundations, comprising approximately 1,500 public foundations and 2,900 non-public foundations (China Foundation Center n.d.).

This shift towards the professionalization of organized philanthropy and governing socio-economic inequality at 'a half-step removed' is underscored by other developments. In 2010, the China Foundation Center was established under the auspices of the Ministry of Civil Affairs, with funding from 35 foundations, to promote financial and operational transparency in the emerging foundation sector (foundationcenter.org.cn). In December 2011, the Ministry of Civil Affairs of the PRC (2011) issued guidelines promoting the transparent reporting of charitable donations. In 2012, the Central Government committed funds of CNY 200 million to develop domestic NGOs (He 2012: 3). Pilot programmes were subsequently started in 19 provinces, allowing NGOs to register directly with civil affairs departments and submit tenders for government funding, instead of having to first find a sponsoring government organization. Also in 2012, the Shenzhen Provincial Government, under the auspices of the Ministry of Civil Affairs, launched an annual China Charity Fair, and the PRC Government introduced a two-year nationwide campaign to promote volunteering, especially around 'Lei Feng Day' in March (Jeffreys and Su 2013).[3] In 2013, the Beijing and Guangzhou Municipal Governments, and the Anhui Provincial Government, introduced provisional regulations encouraging the independent organization of NGOs by banning government officials from joining them ('Guangzhou bans government staff from NGOs' 2013). These changes introduce a new degree of separation between 'government' and 'society', with Chinese media reports indicating that a draft Charity Law, which has been drafted and debated numerous times since 2005, would be submitted to the PRC's legislature for formal review at the end of 2015 ('Charity law draft expected to be reviewed in 2015' 2015).

The PRC's Ministry of Civil Affairs has also recognized and rewarded corporate philanthropy since 2005 through a system of prestigious charity awards – the China Charity Awards (*Zhonghua cishan jiang* 中华慈善奖). Government officials and other individuals receive awards for their charitable activities, whereas entrepreneurs from the private and state-owned sectors are recognized for the extent of their donations. In fact, President Hu Jintao became the first government and Party leader to present philanthropy as crucial to China's economic development and modernization, when he gave a speech to announce the award winners in December 2008. The speech, which a report in the *People's Daily* described as a mobilization directive, called on Chinese citizens from all walks of life to help develop a philanthropic culture in the PRC, in order to realize a moderately affluent and harmonious society as soon as possible (Liu Weitao 2008).

Entertainment and sports celebrities feature more regularly on the China Philanthropy List (*Zhongguo cishan bang* 中国慈善榜), launched in 2005 by the *China Philanthropy Times* (*Gongyishibao* 公益时报). The *China Philanthropy Times* is sponsored by the China Association of Social Workers under the auspices of the Ministry of Civil Affairs (www.gongyishibao.com). The China Philanthropy List recognizes corporations and entrepreneurs based on the extent of their donations, and entertainment and sports stars for promoting public awareness of philanthropy through media publicity. In 2013, the *Chinese Philanthropist* magazine (*Zhongguo cishanjia* 中国慈善家), an independent non-profit venture, issued its first China Celebrity Philanthropist list (*Zhongguo cishan mingren bang* 中国慈善名人榜) ('Meiji 2013 zhongguo cishan mingren bang' 2013).

The PRC's prestigious charity awards and rankings aim to celebrate the newly rich as philanthropists, provide aspirational role models and overcome 'hatred of the wealthy' (*chouhen furen* 仇恨富人). Such 'hatred' is a documented phenomenon in contemporary China because 'ordinary people' tend to assume that those who have become newly rich along with the partial privatization of the economy are 'immoral', having obtained their wealth through corruption or the 'theft' of formerly communal assets. This assumption resulted in the *Forbes*' 'China Rich Lists' of the early 2000s being dubbed the lists of 'China's Most Wanted' (Wu 2007).

The fragile political credentials of the newly rich in China are underscored by the public backlash against corporate and celebrity philanthropy that occurred in the aftermath of the Sichuan earthquake. From mid to late May 2008, multinational corporations with operations in China, such as Coca-Cola and McDonald's, were accused of 'donation-stinginess' in chain letters posted on the internet and disseminated via mobile phone networks. The letters encouraged patriotic citizens to boycott the products of 'exploitative' foreign companies who had failed to 'give back' sufficiently to their host society (Jeffreys 2011: 13–14). While initially directed at multinationals, such criticisms were soon directed towards two of China's richest sports celebrities in the run-up to the Beijing 2008 Olympic Games. Yao Ming, formerly a basketball player with the US National Basketball Association, and Liu Xiang, China's first male Olympic gold medal winner in the track and field, were both accused of donating insignificant sums of money when compared to their vast earnings from sports and product endorsement (Yao Bin 2008).

By early 2009, Chinese netizens were calling on government departments and other organizations to publish earthquake-related 'donation lists' in a populist bid to expose 'dishonest advertising' by corporate and celebrity donors (Jeffreys 2011: 15–16). Subsequent reports that the China Association of Social Workers, which issues the China Philanthropy List, intended to publish a 'name-and-shame list' of companies that had failed to honour their donation pledges, sparked widespread controversy. An online survey of netizens' views on the web portal NetEase.com concluded that nearly 70 per cent supported the 'blacklisting' of companies and celebrities that had failed to honour their pledges (Jeffreys 2011: 16).

Criticisms of corporate and celebrity philanthropy in most cases proved to be premature or unfounded. The perception that multinational companies were more than willing to exploit business opportunities in China, and unwilling to 'give back', was reinforced by a lack of transparency and clarity in the reporting of donations, and the time-delay required to obtain authorization for donations that exceeded the limits set by the corporate social responsibility policies of international companies (McGinnis *et al.* 2009). Media and public outcry over 'fake celebrity pledges' was based in part on a failure to understand that pledges are often given in stages rather than as a bulk sum, for practical reasons relating to donor financial management, legal and administrative procedures, and ensuring that recipient charities have actually commenced the work for which money was pledged (Jeffreys 2011: 8). However, the outcry demonstrates public distrust of the newly rich in China.

In Zhang Ziyi's case, accusations of charity fraud by reportedly millions of netizens led Zhang to hire a team of US-based lawyers to examine her finances and those of the Ziyi Zhang Foundation, and to give an exclusive interview to the *China Daily* in an effort to clear her name (Jeffreys 2011: 7–9). During that interview, a tearful Zhang Ziyi apologized for her lack of experience with organized philanthropy, which had led to administrative delays and encouraged false accusations of charity fraud. She also vowed to continue 'giving back' to the country and society that had subsidized her drama tuition and made her famous. Here, rather than the philanthropy being strictly a mode of disciplining the poor, state and public expectations of philanthropy became a mode of disciplining the newly emplaced rich, and especially those with public profiles.

Indeed, in the wake of the Zhang Ziyi scandal, concerned Chinese netizens escalated matters by widening their scrutiny of elite philanthropy to include the allegedly fraudulent disaster-relief efforts of a range of Chinese entertainment stars, including actor Li Bingbing, singer Hu Yanbing, and movie star Zhao Wei (Jeffreys 2011: 10). Journalists further highlighted the existence of tensions regarding 'the proper administration of wealth' when reporting on the visit of Bill Gates and Warren Buffett to China in September 2010 to talk with Chinese entrepreneurs about The Giving Pledge ('Gates, Buffett talk charity' 2010). Many Chinese entrepreneurs allegedly were reluctant to attend, fearing that public knowledge of such a meeting would mean an automatic obligation to relinquish their wealth. In other words, wealthy people in China were concerned that state and public expectations would *compel them* to be more philanthropic than they might desire to be. This concern is almost inconceivable in western societies; it flows from the not-so-distant history of state-enforced nationalization of private wealth in China, and insecurity over the degree of government and public acceptance of private wealth amid evident poverty.

As the preceding examples demonstrate, entrepreneurs and celebrities in China are viewed as having a social obligation to 'give back *more*' precisely because they have surplus wealth and brand power. At the same time, it is assumed that the philanthropic activities of public individuals should be open to public scrutiny because their money and status requires them to accept responsibility for leading positive social change. The proliferation of elite philanthropy scandals on interactive media formats further suggests that China's netizens view public criticism as a positive incitement for public individuals to do more and better rather than potential or actual discouragement. The rich are to be disciplined by the people, and not the other way around.

In summary, elite philanthropy in present-day China is propelled by a different logic from that which structures elite philanthropy in the USA and in western societies generally. Elite philanthropy is a new phenomenon in the PRC that has been presented, to date, not as a matter of individual choice, but rather as the duty of a successful citizen committed to furthering China's economic reforms and realizing prosperity for all. Corporations and celebrities predominantly give to projects organized by government-affiliated charities and federations – that is, large-scale operations dealing with disaster relief, education, health care, and poverty alleviation – rather than to NGOs, which until recently a history of political controls has ensured tend to be small-scale operations relating to recreation and leisure that are unable to raise public funds (Feng 2013). Government-affiliated charities are funded chiefly by state-owned enterprises, for the simple reason that state-owned enterprises are expected to contribute to them (Shue 1998: 344). Private entrepreneurs contribute voluntarily to government-affiliated charities to facilitate business by obtaining the support and protection of local government authorities, which automatically accrues to and advantages state-owned enterprises 'whose top managers are typically appointed by the government' (Li and Zhang 2007: 795; Su and He 2010: 73–90). For example, entrepreneurs may give generously to causes favoured by local governments to negotiate de facto tax reductions and loans from state and city commercial banks (Shue 2011: 768; Su and He 2010: 87). CEOs and celebrities also contribute to government-affiliated charities because they are asked to donate by local government officials, and may not be able to refuse, and because they may gain improved social standing in recipient and broader communities from associated publicity (Shue 1998: 344–6, 2011: 768). Unlike in western societies, China's governing authorities thus often play a direct rather than an indirect role in structuring the nature and organization of elite philanthropy. These links may be viewed negatively by those who conceive of private philanthropy as the 'third sector' and a wedge against state expansionism, but perhaps positively by those who believe that philanthropy is 'no substitute for strong governmental support for social welfare' (McGoey 2014: 109).

The obligation of wealthy individuals to 'give back' in China also undermines the voluntary principle of philanthropy in western societies, and the assumption that corporations and individuals are free to determine how much of their resources they wish to use on public endeavours. If wealthy individuals are obliged to give back more and publicly, rather than doing so voluntarily based on formal business assessments and personal sentiment, then philanthropy becomes a different and largely unexamined means for ensuring the redistribution of wealth. Alternatively, it can be viewed as placing a populist and informal 'tax' on fame and success. Either way, philanthropy, conceived as a new technique of government in China, deploys a more explicit means of ensuring the self-discipline of individuals and corporations in motivating wealth redistribution than has typically been the case in western societies. Neo-Marxist critiques that presuppose a capricious, unregulated freedom on the part of elite philanthropists lose some of their force in this context.

Conclusion

This chapter uses a governmentality and genealogical approach to examine the development of elite philanthropy in the USA and China, and related public debates about such phenomena. The (western) leftist critique is based on the idea that elite philanthropy is a reflection of entrenched socio-economic inequality and an obstacle to social change because it entrenches the status quo. In China, market-based economic reform was consistent with raising living standards and a revival of political legitimacy for the Communist Party following the proclaimed 'ten-year disaster' of the Cultural Revolution, and the associated rejection of an ideological commitment to class struggle and egalitarianism. Economic reform in China has been transformative in its effects, more by the creation of wealth than by its distribution, much as the leftist critique assumes a radical redistribution of existing wealth would be transformative in mature capitalist economies.

Elite philanthropy is seen in the Chinese context of expanding but unequally distributed wealth as part of the solution to problems thrown up by efforts to reverse a (perceived) failed experiment to distribute wealth equally through society. This discourse of elite philanthropy – which is inherent in both government policy and public criticism of celebrity philanthropists – does not turn on an assumption that the rich deserve their wealth, and redistribute it because of an individual and self-cultivated sense of moral duty, as in the Carnegian view. Rather, wealth creation is seen as the only antidote to entrenched poverty, but its negative distributive consequences are recognized, and philanthropy is viewed as the price that must be paid by elites. Humanitarian assistance is the collective duty of elites, rather than the ethically informed choice of individuals.

This conception in some ways stakes a middle ground between the leftist critique (which decries the hypocrisy of elites giving amid material incentives to do so) and supporters of elite philanthropy (who believe that elites can, as a practical matter, mobilize their own capital and the capital of non-elites in a way that non-elites cannot). It is founded on entrenched distrust of elites in a society with a history of socialist idealism, but also a pragmatic recognition of the potential to redistribute wealth while maintaining the apparatus that creates it.

Charting how ideas concerning elite philanthropy have emerged in China partly undermines the arguments of Žižek (2006) and others (Kapoor 2013;

Nickel 2012). To the extent that it has validity in western contexts, the leftist critique in its general form is premised on an understanding that radical wealth redistribution can be a practical and liberating option. That option is generally viewed as a retrograde step in a country with a history of radical wealth redistribution. At the same time, the emergence of super-rich entrepreneurs is viewed with distrust and cynicism. In this context, mediatized elite philanthropy can be a tool to reduce such distrust and engender acceptance of the liberating but uncertain consequences of reform.

Examples such as Zhang Ziyi also underscore the limits of the liberal-Carnegian-Gates conception of philanthropy in China. Superficially, China can be viewed as importing ideas of American-style philanthropy, superimposed in an ad hoc fashion on a nascent capitalist system, given growing realization of the limits of the PRC Government's welfare provision capability, which has accompanied experimentation with the market mechanism. But the popular criticism of elite philanthropists is different in China to western counterparts. The debt to society of elites is not a historical artefact as it is in western societies, but rather the consequence and work-in-progress of an economic 'new deal'. This 'new deal' imposes a discipline on elites that is revealed most starkly when breaches occur, as in the case of corporate-celebrity philanthropy scandals in China. Hence, the chapter highlights the utility of considering elite philanthropy, and related debates, from the point of view of a different governmental system, in which the means by which philanthropy is deployed as a mode of government is, ipso facto, repositioned.

Acknowledgements

This research was supported under the Australian Research Council's Future Fellowship funding scheme (FT100100238). Thanks to Ivan Roberts for commenting on early drafts of the chapter.

Notes

1 Elite philanthropy in the formative years of the USA had a China connection. Some of the USA's first multi-millionaires and renowned philanthropists, such as John Jacob Astor (1763–1848) and Stephen Girard (1750–1831), made a part of their fortune by being among the first group of Americans to engage in maritime trade with China (Dolin 2012: 92–4). That trade and any possibility for a conjoined history of philanthropic practice were disrupted by the PRC's experiment with revolutionary socialism after 1949.

2 The term '*cishan*' was first documented in the sixth century historical chronicle known as the *Book of Wei* (*Wei shu* 魏书), and entered into the vernacular Chinese language in the early twentieth century via Japan as a term to describe charities run by foreigners in China (Li Ru 2009).

3 Lei Feng, a young soldier with the People's Liberation Army, died in a vehicle accident in 1962. He became famous in 1963, when his alleged diary, which celebrates Mao Zedong Thought and the socialist ideals of altruism and working hard for collective goals, was promoted via a campaign to 'Learn from Comrade Lei Feng' as an

instructional model of exemplary socialist citizenship. Since then, commemorative events such as an annual 'Lei Feng Day' have ensured that everyone in China is familiar with the Lei Feng 'Spirit' of selfless public service. In 2000, the Central Committee of the Chinese Communist Youth League and Chinese Young Volunteers Association renamed Lei Feng Day on 5 March as China Youth Volunteer Service Day, associating it with both the original 1960s campaign to 'Learn from Lei Feng' and the United Nations' International Volunteer Day. In 2012, the fiftieth anniversary of his death, Lei Feng became the 'celebrity face' of a government-led campaign to promote philanthropy/volunteering (see Jeffreys and Su in this book).

References

Alleyne, M.D. (2005) 'The United Nations' celebrity diplomacy', *SAIS Review*, 25, 1: 175–84.

Andrew, D.T. (1989) *Philanthropy and Police: London Charity in the Eighteenth Century*, Princeton: Princeton University Press.

Berlant, L. (ed.) (2004) *Compassion: The Culture and Politics of an Emotion*, New York: Routledge.

Carnegie, A. (1889) 'Wealth', *North American Review*, 340, 391: 653–64.

'Charity law draft expected to be reviewed in 2015' (2015) *Ecns.cn*, 11 March. Online. Available: www.ecns.cn/cns-wire/2015/03-11/157641.shtml (accessed 10 June 2015).

China Foundation Center (n.d.) Data. Online. Available: http://data.foundationcenter.org.cn/foundation.html (accessed 15 June 2015).

'China's new president Xi Jinping calls for "great renaissance"' (2013) *News.com.au*, 17 March. Online. Available: www.news.com.au/world-news/chinas-new-president-xi-jinping-calls-for-great-renaissance/story-fndir2ev-1226599385204 (accessed 10 June 2015).

'Compassion, n.' (2000–) *The Oxford English Dictionary Online*, Oxford: Oxford University Press.

Cooper, A. (2007) 'Celebrity diplomacy and the G8: Bono and Bob as legitimate international actors', Working Paper 29, Centre for International Governance. Online. Available: www.isn.ethz.ch/isn/Digital-Library/Publications/Detail/?ord516=OrgaGrp&ots591=0c54e3b3-1e9c-be1e-2c24-a6a8c7060233&lng=en&id=39553 (accessed 10 June 2015).

Cottle, S. and Nolan, D. (2007) 'Global humanitarianism and the changing aid–media field', *Journalism Studies*, 8, 6: 862–78.

'Current pledgers' (2015) The Giving Pledge. Online. Available: http://givingpledge.org (accessed 15 June 2015).

de Waal, A. (2008) 'The humanitarian carnival: a celebrity vogue', *World Affairs: A Journal of Ideas and Debate*, Fall: 43–55.

Deng Xiaoping (1983) 'Our work in all fields should contribute to the building of socialism with Chinese characteristics', 12 January, *Selected Works of Deng Xiaoping Volume 3* (1982–1992). Online. Available: www.china.org.cn/english/features/dengxiaoping/103381.htm (accessed 10 June 2015).

Dolin, E.J. (2012) *When America First Met China: An Exotic History of Tea, Drugs and Money in the Age of Sail*, London and New York: Liveright Publishing Company.

Edwards, L. and Jeffreys, E. (eds) (2010) *Celebrity in China*, Hong Kong: Hong Kong University Press.

Feng Xiaoming (2013) 'China's charitable foundations: development and policy-related issues', Working Paper No. 485, Stanford Center for International Development.

Online. Available: http://siepr.stanford.edu/?q=/system/files/shared/documents/485_XiaomingFeng.pdf (accessed 10 June 2015).

Fitzgerald, J. (2012) 'Supporting China's expanding non-profit sector', in H.K Anheier and B. Lorentz (eds), *Bridging the Trust Divide: Cultural Diplomacy and Fostering Understanding Between China and the West*, Berlin: Stiftung Mercator, pp. 75–80.

Foucault, M. (1991 [1978]), 'Governmentality' (Lecture at the Collège de France, 1 February 1978), in G. Burchell, C. Gordon, and P. Miller (eds), *The Foucault Effect: Studies in Governmentality*, Chicago: University of Chicago Press, pp. 87–104.

Foucault, M. (2004) *Society Must be Defended*, trans. D. Macey, London: Penguin Books.

'Gates, Buffett talk charity with China's super-rich' (2010) *Associated Press*, 29 September. Online. Available: www.msnbc.msn.com/id/39422689/ns/us_news-giving/t/gates-buffett-talk-charity-chinas-super-rich (accessed 10 June 2015).

Gross, R.A. (2003) 'Giving in America: from charity to philanthropy', in L.J. Friedman and M.D. McGarvie (eds), *Charity, Philanthropy, and Civility in American History*, Cambridge: Cambridge University Press, pp. 29–48.

'Guangzhou bans government staff from NGOs' (2013) *Global Times*, 28 October, p. 5.

Guowuyuan [State Council of the PRC] (2014) *Guowuyuan guanyu cujin cishan shiye jiankang fazhan de zhidao yijian* [Guidance from the State Council on promoting the healthy development of philanthropy], 24 November. Online. Available: www.gov.cn/zhengce/content/2014-12/18/content_9306.htm (accessed 10 June 2015).

He, D. (2012) 'NGO: deregulation for overseas charities "in the pipeline": more funding for NGOs', *China Daily*, 21 August, p. 3.

Hu Jiali and Zhang Lei (2012) 'Gongdan zeren gongjie hexie' [Shared responsibility to build harmonious society], *Zhonghua Gongshang Shibao*, 17 July. Online. Available: http://news.hexun.com/2012-07-17/143633519.html (accessed 10 June 2015).

Jeffreys, E. (2011) 'Zhang Ziyi and China's celebrity philanthropy scandals', *PORTAL Journal of Multidisciplinary International Studies*, 8, 1: 1–21. Online. Available: http://epress.lib.uts.edu.au/journals/index.php/portal/article/view/1627/2292 (accessed 16 June 2015).

Jeffreys, E. and Allatson, P. (eds) (2015) *Celebrity Philanthropy*, Bristol: Intellect.

Jeffreys, E. and Su, X.-Z. (2013) 'China's growing culture of philanthropy', *Asian Currents*, 92: 22–4.

Kapoor, I. (2013) *Celebrity Humanitarianism: The Ideology of Global Charity*, Abingdon: Routledge.

Kiviat, B. and Gates, B. (2008) 'Making capitalism more creative', *Time*, 31 July. Online. Available: http://content.time.com/time/magazine/article/0,9171,1828417,00.html (accessed 10 June 2015).

Li, H. and Zhang, Y. (2007) 'The role of managers' political networking and functional experience in new venture performance: evidence from China's transition economy', *Strategic Management Journal*, 28, 8: 791–804.

Li Ru (2009) 'Lun shehui bianqian beijing xia shuyu "cishan" de chuxian yu puji' [On the history and different uses of the term 'charity' in China], *Dalian Ligongdaxue Xuebao*, 30, 4: 90–4.

Littler, J. (2008) '"I feel your pain": cosmopolitan charity and the public fashioning of the celebrity soul', *Social Semiotics*, 18, 2: 237–51.

Liu Weitao (2008) 'Hu Jintao: fayang rendaozhuyi jingshen reqing canyu cishan huodong' [Hu Jintao: develop the spirit of humanitarianism, engage in philanthropy enthusiastically], *Renmin Ribao*, 6 December. Online. Available: http://cpc.people.com.cn/GB/64093/64094/8471211.html (accessed 10 June 2015).

'Look to the Stars: the world of celebrity giving' (2006–2015) Look to the Stars. Online. Available: www.looktothestars.org (accessed 10 June 2015).

Luscombe, B. (2006) 'Madonna finds a cause', *Time*, 18 August. Online. Available: www.time.com/time/magazine/article/0,9171,1223372,00.html (accessed 10 June 2015).

McGinnis, A., Pellegrin, J., Shum, Y., Teo, J., and Wu, J. (2009) 'The Sichuan Earthquake and the changing landscape of CSR in China', *Knowledge@Wharton*, 20 April. Online. Available: http://knowledge.wharton.upenn.edu/article.cfm?articleid=2213 (accessed 10 June 2015).

McGoey, L. (2014), 'The philanthropic state: market–state hybrids in the philanthrocapitalist turn', *Third World Quarterly*, 35, 1: 109–125.

Magubane, Z. (2008) 'The (Product)Red man's burden: charity, celebrity, and the contradictions of coevalness', *Journal of Pan African Studies*, 2, 6: 1–25.

Marx, K. and Engels, F. (1848) 'Manifesto of the Communist Party', *Marx/Engels Selected Works, Volume 1*, Moscow: Progress Publishers, 1969, pp. 98–137. Online. Available: www.marxists.org/archive/marx/works/1848/communist-manifesto/index.htm (accessed 10 June 2015).

'Meiji 2013 zhongguo cishan mingren bang' [2013 China Celebrity Philanthropy List] (2013) *China Philanthropist*, 19 May. Online. Available: www.icixun.com/spec/2013/csmrb (accessed 10 June 2015).

Ministry of Civil Affairs of the People's Republic of China (2011) '"Gongyi cishan juanzhu xinxi gongkai zhiyin" jinri zhengshi fabu' [Guidelines 'on the disclosure of public information about charitable donations' released today], *Minzhengbu Menhu Wangzhan*, 16 December. Online. Available: www.mca.gov.cn/article/zwgk/mzyw/201112/20111200243894.shtml (accessed 4 February 2015).

Nickel, P.M. (2012) 'Philanthromentality: celebrity parables as technologies of transfer', *Celebrity Studies*, 3, 2: 164–82.

Nickel, P. and Eikenberry, A. (2009) 'A critique of the discourse of marketized philanthropy', *American Behavioral Scientist*, 52, 7: 974–89.

Ostrower, F. (1995) *Why the Wealthy Give: The Culture of Elite Philanthropy*, Princeton: University of Princeton Press.

People's Daily (1946–present) Jinbao dianzi chuban zhongxin, Beijing; Oriprobe Information Services, Windsor, Canada, www.oriprobe.com (accessed 26 February 2015).

'Philanthropy' (n.d.) Philanthropy Australia. Online. Available: www.philanthropy.org.au/about-us/vision-and-mission (accessed 10 June 2015).

Saich, T. (2015) 'Interview with Tony Saich: Chinese philanthropy on the cusp', *China Development Brief*, 12 January. Online. Available: http://chinadevelopmentbrief.cn/articles/interview-tony-saich-part-one (accessed 10 June 2015).

Shue, V. (1998) 'State power and the philanthropic impulse in China today', in W.F. Ilchman, S.N. Katz, and E.L. Queen (eds), *Philanthropy in the World's Traditions*, Bloomington: Indiana University Press, pp. 332–54.

Shue, V. (2011) 'The political economy of compassion: China's "charity supermarket" saga', *Journal of Contemporary China*, 20, 72: 751–72.

State Council (2004) 'Regulations on the Management of Foundations, issued 8 March 2004, effective 1 June 2004'. Online. Available: www.cecc.gov/resources/legal-provisions/regulations-on-the-management-of-foundations-chinese-text (accessed 10 June 2015).

Su, J. and He, J. (2010) 'Does giving lead to getting? Evidence from Chinese private enterprises', *Journal of Business Ethics*, 93, 1: 73–90.

Sun Yuemu (1994) 'Wei cishan zhengming' [Rehabilitating charity], *Renmin Ribao*, 24 February, p. 4.

Wang Zhuoqiong (2008) 'Quake triggers donation deluge', *China Daily*, 5 December. Online. Available: www.chinadaily.com.cn/china/2008-12/05/content_7273896.htm (accessed 4 February 2015).

Watson, A. (2012) 'Building social welfare in China: providing retirement incomes in a transforming economy', in H. McKay and Song Ligang (eds), *Rebalancing and Sustaining Growth in China*, Canberra: ANU EPress, pp. 265–87.

West, D.M. (2007) *Angelina, Mia, and Bono: Celebrities and International Development*, Washington: The Brookings Institution.

Wong, L. (1994) 'Privatization of social welfare in post-Mao China', *Asian Survey*, 34, 4: 307–25.

Wong, L. (1998) *Marginalization and Social Welfare in China*, London and New York: Routledge.

World Bank (2015) Poverty and inequality database, World Bank Group. Online. Available: http://databank.worldbank.org/data/views/variableselection/selectvariables.aspx?source=Poverty-and-Inequality-Database (accessed 12 January 2015).

Wu, Z. (2007) 'China's "most wanted" millionaires', *Asia Times*, 19 September. Online. Available: www.atimes.com/atimes/China_Business/II19Cb02.html (accessed 10 June 2015).

Yao Bin (ed.) (2008) 'Do public lists showing quake donations by the rich serve a purpose? No price on love', *Beijing Review*, 25 June. Online. Available: www.bjreview.com.cn/forum/txt/2008-06/14/content_127482.htm# (accessed 10 June 2015).

Yao, K. and Wang, A. (2013) 'China lets Gini out of the bottle: wide wealth gap', *Reuters*, 18 January. Online. Available: www.reuters.com/article/2013/01/18/us-china-economy-income-gap-idUSBRE90H06L20130118 (accessed 10 June 2015).

Zhonghua renmin gongheguo guomin jingji he shehui fazhan di shi ge wunian jihua gangyao [PRC's Tenth Five-Year Plan for National Economic and Social Development] (2001) National People's Congress, 15 March. Online. Available: www.moc.gov.cn/zhuzhan/jiaotongguihua/guojiaguihua/guojiaxiangguan_ZHGH/200709/t20070927_420874.html (accessed 4 February 2015).

Zhonghua renmin gongheguo guomin jingji he shehui fazhan di shiyi ge wunian guihua gangyao [PRC's Eleventh Five-Year Plan for National Economic and Social Development] (2006) National People's Congress, 16 March. Online. Available: http://news.xinhuanet.com/misc/2006-03/16/content_4309517.htm (accessed 4 February 2015).

Zhonghua renmin gongheguo guomin jingji he shehui fazhan di shier ge wunian guihua gangyao [PRC's Twelfth Five-Year Plan for National Economic and Social Development] (2011) National People's Congress, 16 March. Online. Available: www.gov.cn/2011lh/content_1825838.htm (accessed 4 February 2015).

Zhou Qiuguang and Zeng Guilin (2006) *Zhongguo cishan jianshi* [A Short History of Charity in China], Beijing: Renmin Chubanshe.

Žižek, S. (2006) 'The liberal communists of Porto Davos', *In These Times*, 11 April, www.inthesetimes.com/site/main/article/2574 (accessed 10 June 2015).

Zunz, O. (2012) *Philanthropy in America: A History*, Princeton and Oxford: Princeton University Press.

8 Serving and providing for those 'in need'

'Intermediary' spaces and practices of liaising, collaborating, and mobilizing in urban China

Lisa Hoffman

> The difference between the rich and the poor is too great in China now. Neither government subsidies nor the market alone can solve this problem. We must have volunteers.
>
> (Author interview, Dalian-based academic, May 2010)

Providing for community members who are 'in need' is a critical governmental problem in contemporary societies, including in urban China. Examining how such provisioning happens, through what mechanisms, and according to what norms and rationalities not only helps us to understand mentalities of governing, but also how this problem-space is constituted. As significant shifts are taking place in welfare provisioning in urban China, and as new forms of inequality and human suffering emerge in cities, experiments are enacted to meet the new 'needs' of citizens. Such experiments are helping to shape what I call an 'intermediary' space of social action – a space imbued with politics and compassion that are neither exclusively of the state nor of society, and where governmental practices of *liaising*, *collaborating*, and *mobilizing* are being prioritized.

The governmental problem of urban inequality and disadvantage is not, however, distinct to China, and thus we must make sense of reforms in urban welfare provisioning both within China's own history and as a part of global efforts in the domain of serving and provisioning. This means that solutions for providing for those 'in need' across geographic locations often exhibit *shared* expressions and rationalities of care, and governmental strategies, technologies and styles of thought (Rose *et al.* 2006). For instance, the private transfer of funds through philanthropy, remittances, and investments from wealthy to poorer nations is far outpacing the transfer of public funds, suggesting a global acceptance of non-governmental organizations (NGOs), humanitarian agencies, and individuals as critical for 'doing development'.[1] Discussions of 'human economies' in anthropology also note that while there is an increasing precarity in human life, our contemporary moment is 'accompanied by a structure of feeling that privileges empathy, care, and compassion', whether this care is expressed in terms of liberal altruism or familial relations (Muehlebach 2013: 300; see also

Bornstein 2012; Williams 1977). The practices adopted thus resonate both with a more global rationality of care of how 'best' to address social problems – such as through individual efforts, 'civil society' organizations, and humanitarian relief – and with a shared 'structure of feeling' of compassion, empathy, and the desire to help others. Solutions for welfare provisioning are sought in a simultaneously local and global problem-space of technical answers and affective conditions, producing distinct global assemblages and spaces of social action. In other words, there is a 'shared problematization' of the role of the state in such efforts, and some common interventions in the problem space of urban need, such as volunteering and non-profit work.

This chapter is concerned with the shift in China from state-led and directed welfare provisioning to a more complex governmental assemblage that incorporates diverse mechanisms. It is based on fieldwork conducted in Dalian City in 2009, 2010, and 2012, with a focus on interactions with individuals participating in charitable activities (*cishan huodong* 慈善活动), college students in organized volunteer groups, and organization leaders who are formally promoting philanthropy and volunteerism.[2] The research has notably been with organizations that are considered acceptable by the government – those working on issues of poverty alleviation, disaster relief, care for children, and general inequality in urban regions rather than those advocating for labour reforms or other more sensitive issues. However, instead of emphasizing control (*kongzhi* 控制) and plans (*jihua* 计划) as during high socialism, Chinese state governance now advocates guidance (*zhidao* 指导) and a more customer-oriented service (*fuwu* 服务) by state administrators, and more recently ideas of social governance, drawing on governmental technologies in a variety of systems (Hoffman 2006; Sigley 2006; Jeffreys and Sigley 2009). Reforms in the welfare provisioning for urban residents, especially the shift away from work unit (*danwei* 单位) based services and towards a more 'society-based' system that includes the market, employers, non-governmental (or social) organizations, non-profit organizations (NPOs), government-organized non-governmental organizations (GONGOs), philanthropic giving, and citizen volunteers, are not only shaping this domain, but also the actors engaging in such services.

The chapter begins with a brief overview of the problematization of the socialist state urban welfare system and the recent adoption of a more diverse system of social service provisioning. The second section argues that this problematization has created an intermediary space of social action in which the practices of liaising, collaborating, and mobilizing have become more prominent. These practices signal both the use of more intermediary modes of governing and that new kinds of actors (and actants) are needed to engage in these practices. For instance, liaison work is occurring in municipal experiments in citizen service provisioning and in engaging with social organizations; social organizations are collaborating with formal government entities and efforts; and citizens now identified as volunteers and donors are being mobilized to participate in activities in these kinds of intermediary social spaces. The final section looks more closely at how urban residents make sense of these practices by considering some of the frames and narratives used to explain volunteering and charitable giving. These frames combine references to 'traditional' Chinese culture and socialist politics, and western-defined philanthropy, underscoring the emergent and polysemous character of these practices. I conclude that these practices and norms are shaping a 'politics of giving' in a space that is not 'of' civil society or the state *per se*, but rather in an intermediary space that works across and through these more traditional categories of analysis. It thus requires analytical tools that do not reproduce assumptions about the 'non' governmentalness of social organizations or assume that they have been 'coopted' by the state.

'Societization' of care for those 'in need': creating intermediate spaces for welfare provisioning

To understand why practices such as liaising and collaborating are noteworthy in social welfare distribution and how they are shaping this problem-space, it is important to review recent reforms in welfare provisioning. Under the urban socialist state system, services were delivered through one's workplace, or *danwei*, and directly from the state for those without family support, work, or livelihood (the three nos) (Wong 1994, 2013). With reforms, however, state-owned enterprises identified these costs as excessive and too difficult to sustain. The work-unit-based system of welfare delivery needed to be reformed (Lin *et al.* 1998; Smart and Smart 2001), and new kinds of systems, ranging from citizen efforts to new insurance programmes have been adopted (Trieu 2013). Of note, with these reforms the state's resources were identified as 'limited', and official discourses suggested it was not only the government's responsibility, but also the 'duty of *every person* and social unit to contribute to the welfare enterprise' (Chu 1996: 72, emphasis added). It is this shift from the state as a provider and planner of social services to the state as more of a macro-manager and one among a number of participants in this domain that is of particular interest here (see also Luova 2011; Wong and Tang 2006/2007).

These changes and the development of 'non-work-based social provisions', translated as the 'societization' or 'socialization' of social welfare (*shehui fuli shehuihua* 社会福利社会化), became a critical imperative for reforms as early as the mid-1980s, and led to a series of new directives and regulations (Bray 2006; Hoffman 2013; Ma 2006; Saich 2003, 2008; Wong and Tang 2006/2007; Xu and Jones 2004). Programmes promoted by the Ministry of Civil Affairs in the mid-1980s to develop community-based services (*shequ fuwu* 社区服务), under the slogan of 'social welfare being carried out by society' (*shehui fuwu shehui ban* 社会服务社会办), were an important part of this early effort (Chu 1996: 63; Tao and Drover 1996: 44). Since then there have been a host of reforms leading to the adoption of new modes of service provisioning, including engagement with NPOs and NGOs (called social organizations in China), the development of community-based governance (*shequ* 社区), and a turn to the work of community volunteers. Examples include: new rules about registering social organizations (*shehui tuanti* 社会团体) in 1989; regulations on the registration and management of civilian-run non-enterprise units (*minban feiqiye danwei* 民办非企业单位) in 1998; legalization of foundations (*jijinhui* 基金会) that may take in charitable contributions in 2004; and a blueprint for greater transparency in charitable organizations in 2011 ('Chinese ministry vows more transparency for charitable organizations' 2011).

Volunteering with civilian and social organizations has also gone through changes, with the first such organization established in 1990 in Shenzhen. In 1994 the China Young Volunteers Association was started and a series of rules outlining volunteering were issued in 1999, with updates after the UN-led International Year of the Volunteer in 2001. College students have participated in volunteer activities in significant numbers, leading to government statements on their role in volunteer activities in 2006 and 2008.[3] To help promote volunteering, China also partnered in 2011 with the United Nations Development Programme on the Umbrella Programme 'Strengthening Civic Engagement and Social Innovations through Volunteerism for Development in China' (Fleischer 2011; Lee 2009; Tao and Drover 1996; United Nations Development Programme 2011; United Nations Volunteers 2010).

Provisioning has therefore shifted from a more direct distribution of resources through the work unit and city government to a system that relies more heavily on social organizations and the 'voluntary' mobilization of citizens, and their time, labour, and private assets. Popular reactions after the 2008 earthquake in Wenchuan, Sichuan Province, have contributed to these contemporary manifestations of 'cross-class' care. The post-earthquake response was a particularly important moment for the mass popularization of philanthropic giving by individuals and corporations, and of volunteering by those who had something (time, expertise, enthusiasm) 'to give/donate' to others. Not only did it publicize these practices globally, but the tragedy also introduced many people in China to volunteering and charitable giving on a new scale. Celebrity philanthropy, especially televised appeals and internet presences, played a key role in this popularization (see also Jeffreys in this book). Numerous stories circulated of city residents, and more specifically the middle class, seeing the devastation on television and feeling compelled to help, joining up with more organized efforts (for example, those of NGOs), and generating a new space of disaster tourism for some. News reports estimated that as many as three million people volunteered in some manner, many for the first time (Roney 2012: 88; Watts 2008; Zhang 2012: 228; Zhang *et al.* 2009; Zheng 2009). Yet, questions of trustworthiness, sincerity, and corruption also have been a part of the post-earthquake popular conversation about charitable giving in particular, highlighting the contested nature of such modes of giving.[4]

Responses to the 2008 Sichuan earthquake by non-profits, non-governmental, and social organizations also led to important new state directives about how the state should interact with such actors, both national and international – that is, the government *should collaborate*. This response is notably different from that after the devastating Tangshan earthquake in 1976, when the government emphasized self-sufficiency and refused, especially, aid from foreign entities.

In fact, China first accepted significant foreign support for help after floods in the 1990s (Chu 1996: 79). Hence, the next section highlights the new practices and mechanisms of governing that are emerging in this intermediary space – liaising, collaborating, and mobilizing.

Solving 'urban problems': liaisons, collaborations and mobilizations of individuals and organizations

We may think of the city as a space of experimentation or 'field of intervention' in which various mechanisms, policies, and norms are deployed to address that which has been defined as 'problematic, uncertain, or in need of mediation' (Ong 2011: 10). The problems addressed here are urban inequality, human suffering, and 'social stability', leading to new insurance systems, calls for citizens to donate to others, and state recognition of the 'usefulness' of social organizations. These ways of doing things are embedded in broader mentalities of governing shared across categories that we typically separate in our analyses – most notably, state and (civil) society. While some view the current situation with social organizations in terms of either liberalization *or* Party revitalization (NGO Law Monitor 2015), this chapter focuses on the new kinds of practices and spaces that emerge across these more traditional state–society boundaries. This intermediary space includes a tangible state presence, yet it is in an arena that people consistently identified to me as *not* the state. I outline three important practices in this intermediary space – liaising, collaborating, and mobilizing.

Party campaigns to build a harmonious society, and to strengthen and innovate with social management, are particularly important in shaping interactions with social organizations. In a 2011 speech, President Hu Jintao called for strengthened and innovative social management to 'ensure a harmonious and stable society full of vitality'. Significantly, Hu called on *all sectors* to reach these goals: Party leadership, the government, and non-governmental support and public participation ('Chinese president urges improved social management for greater harmony, stability' 2011). The Twelfth Five Year Plan from 2011 to 2015 explicitly encouraged the state to be 'proactive in reaching out' to social organizations, specifically in 'addressing common social goals' (NGO Law Monitor 2015). Social organizations have reportedly 'proliferated' with these official calls for improving 'social management' and promoting a 'harmonious society', leading to new governance practices of 'eliciting social support and seeking collaboration with society' (Zhang 2012: 221). Other practices include efforts to create community service centres, a more 'grass-roots' strategy to promote community volunteering, the promotion of the profession of social work, and plans to have the government contract with and fund social organizations to do welfare-oriented work (see also Sigley in this book). Of note, in 2013 President Xi Jinping used the term 'social governance' rather than social management innovation, signalling to many that the state was more interested in 'partnership' with, rather than 'management' of, social organizations (NGO Law Monitor 2015).

To discuss the practice of *liaising*, I offer the example of a new urban service centre in Dalian, called the 365 Citizens Building (365 *shimin dalou* 市民大楼). I use this example to highlight both the diversity of actors in this intermediary space and their active involvement in providing solutions to urban problems. In Dalian, one district government drew on models in Beijing and Ningbo to establish the 365 Citizens Building. The number 365 references a 24-hour and seven days per week service for 365 days a year for official city residents, migrant workers, and expatriate residents. It includes offices for city services, dispute resolution, and an all-hours call-in centre, covered by three shifts of 16 people each to help citizens with any issue they have. The administrators of the 365 Citizens Building said the centre's goal was to help anyone living in the district, and not just those with permanent Dalian registrations. They explained that the centre was conceived of and created in response to the central policy that each locality *should experiment* with ways to serve citizens better, and to strengthen and innovate with social management. Inside, the building is shiny and white, with marble-like stone on all surfaces, and clearly marked and orderly office spaces throughout. The multi-storey complex houses city government and Ministry of Civil Affairs staff, as well as the district's Party office. Officially, as explained in the centre's printed introductory materials, the centre's goal is 'strengthening and innovating social management, improving the service level for people's livelihood and constructing [a] quality district' (*jiaqiang he chuangxin shehui guanli, tisheng renmin fuwu shuiping, jianshe pinzhi chengqu de zhongyao pingtai* 加强和创新社会管理，提升人民服务水平，建设品质城区的重要平台).

Projects such as this are clearly part of the state apparatus. The 365 Citizens Building houses official municipal and Party offices and is filled with government employees. The extensive list of regulations, directives, and statements from the central government related to social organizations, volunteering, and charitable giving also illustrates that governance in this domain is still understood as a state project of 'social stability and maintenance of legitimacy' (Luova 2011: 773).

Yet, in interviews, the 365 Building was described as not 'of' the state in the same way as earlier forms of urban administration had been. Individuals who worked in the building prided themselves on helping ordinary citizens *access* the formal city government apparatus – such as water and electricity services – positioning themselves as a liaison to the government for ordinary citizens, as well as an advocate for them in interactions with municipal agencies. For instance, if a resident of the district called and said they did not know how to contact the city government about a problem they had with electricity, the staff at the 365 Centre understood their job as not only getting the right phone number for them, but also making sure the caller received the information and help they needed. It is this kind of in-between liaison role that suggests these practices are experienced and enacted as not necessarily 'of' the state, but still 'about' the state. In the Russian context, Julie Hemment (2012) has described such postsocialist modes of interaction as a 'complex fusion' (and thus not a 'civil society').

This project, which creates a liaison-type role for urban governance, also is embedded in efforts to 'extend' citizen services, and especially volunteer services, from society (*shehui* 社会) to community (*shequ* 社区) (Zhang Jiyuan 2010). For instance, district governments across Dalian have established citizen service centres through the district (*qu* 区), street (*jiedao* 街道), and community (*shequ*) administrations as direct manifestations of these new norms about how provisioning and state–citizen interaction should go. New modes of service provisioning work through the political imperatives of community building and administration, more technical approaches like the legalization of monetary donations to charitable foundations, and modes of social regulation such as building a harmonious society, working 'with' society, and 'sending warmth' campaigns (*song wennuan* 送温暖) (Bray 2006; Xu 2008; Yang 2012). The notion of 'liaison' between the Party-state and the people is indeed a recurrent theme in community- and volunteer-based reforms and underscores the intermediary character of this social space (see also Luova 2011; Xu 2007).

The 365 Building also houses an office, supported by the Ministry of Civil Affairs, to help NGOs, which are often described as social organizations. One man described offices such as this as 'incubators' for social organizations. The offices help people register their organization, evaluate the organization's work plan, and potentially fund the organization's work if it fits within the official priority areas of helping those who need employment, supporting the elderly, serving migrant/temporary workers, helping disadvantaged groups, and working on acceptable environmental projects. The offices also offer training for the organization's staff and outcome/assessment tools, because, as one person explained, those with ideas of how to serve citizens have 'the interest and compassion, but not necessarily the skills' to be successful. This coincides with official efforts to create a more 'professionalized' human resource base for social organizations, especially in terms of training social workers (see also Sigley in this book).

Along similar lines, a man who works with social organizations described his work as an effort to communicate *between* the government and citizens. Over coffee one afternoon he explained that while in 1949 there were many non-governmental, citizen social organizations (*minjian de* 民间的), they were abolished during high socialism and now his work was to build them up again. He recognized that it was difficult to get organizations established because rules required them to have an official government sponsor, but noted that the government in fact *wanted* to encourage the development of what he called 'useful' organizations. He worked hard to meet individuals across the city that were doing good work, focusing on outreach to young people, many of whom did not trust the government. To help establish that trust, he tried to emphasize the 'in-betweenness' of his own role – as a figure to help them *interact with* the government in an official way, similar to the service orientation of the 365 Centre, but also to help them reach their own potential as leaders of social organizations in society, echoing efforts to develop professionalized human resources. While those doing such liaison work do not 'speak the state' as in the highly politicized

Maoist years (Anagnost 1997), their own subjectivity and narratives continue to be connected with state rationalities.

The idea that social organizations did work that the government *did not do* was common. In an interview, an older man who had retired and was spending the majority of his time volunteering felt strongly about this, even though the organization with which he worked was run by someone with a government salary, did work that was prioritized by the government (elderly care), and his own expenses were reimbursed by state funds. He and other people working and volunteering for this organization understood their efforts as *separate from* state projects. They explained the need for their organization and the work it was doing as the government's 'inability' to take care of all the problems present and as the government's 'lack of attention' to some specific problems, echoing official recasting of the state's resources as limited.

In addition to the practice of liaising, *collaboration* between actors identified as the state and not-the-state shape this intermediary space and the subjects within it. Some scholars have argued that recent policies and directives signal that the state indeed takes the role of social organizations, citizen volunteering, and charitable giving seriously (Irish *et al.* 2009). In the case of post-earthquake efforts, one leader of an organization said that:

> The state has created a space for us, it allows us to exist while remaining unofficial not because the government does not know our existence, but precisely because the government does know us and *acknowledges that our existence is necessary.*
>
> (cited in Zhang 2012: 240–1; emphasis added)

Evidence of this includes new regulations and a law on earthquake reconstruction efforts passed by the State Council that emphasized the necessity of 'self-help, government's guidance, and social support', and which acknowledged that the state had 'quickly recognized that *social participation* ha[d] become an integral part of rescue and relief' (Zhang 2012: 231–2; emphasis added). This 'flexible social space' of collaboration and alliance was understood as a positive governmental effort that contributed to the post-earthquake efforts in Sichuan, a noted difference from the Tangshan relief efforts (Roney 2012; Zhang 2012). Moreover, in 2009, China published a white paper suggesting that the government should strengthen 'social mobilization mechanisms' in order to 'give full play to the functions of non-governmental organizations and organizations at the grassroots level as well as volunteers in the sphere of disaster relief', one of the accepted areas of social organization work (cited in Roney 2012: 85). The more recent use of the term 'social governance' signalled to some that the Party 'places society and social organizations more on par with government', recognizing 'that social actors have a part in governance' (NGO Law Monitor 2015). Research also shows that the language of 'collaboration' has positively impacted the expansion of social organizations and citizen volunteers (Roney 2012; Zhang 2012).

Social and non-governmental organizations are therefore increasingly seen as an integral part of governmental solutions and no longer *only* as a threat to the state; they are useful and 'cost-effective' resources for the state (Ding Yuanzhu 2005; Hoffman 2013; Lee 2009; Yang 2005: 16). As the quote that opened this chapter noted, '[n]either government subsidies nor the market alone can solve this problem [of inequality]. We must have volunteers.' Similarly, Yang Lan, the Chinese media sensation who co-hosted the well-publicized dinner with Bill and Melinda Gates, Warren Buffet, and wealthy individuals in China, has argued for a more prominent role for wealthy families, especially through private foundations that may offer education and services to philanthropists and other organizations (Heim 2011). Yet social organizations also evoke memories of professional and trade unions (*hang ye gong hui*), associations of fellow provincials or townsmen (*tong xiang hui*), solidarity or mutual aid societies (*gong ji hui*), and even some well-known secret societies and thus *also of rebellions* (Zi 2009: 49). This history helps to explain both the acceptance of donations 'as a supplement to government welfare spending and also wide-spread suspicion of non-governmental actors' (Zi 2009: 50). The practice of collaboration emphasizes the *complementarity* of NGOs, also neutralizing any potential opposition from them.

The third practice I wish to highlight as important in this intermediary space is *mobilization*. This refers to a variety of incentives, norms and policies that 'encourage' people to participate in addressing social issues and providing direct services. The idea is that people are not 'forced' to participate but rather generate some kind of internal desire to contribute to solving social problems. The idea of mobilization is thus closely tied with the cultivation of individually made, autonomous decisions to participate (for example, in NGO work and volunteering) and a sense of social responsibility to others as well. College students often volunteer for organized activities; I examine this in detail elsewhere (Hoffman 2013). In brief, these young people understood their participation as expressions of human caring, the development of a better self (socially and professionally), and as work that helped to maintain social stability. It required, however, an understanding of the self as an independent agent who *could* get involved, but *did not have to* get involved. Yet such mobilization and citizen participation, especially in the contested space of urban need, is not a 'natural' human characteristic, but must be cultivated and normalized (Hoffman 2010).

Mobilizations of citizens to participate in socially oriented activities are intimately linked with the societization of welfare provisioning, for this mode of provisioning includes the expectation that social organizations and citizens will move into this space of action 'and bear the main burden of service delivery' (Wong and Tang 2006/2007; see also Lee 2000; Ma 2002). Such an understanding of citizen participation raised doubts in many. In interviews with college students, as well as others who volunteered and did paid work with social organizations, people expressed an ambivalence over the nature of 'responsibility' for alleviating urban poverty and disadvantage. Many stated that the state 'had responsibility' even as they accepted the responsibility of an individual to make a difference, or the idea that the government needed support to address all the issues facing China today, or that NGOs were important players in addressing urban inequality (Hoffman 2013). One man said, for instance, that much of this social-problem work should in fact be the government's responsibility, but that it had now moved to the citizens themselves. While there is what can be called an activation, empowerment, and responsibilization of non-state actors in this domain, it is an activation that produces complementarity and not necessarily conflict with the government – but that also requires resources from the government to function. It is an intermediary space of social action.

The politics of giving: compassion and affect in the making of citizen volunteers

A new politics of giving is emerging in relation to these practices of liaising, collaborating, and mobilizing. These politics aim for cross-class interactions rather than the class-specific and friends-versus-enemies politics of the Maoist era. To help promote harmonious social relations (that is, cross-class interactions and provisioning for social stability), organizations such as Dalian's Charity Federation train and register volunteers. To become an official volunteer (*yigong* 义工) with the Federation, each person must attend a training session run by the Federation. Once registered, these volunteers then fan-out across the city to serve where they are needed. Such programmes reflect directives outlined in documents about Community Volunteers' Associations that emphasize the importance of 'service attitude, rights and duties as well as practical skills' in these activities, underscoring the model-citizen-building nature of these practices (Luova 2011: 786).

When I attended an evening volunteer training session in May 2010, we were all instructed to fill out a form with our basic information, such as address, workplace, and contact information, and to provide two photographs. At the beginning of the session we introduced ourselves and said something about why we were there. In addition to reasons such as 'my friend asked me to come' and 'I wanted to do something this summer', several participants said they felt they should 'help society' and 'help others'. The trainer introduced all of the possible projects that we could get involved in, such as a mentoring programme, helping the elderly, or garbage clean-up projects, and then gave us the phone numbers of the coordinators in each city district. We were asked to contact that coordinator directly to get involved in a project. We then all raised our right hands and made a pledge to serve people well and to retain a good spirit about our efforts.

As people left the room after the training, they were asked to make a donation in the box at the front, but the trainer was clear that we should only give what we could afford. If the person in front of us gave CNY 100 but we were a student, we should not do the same as that person. Echoing messages about how people should not volunteer unless they had taken care of their own situation first (food to eat, a place to live), the trainer cautioned us to donate only according to our capacity. Volunteering and charitable giving was to be understood as directly related to one's material condition. In fact, some very active volunteers – with what was called a 'five star' status based on the number of hours they had committed – were occasionally criticized by others who thought they should take more care of their own families and personal business. As this suggests, mobilizing ordinary people to participate in the governmental solution of citizen action is both commonplace and contested.

During the training session other volunteers made laminated identification cards with our photographs, which we were instructed to hang around our necks when engaged in any volunteer activities. The cards identify each person by name and registered number as a 'Dalian Volunteer' (*Dalian yiwu gongzuozhe* 大连义务工作者). The back of the identification card also includes the volunteer motto: 'you are in my heart; helping others is pleasurable' (*yigong geyan: wo xin you ni; zhu ren le ji* 义工格言：我心有你助人乐己). The symbolism of the formal identification, the motto laying against one's heart, and the raising of our hands in a pledge drew on a wide array of norms, politics, and understandings of compassion. The societization of provisioning is not only about new regulations, the legalization of charitable donations, and the prioritization of more intermediary governmental technologies, but also shapes a politics of giving, cross-class interactions, and the subjects who 'participate' in these activities.

These politics draw on a fairly wide array of references, including ideas that such caring for others referenced Confucian humanism, that it came from western, modern, and even Christian values, and that it was a manifestation of 'serving the people' championed by Chairman Mao Zedong. A recent manuscript by an academic in China, for instance, aims to situate contemporary philanthropy in China's cultural traditions (Liu Zhongquan n.d.), referencing Confucian and Taoist understandings of benevolence and reciprocity. Likewise, a glossy publication by the China Charity Federation about the Sichuan earthquake relief efforts notes the importance of 'China's traditions' (*zhonghua chuantong* 中华传统) for the work of today's non-governmental charitable organizations (Li Yulin 2008). While not the dominant discourse, some volunteers framed their participation in terms of their family values and the importance of caring for others. One active volunteer, for instance, explained his participation in terms of a 'cultured' appreciation of Confucian values of benevolence and humanism that came to him from his grandparents. Academics also often reference the Confucian 'roots' of philanthropy, volunteerism, and welfare provisioning in contemporary China, which some argue, emphasize 'obligation, beneficence, reciprocity, and caring' rather than individual rights and justice (Tao and Drover 1996: 35; see also Fleischer 2011). Outi Luova (2011: 775) notes that the Confucian concept of '*yi*' (义), which is used in the term '*yigong*' (volunteer 义工), 'refers to the moral responsibility of a cultivated person to serve society and others of one's own free will' – underscoring the importance of compassion and human feelings in this space.

In another example, an official at the Dalian Charity Federation explained to me that although mutual help was a part of the Mao era, then it was more about a class-based feeling (*jieji ganqing* 阶级感情), rather than a broader human feeling of caring. 'Then it was "*xiao ai*" (小爱), but now it is about "*da ai*" (大爱). That "*xiao ai*" was only for some, even Lei Feng [a 1960s model soldier-worker] was like that' (see also Jeffreys and Su in this book). In other words, caring for others during the Maoist period meant only caring for those with a 'good' class background. It was narrowly defined as a limited love (*xiao ai*), whereas contemporary volunteerism was meant to express a more generalized, universal, and cross-class caring in society (*da ai*). Reinforcing a break with values from the Mao era, a government employee working with social organizations emphatically claimed that the work such organizations did had 'no relation to communism'. 'Mao's time used people' he said. Rather, to use his words: 'the spirit of volunteerism today could be said to come from the west; it's also related to older ideas from imperial China when they recognized that social control was not possible so you needed a lot of civic (*minjian* 民间) solutions'. Such distinctions from the Mao era suggest that people are identifying a shift away from the mass-line politics of friends versus enemies (Dutton 2009) towards a new 'politics of giving' that emphasizes 'cross-class' relations, as well as the more privatized redistribution of resources.

Nevertheless, in other interviews and conversations, people directly referenced Mao and the values embodied in Lei Feng, the soldier who consistently put the interests of others and of the nation before his own, living a life of selfless service. In 'Learn from Lei Feng' campaigns, people were encouraged to follow his example as a model of ideal behaviour. Thus, Lei Feng, Mao-era norms of service, and the mass organization structure itself have genealogical relevance for the contemporary practices of volunteerism, even as people enjoyed dismissing Lei Feng and Learn from Lei Feng campaigns as irrelevant for their lives. When spending time, for instance, with a group of taxi drivers in Dalian who regularly came together to participate in charity events, and who also individually donated their time and services to help others, they proudly told me of being 'model' workers and of winning a Lei Feng honour from the city government. This cohort, generally in their fifties, found great pride and value in these understandings of service, a politics of 'model citizen' subject making that has also been identified with volunteer training for the Beijing Olympics, as well as routine Party work associated with contemporary volunteering (Chong 2011; Rolandsen 2010). Additionally, the government use of the term 'public welfare' (*gongyi* 公益) instead of '*cishan*' to refer to charitable activities (for example, poverty alleviation, disaster relief, education and environmental work) in fields such as the legal system emphasizes an understanding of charitable activities as *public* welfare and *public* interests, which could be said to reference a more Mao-era orientation (Lee 2009: 358, n. 61360).

Other participants in social organizations, as well as some scholars (Chong 2011; Leung *et al.* 2012; Zi 2009), emphasize the 'newness' of charitable and volunteer activities in China, with one official even claiming that prior to the

1990s when people began giving to flood victims, people 'did not have the idea of charitable giving' in China (see also Jeffreys in this book).[5] By 2010, however, individuals who 'mobilized themselves' to help the victims of floods in Gansu described themselves on television reports as 'volunteers', illustrating a kind of 'mainstreaming' and commonplace-ness of volunteering in the country (United Nations Development Programme 2011: 18; see also NGO Law Monitor 2015). This kind of 'mainstreaming' of volunteerism and non-governmental efforts is not limited to China of course, suggesting that there may be a more global 'structure of feeling' and politics of giving associated with these practices.

Despite comments about the 'newness', Joanna Handlin Smith's historical work on charitable activities in Ming–Qing times shows that philanthropy is not simply a 'new' and 'western' activity, but has been practised in a variety of ways in China (Handlin Smith 1998, 2009). Her work also identifies an interesting shift in the late Ming to early Qing in *who* was doing philanthropy, from scholarly Confucian literati elite to merchants (Handlin Smith 1998). Amidst great social change and challenges to the existing social hierarchy with the Manchu takeover, the scholarly elite retreated, opening a space for merchants to engage in such activities, and ultimately in the Republican era for 'modern types of volunteer organizations' to operate (Fleischer 2011: 304). Merchant philanthropy, according to Handlin Smith (1998: 434, 441), was less about 'the worthiness of those members of the elite who led the way' and 'the relationship between donor and heaven', and was more about the relationship 'between donor and beneficiary'.

Handlin Smith's focus on *shifts in social relations*, rather than 'the dichotomy between merchant-gentry initiative and imperial control' (that is, between society and state), is a useful lesson for understanding contemporary modes of serving those 'in need' in China (Handlin Smith 1998: 443). This focus asks us to think not just about *divisions* between state and society, but rather how the meaning of provisioning is shifting to a more intermediary and in-between space, also suggesting a new politics of giving is emerging. The emphasis on personal growth, cross-class interactions and solutions to society's problems, embodies both affective and technical components. Participants learn about desired, proper, expected behaviours, emotions and reactions to social problems. The politics of giving is decidedly *not* class-specific, but rather is about liaising, collaborating and mobilizing *society*. These mechanisms of governing are shaping new mentalities of governing and urban subjects in China.

Conclusion

China's cities are undergoing dramatic transformations as urbanization has become a national economic and development agenda, rural to urban migration expands, and new forms of suffering become increasingly apparent to the general public. The state has also recognized that it cannot sufficiently provide for needy urban residents without the help of ordinary citizens. The engagement of ordinary citizens in these new mentalities of governing is a complex and contested process, involving new governing mentalities and practices of liaising, collaborating, and mobilizing.

These practices are premised on the intermixing of concepts of Confucian benevolence, Maoist service, and international rationales for volunteering and civic engagement, and are helping to shape a new politics of giving and new types of urban subjects. These are social politics that shape cross-class relations and urban subjects who should individually and voluntarily decide to participate in volunteer and charitable activities. Hence, the intermediary space of social action outlined in this chapter is a more complex cross-section of values, politics, and meanings than typical representations of state-versus-civil society arguments posit. It is a space that prioritizes practices of in-betweenness, liaison work, collaboration and mobilization, while also shaping urban subjectivity and politics of giving.

Notes

1 Statistics indicate that private financial flows in 2007 were 'five times larger than public flows' of official development monies going from developed to developing countries (Center for Global Prosperity 2010). The Bill and Melinda Gates Foundation (2013) is a good example of these private flows, with a USD40.2 billion asset trust endowment and grant payments in 2012 of USD3.4 billion.

2 Interviews were conducted with several social organizations focused on social problems as well as environmental groups. Group interviews at three major universities in Dalian were conducted with college students who were active in volunteering. Interviews were also conducted with a number of other volunteers who participated in various community and charitable activities during participation observation.

3 In 2006 a 'Notice on Organizing College Graduates to Help in Education, Agriculture, Medical Services, and Poverty Alleviation in Rural Areas' was issued by the Ministry of Personnel. In 2008, an 'Opinion on Deepening Volunteering Activities' was issued by the Office of the Spiritual Civilization Development Steering Commission of the Chinese Communist Party (United Nations Development Programme 2011: 7). China's Twelfth Five-Year Plan for 2011 to 2015 also explicitly called for more than 10 per cent of all residents to be registered as community volunteers, illustrating that these efforts are not only focused on college students ('Key targets of China's 12th five-year plan' 2011).

4 Film star Zhang Ziyi, for instance, was publicly condemned for not fulfilling her pledges to the relief efforts, and for allegedly keeping funds raised at Cannes (Jeffreys 2011). The Guo Meimei–Red Cross Society of China scandal also garnered wide attention, and is said to have done significant damage to the reputation of charitable giving in China, especially to the dominant GONGOs – the Red Cross and China Charity Federation. This was an internet/microblog-based scandal in which a young woman, Guo Meimei, claimed to work for a 'Red Cross-related company' and flaunted excessive wealth, especially with fancy cars. There was an immediate and intense backlash against the Red Cross Society of China because people assumed she was involved with the corrupt use of charitable donations (Hong and FlorCruz 2011). More recently, controversy erupted when an honorary vice president of the China Charity Federation suggested *requiring* donations by extracting them from people's salaries as a tax (see Wang 2013).

5 It also is important to note that while the term '*cishan*' is translated into English as either charity or philanthropy, these terms have two distinct meanings in the USA, with

charity referring to the 'impulse to personal service' that is rooted in 'concrete, direct acts of compassion and connection to other people', and philanthropy referring to a more 'rationalized' process and organization that 'sought to apply reason to the solution of social ills and needs … [and] aspires not so much to aid individuals as to reform society' (Gross 2003: 31). Much of this rationalized attention in philanthropy was on distinguishing between what were considered the 'deserving' and the 'undeserving' (Gross 2003).

References

Anagnost, A. (1997) *National Past-Times: Narrative, Representation and Power in Modern China*, Durham: Duke University Press.

Bill and Melinda Gates Foundation (2013) 'Foundation fact sheet'. Online. Available: www.gatesfoundation.org/Who-We-Are/General-Information/Foundation-Factsheet (accessed 12 March 2015).

Bornstein, E. (2012) *Disquieting Gifts: Humanitarianism in New Delhi*, Stanford: Stanford University Press.

Bray, D. (2006) 'Building "community": new strategies of governance in urban China', *Economy and Society*, 35, 4: 530–49.

Center for Global Prosperity (2010) *The Index of Global Philanthropy and Remittances 2009: Executive Summary*, Washington: Hudson Institute's Center for Global Prosperity. Online. Available: www.hudson.org/files/documents/2009_index_executive_summary_fnl.pdf (accessed 15 November 2013).

'Chinese ministry vows more transparency for charitable organizations' (2011) *People's Daily*, 16 July. Online. Available: http://en.people.cn/90001/90776/90882/7442206.html (accessed 10 April 2015).

'Chinese president urges improved social management for greater harmony, stability' (2011) *Xinhuawang*, 19 February. Online. Available: http://news.xinhuanet.com/english2010/china/2011–02/19/c_13739874.htm (accessed 12 March 2015).

Chong, G. (2011) 'Volunteers as the "new" model citizens: governing citizens through soft power', *China Information*, 25, 1: 33–59.

Chu, W. (1996) 'The politics of welfare in China: the impact of political concern on welfare development', in T. Wing Lo and J.Y.S. Cheng (eds), *Social Welfare Development in China: Constraints and Challenges*, Chicago: Imprint Publications.

Ding Yuanzhu (2005) 'Preface' and 'China's campus volunteerism and its enabling environment', *China Volunteer Service Journal*, pp. 1–3. Online. Available: www.worldvolunteerweb.org/fileadmin/docdb/pdf/2006/RCVW_English_Journal_1_.pdf (accessed 12 March 2015).

Dutton, M. (2009) 'Passionately governmental: Maoism and the structured intensities of revolutionary governmentality', in E. Jeffreys (ed.), *China's Governmentalities: Governing Change, Changing Government*, Abingdon: Routledge, pp. 24–37.

Fleischer, F. (2011) 'Technology of self, technology of power: volunteering as encounter in Guangzhou, China', *Ethnos*, 76, 3: 300–25.

Gross, R.A. (2003) 'Giving in America: from charity to philanthropy', in L.J. Friedman and M.D. McGarvie (eds) *Charity, Philanthropy, and Civility in American History*, Cambridge: Cambridge University Press.

Handlin Smith, J.F. (1998) 'Social hierarchy and merchant philanthropy as perceived in several late-Ming and early-Qing texts', *Journal of Economic and Social History of the Orient*, 41, 3: 417–51.

Handlin Smith, J.F. (2009) *The Art of Doing Good: Charity in Late Ming China*, Berkeley: University of California Press.

Heim, K. (2011) 'In person: Yang Lan nurtures philanthropy among China's new wealthy', *The Seattle Times*, 24 July 2011. Online. Available: www.seattletimes.com/business/in-person-yang-lan-nurtures-philanthropy-among-chinas-newly-wealthy (accessed 9 April 2015).

Hemment, J. (2012) 'Redefining need, reconfiguring expectations: the rise of state-run youth voluntarism programs in Russia', *Anthropological Quarterly*, 85, 2: 519–54.

Hoffman, L.M. (2006) 'Autonomous choices and patriotic professionalism: governmentality in late-socialist China', *Economy and Society*, 35, 4: 550–70.

Hoffman, L.M. (2010) *Patriotic Professionalism in Urban China: Fostering Talent*, Philadelphia: Temple University Press.

Hoffman, L.M. (2013) 'Decentralization as a mode of governing the urban in China: reforms in welfare provisioning and the rise of volunteerism', *Pacific Affairs*, 86, 4: 835–55.

Hong, H. and FlorCruz, J. (2011) 'Red Cross China in credibility crisis', *CNNWorld*, 7 July. Online. Available: www.cnn.com/2011/WORLD/asiapcf/07/06/china.redcross/index.html (accessed 12 March 2015).

Irish, L., Salamon, L. and Simon, K. (2009) 'Outsourcing social services to CSOs: lessons from abroad', World Bank Report 50385. Online. Available: www-wds.worldbank.org/external/default/WDSContentServer/WDSP/IB/2009/09/17/000333038_20090917230533/Rendered/PDF/503850ESW0WHIT10Lessons0from0Abroad.pdf (accessed 1 June 2015).

Jeffreys, E. (2011) 'Zhang Ziyi and China's celebrity philanthropy scandals', *PORTAL Journal of Multidisciplinary International Studies*, 8, 1: 1–21. Online. Available: http://epress.lib.uts.edu.au/journals/index.php/portal/article/view/1627/2292 (accessed 12 March 2015).

Jeffreys, E. and Sigley, G. (2009) 'Governmentality, governance and China', in E. Jeffreys (ed.), *China's Governmentalities: Governing Change, Changing Government*, Abingdon: Routledge, pp. 1–24.

'Key targets of China's 12th five-year plan' (2011) *Xinhuawang*, 5 March. Online. Available: news.xinhuanet.com/english2010/china/2011-03/05/c_13762230.htm (accessed 12 March 2015).

Lee, D. (2000) 'Legal reform in China: a role for nongovernmental organizations', *The Yale Journal of International Law*, 25, 363: 262–434.

Lee, R. (2009) 'Modernizing charity law in China', *Pacific Rim Law & Policy Journal*, 18, 2: 347–72.

Leung, T., Yip, N., Huang, R., and Wu, Y. (2012) 'Governmentality and the politicisation of social work in China', *British Journal of Social Work*, 42, 6: 1039–59.

Li Yulin (2008) *Zhenqing zuiqianxian: cishan zai wenchuanqu de rezi* [True Love at the Relief Work Front: Charity in Wenchuan Earthquake Rescue and Relief], Beijing: Zhongguo Shehui Chubanshe.

Lin, J., Cai, F., and Li, Z. (1998) 'Competition, policy burdens, and state-owned enterprise reform', *The American Economic Review*, 88, 2: 422–7.

Liu Zhongquan (n.d.) Zhongguo cishan wenhua chuantong yu xiandai xing zhuan xing hou he bo fa [China's Cultural Tradition of Philanthropy and its Modern Transformation], unpublished manuscript, Dalian University of Technology.

Luova, O. (2011) 'Community volunteers' associations in contemporary Tianjin: multipurpose partners of the party-state', *Journal of Contemporary China*, 20, 72: 773–94.

Ma, Q. (2002) 'Defining Chinese nongovernmental organizations', *Voluntas: International Journal of Voluntary and Nonprofit Organizations*, 13, 2: 113–30.

Ma, Q. (2006) *Non-governmental Organizations in Contemporary China: Paving the Way to Civil Society?*, Abingdon: Routledge.

Muehlebach, A. (2013) 'On precariousness and the ethical imagination: the year 2012 in sociocultural anthropology', *American Anthropologist*, 115, 2: 297–311.

NGO Law Monitor (2015) 'China'. Online. Available: www.icnl.org/research/monitor/china.html (accessed 10 April 2015).

Ong, A. (2011) 'Introduction: worlding cities or the art of being global', in A. Roy and A. Ong (eds), *Worlding Cities: Asian Experiments and the Art of Being Global*, West Sussex: Wiley-Blackwell.

Rolandsen, U. (2010) 'A collective of their own: young volunteers at the fringes of the Party realm', in M. Halskov Hansen and R. Svarverud (eds), *iChina: The Rise of the Individual in Modern Chinese Society*, Copenhagen: NIAS Press.

Roney, B. (2012) 'Earthquakes and civil society: a comparative study of the response of China's nongovernment organizations to the Wenchuan earthquake', *China Information*, 25, 1: 83–104.

Rose, N., O'Malley, P., and Valverde, M. (2006) 'Governmentality', *Annual Review of Law and Social Sciences*, 2: 83–104.

Saich, T. (2003) *Enhancing Economic Security in Transition: Pluralism in Service Delivery*, Geneva: International Labour Office.

Saich, T. (2008) *Providing Public Goods in Transitional China*, New York: Palgrave Macmillan.

Sigley, G. (2006) 'Chinese governmentalities: government, governance and the socialist market economy', *Economy and Society*, 35, 4: 487–508.

Smart, A. and Smart, J. (2001) 'Local citizenship: welfare reform urban/rural status, and exclusion in China', *Environment and Planning A*, 33: 1853–69.

Tao, J. and Drover, G. (1996) 'The contestation of values and welfare reform in China', in T. Wing Lo and J.Y.S. Cheng (eds) *Social Welfare Development in China: Constraints and Challenges*, Chicago: Imprint Publications, pp. 29–49.

Trieu, Huong T. (2013) Building a welfare state: a case study of rural migrant medical insurance in urban China. PhD dissertation, University of Michigan. Available: http://deepblue.lib.umich.edu/bitstream/handle/2027.42/97906/htrieu_1.pdf?sequence=1 (accessed 10 April 2015).

United Nations Development Programme (2011) *State of Volunteerism in China: Engaging People through Ideas, Innovation and Inspiration*. Online. Available: www.unv.org/fileadmin/docdb/pdf/2011/corporate/China%20Volunteer%20Report%202011_English.pdf (accessed 23 July 2015).

United Nations Volunteers (2010) *Laws and Policies Affecting Volunteerism Since 2001*. Online. Available: www.unv.org/fileadmin/docdb/pdf/2010/Volunteerism%20laws%20and%20policies%20-%20June%202010.pdf (accessed 13 March 2015).

Wang, R. (2013) 'Why no one trusts government charities in China anymore', *The Atlantic*, 13 March. Online. Available: www.theatlantic.com/china/archive/2013/03/why-no-one-trusts-government-charities-in-china-anymore/273989 (accessed 10 April 2015).

Watts, J. (2008) 'Sichuan earthquake: tragedy brings new mood of unity', *Guardian*, 9 June. Online. Available: www.guardian.co.uk/world/2008/jun/10/chinaearthquake.china/print (accessed 13 March 2015).

Williams, R. (1977) 'Structures of feeling', in *Marxism and Literature*, Oxford: Oxford University Press, pp. 128–35.

Wong, L. (1994) 'Privatization of social welfare in post-Mao China', *Asian Survey*, 34, 4: 307–25.

Wong, L. (2013) *Marginalization and Social Welfare in China*, London: Routledge.

Wong, L. and Tang, J. (2006/2007) 'Dilemmas confronting social entrepreneurs: care homes for elderly people in Chinese cities', *Pacific Affairs*, 79, 4: 623–40.

Xu, F. (2008) 'New modes of urban governance: building community/shequ in post-danwei China', in A. Laliberte and M. Lanteigne (eds), *The Chinese Party-State in the 21st Century: Adaptation and the Reinvention of Legitimacy*, Abingdon: Routledge, pp. 22–38.

Xu, Q. (2007) 'Community participation in urban China: identifying mobilization factors', *Nonprofit and Voluntary Sector Quarterly*, 36, 4: 622–42.

Xu, Q. and Jones, J.F. (2004) 'Community welfare services in urban China: a public–private experiment', *Journal of Chinese Political Science*, 9, 2: 47–62.

Yang, J. (2012) 'Song wennuan (sending warmth): unemployment, new urban poverty, and the affective state in China', *Ethnography* 14, 1: 104–25.

Yang, T. (2005) 'Can volunteerism be promoted through government administration?', *China Volunteer Service Journal Special English Edition*, 16–23. Online. Available: www.worldvolunteerweb.org/fileadmin/docdb/pdf/2006/RCVW_English_Journal_1_.pdf (accessed 13 March 2015).

Zhang Jiyuan (2010) 'Rang cishan yigong shenru shequ' [Allowing charitable volunteering to go deep into communities], *Dalian Charity, Dalian cishan zonghui chubanshe*, 2: 20, 12–13.

Zhang, N. (2012) 'The Wenchuan earthquake, social organizations, and the Chinese state', *Urban Anthropology*, 41, 2, 3, 4: 211–46.

Zhang, R., Rezaee, Z., and Zhu, J. (2009) 'Corporate philanthropic disaster response and ownership type: evidence from Chinese firms' response to the Sichuan Earthquake', *Journal of Business Ethics*, 91, 1: 51–63.

Zheng, Y. (2009) 'Wenchuan earthquake civic donation and the inspiration of modern philanthropy within China', *The China Nonprofit Review*, 1, 2: 247–62.

Zi, Z. (2009) 'Civil society from afar', *Caijing Annual Edition*, China: *Forecasts and Strategies*, 88–9 (this is version I found online to check the text), http://english.caijing.com.cn/upload/english%20annual2009.pdf.

9 Experimental postsocialism

The Chinese hospital as export zone and knowledge park

Melinda Cooper

In more ways than one, health care has emerged as a privileged site of experiment in reform-era China. The hospital was one of the first targets of Deng Xiaoping's experiments in market reform and was later subject to the renewed and intensified liberalization policies of President Jiang Zemin and Premier Zhu Rongji during the 1990s (Huang 2013: 5–81). More recently, under the administration of President Hu Jintao and Premier Wen Jiabao (2003–2013), the health care system as a whole was singled out for special attention as second-generation reformers pointed to the catastrophic effects of uncontrolled market liberalization on 'social harmony' (Office of the World Health Organization Representative in China and Social Development Department of China State Council Development Research Center 2005). Largely as a consequence of these wider institutional reforms, the Chinese urban hospital has refashioned itself in recent years as a site of *actual* clinical experiment, with hospital wards taking on a growing number of clinical trial contracts on behalf of multinational pharmaceutical sponsors.

Once concentrated in the United States of America (USA) and Western Europe, the multinational pharmaceutical industry now offshores a growing number of its clinical trials to the so-called 'emerging economies' of Central and Latin America, Central and Eastern Europe, and East Asia, often distributing parallel 'arms' of a trial in multiple locations around the world in an effort to find a sufficient volume of suitable patients and to accelerate trial completion (Kuo 2012; Petryna 2009; Prasad 2009; Sunder Rajan 2008). Chinese hospitals are fully integrated into this distributed network of contract clinical research: not only can they supply clinical investigators at a much lower price than their North American counterparts, their large patient base also represents an incomparable experimental asset for multinational companies in search of specific patient profiles and accelerated recruitment times (Humphries *et al.* 2006). China's urban hospitals began to conduct commercial clinical trials in the late 1990s, largely under pressure from dwindling budgets, and rapidly expanded their commercial research services throughout the 2000s. By 2011, the China Food and Drug Administration or CFDA (*Guojia shipin yaopin jiandu guanli zongju* 国家食品药品监督管理总局) had certified close to 300 hospitals and many more hospital departments as competent to carry out trials (Djali 2011). Most of these units were based in the large teaching hospitals of Beijing, Shanghai, and Guangzhou, and most were conducting Phase II or III trials on behalf of multinational drug industry sponsors.[1] In barely more than a decade, the elite urban hospital had transformed itself into an experimental export zone, financing part of its ongoing health care operations through the sale of clinical data and other commercial services to the multinational pharmaceutical industry.

In the last five years, the focus of this experimental activity has shifted somewhat as multinational pharmaceutical companies establish fully integrated, long-term research and development centres in China and undertake a growing number of collaborations with Chinese medical researchers (Gu and Shi 2012). The changing policy impetus of the Hu–Wen administration, which emphasized 'indigenous innovation' over offshored scientific services, fostered a new interest in funding and marketing the patentable biomedical innovations developed by Chinese life science researchers. In response to this policy shift, Chinese medical institutions and teaching hospitals established a growing number of dedicated 'translational medicine' centres designed to foster a closer integration between the laboratory and the clinic. It was hoped that these centres would stimulate the 'translation' of China's considerable basic life science capacities into marketable clinical products (Wang *et al.* 2011; Zhao 2013). The promotion of 'translational medicine' has gone hand in hand with a significant expansion of clinical trial infrastructure within the space of the hospital. During the past few years, China's government has invested heavily in dedicated Phase I trial units for first-in-human studies and has allocated grant funding to approximately half of these, with the clear ambition of fostering a competitive market in domestic biomedical innovation (Zhang 2011).

These investments signalled a dramatic rethinking of the strategic role of the hospital in China's economic reforms. For more than a decade, the hospital had operated on the model of a clinical export zone selling low-wage scientific labour and abundant access to human research subjects into a global pharmaceutical market dominated by the USA, Europe, and Japan. Under the Hu–Wen administration, second-generation reformers sought to reclassify the Chinese hospital as a high-tech knowledge park – an employer of high-cost professional labour and the source of high-return proprietary innovations – and to leverage its existing experimental apparatus in the service of international competition. The hospital, in short, has been the site of intense experiments of both a biomedical and institutional kind throughout the reform era, progressively adapting its experimental trial infrastructure to conform to the shifting imperatives of government science policy and the pressures of a global pharmaceutical market.

This chapter develops the concept of 'experimental postsocialism' as a way of understanding the recent history of the Chinese urban hospital. I borrow the term 'postsocialism' from Arif Dirlik (2005: 229–50), who refers to the hybrid state of contemporary Chinese 'government' as a reaction and response to revolutionary Maoism *and* global capitalism, and thus as neither purely socialist nor capitalist. I also draw from the work of Sebastian Heilmann and Elizabeth Perry (2011a, 2011b), who highlight the long history of pragmatist – that is, experimental – philosophy in Chinese political thought. As an epistemology of practice that professes an overt agnosticism with regard to a-priori truths, pragmatism has proved remarkably adaptable to the most ideologically diverse regimes of government in China (liberal, communist, market-socialist, neoliberal). For my purposes, the term 'experimental postsocialism' appears as a particularly apt formulation for understanding the intertwined histories of experimental biomedicine and institutional experimentation in the Chinese hospital.

A focus on the pragmatist legacy in Chinese political thought allows one to understand discontinuity in modern Chinese history without having to overstate the rupture between Maoist and post-Maoist modes of government. Political theorists educated in the idea that a Schumpeterian innovation economy depends on the prior existence of a liberal-democratic form of government are confounded by the coexistence of market reform, innovation policies, and authoritarian intervention in the recent history of Chinese science and technology policy (Segal 2003). Such theorists typically predict that at some point China will need to adopt a liberal-democratic form of government if it is to fully realize its stated techno-scientific ambitions. Yet if one pays attention to the role played by pragmatism in twentieth-century Chinese politics, the coexistence of highly experimental and highly authoritarian forms of government appears less enigmatic. The will to experiment may well be considered the common denominator of successive political regimes in China since the 1920s. What distinguishes these regimes is not the fact of policy experimentalism but the diverse styles of experiment they have adopted and the ends to which they have applied this practice.

The chapter deploys the concept of 'experimental postsocialism' as a prism through which to investigate the restructuring of the Chinese urban hospital over the past three decades. I argue that, by the turn of the millennium, the first generation of market reforms undertaken during the Deng and Jiang periods came to be understood, in retrospect, as a form of 'uncontrolled experiment', one that ultimately proved too costly in terms of social disharmonies and macroeconomic imbalances. The reforms undertaken by the Hu–Wen administration were envisaged, by contrast, as a form of 'controlled experiment', in part because they redefined the promise of clinical research as part of a nationalist agenda of scientific and human development.

Experimental postsocialism

My reference to postsocialist experimentalism is more than metaphorical. Historians of modern China have long recognized the importance of a certain kind of experimentalism to the policy style of the Chinese Communist Party (CCP): both before and after the turn to market liberalization, the central government maintained tight control over the definition of policy objectives while nevertheless delegating policy implementation to decentralized local levels of government, whose experiments were subsequently abandoned or discarded according to the whims of party officials (Selden 1995). Only recently, however, have China scholars highlighted the political importance of applied experimentalism to the continued success of the CCP. In the introduction to an edited collection titled *Mao's Invisible Hand*, Sebastian Heilmann and Elizabeth J. Perry (2011a) argue that the historical experience of Chinese communism differed in fundamental respects from that of Russia and its East European satellites. While sharing the same formal institutions as the Soviet state, the CCP's almost three-decade-long experience of revolutionary mobilization meant that it developed a highly distinctive style of guerrilla governance characterized by continual transformation and rapid adaptation to shifting circumstances. This experimental style of governance, they argue, has continued into the postsocialist era, even while it has been applied to very different ideological ends.

Sebastian Heilmann (2011) traces the intellectual origins of this distinctive policy style to the influence of American pragmatism among Chinese intellectuals and activists, first liberal then Communist, in the early twentieth century. The pragmatist philosopher John Dewey toured the major Chinese cities and universities between 1919 and 1920, where he delivered a series of lectures explaining the importance of the experimental method to modern science (Heilmann 2011: 62–3). In these lectures, Dewey highlighted the difference between 'experience' (rendered in the Chinese translation of his work as *jingyan* 经验) and 'experiment' (*shiyan* 试验), and specified the various kinds of relationship that could be established between them. Importantly, he stressed that while experience and experiment could be considered as dialectic opposites, the relationship between the two was in fact more complex, as experiment itself could also be considered a particular kind of experience – that is, a *controlled* experience (Dewey 1973: 247). As Dewey went on to explain, what is meant by the term 'control' in the experimental method is not so much command as the provisional, and thus revocable, anticipation of results. In the words of Dewey (1973: 248): 'the most important thing in scientific method is the hypothesis, which is something quite different from mere speculation or arbitrary supposition. A hypothesis is devised to control and give direction to experimentation.' Experimental control is always hypothetical or counterfactual in nature, and it is this that distinguishes it from methods of knowledge production which rely on notions of fundamental or a-priori truth.

According to Heilmann (2011), these lectures had an enduring influence on Chinese intellectuals of all political persuasions and were particularly important to the development of Mao Zedong's thinking on practice. Well before the founding of the People's Republic of China (PRC), the CCP had adopted an elaborate model of delegating land reform in the base areas to local 'experimental points' (Heilmann 2011: 65). During the 1942–1943 Rectification Movement, in which the principles of revolutionary strategy were extensively reviewed, the notion of 'creating model experiments' as a basis for policy experimentation and 'proceeding from point to surface' in the adoption of successful experiments, was confirmed as a central tenet of communist policy-making (Heilmann 2011: 68). And by the 1950s, 'the terms "model experiment", "experimental point" as well as "model demonstration", "proceeding from point to surface" and "integrating point and surface" had emerged as key terms in the Chinese Communists' repertoire of policy experimentation' (Heilmann 2011: 70). At least up until the mid-1950s, then, when communist policy-making underwent a distinct period of rigidification, the CCP implemented a practice-based epistemology which privileged on-the-ground policy implementation over theoretical definitions of strategy, without questioning the overall prerogative of the Party-state in the definition of policy objectives.

It is in light of this singular history of social experimentalism that Heilmann and Perry (2011b) seek to explain the otherwise enigmatic success of the CCP in surviving the immense policy upheavals of the reform era. Why, after all, has China not succumbed to the same disastrous fate as the former Soviet Union? How has the PRC – which shared the same formal institutional structures of the Leninist state, with its authoritarian propaganda apparatus, coercive security forces, collectivized production and communal property systems – survived the transition to the 'socialist market economy', artfully combining the Leninist state-form with an economic strategy increasingly attuned to the competitive pressures of the global market?

If we follow the argument developed by Heilmann and Perry (2011b), post-Mao reformers such as Deng Xiaoping and his successors have not abandoned the legacy of communist policy-making but have instead reverted to the period of high experimentalism which characterized the Communist Party up until the mid-1950s. Importantly, the distinction between policy objectives and policy implementation which Mao saw as central to the experimental method has been put to good use by the economic reformers, who have been able to radically alter the political *objectives* of the PRC while remaining completely faithful to its political *methods*. Deng, for example, was fond of characterizing post-1978 economic reform as a 'large-scale experiment' which called for an inductive method of local learning through practice (Heilmann 2011: 84). In this way, he harked back to the high-point of Maoist experimental practice even while overseeing a radical shift in political objectives from the creation of a socialist state to the implementation of a market economy through socialist institutions.

For the purposes of my argument, however, the analysis of Chinese social experimentalism offered in Heilmann and Perry (2011a) needs to be pushed still further to take account of the influence of pragmatism in shaping understandings of actual *medical practice* in China. When Chinese medical doctors and Western-style practitioners clashed over professional status and resources during the 1920s and 1930s, the conflict between the two was framed in terms of the Deweyian distinction between experience (*jingyan*) and experiment (*shiyan*). The conflict came to a head at the first National Health Conference of the National Board of Health in 1929, when the Japanese-trained, western-style doctor Yu Yan (1879–1959) proposed a motion (eventually unsuccessful) to abolish traditional Chinese medicine (Lei 2002). It was Yu Yan, chief proponent of the so-called 'Chinese medical revolution', who popularized the idea that the practical efficacy of traditional Chinese medicine was based on the accumulated pharmacological experience (*jingyan*) of its medical practitioners rather than the received truths of its theoretical tradition. According to the analysis developed by Sean Hsiang-Lin Lei (2002: 341), the Chinese medical revolution should be considered an epistemological event because of the way in which it juxtaposed the Chinese terms *jingyan* and *shiyan* within the emerging discourse of medical science as direct equivalents of the Deweyian concepts of 'experience' and 'experiment'. From this moment on, it came to be accepted as common sense that Chinese medical experience (*jingyan*) needed to be combined with the methods of Western scientific experiment (*shiyan*) to constitute a fully professional scientific practice. 'In this sense', writes Lei (2002: 336), 'the neologistic construction of the Chinese term *jingyan* belongs to neither traditional China nor the modern West. Rather, the concept of *jingyan* is a cultural hybrid created at the moment when traditional Chinese medicine encountered the state'. One could argue the same, of course, for the Chinese concept of *shiyan*.

Yu Yan's appraisal of traditional Chinese medicine was more nuanced than it might at first appear, given the role he played in trying to outlaw it. While he believed that the theoretical component of traditional Chinese medicine could be safely disposed of, he also insisted that much could still be learnt from the pharmacological tradition of Chinese medical formulas, which in his view contained a kind of 'proto-experimentalism', that is, a form of experience derived from uncontrolled, trial-and-error experiment. It was this insight that Mao himself would later develop as an argument in favour of traditional Chinese medicine. Political experiment, Mao would contend, was most successful when informed by the practical experience of the proletariat. As Judith Farquhar (1994: 171) has pointed out, Mao applied the same logic to communist medical science: modern medicine, he argued, would achieve better results if it were combined with the unique body of experience contained in traditional Chinese medicine.

In 1950 Mao applied these ideas to communist health policy by calling for the unification of western (experimental) and Chinese (experiential) medicine in the service of national health (Mao 1986 [1950]). Henceforth, medical science was to be integrated with mass movement and scientific experiment informed by the practical experience of the proletariat. What this meant in terms of actual health policy can be gleaned by considering the mass campaigns launched against infectious disease during this period. The most famous of these, the campaign against bilharzia (schistosomiasis), mobilized local-level Party committees and thousands of non-professional health workers in prevention, treatment, and research units across the country. These field units not only coordinated vast environmental campaigns to eliminate the habitats of parasite-bearing snails, but also conducted mass clinical trials to investigate the relative efficacy of molluscides, 'western' biomedical drugs, and native herbal drugs in treating bilharzia (Farley 1991: 204–5). Among his many other brutal interventions, Mao's anti-bilharzia campaign transformed the Chinese countryside into an enormous field trial and targeted its inhabitants as an experimental population – both subjects and objects of a patriotic pharmacology.

The question of professional expertise and its relationship to the practical experience of the proletariat was deeply contested during this period. The

Chinese medical profession, with its urban bias and reliance on foreign (American, Japanese, and Soviet) training, represented an enduring threat to Mao's model of patriotic mass mobilization and proletarian public health. As a consequence, the fortunes of the Ministry of Health waxed and waned dramatically during the Mao era (Lynteris 2013). Throughout the 1950s, the Ministry sought to accommodate itself to the politics of mass mobilization by invoking a professional ethos of patriotic devotion and self-cultivation which paid due respect to the practical experience of the people. By 1955, however, the CCP had already set up a special committee on schistosomiasis external to the Ministry of Health and when the committee launched its campaign against infectious disease during the Great Leap Forward (1958–1961), it openly defied the advice of medical professionals (Lynteris 2013: 59–65). The catastrophic failure of the Great Leap Forward briefly restored respect for medical professionals, but during the Cultural Revolution the CCP went one step further in its denunciation of intellectuals, identifying professionalism itself as a form of bourgeois property right. As explained by Christos Lynteris, the mass line philosophy of the Cultural Revolution:

> identified skill and expertise as forms of private property, only to proceed to an even more radical identification of the 'self' in and of itself as a bourgeois relic. What followed was a series of attacks in the medical press against [the] self-cultivation model, propagating the abolition of the self as the only true way to the New Man. In the course of the Cultural Revolution (1966–1969), this new doctrine was applied to a wide spectrum of clinical operations, from tumour removal to the control of diabetes, which were rendered battlefields for proving the Maoist truth about the 'self' as against technocrat biopolitics. In turn, medical doctors were called to embrace self-abolition … and engage in long processes of confession and rectification against the 'self' as the ultimate enemy of socialism.
>
> (Lynteris 2013: 90)

At the height of the Cultural Revolution, then, Mao sought to invent a radical pragmatism that was divested of all liberal residues – a pragmatism without professional authority or individual expertise.

Today, the hierarchy between liberal and communist readings of Deweyian experimentalism has come full circle as 'market socialists' redeploy the policy-making strategies of Maoist practice towards decidedly neoliberal ends. Deng Xiaoping repeatedly called for 'vigorous experimentation' in the pursuit of market reform, designating the urban hospital as one of the primary laboratories of institutional change (Heilmann 2011: 64). Under the administration of Jiang Zemin and Zhu Rongji, market reformers sought to commercialize state-owned enterprises and former work units (including the hospital) in the most accelerated of fashions, compelling these formerly public institutions to generate their own income streams with little assistance from the state. In recent years, however, the 'vigorous experimentalism' of the Deng and Jiang eras has come under serious scrutiny as many have questioned the wisdom of pursuing market-reform and innovation policies without government subsidies or protectionism (Chen and Naughton 2013).

In response to these critiques, the Hu–Wen administration initiated a number of policy interventions designed to temper the violent social contradictions which had emerged as a result of Deng's 'vigorous experimentalism'. Although they did not renounce China's experiment in market socialism, their policy discourse tended to characterize first-generation reform as a kind of uncontrolled experiment that had not been properly channelled and mediated by the state. In this respect, the Hu–Wen administration sought to replace the 'vigorous experimentalism' of the early reform era with a form of 'controlled experiment' designed to anticipate and mediate the risks of social disharmony. In what follows, I trace the trajectory of these diverse methods of experiment as they have unfolded in the space of the urban hospital.

The uncontrolled experiment: the hospital as clinical export zone

The liberalization of health care was one of the first and most comprehensive of market reforms undertaken by Deng Xiaoping after 1978. Its effects were all the more resounding given the astonishing success of China's Mao-era campaigns to improve public health through a combination of traditional and Western medicine, preventative, basic health care interventions and collectivized health insurance (Lampton 1977; Huang 2013: 24–52). In the decades following the founding of the PRC in 1949, China massively reduced the incidence of infectious disease and increased life expectancy from an average of 35 to over 60 in the 1970s. During this period, the World Health Organization hailed China's health care system as a model for the entire developing world (Zhan 2011).

After 1949, the urban hospital, like other work sites, was organized as a *danwei* (单位) – an administrative unit that allocated and managed work for a relatively stable internal labour force while also providing for the welfare and family planning of its employees (Bray 2005). In their study of an urban hospital in the years immediately following the Cultural Revolution of 1966 to 1976, Gail Henderson and Myron Cohen (1984: 143) found that the hospital *danwei* combined egalitarian principles of redistributive welfare and shared educational opportunities with a vertically integrated structure of authority 'reminiscent of a feudal estate'. Even after the Cultural Revolution, they observed that promotion was 'egalitarian' but for this very reason more often than not resembled a political decision rather than a reward for professional advancement. Physicians and other staff had few opportunities to move between organizations. In spite of its professional limitations, however, the centrally funded hospital *danwei* managed to offer relatively affordable healthcare to all classes of the population throughout the Mao era.

All this changed in 1978 when the central government began an incremental process of shifting responsibility for medical services onto provincial and local authorities. The enduring effect of these reforms has been a growing disparity between the coastal, urban centres, where tax revenues can be called upon to compensate for at least some funding shortfalls, and the impoverished hinterlands of rural China, where few such alternative sources of income are to be found. Yet even the large urban hospital, the epicentre of China's highly centralized health system, has not fared well under reform, and has abandoned the collectivist principles of the socialist work unit or *danwei* in favour of an entrepreneurial model of health care 'services' (Zhan 2011).

The key turning point occurred in 1989 when the central government formally capped its support for public health care and demanded that hospitals become responsible for covering their own operational costs. In exchange, it was decided that hospitals were to be free to generate income through the sale of drugs and other health care services such as diagnostic tests (Gu and Zhang 2006). For the most part, these reforms have taken the form of institutional marketization – on the model of the so-called 'new public management' – rather than outright privatization (Urio 2012). The PRC did authorize the return of private practice in medicine in 1980 and a small number of private hospitals have been set up, yet public hospitals remain the major player in the hospital sector (Tam 2010: 64). These institutions, however, have been radically transformed from within, as the central government has authorized, indeed compelled, them to turn previously free or low-cost services into profit-making initiatives. In the process, remarks Mei Zhan (2011), the notion of the health care sector as part of the commercial service economy has come to the fore, as previously 'non-productive' health care services have been redefined as lucrative commodities, and erstwhile public spaces have been rediscovered as rent-making assets.

The role of the medical practitioner has dramatically changed as a consequence of these reforms. The salaries of doctors and other medical staff are made up of a fixed wage and a performance-linked bonus or floating wage reflecting the amount of revenue that an individual medical practitioner has been able to bring into the department (Tam 2010: 66). Hospital managers now fix revenue targets for individual departments, setting up different sectors of the institution in competition with each other. In the process of marketization, the vertically integrated, paternalist structures of the hospital *danwei* so vividly described by Henderson and Cohen (1984) have given way to a complex array of horizontal contractual relations between individual wards, services, practitioners and various external clients. In the popular media, it is the increasingly commercial nature of the doctor–patient relationship (mediated by the informal contract of the red envelope or under-the-table bribe) that has come to signify all that is wrong with the contemporary hospital, and indeed the reform process itself (Zhan 2011).

Yet the intrusion of informal and sometimes outright illegal contractual relations into the space of the clinic extends well beyond the immediate encounter between the doctor and the patient. Waikeung Tam (2010: 68–9), for example, recounts that the leasing out of entire clinical departments to outside contractors has become common practice since the 1990s, despite repeated efforts by the

Ministry of Health to ban it. Other institutions have resorted to the legal practice of creating VIP floors, which offer private rooms, private toilets, and other special amenities to patients willing to pay more (Cong and Hu 2005).

It is in the context of these wider institutional changes that a market for contract clinical research has evolved. During the past decade, the multinational pharmaceutical industry has increasingly moved to offshore clinical trials from the USA and Western Europe to peripheral destinations such as the former Soviet Union, Latin America, India and China, where the costs of employing clinical professionals, institutional space, and human research subjects are much lower (Kuo 2012; Petryna 2009; Prasad 2009; Sunder Rajan 2008). In recent years China's clinical trial market has grown at a faster rate than any other emerging or established market (Thiers *et al.* 2008).

The revenue-raising imperative that weighs on hospitals means that clinical trials are becoming a vital source of income for the beleaguered Chinese hospital and an informal means of resolving conflicts between the medical practitioner and the patient. By acting as Principal Investigators on a pharmaceutical industry-sponsored drug study, doctors not only receive a sizeable bonus or 'floating wage', but also the chance to be published in a reputable international medical journal (author interview 2008a, 2008b, 2013a). In the meantime, uninsured or underinsured patients derive at least a relative benefit from the arrangement by receiving medicines that are both foreign-manufactured (and thus considered 'safer' than Chinese-manufactured products) and free of cost, along with free health care for the duration of the trial (author interview 2008a, 2008b). In the absence of alternative means of accessing drugs, many patients have jumped at the chance to participate in trials, even though the therapeutic usefulness of the drugs is by no means assured and the actual distribution of drugs (as opposed to placebo) in a double-blinded randomized trial is unknown to both the investigator and the patient (Berton 2006; Vaidya *et al.* 2007: 23; Xu *et al.* 2006: 371).

In many respects, the expansion of multinational clinical trials into China is an artefact of changes in international governance. In 1995 the International Conference on Harmonization (ICH), a consortium of pharmaceutical companies and drug regulators from Western Europe, the USA, and Japan, established a standard set of rules for the conduct of clinical trials, the manufacture of drugs, and bioethics approval, including Good Laboratory Practice (GLP) and Good Clinical Practice (GCP) guidelines (Abraham and Reed 2002; Daemmrich 2004: 151–66). ICH guidelines have subsequently been adopted by prospective drug markets worldwide, including China, in an effort to take advantage of the expanded commercial opportunities of multiple market registration for new drugs. These efforts at forging global standards have transformed the experimental results of clinical research into fully exchangeable data, whose translatability across regulatory borders and drug consumer markets is rendered as smooth as possible.

Having adopted the global standard of GCP in 2003, China's government has also made concerted efforts to transform China into an attractive destination for multinational clinical trials. It has implemented drug approval regulations conforming to those of the US Food and Drug Administration; created an accreditation system for clinical trial sites in hospitals; established special technology zones for contract research organizations (Zhongguancun Life Science Park in Beijing and Zhangjiang Biopharmaceutical Park in Shanghai); and pursued a high-profile anti-corruption case against the former head of the China Food and Drug Administration, who was accused of fraudulent drug approvals (he has since been sentenced and executed) (Huang 2013: 112–34; Scott 2011; Zhang and Wu 2012; Zhou 2005). One regulatory intervention in particular has been decisive. Prior to 2003, new drugs could only be marketed in China if they had already been tested and approved for marketing in Europe and the USA. Changes to domestic regulation in 2003 made it possible to include China in multinational drug trials without a time lag (Humphries *et al.* 2006). As a result, clinical trial data collected in China are now being used not only for the domestic approval of drugs already accepted in the USA, but also as a platform for developing new drugs for the international market.

The reform-era Chinese hospital represents an attractive production site for the multinational pharmaceutical sponsor precisely because it retains at least some of the features of the old hospital *danwei*: a professionally qualified work force, centralized management, massive case loads, and a concentration of specific patient profiles in specialized departments. In contrast to the USA, where clinical trials have been outsourced to private institutions or delegated to physicians in private practice, all Chinese clinical trials (Phases I, II, and III) take place in large urban government hospitals, which are invariably affiliated with a medical school. Despite recent efforts to create a more decentralized GP or general practitioners' system based in community health clinics, hospitals remain the destination of choice for most Chinese patients: no referral is needed to visit a hospital and patients regularly travel from remote rural destinations to consult the more qualified staff that can be found in the large urban centres. These hospitals have multiple specialty departments and can house between 1,000 and 2,000 beds, making them considerably more efficient than the current US model of later phase trials run from private physicians' offices. As of 2011, the CFDA had accredited 278 clinical trial institutions, more than double the number it had approved in the late 1990s (Djali 2011).

In the past few years, China has seen a rapid increase in Phase I units for first-in-human studies of new, previously untested drugs, as multinational pharmaceutical companies undertake comprehensive drug development programmes on Chinese soil.[2] All Phase I units in China are based in hospital grounds and are either run by hospital staff or cooperatively organized with a private contract research organization (CRO) specialized in the on-site coordination of trials (Zhang 2011). Shanghai Clinical Research Center, for example, is a 56-bed unit located within the confines of Xuhui Central hospital. Much like comparable institutions in the USA, the unit has a small intensive observation ward equipped with 12 beds, an entertainment area for trial subjects, a blood-drawing room, an emergency room for 'adverse events', and state-of-the-art EMG (electromyography) and ECG (electrocardiography) facilities. The unit's website includes a recruitment page featuring pastel-coloured, airbrushed photos of smiling families against a verdant backdrop of trees. Below the images a caption reads 'Here you help to create a better future!' ('Volunteers at SCRC' 2008–2015).

Other units are located in government hospitals but run by international Phase I groups, who typically manage a chain of similar Phase I units in strategic locations around the world. One such company, the US-based FrontageLab, has a 72-bed Phase I–IIa clinical trial unit in New Jersey and a 130-bed, hospital-based Phase I–IIa facility located in the First Affiliated Hospital of Zhengzhou University, a 6,000-bed facility considered to be one of the top hospitals in China ('Clinical trials in the U.S. and China' 2013). Another private US-based clinical trials company, START (South Texas Accelerated Research Therapeutics), which already operates Phase I units on the USA–Mexico border and in Madrid, has recently opened a Phase I unit in Fudan University Cancer Centre, Shanghai's largest cancer centre (Carlson 2011). A private–public partnership between Fudan University, START, and Cenova Ventures, a health investment fund backed by local and central governments in China, this operation is unique in China. As such, it not only testifies to the PRC's willingness to experiment with new institutional forms but also to the emergence of transnational synergies between Phase I trial markets.

Taken together, these examples of multinational investment in China are representative of an emerging global production chain in clinical research, one which aspires to leverage a 24-hour per day network of public and private clinics, physicians' offices, and hospital wards for the production of data that can be lodged with multiple regulatory agencies at the same time. The harmonization of regulatory, clinical, and ethical standards has made it possible for CROs to set up operations in various strategic locations around the world, in each case taking advantage of the changing social and economic conditions that have served to repurpose the specific medical institution (the private doctor's office or the socialist hospital) as an experimental production site.

Having abandoned the collectivist model of the *danwei*, the Chinese hospital now survives as a hybrid institution in which the formal structures of the socialist health care complex are maintained in place by recombining forces with the multinational, private research sector. As David Stark (2001) argues with respect to the former Soviet Union, the postsocialist transition to a neoliberal model of growth has not, in practice, involved the rapid and all-encompassing implementation of market reform and privatization. Rather, 'market socialism' has blurred the boundaries between organizational forms, legitimating principles, and standards of valuation, making it impossible to distinguish between private and public goods in any final way. As Stark (2001: 82) goes on to argue, the resultant ambiguity of assets means that one institution is able to deploy its infrastructure towards multiple ends. The reform-era Chinese hospital offers the perfect example of such a strategy of 'organizational hedging': operating within the general legitimating principles of collectivist public health care, it has also transformed itself into a *clinical export zone* in which physicians are called upon to serve the dual role of health care provider and clinical investigator, and patient bodies are leveraged as both clients of health care services and experimental assets.

The reform era has rehabilitated the professional independence of the medical practitioner, redefining the status of the physician as a function of individual expertise and delinking wages from collectivist notions of public service. Yet all too often this new-found autonomy is associated, in the eyes of the public, with an overt and unrestrained self-interest (Hui 2010). Medical practitioners have responded to this pervasive mistrust by seeking to revive the notions of Confucian self-cultivation and professional ethics that were once championed by the Ministry of Health as an alternative to Mao's mass-line (Lynteris 2013). Yet the absence of thoroughgoing reform to address the profound inequalities in public access to health care has, until recently, rendered such gestures largely ineffective.[3]

Towards the controlled experiment: indigenizing life science innovation

During the last decade, the social, political and indeed public health risks associated with the first generation of 'market socialist' interventions have become increasingly clear even to the most reform-oriented of economists. Critics of market reform consistently single out the health care sector as the symptom of all that went wrong with the first wave of 'market socialism' (Gu and Zhang 2006). By the turn of the century, the problems plaguing the urban hospital (overcrowding, inflated drug prices, medical negligence, and corruption) were notorious, as were the failures of the social welfare system (see also Hoffman, Jeffreys and Sigley in this book). It was generally recognized that China's low rates of consumption and high rates of saving could be attributed in large part to the catastrophic effects of illness on household budgets: the impact of large numbers of uninsured or underinsured citizens in any calculation of China's future macroeconomic prospects was impossible to ignore (Office of the World Health Organization Representative in China and Social Development Department of China State Council Development Research Center 2005: 22). It was also becoming abundantly clear that the introduction of commercial research into Chinese hospitals had done little to elevate China's position in the global hierarchy of life science research: Chinese clinical investigators had entered the global knowledge economy in the lowly guise of contract researchers – that is, as scientific service workers – rather than generators of high-value patents.

As if to underscore the urgency for reform, the outbreak of the severe acute respiratory syndrome virus (SARS) in 2003 revealed fatal flaws in both the public health and medical research systems. Communication between public hospitals and ministries was chaotic; infected patients failed to present at hospitals for fear of high medical bills; and the hierarchical nature of Chinese scientific institutions meant that precious time was wasted deferring to the opinion of respected elder scientists instead of pursuing all research options into the provenance of the virus (Cao 2004). The mismanagement of the SARS crisis pointed to a series of systematic flaws in the organization of health care and life science research which had emerged as a result of first-generation reform. In response to these domestic concerns, a 2005 report cosponsored by the World Health Organization and the State Council offered a devastating indictment of the social and economic consequences of China's market-oriented health care reform, identifying health care inequalities as one of the most significant sources of China's 'disharmonious social relationships' (Office of the World Health Organization Representative in China and Social Development Department of China State Council Development Research Center 2005).

It was in this atmosphere of heightened critique that Hu Jintao and Wen Jiabao came to power. Almost immediately upon entering office, the administration announced a new 'indigenous innovation' agenda designed to recalibrate the interests of national development and market success in Chinese science policy. The discourse of 'indigenous innovation' was nationalist in tone but Schumpeterian in method – calculated to neutralize emerging nationalist, populist, and anti-liberal sentiments in the Chinese public, without renouncing the project of liberalization itself (Chen and Naughton 2013; see also Sigley in this book, on 'indigenizing' social work).

In a speech delivered at the opening of China's Fourth National Conference on Science and Technology in January 2006, President Hu spoke of China's need to 'adhere to a new path of innovation with Chinese characteristics and strive to build an innovation-oriented country' (Liang *et al.* 2010). Following this announcement, the State Council (2006) published a 'Medium to Long-Term Programme on National Science and Technology Development 2006–2020' (hereafter the 2006 Programme), which outlined its ambition to transform China into 'an innovation oriented society by the year 2020' and a world-leading innovator in the long term. A few years later, China's Twelfth Five-Year Plan for 2011 to 2015 predicted that China's coastal regions would soon cease to play the role of the 'world's factory' and instead compete with the USA and the European Union in high-end, value-added research and development (Zhonggong zhongyang 2010). Such hyperbole reflected the view of a growing number of Chinese economists that science policy during the 1990s had blundered in assuming that innovation could be fostered without significant levels of state funding in basic research (Chen and Naughton 2013: 9).

The 2006 Programme (State Council 2006) designated 16 mega-projects for exceptional levels of state funding, including the 'New Drug Creation and Development Programme', launched in 2008 under the leadership of the Ministry of Health, which provided generous government subsidies to promote the development of patentable drugs for ten major disease categories (Cyranoski 2008; Hughes 2010). The programme supports partnerships between academic institutions and private pharmaceutical companies (often multinational), but crucially requires patent-sharing agreements with Chinese researchers as a condition of funding. It was renewed and expanded under the Twelfth Five-Year Plan (2011–2015) which, in the wake of the global financial crisis, set aside CNY 16 billion to fund seven emerging strategic industries, among them biomedical innovation and new drug development (Jia 2010).

Alongside these centralized funding programmes, many of China's leading universities and medical colleges have independently opened up 'translational medicine centres' designed to foster intense collaboration between basic life science researchers and hospital-based clinicians (Wang *et al.* 2011; Dai 2011). More than 40 such institutions have been established since 2009, including major centres at Peking University Health Science Centre, Peking Union Medical Centre, and Shanghai Jiaotong University School of Medicine (Zhao 2013).

The concept of 'translational medicine' was first advanced by the USA National Institutes of Health (NIH) in 2004 under the leadership of Elias A. Zerhouni (2005), in response to what was perceived as a disabling division of labour between basic life science research and clinical application. Until then, most basic life science research in the USA was carried out in academic laboratories while research into clinical applications had been ceded to the private pharmaceutical industry. The promotion of 'translational medicine' was designed to foster a much closer working collaboration between clinical researchers and life scientists, with the ultimate goal of accelerating commercial innovation.

In China, the commercial potential of this initiative is greatly enhanced by the size of its population. Professor Zhao Yupei of Peking Union Medical College Hospital defines China's large patient base as one of the 'national resources' at the disposal of its translational medicine agenda.

> The large base number of the Chinese population provides sufficient numbers of patients for comprehensive clinical trials that can be conducted more rapidly and, thus, result in discoveries that would require a much longer time frame than in countries with substantially smaller populations.... Additionally, because the Chinese race is typical among the Asian ethnic groups, studies involving Chinese patients have great potential value for advancing global translational medical research.
>
> (Zhao 2013: 31)

Minister of Health Chen Zhu (2011) has been particularly outspoken in promoting the concept of 'translational medicine' as a guiding principle for China's investments in life science research. Indeed, since his appointment in 2008, Chen has pursued a vigorous campaign in favour of the creation of a Chinese equivalent to the American NIH. This campaign has not yet borne fruit but, in the meantime, Chen has succeeded in launching a medical research department within the Natural Science Foundation of China, reputed to be the most independent and democratic of China's science-funding institutions. In 2010 alone, the newly created medical department disbursed close to CNY 1 billion in grants, privileging projects with potential clinical applications over more speculative research (Guo 2010; Jiao 2010; Wang *et al.* 2011).

Much of China's interest in translational medicine has been pursued in collaboration with the NIH itself, along with other leading medical institutions in the USA. The Sino-American Symposium on Translational Medicine, first held in Beijing in 2010, and co-organized by the Chinese Academy of Medical Sciences, the US NIH and the private Global MD Organization, is one such venue for these collaborations. In general, China's new translational research centres are affiliated with a US-based university or research hospital and have established ongoing research and training exchanges for students and physicians (Ognibene *et al.* 2011; Shi and Dai 2013). For example, the translational research centre of Peking Union Medical College, which was established in 2010, conducts joint projects with the Institute of Basic Medical Sciences of the Chinese Academy of Medical Sciences and has an ongoing collaboration with the University of California San Francisco; Peking University Clinical Research Institute has a Memorandum of Understanding with the University of Michigan (author interview 2013b); Sun Yat-Sen University is affiliated with Johns Hopkins University; while the Yale Center for Clinical Investigation conducts exchanges with various Chinese universities and research hospitals.

Exemplary of this new institutional model is the Peking University Clinical Research Institute (PUCRI), founded by Peking University Health Science Centre in 2008. Peking University has the unique advantage of having eight affiliated hospitals, some of them dedicated to one specialty area only (by contrast, the other major medical school, Peking Union Medical College, only has one hospital). Like other major urban hospitals, it has been hosting contract clinical trials for more than a decade now, has numerous accredited departments, and an on-site Phase I unit that sees a steady stream of contract work. Only recently, however, has the university administration sought to mobilize this infrastructure on behalf of academic clinical research – by all accounts extremely underdeveloped in China until now (author interview 2013b).

PUCRI styles itself as an academic research organization (ARO), distinct from the traditional CRO in that it is practised in the workings of both academic and commercial research. Its institutional model is something of a hybrid – PUCRI performs numerous contractual services for the pharmaceutical industry (including drug development courses and clinical trials) and partially funds its academic programme through these commercial activities (author interview 2013c). Its academic programme is designed to build up clinical research skills within its affiliated hospitals. It involves close working relationships with individual physicians, who receive intensive, ongoing training in the everyday practice of clinical research, project support, data management, and help with the statistical interpretation of data. Alongside this one-to-one training, PUCRI is also developing an extensive programme of postgraduate training in clinical research, including a proposed Masters Degree – forms of professional training that were until now non-existent in China (author interview 2013b; Hu *et al.* 2011; Huang *et al.* 2013).

Other translational research institutes are more heavily involved in testing new drug candidates developed by the Chinese bio-pharmacological companies. Thanks to generous state funding of drug innovation, academic spinoffs have proliferated in recent years. The Third Xiangya Hospital, one of the three affiliated hospitals of Central South University in Hunan province, specializes in rare and critical illnesses. In 2008, it entered into partnership with the domestic CRO Tigermed to provide a collaborative Phase I unit dedicated to first-in-human studies of proprietary drugs developed in China. It has completed more than 40 investigational studies of new drugs, many of these for complex protein therapies, and has recently set up a clinical research programme for postgraduate students (Yuan 2013). PUCRI and Xiangya are only two examples of the distinctive conglomerates of academic and commercial research that are emerging in China, as the infrastructures created to house contract clinical research in the first decade of the twenty-first century are now being adapted to serve the project of 'indigenous innovation' and 'scientific development'.

The nature and scope of private pharmaceutical investment in China has evolved in line with this changing research environment. Multinational pharmaceutical companies continue to place relatively simple-to-perform, later-phase trials in urban hospitals, contracting them out to medical practitioners on a case-by-case basis. These trials follow protocols that have been entirely designed by the multinational pharmaceutical company and test drugs that have been invented in the USA or Western Europe. The Chinese hospital has no proprietary claim over the drug to be tested and the clinical investigator is hired as a contract researcher, with little or no creative input into the design of the trial. In recent years, however, the same companies have entered into a growing number of joint ventures with China's translational medicine centres to develop innovative drugs and therapies discovered by Chinese life science researchers (Hughes 2010; Qian *et al.* 2012). These collaborations involve joint IP-sharing agreements and establish a true partnership between Chinese research institutions and their industry collaborators.

For example, Roche established a research centre in China in 2004, hiring Chinese scientists as lower-cost but highly qualified service labour to develop promising chemical compounds that had been discovered overseas. By 2007, however, the company had changed its strategy and begun collaborating with Chinese academic research centres in the development of new therapies in oncology and virology (Hughes 2010: 581). In 2006, AstraZeneca created its own USD100 million translational research centre, the Innovation Center China, which focuses on developing drugs targeting the kinds of cancers that are most prevalent in East Asia – liver, gastric, and lung cancers. The centre employs in-house clinical investigators – many of them Chinese investigators trained overseas – while also engaging with external research centres and hospitals (Gu and Shi 2012).

Commercial investment in China's biomedical and pharmaceutical sectors has been bolstered by the introduction of a comprehensive health reform programme in 2009, which promises to provide universal basic health care coverage by 2020. After more than two decades of dwindling health insurance coverage, this major overhaul of the health system promises to transform China into a major consumer market for therapeutic drugs and other pharmaceutical products.

Concluding remarks

As a result of the reform policies initiated by the Hu–Wen administration, the reform-era Chinese hospital has intensified its experimental activities and expanded its clinical research infrastructures. Far from disavowing the intense experimentalism of China's first generation of hospital reforms, the proponents of 'indigenous innovation' have multiplied the experimental sites available in the urban hospital and dedicated enormous resources to the professionalization of pharmacological and clinical research. What has changed, however, is the long-term focus of this experimentalism. Until recently, the hospital has operated as an export-oriented research zone and source of low-cost scientific labour for the multinational pharmaceutical industry. Today, hospital and university administrators are striving to repopulate this space with internationally competitive, professional knowledge workers and redefine it as a source of national, globally competitive innovation.

In short, China's second generation reformers have sought to repatriate the dividends of experimental investment by leveraging existing clinical infrastructures towards the ends of national economic growth and domestic health care consumption. In so doing, they have redefined China's patient population as a national experimental asset rather than a source of exportable data – both subject and object of a controlled experiment in post-revolutionary socialist reform. The ongoing mobilization of experimental subjects continues to rely on persistent inequalities in the distribution of wealth and health insurance, even after recent efforts to reform health care. And yet the discourse of 'indigenous innovation' seeks to neutralize radical critique by enrolling China's population in a national development agenda that promises, at some point, to improve health for all.

Acknowledgements

This research was supported under the Australian Research Council's Future Fellowship funding scheme (FT100100543).

Notes

1 Clinical trials take place in three phases. Phase I or first-in-human studies follow upon animal studies and seek to establish the safety of a drug or therapeutic product for human consumption. These studies are conducted on healthy subjects and present the greatest risk to the research subject, as by definition they involve drugs whose risk profile has not yet been established. After initial safety studies have been conducted, Phase II and III studies are conducted on patients who are suffering from the targeted ailment. These studies seek to establish the efficacy and ideal dosage of the drug being tested.

2 The CFDA prohibits Phase I, first-in-human studies of drugs developed outside of China. However, multinational companies can undertake Phase I trials of drugs they have developed in their China-based research and development institutions. As a growing number of multinational companies establish comprehensive drug development programmes in China, the number of Phase I trials has risen accordingly.

3 In China today, debates around the role of doctors and medical ethics have thrived alongside the rampant commercialization of health care services. Indicative of this trend, the Law on Medical Practitioners, passed in 1999, defines medical practice as an autonomous profession, calls for a standardization of professional status and titles, and asserts that doctors 'should possess good occupational morals and professional medical knowledge, practice humanitarianism, and perform the sacred duties of preventing and treating diseases' (National People's Congress 1999: Article 3). In 2002, the first professional association for Chinese medical practitioners, the Chinese Medical Doctor's Association (CMDA), was founded under a charter which states that medical professionalism depends on the ethical conduct of individual practitioners and the cultivation of trust between doctor and patient (Cao 2011; Hsiao and Hu 2011). The CMDA has subsequently published numerous guidelines on the proper ethical conduct of medical professionals.

References

Abraham, J. and Reed, T. (2002) 'Progress, innovation and regulatory science in drug development: the politics of international standard-setting', *Social Studies of Science*, 32, 3: 337–69.

Author interview (2008a) Interview with CRO representative conducted by Melinda Cooper, 14 November, Beijing.

Author interview (2008b) Interview with CRO representative conducted by Melinda Cooper, 18 November, Beijing.

Author interview (2013a) Interview with Peking University Academic Phase 1 Centre assistant director conducted by Melinda Cooper, 25 June, Beijing.

Author interview (2013b) Interview with Peking University Clinical Research Centre clinical researcher conducted by Melinda Cooper, 25 June, Beijing.

Author interview (2013c) Interview with Peking University Clinical Research Centre (PUCRI) data management specialist, 25 June, Beijing.

Berton, E. (2006) 'More Chinese get free drugs in clinical trials', *Wall Street Journal Online*, 14 February. Online. Available: http://online.wsj.com/article/SB113988758015373215.html (accessed 11 May 2015).

Bray, D. (2005) *Social Space and Governance in Urban China: The Danwei System from Origins to Reform*, Stanford: Stanford University Press.

Cao, C. (2004) 'SARS: "Waterloo" of Chinese science', *China: An International Journal*, 2, 2: 262–86.

Cao, C. (2011) 'The Chinese Medical Doctor Association: a new industrial relations actor in China's health service?', *Relations Industrielles/Industrial Relations*, 66, 1: 74–97.

Carlson, R.H. (2011) 'START Phase I trial group opens centre in Shanghai', *Oncology Times UK*, 8, 4: 6.

Chen, L. and Naughton, B. (2013) 'The emergence of Chinese techno-industrial policy: from megaprojects to strategic emerging industries, 2003–2011', unpublished paper.

Chen, Z. (2011) 'National plan on translational medicine in China: promoting health care reform and improving people's health', in S. Sanders (ed.), *Selected Presentations from the 2011 Sino-American Symposium on Clinical and Translational Medicine*, Washington: Science/AAAS, pp. 7–8.

'Clinical trials in the U.S. and China' (2013) Frontage. Online. Available: www.frontagelab.com/clinical-trials-us-china.asp (accessed 12 May 2015).

Cong, Y. and Linying Hu (2005) 'The VIP floors', *Hastings Center Report*, 35, 1: 16–17.

Cyranoski, D. (2008) 'China rushes through major funding system', *Nature*, 455, 7210: 142–3.

Daemmrich, A.A. (2004) *Pharmacopolitics: Drug Regulation in the United States and Germany*, Chapel Hill: University of North Carolina Press.
Dai, K. (2011) 'The development strategy of translational research based on China's current national situation', in S. Sanders (ed.) *Selected Presentations from the 2011 Sino-American Symposium on Clinical and Translational Medicine*, Washington: Science/AAAS, pp. 15–16.
Dewey, J. (1973) *Lectures in China, 1919–1920*, Honolulu: University Press of Hawaii.
Dirlik, A. (2005) *Marxism in the Chinese Revolution*, Lanham: Rowman and Littlefield.
Djali, S. (2011) 'Capacity building for global clinical trials', *ChinaTrials 2011: Global Clinical Development Summit*, 9 November, Beijing.
Farley, J. (1991) *Bilharzia: A History of Imperial Tropical Medicine*, Cambridge: Cambridge University Press.
Farquhar, J. (1994) *Knowing Practice: The Clinical Encounter of Chinese Medicine*, Boulder: Westview Press.
Gu, E. and Zhang, J. (2006) 'Health care regime change in urban China: unmanaged marketization and reluctant privatization', *Pacific Affairs*, 79, 1: 49–71.
Gu, Y. and Shi, W. (2012) 'Asian innovation: a unique opportunity for the pharmaceutical industry', *Drug Discovery World*, Fall. Online. Available: www.ddw-online.com/business/p191008-asian%20innovation%3A%20a%20unique%20opportunity%20for%20the%20pharmaceutical%20industry.%20%20fall%2012.html (accessed 11 May 2015).
Guo, L. (2010) 'China boosts medical research', *The Lancet*, 375, 9716: 532–3.
Heilmann, S. (2011) 'Policy-making through experimentation: the formation of a distinctive policy process', in S. Heilmann and E.J. Perry (eds), *Mao's Invisible Hand: The Political Foundations of Adaptive Governance in China*, Cambridge, MA: Harvard University Press, pp. 62–101.
Heilmann, S. and Perry, E.J. (eds) (2011a) *Mao's Invisible Hand: The Political Foundations of Adaptive Governance in China*, Cambridge, MA: Harvard University Press.
Heilmann, S. and Perry, E.J. (2011b) 'Embracing uncertainty: guerilla policy style and adaptive governance in China', in S. Heilmann and E.J. Perry (eds), *Mao's Invisible Hand: The Political Foundations of Adaptive Governance in China*, Cambridge, MA: Harvard University Press, pp. 1–29.
Henderson, G.E. and Cohen, M.S. (1984) *The Chinese Hospital: A Socialist Work Unit*, New Haven: Yale University Press.
Hsiao, W.C. and Hu, L. (2011) 'The state of medical professionalism in China: past, present, and future', in W.P. Alford, K. Winston, and W.C. Kirby (eds), *Prospects for the Professions in China*, Abingdon: Routledge, pp. 111–28.
Hu, Y., Yueqin, H., Ding, J., Liu, Y., Fan, D., Li, T., Shou, C., Fan, J., Wang, W., Dong, Z., Qin, X., Fang, W., and Ke, Y. (2011) 'Status of clinical research in China', *The Lancet*, 377, 9760: 124–5.
Huang, S., Chen, Q., Yan, J., and He, X. (2013) 'Medical research in China: where does it go?' *American Journal of Medical Quality*, 28, 2: 172–3.
Huang, Y. (2013) *Governing Health in Contemporary China*, Abingdon: Routledge.
Hughes, B. (2010) 'China spurs pharma innovation', *Nature Reviews Drug Discovery*, 9, 8: 581–2.
Hui, E.C. (2010) 'The contemporary healthcare crisis in China and the role of medical professionalism', *Journal of Medicine and Philosophy*, 354: 477–92.

Humphries, M., Niese, D., and Dai, P. (2006) 'China as a growing research base for innovation in medicines development', *International Journal of Pharmaceutical Medicine*, 20, 6: 355–9.

Jia, H. (2010) 'China's $2.4 billion splurge', *Nature Biotechnology*, 28, 10: 990.

Jiao, L. (2010) 'After long march, scientists create "Chinese NIH" ', *Science*, 327, 5962: 132.

Kuo, W.-H. (2012) 'Transforming states in the era of global pharmaceuticals: visioning clinical research in Japan, Taiwan, and Singapore', in K.S. Rajan (ed.) *Lively Capital: Biotechnologies, Ethics and Governance in Global Markets*, Durham: Duke University Press, pp. 279–305.

Lampton, D.M. (1977) *The Politics of Medicine in China: The Policy Process, 1949–1977*, Berkeley: University of California Press.

Lei, S. (2002) 'How did Chinese medicine become experiential? The political epistemology of jingyan', *Positions: East Asia Cultures Critique*, 10, 2: 333–64.

Liang, H., Ding, J., and Xue, Y. (2010) 'China's drug innovation and policy environment', *Drug Discovery Today*, 16, 1–2: 1–3.

Lynteris, C. (2013) *The Spirit of Selflessness in Maoist China: Socialist Medicine and the New Man*, London: Palgrave Pivot.

Mao Zedong (1986 [1950]) 'Inscription for the first national conference on health care (August 1950)', in *The Writings of Mao Zedong, 1949–1976: Volume 1, September 1945–December 1955*, New York: M.E. Sharpe, p. 131.

National People's Congress (1999) *Law of the People's Republic of China on Medical Practitioners*, 26 June. Online. Available: www.asianlii.org/cn/legis/cen/laws/lotprocomp511 (accessed 16 June 2015).

Office of the World Health Organization Representative in China and Social Development Department of China State Council Development Research Center (2005) *China: Health, Poverty and Economic Development*, Beijing, December. Online. Available: www.who.int/macrohealth/action/CMH_China.pdf (accessed 11 May 2015).

Ognibene, F.P., Shi, T., and Gallin, J. (2011) 'Global outreach in clinical research by the NIH Clinical Center: building training partnerships with China', in S. Sanders (ed.), *Selected Presentations from the 2011 Sino-American Symposium on Clinical and Translational Medicine*, Washington: Science/AAAS, pp. 8–10.

Petryna, A. (2009) *When Experiments Travel: Clinical Trials and the Global Search for Human Subjects*, Princeton: Princeton University Press.

Prasad, A. (2009) 'Capitalizing disease: biopolitics of drug trials in India', *Theory, Culture and Society*, 26, 5: 1–29.

Qian, M., Wu, D., Wang, E., Marincola, F.M., Wang, W., Rhodes, W., Liebman, M., Bai, C., Lam, C.W., Marko-Varga, G., Fehniger, T.E., Andersson, R., and Wang, X. (2012) 'Development and promotion in translational medicine: perspectives from 2012 Sino-American Symposium on clinical and translational medicine', *Clinical Translational Medicine*, 1: 25.

Scott, G. (2011) 'China fast becoming No. 1 market for pharma: interview with Gregg Scott (podcast)', Mendelspod.com, 27 October. Online. Available: http://mendelspod.com/podcast/chinabio# (accessed 11 May 2015).

Segal, A. (2003) *Digital Dragon: High-Technology Enterprises in China*, Ithaca: Cornell University Press.

Selden, M. (1995) *China in Revolution: The Yenan Way Revisited*, Armonk: M.E. Sharpe.

Shi, T.Z. and Dai, K. (2013) 'Training translational investigators in China', in B. Alving, K. Dai, and S.H.H. Chan (eds), *Translational Medicine: What, Why and How – An International Perspective*, Basel: Karger, pp. 47–55.

Stark, D. (2001) 'Ambiguous assets for uncertain environments: heterarchy in postsocialist firms', in P. DiMaggio (ed.), *The Twenty-First-Century Firm: Changing Economic Organization in International Perspective*, Princeton: Princeton University Press, pp. 69–104.

State Council of the People's Republic of China (2006) 'Guojia zhongchangqi kexue he jishu fazhan guihua gangyao (2006–2020)' [Medium-to-Long Term Programme of National Science and Technology Development 2006–2020], 9 February 2006. Online. Available: www.gov.cn/jrzg/2006-02/09/content_183787.htm; http://sydney.edu.au/global-health/international-networks/National_Outline_for_Medium_and_Long_Term_ST_Development1.doc (accessed 11 May 2015).

Sunder Rajan, K. (2008) 'Biocapital as an emergent form of life: speculations on the figure of the experimental subject', in S. Gibbon and C. Novas (eds), *Biosocialities, Genetics and the Social Sciences*, Abingdon: Routledge, pp. 157–87.

Tam, W. (2010) 'Privatizing health care in China: problems and reforms', *Journal of Contemporary Asia*, 40, 1: 63–81.

Thiers, F.A., Sinskey, A.J., and Berndt, E.R. (2008) 'Trends in the globalization of clinical trials', *Nature Reviews Drug Discovery*, 7, 1: 13–14.

Urio, P. (2012) *China, the West and the Myth of New Public Management*, Abingdon: Routledge.

Vaidya, A., Liapi, A., and Kermani, F. (2007) *The Chinese Biotechnology, Life Science and Pharmaceutical Industry (UK Trade and Investment Life Sciences Sector Group)*, London: UK Trade and Investment.

'Volunteers at SCRC' (2008–2015) Shanghai Clinical Research Center. Online. Available: www.scrcnet.org/Volunteers_en.asp (accessed 12 May 2015).

Wang, X., Wang, E., and Marincola, F.M. (2011) 'Translational medicine is developing in China: a new venue for collaboration', *Journal of Translational Medicine*, 9: 3.

Xu, J., Li, B., Qiang, M., Liu, H., and Cong, Y. (2006) 'Human subjects protections in clinical drug trials in China: a focus on the institute level', *International Journal of Pharmaceutical Medicine*, 20, 6: 367–72.

Yuan, H. (2013) 'Hospital GCP-Centre: collaboration with industrial partners to advance drug clinical trials', *The 4th Sino-American Symposium on Clinical and Translational* Medicine, 22 June, Beijing.

Zerhouni, E.A. (2005) 'Translational and clinical science: time for a new vision', *New England Journal of Medicine*, 363, 15: 1621–3.

Zhan, M. (2011) 'Human-oriented? Angels and monsters in China's health-care reform', *East Asian Science, Technology and Society: An International Journal*, 5, 3: 291–311.

Zhang, D. (2011) 'Phase I operation in China: opportunities and challenges', *ChinaTrials 2011: Global Clinical Development Summit*, 9 November, Beijing.

Zhang, F. and Wu, F. (2012) '"Fostering indigenous innovation capacities": the development of biotechnology in Shanghai's Zhangjiang High-Tech Park', *Urban Geography*, 33, 5: 728–55.

Zhao, Y. (2013) 'National agenda and strategies for the development and implementation of translational medicine', in B. Alving, K. Dai, and S.H.H. Chan (eds), *Translational Medicine: What, Why and How – An International Perspective*, Basel: Karger, pp. 29–35.

Zhonggong zhongyang [Central Committee of the Communist Party of China] (2010) 'Zhonggong zhongyang guanyu zhiding guomin jingji he shehui fazhan di shier ge wu nian guihua de jianyi' [Central Committee of the Communist Party of China proposal for formulating the Twelfth Five-Year Plan for National Economic and Social Development]. Online. Available: http://dangshi.people.com.cn/GB/13067740.html (accessed 12 May 2015). English translation available at www.britishchamber.cn/sites/default/files/full-translation-5-yr-plan-2011-2015.doc (accessed 12 May 2015).

Zhou, Y. (2005) 'The making of an innovative region from a centrally planned economy: institutional evolution in Zhongguancun Science Park in Beijing', *Environment and Planning A*, 37, 6: 1113–34.

10 The biopolitics of China's HIV governance

Haiqing Yu

This chapter looks at a well-studied topic – China's governance of the human immunodeficiency virus (HIV) and the acquired immune deficiency syndrome (AIDS) – through the wider lens provided by the Foucauldian concept of governmentality. It reviews major literature on the actions and initiatives of the diverse individuals and organizations involved in combating the spread of HIV and associated discriminatory practices. It invites people to rethink the politics of inequality by linking the moral and political economy of infectious diseases and public health governance. It uncovers the governmental logic that guides policy intervention on HIV and AIDS in China with reference to both the Foucauldian concept of dividing practices and the Chinese discourse of *suzhi* (素质 human quality), and inverse ranking practices that place AIDS at the top of a pathological hierarchy of infectious diseases and people living with HIV at the bottom of a moral hierarchy.

As the work of Michel Foucault (1982, 2008) has shown, the terms 'government' and 'governance' refer not only to political structures or the state and its apparatuses, but also to the management of populations and individuals by means other than coercion. Often, this requires a subtle implementation of dividing and ranking practices along the lines of gender, class, and morality, to normalize and rationalize policy interventions. If we wish to understand the biopolitics of HIV governance in China, we need to explore the rationality that underlies such practices.

Biopolitics, in the Foucauldian sense, refers to systems of intertwined knowledge and power concerned with the administration of biological life at the level of populations (Dean 1999: 99). In Foucault's analysis, biopolitics appears as a key element within newly emergent liberal modes of governmentality. This involved a historical transition whereby 'the ancient right to take life or let live was replaced by the power to foster life or disallow it' (Foucault 1990: 138). Melinda Cooper (2008a) extends the link between biopolitics and governmentality in her examination of biotechnology and capitalism in the neoliberal era. She argues that the shift from labour to biological life and the extraction of surplus value from biological life characterizes neoliberalism; that the extraction of surplus value from biological life requires life being classified, manipulated, and controlled. To use Cooper's words, 'the promise of a surplus life will be predicated on a corresponding move to devaluate life' (Cooper 2008a: 45).

The chapter first outlines China's changing HIV demography and government responses, showing how the 'sexualization' of HIV has encouraged the inclusion of market-oriented and self-governing approaches to state-centred responses. It then shows how the discourse of *suzhi* and the rhetoric of crisis essentialize the HIV-positive and 'at-risk' groups of the Chinese population as an unruly and devalued 'other', while promising a life of surplus and quality for others. It also tethers the logic of dividing practices to ranking practices that place people living with HIV and AIDS at the bottom of a moral hierarchy and places the AIDS epidemic at the top of a pathological hierarchy of infectious diseases. This pair of inverse ranking schemes underscores the extent to which the ethical and the biological are linked through strategies of governance in contemporary China.

China's changing HIV demography

Since the first case of HIV was reported in the People's Republic of China (PRC) in 1985, the governance of HIV in China has progressed through four different stages. These stages reflect the changing demography of China's HIV epidemic, which was initially associated with intravenous drug users and the recipients of contaminated blood products, and is now associated with sex workers and their clients, partners, and spouses, as the incidence of sex-related transmission has increased. They also reflect a shift away from governing strategies based on policing borders according to racial and ethnic dichotomies, such as Chinese versus non-Chinese and Han versus non-Han bodies, towards strategies based on social-psychological models and multi-partnerships in health care provision (Jeffreys and Yu 2015: 123–9). They further signify a shift away from Leninist biopolitics – politics that are state-centred and predominantly bureaucratic and mobilizational in approach – towards a form of neoliberal biopolitics, which stresses regulating and administering social conduct through individual responsibilities and market-oriented means (Greenhalgh and Winckler 2005). Such a shift started in the late 1970s when the PRC gradually shifted away from a highly centralized Maoist approach to government and towards a more decentralized and market-oriented approach. In other words, the task of governing the population has extended from state bureaucracies to incorporate markets, professional disciplines, and individuals.

When the topic of AIDS first surfaced in China between 1985 and 1989, policies directed at containing the spread of the HIV virus turned on a logic of 'policing' and 'distancing'. During this period, all reported cases were 'foreign' in nature – they were literally imported into the nation by overseas Chinese and foreign travellers (Wang 2000; Wang 2007: S3). Hence, HIV governance was primarily concerned with policing Chinese borders through visa controls that required the compulsory HIV testing of people entering into the PRC (Tsinghua International Center for Communication Studies 2005: 16).

During the second stage, between 1989 and 1993, new cases of HIV infection were identified among intravenous drug users in southwest and northwest China, which have direct links to the world's two largest heroin and opium drug trafficking routes known as the Golden Triangle and the Golden Crescent (Hayes 2005; Yu 2012: 4). While AIDS had clearly become a domestic issue, its geographical location in China's border regions, and association with 'marginalized' practices and populations (intravenous drug use by ethnic minorities especially in Yunnan Province and the Xinjiang Uyghur Autonomous Region), ensured that it continued to be portrayed in China's media as a 'distanced' disease or a 'minority' problem (Hood 2011a; Hyde 2007; Rudelson 2003). These policing and distancing strategies refer to what is now known as 'the era of denial' (Hague 2008: 140).

Approaches to the governance of HIV in China started to change during stage three (1994–2000), when large numbers of rural people in central provinces were found to be infected with HIV. The infected mostly consisted of former blood donors and their spouses and children (suggesting mother-to-child transmission), and the recipients of contaminated blood products. This new vector of infection emerged as a result of uneven development and criminally lax hygienic practices (Hood 2011b: 45–56). Impoverished agricultural workers were recruited by illegal blood brokers known as 'blood heads' and encouraged by local government authorities to sell blood to local blood collection stations that operated mostly in China's central provinces, especially Henan (Su 2010). These blood stations were poorly equipped and often unregulated and unsanitary. To reduce production costs and enhance profit margins, some stations pooled the blood of thousands of untested donors from which they would extract plasma, the foundational building block of many blood products, and then reinject donors with some of the remaining blood mixture to aid their recovery time. As a result of these practices, blood-borne diseases such as Hepatitis B and HIV spread rapidly within blood-selling families and communities. By the mid-1990s, an estimated 35–45 per cent of all the commercial blood donors in Henan Province had contracted HIV or AIDS (Hayes 2005: 5). While villagers were getting sick and dying of a 'mysterious disease', local government authorities attempted to 'cover-up' the extent of the problem.

By the end of the 1990s, all of China's provinces, autonomous regions, and municipalities had reported cases of HIV, with transmission through contaminated blood being the leading cause of infection and associated deaths. The growing rate of infection and deaths, displays of social discontent, and pressures placed on the PRC Government by international and domestic activists, ensured that denial was no longer a viable approach to governance (Rosenthal 2001). In 2001, the PRC Government issued its first Action Plan on HIV/AIDS Prevention and Containment (2001–2005). In 2002, the PRC Government began to speak openly about the PRC's growing AIDS crisis after an internal health report was leaked by Wan Yanhai, a leading AIDS activist (Gittings 2002). On 1 December 2003, Premier Wen Jiabao made history in the PRC by visiting AIDS patients in Beijing Ditan hospital. The visit was widely covered in the Chinese media (Zhang 2009). Also in December 2003, the PRC initiated its 'Four Free and One Care' (*si mian yi guanhuai* 四免一关怀) policy, that is, free antiretroviral (ARV) drugs, free prevention of mother-to-child transmission, free voluntary counselling and testing, free schooling for children orphaned by AIDS, and care for people living with HIV and AIDS.

The change of state policy towards HIV and AIDS as signified by the personal engagement of high-ranking state officials with AIDS-related issues has increased dramatically the visibility of the subject of AIDS in the Chinese media since 2003 (Liu and Zhang 2005; Zhang 2009). The growth in media representations of AIDS has helped to raise public awareness about the disease. However, many reports still tend towards sensationalism and bias, and continue to 'other' those who are infected – associating HIV and AIDS with foreigners, Chinese ethnic minority groups, poor and greedy 'peasants', and drug users, sex workers, and homosexuals (who are presented as moral and sexual decadents) (Ren *et al.* 2010). This stereotyping of people living with HIV and AIDS has been challenged by some progressive newspapers such as the *Southern Metropolitan News*, which frames AIDS in terms of social and political issues (Zhang 2009). But stereotypes continued to influence popular understandings of the disease as China moved into the fourth stage of its HIV governance, from 2003 onwards.

The fourth stage corresponds with rising rates of HIV infection through sexual transmission. This rise was linked not only to cases of infection among the spouses and sexual partners of intravenous drug users and former blood donors, but also to China's illegal but booming commercial sex business (Zhonghua renmin gongheguo weisheng bu 2011). Commentators estimate that there are between two million and 20 million sex workers in China, although Chinese law bans the sex industry (Lau 2014).

According to statistics provided by the PRC's Ministry of Health, UNAIDS, and the World Health Organization, sexual transmission is now the main route of HIV infection in the PRC (Zhonghua renmin gongheguo weisheng bu 2011: 14). There were 780,000 reported cases of HIV and AIDS in China in 2011. Nearly 64 per cent of those cases were sexually transmitted and over 17 per cent were the result of sexual transmission between same-sex partners.

Rising rates of HIV infection through sexual transmission have encouraged the 'sexualization' of AIDS in China. Joan Kaufman *et al.* (2006: 3–4) identify seven risk factors for the development of a widespread sexual epidemic, which are associated with China's opening up, its uneven and unequal development, and changing social attitudes towards sex and marriage. These are:

> (1) the size of China's young sexually active population; (2) changing sexual behaviours and norms; (3) widespread prostitution; (4) massive internal migration; (5) low knowledge about transmission routes among the general population; (6) even lower perception of self-risk among the general population; and (7) an HIV epidemic among men who have sex with men (MSM) that has only recently been recognized.
>
> (Kaufman *et al.* 2006: 3–4)

In this context, Chinese health authorities and officials, non-governmental organizations (NGOs) and self-help groups, and international agencies working with the United Nations (UN) and foreign governments, have started working together to design and implement HIV prevention, education, and care programmes (Gill *et al.* 2007; Jeffreys and Su 2011). These public–private collaborations chiefly target those identified as 'most at-risk': that is, migrant workers; long-distance truck drivers; intravenous drug users; former blood donors; sex workers and their clients; men who have sex with men; homosexuals; university students; and people who engage in casual, premarital, extramarital, or non-monogamous sex (Gill *et al.* 2007). Hence, as the HIV epidemic has become 'sexualized', it has been increasingly classified through dividing practices that separate those 'at risk' from 'us'.

Changing government responses to HIV governance

The PRC Government was pushed to adopt multi-partnership and more comprehensive approaches to governing HIV by the nation's changing HIV demography and international attention, especially following the publication of a UNAIDS 2002 report that described the potential for an AIDS pandemic in China as a 'titanic peril' (UNAIDS 2002). A large body of scholarly and specialized work has shown that China's HIV governance has since moved from denial to taking positive actions, and from a health-oriented response to a multi-government, socially inclusive, and humanitarian response (Chan 2011; Gill 2006; Hood 2011a; Jeffreys and Su 2011; Jing and Worth 2010; Kaufman *et al.* 2006; Tsinghua International Center for Communication Studies 2005; Wu *et al.* 2007). This includes: identifying and targeting at-risk groups; establishing a national monitoring and surveillance system to aggregate and interpret data collected from surveillance sites, including STD clinics and local Centers for Disease Control and Prevention (CDC); implementing comprehensive drug-rehabilitation services; abolishing the quarantining of AIDS patients; removing the category of homosexuality from medicalized lists of pathological disorders; launching a nationwide HIV education and prevention campaign; and stepping up laboratory and epidemiological research (Cui *et al.* 2009; Gill 2006; Hague 2008; Jeffreys and Huang 2009; Kaufman 2010).

The PRC Government had demonstrated its commitment to taking more action to control the spread of HIV and AIDS, and to do so with more transparency, even before the outbreak of SARS in 2003, which scholars argue marks a turning point in China's health governance more generally (Kaufman 2010). This trend has continued into the second decade of the twenty-first century, as China is seen to be increasingly integrated into the global health governance regime through its participation in forums and signatory bodies led by the UN. China's governing authorities have issued HIV-related policies and laws to conform to 'international' standards, and have allowed NGOs to carry out HIV prevention work (Kaufman 2009; Meng 2012; Wu 2005). In addition to substantive policy initiatives, authorities have used media and communication networks to present their engagements with HIV governance in a largely positive light, for both domestic and international audiences (Liu and Zhang 2005; Zhang 2009).

The governance of HIV in China now consists of two distinct strands: the first is a hierarchical, vertically integrated, and normalized approach centred on the Chinese state, especially the Ministry of Health and its CDC offices. Although the PRC's Ministry of Health has contributed to the introduction of numerous laws and policies to help prevent the spread of HIV and AIDS in China, it lacks both the authority and the budget (despite recent increases) to effectively implement its HIV governance strategies, especially at the local level (Cui *et al.* 2009; Gill 2006; Hague 2008; Kaufman 2010; Kaufman *et al.* 2006). Local government officials often cover up the existence of AIDS in their areas of jurisdiction, either because they wish to avoid possible criticism or simply do not see it as worthwhile to commit local personnel and resources (Hayes 2005). For example, under the 'Four Free and One Care' policy and the Comprehensive AIDS Response programmes, people living with HIV and AIDS should have access to free ARV treatment, voluntary counselling and testing, treatment to prevent mother-to-child transmission, schooling for children orphaned by AIDS, and medical care and economic assistance for HIV-affected households (Ministry of Health, People's Republic of China 2006). However, these benefits are not implemented evenly and effectively. In some places there are multiple fees charged for related health services, patients pay for tests and treatments of opportunistic infections such as tuberculosis and pneumonia, AIDS orphans do not receive adequate care and schooling, and people living with HIV and AIDS have been refused treatment (Gill 2006; Jing and Worth 2010; Kaufman *et al.* 2006).

A second strand of HIV governance has emerged as the result of outsourcing to public–private collaborations in healthcare provision. A range of non-state actors are now responsible in practice for the implementation of HIV education and behavioural intervention programmes. The number of international NGOs and charitable foundations that are authorized to engage in AIDS-related work within China has increased steadily since 1994 (Wu 2005: 919); and more than 600 domestic organizations, including grass-roots, community, and university-based organizations, were working on AIDS in China in 2010 (National Center for AIDS/STD Control and Prevention and CHAIN 2010). In most cases, these international and domestic groups form a partnership with government organizations to carry out HIV prevention work. Contrary to the widespread perception that such partnerships are marked by irresolvable conflict, many of the NGOs involved consider their relations with government authorities in relatively positive terms – cooperative more often than not – and are optimistic about the ongoing effectiveness of their partnerships (Kaufman 2009).

Based on these developments, some commentators have noted the potential for a rapid change in relations between government and social organizations (Schwartz and Shieh 2009). This potential is founded on the view that NGOs provide a grass-roots forum for the voices of ordinary citizens to be heard, and, as intermediaries, also channel international funding and democratic practices to the local level. As one commentator puts it, with the 'right encouragement' from the PRC Government, or 'in the absence of specific regulatory or political discouragement – these organizations, already ingenious at meeting current challenges, face promising prospects' (Bentley 2004). This growth is occurring in the AIDS NGO sector, which is composed of an increasingly independent GONGO (government organized NGO) sector, a set of active legal advocacy NGOs ('some with international funding and links to global legal advocacy networks'), groups representing people living with HIV and AIDS, and 'a growing number of grassroots service NGOs with specific focus on most at-risk populations like MSM, migrants and youth' (Kaufman 2009: 162). In recent years, a new partnership between international organizations, China's health authorities and domestic social service organizations has been formed through a market-driven model in health governance called *goumai fuwu* (购买服务), involving the competitive contracting or outsourcing of HIV education and testing to private service providers as a means to scale-up HIV testing among high-risk groups (Fan 2014). The growth of pragmatic partnerships between grass-roots AIDS NGOs and local CDCs may help to improve not only service provision, but also socio-political acceptance of the potential value of NGO roles in service provision, education, and advocacy (Kaufman 2009: 162–7).

However, the roles of NGOs in the new HIV governance regime are limited by the normalized state-centred structure and their own operational and financial constraints. The commodification of HIV governance, as exemplified in the use of a contracting system to scale-up testing among men who have sex with men, inevitably subjects certain pockets of the population to the state-centred web of surveillance and discourse of AIDS, while subjecting social service organizations to the money–power–politics matrix (Fan 2014). The organizations that get 'contracts' are typically those that 'reach' and 'find' (through testing) the largest number of people living with HIV. Local AIDS activists and NGOs who are not entangled in the state-dominated power–knowledge structure often face institutional obstacles and in some cases local government harassment and censorship, as reported by Human Rights Watch (2005). In Henan Province, AIDS activists faced harassment and even detention by local authorities for speaking to the media, demanding government responsibility for AIDS orphans, or seeking access to ARV treatments on behalf of AIDS patients (Human Rights Watch 2005: 12–28). Furthermore, inter-organizational solidarity and thus the capacity for broader outreach work is hampered by lack of funding; in-fighting among groups over funding, local ownership, and media visibility; shortage of trained staff and a frequent turnover of volunteers; and poor understanding of fundraising and operational capacity (Kaufman 2009: 169; see also Liu and Kaufman 2011). Despite the recent use of celebrities in public awareness campaigns to popularize HIV education, treatment, and anti-discrimination messages (Hood 2010; Jeffreys and Yu 2015: 133–7), citizen participation and influence in government-organized AIDS work 'still have a long way to evolve' (Kaufman 2010: 82).

In summary, the withdrawal of the state from Mao-era commitments to universal, albeit often rudimentary, medical provision has meant that strategies for managing health, including the AIDS crisis, have increasingly been devolved to non-state actors and individuals. NGOs are now encouraged to carry out work in AIDS education, care, and prevention, particularly among groups of people defined as 'most at-risk', but the scope of that work is still restricted by the political structure. Individuals are also increasingly asked to take responsibility for their own economic future and health through discourses and practices that emphasize care of the self, or the exercise of self-governance and self-responsibility in managing one's sexual and overall health. While this 'neoliberal' emphasis aims to empower individuals to manage their own health, it also works to rationalize and normalize social control based on the division of China's population into populations of 'higher' and 'lower' human quality through the discourse of *suzhi*.

Dividing practices

The work of Michel Foucault (1982) shows that dividing practices have been central to modern discourses in medicine, psychiatry, and criminology, and have been materialized through corresponding institutions – the hospital, the asylum, and the prison – designed to separate out the sick, the insane, the hysteric, the delinquent, and the criminal. Through the deployment of binary divisions such as healthy/ill, sane/mad, and law-abiding/criminal, the subject is either divided inside oneself or divided from others (Foucault 1982: 778). Dividing practices categorize the individual, marking them by imposed or self-internalized criteria, which are both taken as 'truths' and make particular individuals the focus of corrective interventions. Dividing practices thus refer to power exercised over individuals, and are an individualizing tactic.

The discourse of *suzhi* is a linchpin in the dividing practices of China's HIV governance. This official as well as popular discourse permeates and organizes everyday life in China through discussions of such wide ranging topics as birth control, education, self-cultivation in the *qigong* tradition, self-help manuals and AIDS. It 'justifies social and political hierarchies of all sorts' by dividing individuals into those of 'high' and 'low' quality based on an abstract set of physical, psychological, and cultivated qualities (Kipnis 2006: 295). These qualities are evaluated along multiple vectors, including: age, gender, place of birth, class, education, ethnicity, health, sexuality, wealth, bodily practices, morality, and civility, reflecting both 'contested public standards' and the 'politics of arbitrary personal power' and 'administrative fiat' (Kipnis 2007: 392; see also Jacka 2009). The discourse of *suzhi* also legitimizes socio-economic inequality as China's citizens are now defined by their individual progress in improving their *suzhi*, which is understood in terms of their physical, material and educational attainments or biocapital, not by their membership of a collective political body (Anagnost 2008).

Scholars describe the discourse of *suzhi* as a form of 'neoliberal governmentality' that is closely tied with the competitive environment of both global capitalism and China's 'socialist market economy' (Yan 2003; Sigley 2009). In the words of Ann Anagnost (2004: 192): 'Suzhi is the quintessential expression of how subjects are set up for the rational choice making that grounds China's capitalist transformation'. The discourse of *suzhi* encourages members of China's urban middle class, in particular, to cultivate an entrepreneurial subjectivity and accept responsibility for their own 'profits and losses', including managing their own careers and health. While the categorization of individuals based on an abstract set of criteria is predatory and arbitrary, *suzhi* as a dividing practice has become 'normalized' as individuals internalize the distinctions which mark off aspirant middle-class consumers from their 'low-quality' fellow citizens, typically those of rural origin.

Virtually everybody in China has become enmeshed in this new discourse of individual self-improvement and self-governance; however, not everybody has equal access to the resources required to 'improve themselves'. The reform policies initiated in China from 1979 onwards have removed import and export barriers and encouraged entrepreneurialism, while reducing investment in public service provision, such as health care. Rapid economic development on the eastern seaboard has also seen the largest internal migration in Chinese history, as millions of young and middle-aged men and women move from the rural hinterland to developing urban centres to seek jobs (Chan 2013). These migrant workers often cluster in urban slum areas as factory workers and construction workers.

In the cultivation of high quality, it is often the body that becomes the asset of regenerative resources and surplus value, whether in the form of selling physical labour, or blood, organs, and sex. Many people of rural background become migrant workers, sex workers, and money boys (men who provide commercial sexual services, usually to other men) – major categories of 'at-risk' individuals in the discourse of HIV governance. For some of the 'left-behind' population in poor areas, survival has become a game of self-exploitation, involving the selling of blood and participation in clinical trials (Cooper 2008b; see also Cooper in this book). The objective is to improve their material conditions and to gain more *suzhi* so that, like their urban counterparts, they too can become 'good' and 'useful' consumer citizens.

The desire for self-improvement encourages people at both ends of the *suzhi* spectrum to cultivate their bodily assets, with one end *working with* their bodies and the other *working on* their bodies (see also Woronov in this book). For the urban middle class, educational and financial attainment is no longer the predominant concern in the accumulation of *suzhi* capital. Health and beauty care increasingly fuels their drive to enhance their biocapital through the use of biotechnological products, including plasma products. The increasing demand for pharmaceutical products in virotherapy and therapeutic antibodies, as well as anti-ageing skincare products, has contributed to the heavy investment in pharmaceutical and biomedical innovation in China and worldwide from the biotech industry. Such investment is conditioned on the extraction of surplus value from the biological life of less costly bodies (Cooper 2008b).

The 'low' *suzhi* people from China's rural hinterland and the 'floating population' of rural-to-urban migrant workers are most actively engaged in the biomedical labour of China's transforming economy. This has encouraged a corresponding move to devaluate life in these people, as suggested by the involvement of local government authorities in blood-collection practices in Henan Province and their subsequent denial and cover-up of AIDS-related deaths. Following this logic, biotechnology becomes 'vampiric' when its value is extracted from social inequality – the inequality in China between those people who are categorized as middle class with 'high' *suzhi* and those who are categorized as having 'low' *suzhi* (Anagnost 2006).

Within the dominant discourse of AIDS in China, poverty, disease, and marginalization are presented as the result of having low *suzhi*. As such, they are associated with individual failure in educational, cultural, and financial attainment, and inability to compete in the market economy or contribute to national development. Such failure, in turn, as the logic of *suzhi* discourse goes, leads to 'bad' choices in personal behaviour. This kind of logic is applied not only to migrant workers, but also to the 'less desirable' urbanites such as intravenous drug users, sex workers, money boys, and men who have sex with men. Women in prostitution, once seen as victims of socio-economic inequalities, are now portrayed as the victimizers of public health, while the role of male clients in hindering the adoption of safer sex practices is overlooked (Choi 2011). Similarly, men who have sex with men, homosexuals, and money boys are often stigmatized for their non-normative sexual behaviour, rural origins, or involvement in the sex trade, and hence as perceived high-risk groups for sexually transmissible infections (STIs) and HIV transmission (Jeffreys 2007). These marginalized 'most at-risk' groups are presented in mainstream discourses as posing a threat to the 'imagined immunity' and 'imagined solidarity' of the dominant majority of the Chinese population (Hood 2011a).

As a dividing practice, *suzhi* is internalized not only by the urban middle class to mark themselves off from their 'low-quality' counterparts, but also by the 'low-quality' other who view themselves as lacking in or lagging behind in the accumulation of *suzhi* capital. Like sufferers of occupational disease, the 'at-risk' individuals fail to be categorized in the 'normal' political, economic, and cultural practices. They 'occupy a socially constructed and maintained space designated for those who are abnormal, or fundamentally, the other' (Ho 2014: 823). They are subject to 'policing and violence while simultaneously banished from society by a variety of formal and informal mechanisms of exclusion: legal, economic and social' (Ho 2014: 823). In the HIV discourse, the judgement is not just put on the failure of the at-risk individuals to express their entrepreneurialship as self-improving and self-governing subjects or their patriotism as disciplined and hardworking subjects for the collective interests. The judgement is often moral. It is assumed that certain types of people, for example poor ruralites, peddlers, and small traders, are 'at-risk' of contracting HIV because they are people of questionable morality with limited conceptions of public responsibility (Hsu 2006; Osburg 2013: 129–33).

The dividing practices that inhere in China's HIV governance thus categorize individuals based on their socio-economic background and position, their capacity to accumulate *suzhi* capital (especially high moral *suzhi*), and their frequency of bodily movement among and interactions with the 'low-quality' sections of the population. High risk of HIV transmission is associated with high levels of mobility and invisibility in human movement and interactions (or ungovernability). The discourse of *suzhi* is an integral part of the 'techno-scientific reasoning' that characterizes economic planning and the administrative regulation of the population in China (Sigley 2009). It reinforces and legitimates inequality, and reifies 'decidedly unliberal' hierarchies (Kipnis 2007: 390).

These dividing practices are reflected in media coverage. AIDS is now front-page news; it is no longer 'hidden' or portrayed as a non-Chinese problem or 'state secret' (Liu and Zhang 2005). However, it is still kept at a 'distance' in both official and lay discourses as a 'non-Han Chinese' and 'non-mainstream' type of disease. China's media continue to frame HIV from a state-centred approach that focuses on health policy and expert advice on prevention and treatment, and provides little discussion of the AIDS situation on the ground (Dong *et al.* 2008; Li 2009; Liu and Zhang 2005; Tsinghua International Center for Communication Studies 2005).

This 'normalized' approach to AIDS reportage has created a media environment where health news is abundant but of little practical use either to people in pursuing their medical and legal rights, or to the general public in raising levels of HIV awareness (Tsinghua International Center for Communication Studies 2005). It also creates a logic of 'blaming the victim', where the victims of China's uneven development are blamed for their 'pathological abnormality'. This problem is exacerbated by the frequency with which the media report negative stories about HIV needles found on public buses or beaches, and about schools that refuse to admit AIDS orphans or children whose parents are infected with HIV (Tsinghua International Center for Communication Studies 2005). The 'distancing' perspective and 'othering' approach adopted by the media and in official educational campaigns have tended to dehumanize sufferers even when the objective is ostensibly anti-stigmatization (Ren *et al.* 2010).

At the same time, the perceived threat posed by 'at-risk' groups to the rest of the population is used to justify extraordinary measures for social control and institutional intervention. Although the governance of HIV in China appears to have aligned with global norms, its decentralized structure, its contradictory policies, and the ongoing media stigmatization of people living with HIV and AIDS have exacerbated the distancing perspective and heightened the fear of sexualized disease in the popular imagination. As a result, real and virtual zones of abandonment have been created where the 'living dead' can be consigned to avert the perceived threats they present for public health and social order. This point is demonstrated by the existence of AIDS villages in Hunan Province, where AIDS patients are left to die with minimum care or human dignity (Chen 2003).

In this respect, China resembles Brazil, where 'borders' continue to be policed in order to separate those infected with HIV from those who are not infected (Biehl 2001). Thus, even as activists, NGOs, and CDC officials collaborate to provide medical and financial assistance on a national scale, the low-*suzhi* and pathologized others have been systematically identified and excluded – beginning with the association of AIDS with foreigners, then with ethnic minorities, then with villagers in central China, and now with 'sexual minorities' in urban areas (homosexuals, sex workers, and sexually active migrant workers). Rather than acknowledging its links to the deeper structural inequalities which have emerged as a result of the neoliberal development strategies pursued by China's governing authorities, AIDS is still presented in mainstream discourse as a disease associated with people of low *suzhi* and with immoral or irresponsible behaviours.

The aspirations of migrant workers, sex workers, and former blood donors for attaining higher *suzhi* are therefore limited by the structural inequalities and social biases that have created 'a growing disparity in the body of the nation between the haves and have-nots' (Anagnost 2008: 499), and, correspondingly, between the disease-immune and the disease-prone. In other words, the citizenship of people who are categorized as the 'at-risk' groups in the AIDS discourse has been delimited by the indelible marks of their low quality/*suzhi*, marginality, and perceived predisposition for HIV contamination and spread.

Ranking practices

China's HIV governance is characterized not only by dividing practices that classify and categorize individuals into 'at-risk' and 'normal' groups based on the discourses of *suzhi*, but also by what I call ranking practices that place people living with HIV and AIDS in a moral hierarchy and the AIDS epidemic in a pathological hierarchy. Similar to dividing practices, ranking practices are based on vectors such as class, wealth and education. Unlike dividing practices, ranking practices categorize collective groups of people rather than individuals. By making a particular group of people and disease the focus of attention ostensibly to channel funding and support to avert an epidemic, they justify social and political hierarchies of diseases, with those at the top of the hierarchy gaining more moral and financial support than those at the bottom. Both dividing and ranking practices are reflexive of the political economy of infectious diseases in China. As the unarticulated and unspeakable logics of China's HIV governance, they also underline the biopolitics of China's public health governance.

The first layer in such ranking practices concerns the morality discourse in HIV governance. In the moral hierarchy of AIDS, 'innocent' victims are ranked at the top and 'non-innocent' reprobates at the bottom. 'Innocent' victims, particularly AIDS orphans and recipients of contaminated blood products, are often presented and treated differently from their perceived non-innocent counterparts – those who are infected through 'greed' (poor rural people) or 'immoral' and 'irresponsible' behaviours (sex workers, drug addicts, and people who pass the virus to their spouses). Most of the people living with HIV and AIDS who openly appear on Chinese television, that is, without wearing sunglasses or any technical treatment to prevent facial and vocal recognition, belong to the 'innocent' group of victims ('Song Pengfei: Xiao kan weilai' 2003; 'Zhimian aizi' 2003).

People at the bottom of this moral hierarchy, such as sex workers and drug addicts, not only endure physical suffering and social exclusion, but are further dehumanized because of the perceived threat they pose to China's future (Anagnost 2006). They are a focus of both health campaigns and extraordinary means supposedly to safeguard public health and social order. Drug users are routinely dealt with by police in a largely punitive manner – being detained for up to six months in detoxification centres and to up to two years in re-education through labour camps – despite the central government's endorsement of harm-reduction interventions among intravenous drug users (Hammett *et al.* 2006: 219). People who knowingly sell or buy sex while infected with serious sexually transmissible infections, including syphilis and gonorrhoea, face detention and potential jail sentences of up to five years, according to the 1997 Criminal Law of the PRC (Choi 2011: 100). Female sex workers, especially those from less-politically connected entertainment venues, drug-using sex workers, and street walkers, are often the prime target of selective police enforcement, facing arrests and fines (Choi 2011: 102). This entrenches the gendered social stigmatization of female sex workers as carriers of disease and may discourage them from being tested for STIs, including HIV.

Men who have sex with men are ranked low in the moral hierarchy and ranked high in the pathological hierarchy of China's AIDS discourse. Many such men enter heterosexual marriages and have a child because of social and family pressures (Jeffreys and Yu 2015: 89), creating multiple complications in their public and private lives. However, they are ranked low in the moral hierarchy of HIV governance because of social discrimination against homosexuality and engagement in non-normalized sexual behaviours (multiple sexual partners and unprotected sex). They are targets of police-led campaigns against crime and also targeted for blackmail by criminal gangs because exposure of their sexuality would bring opprobrium to their family, and might result in loss of employment and social status (Li 2006: 86–94; Wang 2000).

The fear of AIDS that permeates Chinese same-sex communities and the shame that is attached to being an HIV-seropositive gay has forced men who have sex with men into an even darker closet, where they become even more isolated and marginalized. This has exposed their peers and female sexual partners to greater risk of HIV infection. It is in this context that intervention efforts have been stepped up in recent years, particularly in the area of testing, in the population of men who have sex with men. Many MSM-focused community-based organizations have been established, often by government agencies, to carry out the testing tasks for China's CDCs and to channel AIDS funding from the government and international donors (Fan 2014: 89). This has placed MSM high in the pathological hierarchy of China's HIV governance, but also prevents HIV and MSM-focused organizations from developing an identity outside of the rubric of disease prevention.

The second layer in the ranking practices thus concerns the political economy of infectious diseases in China. AIDS occupies a special place and is ranked high in the pathological hierarchy of China's public health governance, not only because of the magnitude of its threat to public health, social order, and economic development, but also because of the discursive and representational power it can generate. International attention to the 'Titanic peril' of China's HIV epidemic and subsequently increased funding from international donors and organizations may be an external factor in the economic imperative to rank HIV and AIDS high in the pathological order. An internal factor placing HIV and AIDS high in the pathological hierarchy of China's public health governance is the social and economic costs associated with rising rates of HIV infection rate among the urban population, and the potential for co-infection and increased rates of other diseases that spread through blood or bodily fluids, especially tuberculosis and hepatitis B and C. Like HIV, these diseases can infect people of any age, race or class, including the 'high-*suzhi*' middle class who dominate political, economic, and intellectual life in China. Members of this class and CDC health officials are aware of the high risk of co-infection and triple infection among people living with HIV and AIDS with tuberculosis and hepatitis B and C, and hence take seriously the potential threat posed to public health and individual families in terms of increased mortality rates (Guo *et al.* 2010). It is mainly through these individuals, their supporters, and spokespeople in the academic and public health systems that discussions and discourses about HIV have gained access to the broader public, reaching beyond academic fora and online communities (Jeffreys and Yu 2015: 81–2). Economic imperatives and the representational power of the high-*suzhi* middle class have helped to project HIV as a national crisis.

Crisis, as Patricia Thornton (2009) argues, is a mode of governance rather than a reflection of the real lived situation. The history of the PRC is marked by a constant invocation of 'crisis mode' or 'crisis mentality' to initiate policy changes and to strengthen the ruling capacity of the Party (Thornton 2009). But whereas Mao Zedong deployed the rhetoric of crisis within a revolutionary discourse in order to normalize radical policies such as the Great Leap Forward, the current leadership shape rhetorics of crisis around perceived threats to social harmony and stability. The 'state of exception' created by crises functions to consolidate the central government's power and authority over the fragmented and decentralized bureaucracy and local governments, while the latter have continued to work at cross-purposes with the central government and its policies. Hence selective implementation of policies, and evasion and obfuscation from local officials and even members of the public, have short-circuited 'normal politics' in the name of public opinion and the wellbeing of the local population. This became evident during the SARS crisis when migrant workers and poor rural petitioners temporarily staying in Beijing were targeted by local authorities for special handling, while thousands of travelling students, family members of officials and businesspeople, who could just as easily transmit the disease, were largely overlooked (Thornton 2009).

Selective targeting is also a feature of China's HIV governance. The government remains the main service provider and facilitator in the AIDS response, principally through China's CDC and its provincial and local branches (Kaufman 2009). However, its effort to fight the epidemic is undermined by the activities of officials and their business allies, or people of perceived high *suzhi* who have the documented capacity to break rules and abuse power, and have multiple sexual partners. These men, especially successful businessmen, often feature as exemplary models and 'celebrity CEOs' in the Chinese media. But as David Davies (2010) points out, their celebrity is shadowed by the suspicion of their rule-breaking, quasi-legal rent-seeking, and corrupted paths towards wealth and fame. Sex is often implicated in the path towards success for these men. Zheng Tiantian (2006: 168) further suggests that male government officials and corporate figures routinely hire commercial sex workers as part of masculinist (and elitist) 'business rituals' designed to establish 'mutual trust' (Zheng 2006: 182; see also Uretsky 2008). These men's behaviour constitutes a well-documented risk factor in HIV transmission, but they are not considered as a target group in HIV prevention programmes because of their high social status (Micollier 2012: 116).

As in other parts of the world, the primacy accorded to AIDS by such moral and pathological framings also forestalls the inclusiveness of less 'sexy' and less 'privileged' diseases in China's public health governance. For example, official statistics suggest that over 750,000 Chinese miners have pneumoconiosis (black lung), an incurable but preventable disease caused by prolonged breathing of coal dust ('Woguo chenfeibing renshu buduan zengduo, weiquan wenti cheng zuli' 2011). More attention needs to be focused on framing suffering as shared experience rather than creating a state of exception by dividing and ranking people according to a certain set of vectors. The changing demography of HIV in China calls for new approaches to the governance of HIV that are devoid of biases along the lines of gender, sex, class, and ethnicity (Gill *et al.* 2007; Lu *et al.* 2008). It requires a more resourced and an all-embracing approach to HIV education that not only targets the identifiable 'at-risk' population, but also their 'high-*suzhi*' counterparts who consume the surplus value of their biological life.

Conclusion

The biopolitics of China's HIV governance reveals how the national government deals directly in the power over life by dividing and ranking the population so as to exercise power over the national body and produce particular kinds of citizens. Through two particular strategies of governance – dividing practices and ranking practices – authorities have revived old spectres and exacerbated existing economic and moral divides. They have spurred the vilification of homosexuality and licensed the policing of sex workers, migrant workers, and drug users. Public discussions of HIV-related topics such as safer sex practices and unconventional sexual behaviours also remain awkward and are subject to censure. Issues that need to be addressed in order to improve China's governance of the sexualized epidemic include: the persistence of gender stereotypes, the naturalized definition of normative sexual behaviours, the lack of representations from the 'margins' such as sex workers in HIV and AIDS policy and research programmes, and the lack of social and human science approaches to HIV governance (Micollier 2012).

The majority of China's HIV carriers and AIDS sufferers continue to endure socio-psychological and financial suffering, injustice, and discrimination. HIV-affected villagers are still struggling for the provision of basic health care and subsistence, despite various policies issued by the central government (Hood 2013). AIDS activists and health professionals face harassment and punishment for their efforts to bring the plight of China's rural people to the public's attention (Hood 2012). Journalists face physical and administrative retribution for paying attention to 'devalued' groups of the population who are ranked low in the moral and high in the pathological hierarchies of infectious diseases, for example by being demoted, banned from work, beaten, or having their equipment destroyed (Wu and Jia 2010).

The pairing of the discourse of *suzhi* and crisis rhetoric with the power to divide and rank the population legitimizes a neoliberal mode of HIV governance. The individual body becomes an accumulated form of biocapital, with some understood as having more 'value' than others and having 'value' for others (Anagnost 2006: 521, 532). Some are condemned for contracting transmissible diseases like HIV and hepatitis B, and thus lose their vitality and ability for reproduction of the biovalue desired by the biotechnology enterprise and biopolitical regime. This is reflected in the existence and outcomes of China's blood economy. As Anagnost (2006: 525–6) points out, it suggests that

> what has been produced by the biotechnological enterprise is a new economy of life and death that forces us to consider how the active production of inequality has both been the condition of possibility for it while also exacting a retroviral revenge.

This 'retroviral revenge' is not limited to a transmissible virus or disease that can impact on anyone; it also comes in various forms of biomedical activism. The spread of HIV and the subsequent responses of China's governing authorities have been accompanied by struggles at the grass-roots level for survival and recognition, as evidenced in the emergence of humanitarian activism, philanthropy, and bio-activism (Hood 2010; 2012). Chinese 'non-normative' sexual groups have adopted 'nomadic strategies' to carry out their grass-roots activism. They are making alliances across different social groups to engage in non-normative politics by using digital media, business, and social networks, securing funding from AIDS-related international organizations and mobilizing the discourse of 'pride' (Rofel 2013). A range of celebrities have also appeared publicly as AIDS campaign spokespersons (Hood 2010; see also Jeffreys and Yu 2015: 133–7).

Such bio-activism is organized around the politics of suffering and forged around 'politicized biology', as in the case of Brazil (Biehl 2004: 122). It helps to foster a culture of tolerance in Chinese society, serves to critique China's HIV governance from within, and promotes new forms of biosociality as HIV carriers and their supporters traverse the country to support each other and contest their marginal status. Vibrant expressive genres have sprung up as a result – film, theatre, art, documentary, literature, and music – that try to construct a 'positive' identity (Hood 2012). They have triggered energetic forms of heterogeneous alliances with international movements, NGOs and volunteers, as well as with various corporate public relations efforts.

Michel Foucault (1982: 794) states that:

> Every power relationship implies, at least *in potentia*, a strategy of struggle.... Each constitutes for the other a kind of permanent limit, a point of possible reversal ... between a relationship of power and a strategy of struggle there is a reciprocal appeal, a perpetual linking and a perpetual reversal.

The power to divide and the state of exception are limited by a perpetual linking and reversal between the 'at-risk' or 'rogue' segments of the population and the 'healthy' or 'high-quality' groups of people.

Increasingly, HIV activists, carriers, and their supporters are engaging in various forms of counter biopolitics or bioactivism. As Jean Comaroff (2007: 211) states:

> If life itself has become the prime medium for exerting authority, it is also the stuff of collective action and aspiration: vide the various kinds of activism that have sprung up around the world to deal with AIDS, activism that insists on making visible the deleterious effect of exclusion on ailing bodies and beings.

The politics of survival and the will to assert one's visibility and rights will continue to fuel everyday struggles for equality and fairness among those pathologized by the biopolitics of China's HIV governance.

References

Anagnost, A. (2004) 'The corporeal politics of quality (suzhi)', *Public Culture*, 16: 189–208.

Anagnost, A. (2006) 'Strange circulations: the blood economy in rural China', *Economy and Society*, 35, 4: 509–29.

Anagnost, A. (2008) 'From "class" to "social strata": grasping the social totality in reform era China', *Third World Quarterly*, 29, 3: 497–519.

Bentley, J.G. (2004) 'Survival strategies for civil society organizations in China', *The International Journal of Not-for-Profit Law*, 6, 2. Online. Available: www.icnl.org/research/journal/vol. 6iss2/art_1.htm (accessed 10 July 2015).

Biehl, J. (2001) 'Vita: life in a zone of social abandonment', *Social Text*, 68: 131–49.

Biehl, J. (2004) 'The activist state: global pharmaceuticals, AIDS, and citizenship in Brazil', *Social Text*, 80: 105–32.

Chan, K.W. (2013) 'China, internal migration', in I. Ness and P. Bellwood (eds), *The Encyclopedia of Global Human Migration*, Oxford: Wiley-Blackwell.

Chan, L.H. (2011) *China Engages Global Health Governance: Responsible Stakeholder or System-Transformer?*, New York: Palgrave Macmillan.

Chen Weijun (2003) *To Live is Better Than to Die* [*Hao si buru lai huozhe*], documentary film, 88', China. Online. Available: https://www.youtube.com/watch?v=whoq3L7qfl8 (accessed 10 July 2015).

Choi, S.Y.P. (2011) 'State control, female prostitution and HIV prevention in China', *The China Quarterly*, 205: 96–114.

Comaroff, J. (2007) 'Beyond bare life: AIDS, (bio)politics, and the neoliberal order', *Public Culture*, 19, 1: 197–219.

Cooper, M. (2008a) *Life as Surplus: Biotechnology and Capitalism in the Neoliberal Era*, Seattle: University of Washington Press.

Cooper, M. (2008b) 'Experimental labour: offshoring clinical trials to China', *East Asian Science, Technology and Society: An International Journal*, 2, 1: 73–92.

Cui, Y., Liau, A., and Wu, Z.Y. (2009) 'An overview of the history of epidemic of and response to HIV/AIDS in China: achievements and challenges', *Chinese Medical Journal*, 122, 19: 2251–7.

Davies, D. (2010) 'China's celebrity entrepreneurs: business models for "success" ', in L. Edwards and E. Jeffreys (eds), *Celebrity in China*, Hong Kong: Hong Kong University Press, pp. 193–216.

Dean, M. (1999) *Governmentality: Power and Rule in Modern Society*, London: Sage.

Dong, D., Chang, T.K., and Chen, D. (2008) 'Reporting AIDS and the invisible victims in China: official knowledge as news in the People's Daily, 1986–2002', *Journal of Health Communication*, 13, 4: 357–74.

Fan, E.L. (2014) 'HIV testing as prevention among MSM in China: the business of scaling-up', *Global Public Health: An International Journal for Research, Policy and Practice*, 9, 1–2: 85–97.

Foucault, M. (1982) 'The subject and power', *Critical Inquiry*, 8, 4: 777–95.

Foucault, M. (1990) *The History of Sexuality, Volume 1: An Introduction*, trans. R. Hurley, New York: Vintage Books.

Foucault, M. (2008) *The Birth of Biopolitics: Lectures at the Collège de France 1978–1979*, New York: Palgrave Macmillan.

Gill, B. (2006) 'Assessing HIV/AIDS initiatives in China: persistent challenges and promising ways forward', a report of the CSIS Task Force on HIV/AIDS. Online. Available: http://csis.org/files/media/csis/pubs/assessing_aids_initiatives_in_china-gill-web.pdf (accessed 10 July 2015).

Gill, B., Huang, Y., and Lu, X. (2007) 'Demography of HIV/AIDS in China', a report for the Task Force on HIV/AIDS, Center for Strategic and International Studies. Online. Available: http://csis.org/files/media/csis/pubs/070724_china_hiv_demography.pdf (accessed 10 July 2015).

Gittings, J. (2002) 'China admits "blood stations" caused steep rise in AIDS', *Guardian*, 10 September. Online. Available: www.theguardian.com/world/2002/sep/10/aids.china (accessed 10 July 2015).

Greenhalgh, S. and Winckler, E.A. (2005) *Governing China's Population: From Leninist to Neoliberal Politics*, Stanford: Stanford University Press.

Guo, L., Zhou, F., Li, X., and Jin, Q. (2010) 'HIV/TB co-infection in mainland China: a meta-analysis', *PLoS ONE*, 5, 5. Online. Available: http://journals.plos.org/plosone/article?id=10.1371/journal.pone.0010736 (accessed 10 July 2015).

Hague, R. (2008) 'The governance of AIDS in China: assessing the impact of global norms', unpublished PhD thesis, University of New South Wales.

Hammett, T.M., Chen, Y., Ngu, D., Cuong, D., Van, L.K., Liu, W., Meng, D., Quyen, H.N., Broadhead, R.S., and Des Jarlais, D.C. (2006) 'A delicate balance: law enforcement agencies and harm reduction interventions for injection drug users in China and Vietnam', in J. Kaufman, A. Kleinman, and T. Saich (eds), *AIDS and Social Policy in China*, Cambridge, MA: Harvard University Asia Center, pp. 214–32.

Hayes, A. (2005) 'AIDS, "bloodheads" and cover-ups: the "ABC" of Henan's AIDS epidemic', *Australian Quarterly: Journal of Contemporary Analysis*, 77, 3: 12–16.

Ho, W.-C. (2014) 'Biopolitics, occupational health and state power: the marginalization of sick workers in China', *The China Quarterly*, 219: 808–26.

Hood, J. (2010) 'Celebrity philanthropy: the cultivation of China's HIV/AIDS heroes', in L. Edwards and E. Jeffreys (eds), *Celebrity in China*, Hong Kong: Hong Kong University Press, pp. 85–102.

Hood, J. (2011a) *HIV/AIDS, Health and the Media in China: Imagined Immunity through Racialized Disease*, Abingdon: Routledge.

Hood, J. (2011b) 'China's AIDS underclass (*Aimin*): preserving power and inequality through media portrayals of HIV/AIDS', unpublished PhD thesis, University of Technology Sydney.

Hood, J. (2012) 'HIV/AIDS and shifting urban China's socio-moral landscape: engendering bio-activism and resistance through stories of suffering', *International Journal of Asia Pacific Studies*, 13, 1: 125–44.

Hood, J. (2013) 'Between entitlement and stigmatization: the lessons of HIV/AIDS for China's medical reform', in W. Sun and Y. Guo (eds), *Unequal China: The Political Economy and Cultural Politics of Inequality*, Abingdon: Routledge, pp. 139–53.

Hsu, C. (2006) 'Cadres, getihu, and good businesspeople: making sense of entrepreneurs in early post-socialist China', *Urban Anthropology and Studies of Cultural Systems and World Economic Development*, 35, 1: 1–38.

Human Rights Watch (2005) 'Restrictions on AIDS activists in China', *Human Rights Watch*, 17, 5. Online. Available: www.hrw.org/reports/2005/china0605/china0605.pdf (accessed 10 July 2015).

Hyde, S.T. (2007) *Eating Spring Rice: The Cultural Politics of AIDS in Southwest China*, Berkeley: University of California Press.

Jacka, T. (2009) 'Cultivating citizens: suzhi (quality) discourse in the PRC', *Positions: East Asia Cultures Critique*, 17, 3: 523–35.

Jeffreys, E. (2007) 'Querying queer theory: debating male–male prostitution in the Chinese media', *Critical Asian Studies*, 39, 1: 151–75.

Jeffreys, E. and Huang, Y. (2009) 'Governing sexual health in the People's Republic of China', in E. Jeffreys (ed.), *China's Governmentalities: Governing Change, Changing Government*, Abingdon: Routledge, pp. 151–73.

Jeffreys, E. and Su Gang (2011) 'China's 100 percent condom use program: customising the Thai experience', *Asian Studies Review*, 35, 3: 315–33.

Jeffreys, E. with Yu, H.-Q. (2015) *Sex in China*, Cambridge: Polity Press.

Jing, J. and Worth, H. (2010) *HIV in China: Understanding the Social Aspects of the Epidemic*, Sydney: UNSW Press.

Kaufman, J. (2009) 'The role of NGOs in China's AIDS crisis', in J. Schwartz and S. Shieh (eds), *State and Society Response to Social Welfare Needs in China*, Abingdon: Routledge.

Kaufman, J. (2010) 'Turning points in China's AIDS response', *China: An International Journal*, 8, 1: 63–84.

Kaufman, J., Kleinman, A., and Saich, T. (2006) *AIDS and Social Policy in China*, Cambridge, MA: Harvard University Asia Center.

Kipnis, A. (2006) 'Suzhi: a keyword approach', *The China Quarterly*, 186: 295–313.

Kipnis, A. (2007) 'Neoliberalism reified: suzhi discourse and tropes of neoliberalism in the People's Republic of China', *Journal of the Royal Anthropological Institute*, n.s., 13, 2: 383–400.

Lau, M. (2014) 'China's sex industry flourishing despite dangerous conditions and corrupt police', *South China Morning Post*, 3 March. Online. Available: www.scmp.com/news/china/article/1439543/chinas-sex-industry-flourishing-despite-dangerous-conditions-and-corrupt (accessed 10 July 2015).

Li, L. (2009) 'Mass media and HIV/AIDS in China', *Journal of Health Communication*, 14, 5: 424–38.

Li, Y. (2006) 'Regulating male same-sex relationships in the People's Republic of China', in E. Jeffreys (ed.), *Sex and Sexuality in China*, London and New York: Routledge, pp. 82–101.

Liu, Q. and Kaufman, J. (2011) 'AIDS NGOs in China: leading the way in forging new working partnerships with government'. Online. Available: www.hks.harvard.edu/news-events/events-calendar/%22aids-ngos-in-china-leading-the-way-in-forging-new-working-partnerships-with-government%22 (accessed 10 July 2015).

Liu, X. and Zhang, J. (2005) 'From hidden corner to front page: the People's Daily's framing of AIDS from 1985–2003', *China Media Research*, 1, 1: 27–42.

Lu, L., Jia, M., Ma, Y., Yang, L., Chen, Z., Ho, D., Jiang, Y., and Zhang, L. (2008) 'The changing face of HIV in China', *Nature*, 455, 2 October: 609–11.

Meng, J. (2012) 'HIV governance through law: achievements and challenges of China's legal environment', *International Journal of Asia-Pacific Studies*, 8, 1: 57–75.

Micollier, E. (2012) 'Sexualised illness and gendered narratives: the problematic of social sciences and humanities in China's HIV and AIDS governance', *International Journal of Asia Pacific Studies*, 8, 1: 103–24.

Ministry of Health, People's Republic of China, Joint United Nations Programme on HIV/AIDS, and the World Health Organization (2006) '2005 update on the HIV/AIDS epidemic and response in China'. Online. Available: http://data.unaids.org/publications/external-documents/rp_2005chinaestimation_25jan06_en.pdf (accessed 10 July 2015).

National Center for AIDS/STD Control and Prevention and CHAIN (China HIV/AIDS Information Network) (2010) 2010 China HIV/AIDS CSO/CBO Directory, published by China CDC and CHAIN internal press.

Osburg, J. (2013) *Anxious Wealth: Money and Morality Among China's New Rich*, Stanford: Stanford University Press.

Ren, C., Hust, S.J.T., and Zhang, P. (2010) 'Stigmatizing HIV/AIDS in the 21st century? Newspaper coverage of HIV/AIDS in China', *China Media Report Overseas*, 1 October.

Rofel, L. (2013) 'Grassroots activism: non-normative sexual politics in post-socialist China', in W. Sun and Y. Guo (eds), *Unequal China: The Political Economy and Cultural Politics of Inequality*, Abingdon: Routledge, pp. 154–67.

Rosenthal, E. (2001) 'Suddenly, AIDS makes the news in China', *New York Times*, 5 December. Online. Available: www.nytimes.com/2001/12/05/world/suddenly-aids-makes-the-news-in-china.html (10 July 2015).

Rudelson, J. (2003) 'HIV/AIDS as a regional security threat', Center for Strategic and International Studies. Online. Available: www.csis.org/media/csis/events/030605_rudelson.pdf (accessed 13 March 2015).

Schwartz, J. and Shieh, S. (eds) (2009) *State and Society Responses to Social Welfare Needs in China: Serving the People*, Abingdon: Routledge.

Sigley, G. (2009) 'Suzhi, the body, and the fortunes of technoscientific reasoning in contemporary China', *Positions*, 17: 537–66.

'Song Pengfei: xiao kan weilai' [Song Pengfei: smiling at the future] (2003) China Central Television, 2 December. Online. Available: www.cctv.com/news/china/20031202/101718.shtml (accessed 10 July 2015).

Su, C. (2010) '"Red oil": blood and the role of a machine in the HIV outbreak in central China', in J. Jing and H. Worth (eds), *HIV in China: Understanding the Social Aspects of the Epidemic*, Sydney: University of New South Wales Press, pp. 102–16.

Thornton, P.M. (2009) 'Crisis and governance: SARS and the resilience of the Chinese body politic', *The China Journal*, 61: 23–48.

Tsinghua International Center for Communication Studies (2005) 'Zhongguo meiti aizibing gongzuo xianzhuang pinggu baogao' [Evaluation Report of Chinese Media Reporting on AIDS]. Online. Available: www.chain.net.cn/document/20070702115008125353.pdf (accessed 13 March 2015).

UNAIDS (2002) 'HIV/AIDS: China's titanic peril'. Online. Available: www.hivpolicy.org/Library/HPP000056.pdf (accessed 10 July 2015).

Uretsky, E. (2008) '"Mobile men with money": the socio-cultural and political-economic context of high-risk behaviour among wealthy businessmen and government officials in urban China', *Culture, Health and Sexuality*, 10, 8: 801–14.

Wang, L. (2007) 'Overview of the HIV/AIDS epidemic, scientific research and government responses in China', *AIDS*, 21, Suppl. 8: S3–S7.

Wang, Y. (2000) 'A strategy of clinical tolerance for the prevention of HIV and AIDS in China', *Journal of Medicine and Philosophy*, 25, 1: 48–61.

'Woguo chenfeibing renshu buduan zengduo, weiquan wenti cheng zuli' [Increasing number of black lung disease sufferers are obstructed in their right defense] (2011) Sohu.com, 21 February. Online. Available: http://business.sohu.com/20110221/n279441286.shtml (accessed 10 July 2015).

Wu, F.S. (2005) 'International non-governmental actors in HIV/AIDS prevention in China', *Cell Research*, 15, 11–12: 919–22.

Wu, C. and Jia, J. (2010) Aizibing, "xianshen" meijie de hefaxing yu quanli xingdong de keneng: jiyu *Renmin ribao* yu dushibao de wenben yanjiu' [AIDS, legitimacy of representative media and possibility for enactment of rights: textual analysis of *People's Daily* and other metropolitan newspapers], *Kaifang Shidai*, 11: 106–32.

Wu, Z., Sullivan, S., Wang, Y., Rotheram-Bonus, M.J., and Detels, R. (2007) 'Evolution of China's response to HIV/AIDS', *The Lancet*, 369: 679–90.

Yan, H. (2003) 'Neoliberal governmentality and neohumanism: organizing suzhi/value flow through labor recruitment networks', *Cultural Anthropology*, 18, 4: 493–523.

Yu, H. (2012) 'Governing and representing HIV/AIDS in China: a critical review', *International Journal of Asia Pacific Studies*, 8, 1: 1–33.

Zhang, M. (2009) 'Hou SARS shidai zhongguo dalu aizibing yiti de meiti chengxian: kuangjia lilun de guandian' [Media representations of HIV and AIDS agendas in post-SARS China: perspectives of framing theories], *Kaifang Shidai*, 2. Online. Available: www.usc.cuhk.edu.hk/PaperCollection/Details.aspx?id=7245 (accessed 10 July 2015).

Zheng, T. (2006) 'Cool masculinity: male clients' sex consumption and business alliance in urban China's sex industry', *Journal of Contemporary China*, 15, 46: 161–82.

'Zhimian aizi' [Face to face with AIDS] (2003) China Central Television, 2 February. Online. Available: www.cctv.com/tvguide/onlinestory/rwgs/20030128/100424_1.shtml (accessed 10 July 2015).

Zhonghua renmin gongheguo weisheng bu, lianheguo aizibing guihua shu, shijie weisheng zuzhi [Ministry of Health (PRC), UNAIDS, and the World Health Organization] (2011) '2011 nian zhongguo aizibing yiqing guji gongzuo baogao' [Report on China's AIDS epidemic estimate in 2011]. Online. Available: www.moh.gov.cn/cmsresources/mohyzs/cmsrsdocument/doc13944.pdf (accessed 10 July 2015).

11 'Model consumers'

Beauty bloggers, everyday experts, and governmentality in urban China

T.E. Woronov

Thirty-three-year-old Feng He seems an unlikely candidate to be an 'expert' in the changing governmental regimes of contemporary China. A native of Chengdu, the cute and perky Feng has a degree in marketing and international trade from the University of Auckland, and is a former English teacher at one of China's Xin Dongfang[1] test prep centres. But her expertise lies in neither English teaching nor international trade. Instead, in her online guise as 'Xiao Nini', Feng is one of China's most famous beauty bloggers, one of a new group of mostly female online personalities known as '*daren*' (达人), a Chinese translation of internet-based urban fashionistas or 'It Girls'. *Daren* are beauty and fashion experts[2] who advise their blog and Weibo[3] followers on how to purchase and apply makeup, which foreign and domestic brands of skin care products will keep their skin soft and young, what accessories to match with which designer clothes, where to travel for great shopping, and what kinds of foods to eat to stay slim and lovely. Although each *daren* tends to specialize in advice in different areas, a conscientious web surfer can turn to them for suggestions on every aspect of consumption necessary to become a beautiful member of the new Chinese middle class. The lifestyle advice they provide is almost entirely about appropriate commercial consumption: what to buy, where to buy it, and how to navigate through the new proliferation of fashion and beauty products that are available in large Chinese cities today.

Entrepreneurial *daren* such as Feng He (aka Xiao Nini) have parlayed their knowledge of the beauty industry and their internet fame into lucrative careers. Xiao Nini (2012) began blogging in 2007 about her love of makeup and beauty products, and her experiences travelling in Anglophone countries. Today she presides over a beauty-focused media empire, and her blog has received over 62 million visitors (Xiao Nini 2015). Her recent book, a compilation of diet, skin care, makeup, and cooking tips, available only through her Weibo and blog sites, has been reprinted three times in less than one year (Xiao Nini 2012). Xiao Nini has also made numerous appearances as a guest expert on one of China's most popular beauty, diet, cooking, and fashion television shows, Hunan Television's *I am a Great Beauty* (*Wo shi da meiren* 我是大美人) ('Shipin: Hunan dianshitai wo shi da meiren Xiao Nini laoshi tuijian Dr. Lumen duo' n.d.).

This chapter examines the *daren* phenomenon as a Chinese example of what are known as 'everyday' or 'popular' experts, a growing number of specialists around the globe who provide lifestyle advice across media platforms that include magazines, television reality and makeover shows, and the internet (Lewis 2008; Lewis *et al.* 2012; Ouellette and Hay 2008; Xu 2007). Studies of these 'everyday' experts have largely been based in research on reality television, and only recently have extended into studies of new forms of internet communication, including websites, blogs, internet sales, and Youtube sites (Lewis 2008). Research in China has generally followed this pattern, where studies of lifestyle expertise have so far focused on reality television and magazines (Song and Lee 2010, 2012; Sun and Zhao 2009). However, internet use is growing exponentially in urban China today, with an estimated 632 million users by the end of June 2014 (China Internet Network Information Center 2014). Cyberspace is therefore an increasingly important site from which to view the ways that lifestyle experts provide advice on negotiating the growing consumer market and the pedagogy of consumption.

I argue that *daren* are internet entrepreneurs who provide their Chinese audience with new models of how to be 'entrepreneurs of the self' (Rose 1996). The popularity of *daren* is directly linked to new regimes of biopolitics where responsibility for care for the self has partly devolved from the state onto individuals. These regimes constitute modern urban Chinese subjects as consumers, who care for the self in increasingly gendered terms. Middle-class Chinese must learn how to manage the proliferation of new products available, and the concomitant anxieties – and pleasures – of how to use consumer goods to craft new urban identities. *Daren* provide guidance on how to do this by drawing on both the concept of a 'model' (*mo'te* 模特) – a beautiful woman who poses in magazines, commercials, and fashion shows – and more traditional Chinese conceptions of the 'model' (*mofan* 模范) as a pedagogic guide to emulate for correct living (Bakken 2000; Landsberger 2001; Munro 1969). Much as the image of model workers (*laodong mofan* 劳动模范) in Maoist-era China had a pedagogic function, to exemplify (gendered) socialist subjects as productive labourers for the Chinese public to emulate (Chen 2003; Landsberger 1995), today *daren* are model consumers who show observers (in this case, visitors to their blogs, Weibo and Taobao – respectively China's equivalent of 'Twitter' and 'e-Bay' sites) how to make the right consumer choices, and how to purchase and wear the fashions and cosmetics necessary to be exemplary middle-class urban beauties. Rather than being posed by state authorities as workers in state-defined production regimes, *daren* pose as model consumers in highly individuated, gendered consumption regimes.

In order to understand how these bloggers are part of a growing cadre of 'everyday experts' in China today, and how these are part of a new form of government of the self, it is first necessary to understand how the genre of lifestyle experts has developed globally, and how the bloggers are part of a much larger social and political transformation in China. The chapter consequently first outlines the global scholarship on 'everyday experts' and reviews the growing gendered regimes of biopolitics that constitute middle-class urban Chinese as consumers, creating the perceived need for expert beauty advice online. It then describes some of the more popular *daren* blogs, to give a sense of how this form of expertise as a new internet genre delivers beauty advice to readers. The final section places this genre in a historical context, arguing that *daren* as experts are only the most recent in a long-term process of posing models, whose images help constitute Chinese as appropriate subjects.

Everyday expertise and the government of the self

Communications scholars have observed a growing trend in what has been called 'lifestyle media' across the world, designed to teach audiences how to improve their lives by managing a range of everyday tasks, including home decorating, fashion, diet, makeup, and exercise (Bell and Hollows 2005; Lewis 2008; Lewis *et al.* 2012; Ouellette and Hay 2008; Palmer 2004). As these scholars have noted, the growth of lifestyle media in western societies is linked to a larger social transformation involving neoliberal modes of governance of the self. The very idea of creating a 'lifestyle' is part of the ongoing 'conduct of conduct' and forms of self-regulation that are part of neoliberal governance (Foucault 2008).

The concept of 'care for the self' is central to these new lifestyle media cultures for two key reasons. First, the growth of lifestyle media is part of a larger, dispersed network of technologies brought to bear upon a subject 'that does not need to be governed by others but will govern themselves, master themselves, care for themselves' (Lewis 2008; see also Rose 1996). Thus, while the term 'lifestyle' is used in a range of different contexts, from health to cooking to home decorating, it is essentially underpinned by a conception of identity that foregrounds personal choice and the malleable nature of the self (Bell and Hollows 2005; Lewis *et al.* 2012: 540). Second, cultures of self-governance and self-surveillance are part of a larger neoliberal strategy of freedom and empowerment; in this context governance of the self should be understood as productive rather than punitive. Culturally, media facilitates this: 'by focusing on what you are and what you can achieve you can be happy … in an enterprise culture which envisages the *self as a project*' (Palmer 2004: 185–6). Help is now available from lifestyle experts who 'legitimate and provide the tools and techniques for the government of the self' (Lewis 2008: 15).

These tools and techniques revolve around appropriate consumption, for the marketplace is the site where individuals can realize themselves fully through making the right choices as consumers. 'Ordinary' or 'everyday' experts are marked less by their credentials or specialist backgrounds than by their ability to guide consumers through choices in the realm of the quotidian; their domains of expertise include household goods, skin care and beauty products, everyday meals, and fashion. Unlike the specialists that Michel Foucault (1994), Nikolas Rose (1999) and Timothy Mitchell (2002) have described as essential to framing the growth of the modern liberal polity, the new lifestyle experts in the neoliberal media age are self-proclaimed rather than credentialed, and operate in the realm of the mundane, not the technical or the esoteric. They specialize in guiding individuals in making appropriate market-based consumer choices to construct the 'best' possible self.

While the category of lifestyle media and 'everyday experts' is spreading around the world, the growing popularity of this new form of expert in China needs to be more broadly understood as 'emerging out of a complex conjuncture of historical, social, and cultural developments' (Lewis 2008: 5). In China, the cultural move towards personal development marked by the growth of *daren* is part of a larger reform-era process of partly devolving government responsibility from the state to the individual. As Elaine Jeffreys and Gary Sigley (2009: 10) describe, this transformation in governance has been occurring since the market reforms were first implemented in the 1980s: 'The socialist market economy does not signal a retreat of the state; it requires a powerful government that simply intervenes in different ways'. Li Zhang and Aihwa Ong (2008) have labelled this transformation as 'government at a distance'.

As with all cultures of self-governance, this strategy is not (only) repressive, but productive, a form of biopower that has produced the Chinese population as the object of policies intending to raise the general health and welfare of the nation (Foucault 2008; Greenhalgh and Winckler 2005; Hoffman 2010; Jeffreys 2009; Jeffreys and Sigley 2006, 2009; Sigley 1996, 2009; Woronov 2009). The market is central to these processes. In ways that increasingly resemble the capitalist west, the market economy is 'creating a space for people to exercise a multitude of private choices' in urban China (Zhang and Ong 2008: 2). Today, the urban Chinese population has been partially reconstructed as the object of new disciplines of the body that collectivize and individuate subjects through gendered regimes of consumption that are radically different from the recent past.

Extensive research has documented the 'consumer revolution' that has transformed the urban landscape and China's cultural forms (Davis 2000, 2005; Dirlik 2001; Hanser 2005; Latham *et al.* 2006; Pun 2003; Wang 2008; see also Cartier in this book). Consumption is a central part of urban people's lives. One analyst predicts that 'By 2020 and within the course of one decade, real consumption will have doubled to $4.8 trillion and China will then be the world's second-biggest consumer market after the United States' (Atsmon *et al.* 2011). Another market research firm predicts that between 2010 and 2020, the number of households in China with an annual disposable income above USD10,000 '(in nominal terms) will almost quadruple – from 57.1 million households in 2010 to 222 million by 2020' (Euromonitor International 2010).

This transformation to a consumer culture has been carried out through a concerted effort by the Chinese state, as part of the 'government at a distance' project of the reform era. As Pun Ngai (2003) argues, China's government has seen consumption as key not only to transforming the domestic economy, but also to producing a global, urban citizenry. Starting early in the reform era, the nation's leaders instituted programmatic efforts to encourage the high-saving Chinese population to go out and spend (Croll 2006; Davis 2000; Pun 2003; Hanser 2008; Latham *et al.* 2006; Zhang 2010). In the view of the state, transforming the populace into better consumers – of goods, services, and even life experiences (such as travel) – would both stimulate the new consumer economy, and remake urban Chinese into better subjects for the nation's efforts to link with the global economy. In Pun's words:

> Consumption ha[d] suddenly become the target for national mobilizations at the close of the century in a curious inversion of the mass mobilizations launched under Mao in the 1950s and 1960s when calls to raise production targets set all of society on the move. This new call is no less a political mobilization *(yundong)* to stimulate economic growth through consumer spending.
>
> (Pun 2003: 473)

China's Twelfth Five-Year Plan for 2011 to 2015 continued the long-term trend of government oversight and encouragement of consumerism. It actively sought to transform the Chinese economy from one driven by exports to one supported by domestic consumption, and proposed a number of state interventions to drive consumerism (Casey and Koleski 2011).

Pun's central point, however, is that this transformation of Chinese people from socialist to consumerist subject does not represent a natural 'freeing' of consumers (see also Davis 2000), but is instead a new form of governmentality in China (Pun 2003). The production of a new, consumerist populace is part of the state's transformation during the reform era to forms of neoliberal governance of self-transformation. In ways that increasingly resemble western societies as described above, Chinese people now are constituted as subjects who are encouraged to transform themselves into self-propelled consumers, and to seek happiness and fulfilment through market choices.

These new consumption regimes are also deeply gendered. Concomitant with the growth of the consumer subject, changing discourses of naturalized gender difference, linked to a concept called 'market feminism', have naturalized women as desiring subjects who find their satisfaction through shopping (Cartier 2008, 2009; Evans 2006; Hanser 2005; Otis 2011; Rofel 2007; X. Wang 2003; Z. Wang 2003). This consumer feminism 'promoted commercialized forms of self-expression and the implication that gender equity could be achieved only under conditions of material satisfaction' (Cartier 2009: 381). As a result, recent market research indicates that women today are notably different shoppers than men. The *China Daily* reports that: 'Urban Chinese women are spending more and saving less as they poured 63% of their incomes into consumer goods ranging from clothes to cosmetics' (Cheng 2010). This article continues to discuss a 2010 survey which showed that 'urban Chinese women put less money in their bank accounts and developed a growing passion for spending, which is totally different from the patterns just a few years ago', and that respondents, all residing in China's largest cities, spent an average of CNY 21,900 (USD3,220) 'on consumer goods last year' (Cheng 2010).

I suggest that the discourse of 'market feminism' that has inscribed women as privileged *consumers* in China today is also linked to a larger transformation in gender discourse, which posits *beauty* as essential to contemporary women's identity. As one scholar summarizes: 'The Maoist insistence on gender equality has all but evaporated, giving way, to an alarmingly rapid emergence or revival of blatant gender inequality … a revival of the cultural reinscription of sexual difference that validates and naturalizes gender discrimination' (X. Wang 2003: 147). Anthropologist Yang Jie's (2010) recent work, which focuses on gendered representations of consumer subjects based on their cosmetics, fashion, and consumption patterns, helps explain how this works. As with the constitution of the consumer subject, her work on gender discourse shows that it is part of a post-Mao state rationality that celebrates women's bodies as representations of consumer capitalism. Highlighting the fact that 'the female body sells products, beauty sells products, and eroticism and sexuality sell products' (Yang 2010: 334; see also Brownell 1998, 2001), discourses of the importance of female beauty reinforce the essential role of the female body, feminine beauty, and feminine youth in developing consumer capitalism in China (Evans 2006). As Yang notes, this discourse both constitutes and legitimates China's female beauty economy (*meinü jingji* 美女经济), which can include everything from 'beauty pageants and modelling competitions to advertisements, cosmetics, plastic surgery, beauty and health care services, and television and cinema, which link women's beauty with the economy' (Xu and Feiner 2007: 334). In the words of Harriet Evans (2006: 173): 'The fashionable figure of the modern beauty is an emblem of China's consumer culture.'

This combined focus on the importance of beauty, and the stress on consumption to generate appropriately modern urban subjects, have together produced a very strong market in China for cosmetics and other beauty products. The beauty industry, which includes spending on hair and skin care, and spas and gyms, accounted for over CNY 300 billion (around USD45 billion) in 2008. That year, beauty products comprised 1.1 per cent of China's total gross national product, and was the second-fastest growing segment of the economy after real estate (Hopkins 2007; Xu and Feiner 2007; Di 2008). Today, China is reported to be the third-largest market in the world for cosmetics, after the USA and Japan (China Cosmetics Beauty Expo 2012).

The avalanche of new consumer goods has been coterminous in China with the growth of new technologies: the blogosphere, online shopping portals (and a modernized banking system that enables online purchases), and the tremendous popularity of Sina Weibo. As internet scholar Minh-Ha Pham (2011) notes, greatly increased access to the internet globally sets up the potential for almost anyone to offer advice. Blogging is 'a phenomenon at the nexus of computer-mediated communication technologies and consumer culture' (Pham 2011: 3). In this arena, where new technologies meet a very rapidly growing consumer sector, there is growing technological space for lifestyle experts.

China's *daren* thus exist at the confluence of many different factors and discursive effects. The growth of the internet, which enables anyone to offer advice, has occurred concurrently with the neoliberal project of producing consumer subjects. This, along with the naturalization of 'market feminism' and the discourse of women as naturally desiring beauty, has laid the groundwork for a new kind of lifestyle expert to arise: the beauty blogger. *Daren* have emerged through these new technological platforms as lifestyle experts whose goal is to teach the new middle classes how to discern and then purchase the right products to become urban beauties.

China's *daren* bloggers: the pedagogy of beauty and fashion

The Chinese blogosphere is enormous, with the sector specifically devoted to fashion and beauty growing apace. China's best-known internet companies, including Sohu, Baidu, and Sina, all host massively popular *daren* blogs (some with tens of millions of hits each), while a beauty-specific site called Onlylady.com hosts dozens of extremely popular beauty, skincare, and makeup blogs (http://blog.onlylady.com). Chinese netizens also increasingly follow their favourite *daren* on Sina Weibo, where the most popular fashionistas may each have millions of followers (known as 'fans') (e.g. XiaoP Laoshi 2013–2015). Anyone seeking advice can enter one of many popular search terms (including 'fashion', 'makeup', 'skincare', or '*daren*') into a Weibo or general Chinese search engine to return literally millions of hits. Because of the sheer size of these new media domains, I will describe a few of the most popular fashion and beauty blogs to give a sense of the range of *daren* sites as a genre. My discussion focuses largely on blogs, rather than the extremely popular Weibo posts, which, because of their truncated (Facebook-style) length, tend to include less content than the larger blog pages.

The blog site of fashion blogger Ahqiuqiu (2015), for example, had received over 38 million hits by early 2015, and contains many of the visual and textual elements that exemplify the genre. A Shanghai-based fashionista, Ahqiuiqiu also has 350,000 Weibo followers. Her blog includes a typically slangy, ironic self-description, stating that while her parents named her 'Zhang Juan' she named herself 'Ah Qiu Qiu'. She claims that her past jobs have included hosting radio and television shows in Shaanxi Province, editing a Chinese-language fashion magazine in France, and jobs as a fashion stylist, wardrobe manager, and DJ; she then says that her favourite job title is 'happy dog mom'. The ironic tone, vocabulary, and work history mark her as urban and hip, with a middle class, vaguely fashion-associated international career. Typical of many of the *daren* blogs, Ahqiuqiu appears to provide a lot of information, but actually divulges little personal data about her background. Also typical of many of the *daren* blogs, this one includes links to a Taobao site where she sells some of the fashion items she models on the blog.

The images posted daily on Ahqiuqiu's site show an exceptionally thin, petite woman who appears to be in her early thirties; her perfect skin and makeup, and absolutely straight, shoulder-length hair are all standard markers of urban female Chinese beauty today. She occasionally poses carrying a small, extremely well-groomed fluffy dog, a common prop on *daren* sites, and a common marker of middle-class status in Chinese cities today (Ahqiuqiu, 1 April 2013). In her photographs Ahqiuqiu tends to look serious and unsmiling, perhaps to stress her urban hipster (*chaoren* 潮人) status. The photos are very well lit and posed, and appear to be the work of a professional photographer. Generally, she poses in unmarked urban spaces, such as street scenes or store dressing rooms. The images combine full-length poses of clothes with close-ups of shoes, jewellery, and handbags, to give viewers a sense of total fashion. The overall effect is, frankly, stunning; the clothes and accessories Ahqiuqiu models are clearly extremely expensive and well-designed, and she puts together outfits with flair and wears them with tremendous panache.

The blog's text tends towards the didactic. One post reads: 'I like big sweaters with a strong sense of design.... This one has a large pattern but narrow sleeves so it shines when I put it on. Fashion is ultimately all about details!' (Ahqiuqiu, 23 March 2013). Another post notes that while trench coats are 'a kind of magic', wearers have to pay extra attention to how to tie the belt: 'tying it casually is best. Please don't formally tie it into the buckle!' (Ahqiuqiu, 24 March 2013). She then warns: 'Solid black stockings will make you look classic. Don't touch patterned stockings unless you're a master!' (Ahqiuqiu, 23 March 2013).

Another very popular fashion blog is by identical twins Wei Dan and Wei Qing (2015) of Chongqing, whose site LadyAngel (呛口小辣椒 *qiangkou xiaolajiao*; subtitled 'I Love My Life' in English) has received over 400 million hits. Their site is constructed much like Ahqiuqiu's, with new photographs of one of the thin, poised, immaculately groomed young women in exquisite clothes posted every few days. This blog, however, is much more international; the twins have blogged effusively about their travels in France, Germany, Italy, Japan, New Zealand, and Thailand since 2012.

Less strictly about fashion, LadyAngel is more of a lifestyle blog. Unlike the strictly fashion-focused bloggers, they mix descriptions of clothes and accessories with discussions of their favourite foods, travel destinations, and exotic locales. Along with images of clothes, jewellery, shoes, skincare products, and handbags, their blog includes photographs of some of the special meals they have had while travelling, and photos of some of their favourite shops. Visually, the LadyAngel site presents a montage of images of perfect female beauty living perfect, globe-trotting, upscale lives, narrated with genteel calm. A typical post shows a photograph of one of the twins, wearing exquisite designer clothes, draped on a sofa in a luxury hotel room next to an enormous flower arrangement, with tousled hair, perfect makeup, and strappy heels; other popular settings are in gardens, dressing rooms in luxury shops, and outdoor cafes (Wei Dan and Wei Qing, 31 March 2013). The twins appear comfortable and at ease in all these settings, always naturally poised and elegant.

As with their photographs, the text of LadyAngel's blogs is less fashion-oriented than Ahqiuqiu's, and more travel- and lifestyle-focused. Their visit to New Zealand in 2013, for example, says:

> Picking cherries in orchards was the most interesting experience in New Zealand. Half an hour car-drive from Queenstown, there are lots of orchards.

> There's a variety of fresh fruit for sale. Some of the orchards are open to tourists. You can take the fruit basket into the orchard and pick the fresh fruit yourself. This makes it so much fun. It's sweeter to eat the fruit you pick yourself.
>
> (Wei Dan and Wei Qing, 13 March 2013)

The twins' photos, travelogs, and twee descriptions of their favourite things all support a growing media empire. Clicking on any blog photograph brings the viewer to the highly sophisticated LadyAngel Taobao site, where shoppers can purchase low-cost (CNY 150–700) clothes and accessories. The twins also model all the Taobao sales photos in the same locations as the blog photographs; although they are posed less formally, the international settings of the sales photos add a dimension of exotic glamour for Chinese viewers. Several outfits, for example, are modelled in front of a street sign that reads 'Downtown Prague buses'; others are posed in front of a rack of French-language greeting cards. Shoppers are thus able to purchase some of the bloggers' international panache along with the stylish and reasonably priced clothes and accessories. The Taobao site seems to promise an entire fantasy package that includes the global lifestyle, casual elegance, and languid indulgences pictured on the blog. Total sales from the site are unknown, but the twins' reach is growing. Along with prominent appearances at major fashion shows (including Dior and Chanel) in Shanghai and Beijing, the twins recently expanded their 'brand' to an online partnership with the Chinese bakery Couture, to launch a line of designer cakes ('Couture' n.d.).

Another very popular blogger, 'Xiaoman', takes an almost diametrically opposite approach to that of the LadyAngel site (Xiaoman 2015). Rather than focusing on fashion, Xiaoman is a makeup and skincare blogger who has attracted an enormous following – over 130 million blog hits – for her sarcastic, slangy, and sometimes outright rude blog posts. Although she occasionally makes references to shopping in British pounds or buying goods at Sainsbury's, which hints that she lives in the UK, Xiaoman has provided almost no information about herself, and the site does not generally include pictures of herself using the products she reviews. Unlike the lush romanticism of LadyAngel or the no-nonsense directives of Ahqiuqiu, Xiaoman's blog is full of up-to-the-moment internet slang and hipster references to current soap operas, novellas, and starlets, and is intended to amuse. For example, blogs posted during April 2013 tested several products that had won a Japanese online consumer cosmetics award called the Cosme (www.cosme.net). Xiaoman's comments on the top-ranked product, a Nars eye foundation, give a sense of her rhetorical style:

> My love at first sight for Nars didn't last long – when the hot summer came, Comrade Nars couldn't hold me anymore. I didn't notice until a friend stared at my eyes, hesitated then asked if I had smoky eye makeup. I was shocked and quickly got out a mirror and looked at myself: indeed, my eyes looked like they'd been punched or like our national treasure the giant panda. Suddenly I felt I'd made a silly mistake, upset, confused, I needed a

> drink … oh sorry … I lost my lines…. But it was Number 1 at Cosme and had won so many hearts. I can't believe it was defeated by my oily eyelids. At that moment, I wasn't sure if I should be sad for Nars' loss, or proud of my unbeatably oily eyelids.
>
> (Xiaoman 28 February 2013)

A later blog post includes a full-page nationalistic rant against the company Urban Decay, which had refused to enter the Chinese market because of the governmental requirement in China that all cosmetics first be tested on animals. Although the testing requirement caused an uproar in the global beauty blogosphere, Xiaoman was quick to point a finger at corporate hypocrisy:

> Wait a minute! Let's leave the argument about the morality of animal testing and first ask about Urban Decay wanting to suck money out of China! They hurried to enter China because they know that Chinese have money and love to spend it on silly things. Gee, Urban Decay wants to be a bitch and at the same time set up a memorial arch for itself.
>
> (Xiaoman 28 February 2013)[4]

Xiaoman's makeup reviews are a direct contrast to another very popular Weibo poster, Teacher XiaoP (XiaoP *laoshi*) (XiaoP Laoshi 2013–2015). A young man who appears to be in his early thirties, Teacher XiaoP, as his title reminds readers, is a professional makeup artist whose Weibo posts support a website, television specials, and Youku video-hosting feeds. A well-groomed man, originally from Taiwan, Teacher XiaoP poses in a tuxedo on his Weibo site with the asexual charm of a Japanese manga character or Korean boy-band star. His more than 36 million Weibo followers read posts where he shares beauty secrets without a hint of irony or sarcasm. Teacher XiaoP does not have a blog; instead, his Weibo site is only a portal to a much larger website, www.pimei.com, which he uses to consolidate a vast array of fashion- and beauty-related social media projects, linking video, online sales, and interactive media on a range of topics.

The genius of Teacher XiaoP's posts is the calm, matter-of-fact techniques and tips he offers to solve the myriad beauty problems that readers never realized they had. This Weibo post on keeping hands soft is a typical example:

> If your hands are oily, can't absorb hand cream and if you have white skin between your fingers after you apply hand cream, then you should do a hand exfoliation. Honey can nourish and whiten skin. Mixed with sugar it can remove aging or dead skin very well. This sugar-honey scrub programme is the secret weapon of a DIY hand spa. Used on a regular basis, you too can have soft, white, smooth delicate hands.
>
> (XiaoP Laoshi 2013–2015, posted 11 March 2013)

While these blogs are characterized by many differences in tone and approach, *daren* are marked by important similarities. *Daren* rarely (if ever) discuss on their blogs their family backgrounds or where they come by the money to buy the fashions and products they model. Yet they are clearly a part of China's growing middle classes and this positioning is an essential part of the pedagogy and expertise in 'care of the self' that they provide.

Advising a new middle class: *daren* and class expertise

Daren are firmly located in China's new middle classes; this is clear from at least three aspects of their blogs. First, it is an expensive endeavour to begin a career as a *daren*. For their blogs to attract readers, *daren* need access to extensive collections of clothes, accessories, makeup, and skin care products, and to exotic life experiences (such as overseas travel). Second, many *daren* acknowledge that they rely on professional photographers for the high-quality photographs on their blogs, and while they rarely mention this online, many *daren* are also assumed to hire professional makeup artists as well. Finally, many of the well-known *daren* are very well educated – LadyAngel twin Wei Dan, for example, has a law degree from Sichuan University, while Xiao Nini was educated in New Zealand.

As experts in purchasing makeup, skin care, fashion, and home furnishings, *daren*'s expertise is linked to quotidian, everyday life, but they are *daren* precisely because they are not 'ordinary' – they have access to products, goods, and services about which they have become experts. Some of the most popular *daren* became famous for modelling clothes from companies including Chanel, Dior, and Vivienne Westwood, and recommending very expensive skin care products from exceptional companies like La Mer. As discussed above, LadyAngel bloggers Wei Dan and Wei Qing have based their media empire on stories about their global travels. *Daren* thus embody aspirational norms rather than 'real' daily life for their millions of fans. Yet the aspirational and class aspects of their modelling are buried beneath a discourse of normative beauty standards.

While *daren* are sometimes described as 'the girl next door' ('Qiang kou xiao lajiao' 2015), they are actually representatives of a particular (upper-middle) class position and a particular kind of taste (see Palmer 2004). They are part of a logic that consumers are all 'free' to choose on the open market, if only each shopper had the right guidance to make the right choices. This, of course, hides the class basis for these choices in the guise of 'taste', and naturalizes class difference, for these are entirely middle-class competencies and values (Song and Lee 2010).

In many ways, the *daren* blogs recapitulate the ways the discourse of 'class' has been attenuated in China today (Anagnost 2008); social hierarchy is visible everywhere, but is discursively relegated to natural forms of social difference. Thus, while money is essential to the *daren*'s work, it largely goes unmentioned as a topic in their blogs. In China, unmarked images of the *daren* casually draped in thousands of dollars of imported fashion and makeup are linked to the erasure of class as a category of social analysis and identity.

This logic is not confined to the bloggers; globally, scholars of lifestyle media argue that the growth of the genre is part of the larger, neoliberal post-class emphasis on freedom and individuality that turns the self into an individual project, rather than the production of identity through membership in groups such as classes (Lewis 2008: 8; Palmer 2004). 'Taste' is understood as a naturally occurring quality, and beauty is equally available to all, if only they watch the right media, click on the right websites, and purchase the right products. According to this discourse, the body is a site that can be transformed, improved, and controlled simply through individual action and choice.

Yet the economics of these blogs and websites creates a potential problem, for *daren* must tread a fine line to maintain their credibility with readers. They are revered for their objective opinions, and their objectivity supposedly derives partly from their amateur status, especially for skincare bloggers.[5] Yet their opinions are sought precisely because of their access to extraordinary amounts of very expensive products, access which renders their objectivity suspect. The *daren* therefore all run the risk of being labelled a '*tuo'er*' 托儿, a neologism for 'shilling' a product that they have been paid to promote. For example, one extremely popular blogger, 大C, was forced to close both her blog and Taobao sites in 2009 after she was accused of taking kick-backs from companies whose fashions she promoted.[6]

In spite of the difficulties to become a *daren*, one of the many accomplishments achieved by successful bloggers is the way they have joined their contemporaries in western societies to expand the categories of 'beauty' and 'lifestyle' far beyond the original conceptions of the terms. Perhaps one key to their popularity is the way that *daren* demonstrate that beautiful skin or well-crafted makeup must be linked to the right fashions, right food, and right cosmopolitan experiences; *daren* present images of entire lifestyles for readers to emulate (see also Lewis 2008). Travel, healthy food, weight loss, workouts, and accessories are all important parts of self-construction and self-presentation for the Chinese middle classes today; rather than advertising which focuses solely on one product, the *daren* help readers understand how to put together all aspects of their lives for beautiful results. The expansion of the category of beauty therefore helps readers negotiate the confusing thicket of products and practices available on the changing market, and expands the 'care of the self' to encompass all aspects of life. In this way, *daren* are closely linked to their counterparts in western societies, where popular experts like Oprah, Martha Stewart, and other lifestyle celebrities expand the range of intervention in everyday lives to instruct viewers in how to beautify homes, skin, waistlines, and relationships.

As experts, *daren* tend to focus on their own bodies; they are experts, quite literally, of themselves. Although many of the well-known *daren* are well educated, and some are professionals in the fashion or makeup industry, most of the *daren* derive their expertise from what they look like in the newest fashions, how different makeup looks on their faces, and the results achieved when they applied the latest skin care products.[7] The care of the self is, in their cases, literal: they display the care they embody, and present it as a new aesthetic norm for readers.

Key to this are the ways that *daren* focus on beauty as a source of pleasure, rather than on the anxieties associated with remaking the self through consumption. The banner across the first page of LadyAngel's blog says (in English) 'I Love My Life', and further down the page reads (again, in English) 'ZZ loves all the extraordinary things. It is even hotter than the chilli and more fashionable. It's called happiness' (Wei Dan and Wei Qing 2015). The *daren* blogs are full of the joys of self-expression through shopping, of sharing new discoveries in stores and through world travel, and the pleasures of remaking the self into someone thinner, younger, more beautiful, and more fashionable. Readers may visit these sites out of anxiety – over how to be thinner, how to make the right choices among the myriad products available, or over how to get the best results for limited financial resources; this awaits more empirical research. But once they have clicked onto these sites, the message is very clear: care for the self should be fun and rewarding. As blogger JJ.ing's banner announces on her home page: 'Be your true self, do not feel inferior, not confused, not anxiety [sic]' (Jinshao 2013).

This is surely a kind of 'market exuberance' that reflects not only the plethora of consumer goods now available, but which dictates the appropriate emotional stance towards consumption and care for the self (Zhang and Ong 2008: 10). The biopolitics of the beautiful subject require young urban women who see self-construction as a pleasurable task. Part of the *daren*'s expertise lies in their ability to model precisely how much fun the new gendered techniques of the self can be. In this way, the Chinese middle-class woman is instructed in how to present the right kinds of affect for the neoliberal era (see also Berlant 2011).

Biopolitics and models consumers: historical antecedents

In a study of images of women model workers in the 1950s, Tina Mai Chen (2003) argues that 'individual models represented metonymically the new Chinese body politic', in a political climate where all Chinese had the potential to become an exemplar. At that time, the mass media and Maoist egalitarian politics together created 'a set of prevailing images whereby model workers constituted an iconography of the state, with the individual models assuming status as everyday icons' (Chen 2003: 270). Chen conceptualizes images of women who were China's first welders, tractor drivers, and train engineers as symbols of the relationship between experience and representation. These 'first women' represented morality and value within socialist China by displaying images of bodies that represented socialist experience: they demonstrated visually the ways that women embodied the experience of socialism and had as a result been transformed into new kinds of subjects. In Chen's analysis, everyday icons of model workers served as a system of symbolic representation of the values of the socialist system. Posed beside her tractor or train engine, the female model worker 'became an instrument through which to achieve socialist construction by establishing a symbiotic relationship between her body and machinery'.

Today, perhaps, the *daren* as model consumer may be considered an instrument for representing a form of capitalist construction by establishing a symbiotic relationship between her body and the 'machinery' of beauty: makeup, skincare, fashion, accessories. She is the model consumer of the 'socialist market economy', building a better body and a better self, through post-industrial processes based in individual efforts of consumption on the global market (see also Cartier in this book). There is, of course, a limit to the analogy; a Weibo photograph of a *daren* draped across a Ferrari is not the direct functional equivalent of model worker Liang Jun posed on her tractor in the early 1960s (e.g. 'Zhubo Linda' 2012). But *daren* may also be considered everyday icons who represent a changing morality and value system: consumer morality in a value system that favours beauty, youth, and consumer savvy.

Just as the 'first women' did during the Cultural Revolution, the transformations the *daren* effect in their own bodies model changes that are supposedly available to anyone else who wants to emulate them. Their bodies are simultaneously instruments for achieving goals of capitalist-style modernity and beauty and models of how to get there. *Daren* model the new values of the care for the self and the technologies of how to achieve this; their blogs are contemporary icons of the conceptual relationship between representation and the experience of buying and using makeup, skincare, fashion, and accessories.

Conclusion

I have argued that the *daren* phenomenon should be understood in the context of changing governmental regimes that displace responsibility for health and welfare from the socialist state onto individual Chinese subjects. Centred on a new logic of 'care for the self', these regimes produce urban Chinese as gendered consumers, who must learn how to consume appropriately among the plethora of new goods available in the rapidly expanding consumer markets. *Daren* present themselves as model consumers who can dispel middle-class anxiety through displaying the potential pleasures associated with mastering the complexities of the new beauty economy. In playing this role, they exemplify how new forms of expertise are generated within the realm of the domestic and the everyday. The *daren* phenomenon thus helps to demonstrate the ways that the new economy *produces* desiring consumers, rather than simply freeing consumers to buy what they wish (Rofel 2007).

Tania Lewis *et al.* (2012: 539) argue that lifestyle media in Asia 'steps in where the state retreats from the care of its citizens in areas such as housing, education and health care'. To use their words: 'In the context of the privatization and individualization of Chinese society, such programming fulfils the need for potentially lucrative "soft" TV content while also demonstrating middle-class values and tastes to urban socio-economic elites' (Lewis *et al.* 2012: 539; see also Sun and Zhao 2009). The expertise provided by lifestyle media, including *daren* blogs, naturalizes class difference that 'helps citizen-subjects to survive market turbulence and cope with the gradual withdrawal of state resources'

(Lewis *et al.* 2012: 539). These authors hint that the erasing of class inequality through a valorization of 'taste', rooted in the individual and expressed through market choices, may mute the potential for social unrest in China. Presumably, blog readers who take to heart the injunctions to consume avidly, to love their lives, and to continuously improve their beauty are not also disgruntled social or political activists. In this respect, 'ordinary' experts may be as effective in disciplining docile subjects in China as their more credentialed and professionalized forbearers elsewhere.

My approach also links *daren* blogs to the growing global study of digital politics, including research on the internet. While studies of blogs are fairly recent, most of this fledgling research has focused only on English-language blogs that deal with political topics for the purpose of exploring the potentials of cyberdemocracy, where everyone is assumed to be equal, and everyone is assumed to have an equal say. I follow a different trajectory, based on the work of Pham (2011) and others who look instead at cultural blogs that focus on gendered and racial topics. The objective of this approach is to examine the potential politics of 'digital subject formations' (Nakamura 2007), and to address questions that are applicable to gendered and racialized internet use globally. In China today, under regimes of governmentality that are producing (gendered) subjectivities partly through the pleasures of consumption (Pham 2011: 9), and where the politics of race, gender, and language on the internet pose radically different questions than they do in other (western) settings, there are still many questions to answer. In this chapter I have shown how some of these questions can be fruitfully addressed through a governmentality framework which illuminates the ways in which the internet provides a platform for the emergence of new forms of everyday expertise concerned with the conduct of consumption.

Acknowledgements

I must thank several people for their help through the many iterations of this chapter. Ruby Hong Na and Chen Shuxia provided invaluable research support, and Shuxia translated several of the *daren* sites. Leticia Veloso, Jennifer Roth-Gordon, Gary Sigley, and especially Lisa Hoffman provided extremely helpful comments on previous drafts. I thank the volume editors – David Bray and Elaine Jeffreys – for advice and feedback. The research for this chapter was generously funded by the China Studies Centre at the University of Sydney.

Notes

1 Xin Dongfang (New Oriental) is the largest private educational services company in China, specializing in preparing Chinese students to take the standardized admission tests required for entry into foreign universities.

2 According to Baidu Baike or Baidu Encyclopedia, the term '*daren*' can be directly translated as 'expert' ('Daren' 2015). The contemporary use of the term in China comes from Taiwan, which in turn derived '*daren*' from Japanese, where the character '*da*' is used to represent the first syllable of the English word 'talent'. The term is also

used widely in China as part of the title for television reality talent programmes, mostly for singers.

3 Sina Weibo is similar to a Chinese version of Facebook and Twitter.

4 Urban Decay has since been purchased by global cosmetics giant L'Oreal, which may change their marketing decisions in China.

5 See Xu (2007) for a discussion of how the problem of consumer fraud is central to the new consumer/lifestyle television media in China.

6 See http://blog.renren.com/share/251518475/4400373207. For a discussion of this kind of censoring in the context of European bloggers, see Pham (2011).

7 Note that even the fashion professionals who maintain popular blogs also pose on those blogs and serve as fashion models. The best example of this – and the most popular – is blogger Han Huohuo (2014), a former fashion editor with the Chinese edition of *Marie Claire* magazine.

References

Ahqiuqiu (2015) *Ahqiuqiu de shixiang rizhi* [Ahqiuqiu's Fashion Journal]. Online. Available: http://aqiuqiuvip.blog.sohu.com (accessed 10 July 2015).

Anagnost, A. (2008) 'From "class" to "social strata": grasping the social totality in reform-era China', *Third World Quarterly*, 29, 3: 497–519.

Atsmon, Y., Magni, M., Liu, M., and Li, L. (2011) '2011 annual Chinese consumer study: new frontiers of growth', *McKinsey China Insights*. Online. Available: https://solutions.mckinsey.com/insightschina/_SiteNote/WWW/GetFile.aspx?uri=%2Finsightschina%2Fdefault%2Fen-us%2Fabout%2Four_publications%2FFiles%2Fwp2055036759%2FMcKinsey%20Insights%20China%20-%202011%20Annual%20Consumer%20Study%20-%20EN_1efd3213-1835-465e-baa2-c2a37c1c8a3e.pdf (accessed 10 July 2015).

Bakken, B. (ed.) (2000) *The Exemplary Society: Human Improvement, Social Control, and the Dangers of Modernity in China*, Oxford: Oxford University Press.

Bell, D. and Hollows, J. (eds) (2005) *Ordinary Lifestyles: Popular Media, Consumption and Taste*, Maidenhead: Open University Press.

Berlant, L. (2011) *Cruel Optimism*, Durham: Duke University Press.

Brownell, S. (1998) 'The body and the beautiful in Chinese nationalism: sportswomen and fashion models in the reform era', *China Information*, 13, 2–3: 36–58.

Brownell, S. (2001) 'Making dream bodies in Beijing: athletes, fashion models, and urban mystique in China', in N. Chen, C. Clark, S. Gottschang, and L. Jeffery (eds), *China Urban: Ethnographies of Contemporary Culture*, Durham: Duke University Press, pp. 123–42.

Cartier, C. (2008) 'The Shanghai–Hong Kong connection: fine jewelry consumption and the demand for diamonds', in D.S.G. Goodman (ed.) *The New Rich in China: Future Rulers, Present Lives*, Abingdon: Routledge, pp. 187–200.

Cartier, C. (2009) 'Production/consumption and the Chinese city/region: cultural political economy and the feminist diamond ring', *Urban Geography*, 30, 4: 368–90.

Casey, J. and Koleski, K. (2011) *Backgrounder: China's 12th Five-Year Plan*, Washington: US–China Economic and Security Review Commission.

Chen, T.M. (2003) 'Female icons, feminist iconography? Socialist rhetoric and women's agency in 1950s China', *Gender and History*, 15, 2: 268–95.

Cheng, Y. (2010) 'Urban women catch shopping fever, survey finds', *China Daily*. Online. Available: www.chinadaily.com.cn/business/2010-08/25/content_11198163.htm (accessed 10 July 2015).

China Cosmetics Beauty Expo (2012) 'Fact sheet'. Online. Available: www.cbebaiwen.com/en/en/facts/china-beauty-market.html (accessed 19 February 2015).

China Internet Network Information Center (2014) 'Statistical report on internet development in China', July 2014. Online. Available: www1.cnnic.cn/IDR/ReportDownloads/201411/P020141102574314897888.pdf (accessed 10 July 2015).

'Couture' (n.d.) Online. Available: www.couturecakes.com.cn/qkxlj (accessed 26 July 2013).

Croll, E. (2006) 'Conjuring goods, identities and cultures', in K. Latham, S. Thompson, and J. Klein (eds), *Consuming China: Approaches to Cultural Change in Contemporary China*, London: Routledge, pp. 22–39.

'Daren' (2015) Baidu Baike. Online. Available: http://baike.baidu.com/view/2453.htm (accessed 19 February 2015).

Davis, D. (ed.) (2000) *The Consumer Revolution in Urban China*, Berkeley: University of California Press.

Davis, D. (2005) 'Urban consumer culture', *The China Quarterly*, 183: 692–709.

Di, J. (2008) *Annual Report on Development Assessment of China's Hair and Beauty Industry*, Beijing: Department of Commercial Services Administration, Ministry of Commerce, People's Republic of China.

Dirlik, A. (2001) 'Markets, culture, power: the making of a "second cultural revolution" in China', *Asian Studies Review*, 25, 1: 1–33.

Euromonitor International (2010) 'Top 10 largest economies in 2020', 7 July. Online. Available: http://blog.euromonitor.com/2010/07/special-report-top-10-largest-economies-in-2020.html (accessed 10 July 2015).

Evans, H. (2006) 'Fashion and feminine consumption', in K. Latham, S. Thompson, and J. Klein (eds), *Consuming China: Approaches to Cultural Change in Contemporary China*, London: Routledge, pp. 173–89.

Foucault, M. (1994) *The Birth of the Clinic: An Archaeology of Medical Perception*, New York: Vintage Books.

Foucault, M. (2008) *The Birth of Biopolitics: Lectures at the Collège de France 1978–1979*, New York: Palgrave Macmillan.

Greenhalgh, S. and Winckler, E. (2005) *Governing China's Population: From Leninist to Neoliberal Biopolitics*, Stanford: Stanford University Press.

Han Huohuo (2014) 'It's amazing … (blog)', *Sina.com*. Online. Available: http://blog.sina.com.cn/hanshang (accessed 19 February 2015).

Hanser, A. (2005) 'The gendered rice bowl: the sexual politics of service work in urban China', *Gender and Society*, 19, 5: 581–600.

Hoffman, L. (2010) *Patriotic Professionalism in Urban China*, Philadelphia: Temple University Press.

Hopkins, B.E. (2007) 'Western cosmetics in the gendered development of consumer culture in China', *Feminist Economics*, 13, 3–4: 287–306.

Jeffreys, E. (ed.) (2009) *China's Governmentalities: Governing Change, Changing Government*, Abingdon: Routledge.

Jeffreys, E. and Sigley, G. (2006) 'China and governmentality: a special issue', *Economy and Society*, 35, 4.

Jeffreys, E. and Sigley, G. (2009) 'Governmentality, governance and China', in E. Jeffreys (ed.) *China's Governmentalities: Governing Change, Changing Government*, Abingdon: Routledge.

JinShao (2013) 'JJ.ing to strive for happiness', JJ.ing Blog. Online. Available: http://jinshao.blog.blog.163.com (accessed 30 April 2013).

Landsberger, S. (1995) *Chinese Propaganda Posters: From Revolution to Modernization*, Amsterdam: The Pepin Press.

Landsberger, S. (2001) 'Learning by what example? Educational propaganda in twenty-first century China', *Critical Asian Studies*, 33: 541–71.

Latham, K., Thompson, S., and Klein, J. (eds) (2006) *Consuming China: Approaches to Cultural Change in Contemporary China*, London: Routledge.

Lewis, T. (2008) *Smart Living: Lifestyle Media and Popular Expertise*, New York: Peter Lang.

Lewis, T., Martin, F., and Sun, W. (2012) 'Lifestyling Asia? Shaping modernity and self-hood on life-advice programming', *International Journal of Cultural Studies*, 15, 6: 537–66.

Mitchell, T. (2002) *Rule of Experts: Egypt, Techno-Politics, Modernity*, Berkeley: University of California Press.

Munro, D. (1969) *The Concept of Man in Early China*, Stanford: Stanford University Press.

Nakamura, L. (2007) *Digitizing Race: Visual Cultures of the Internet*, Minneapolis, MN: University of Minnesota Press.

Otis, E. (2011) *Markets and Bodies: Women, Service Work, and the Making of Inequality in China*, Stanford, CA: Stanford University Press.

Ouellette, L. and Hay, J. (2008) 'Makeover television, governmentality and the good citizen', *Continuum: Journal of Media and Cultural Studies*, 22, 4: 471–84.

Palmer, G. (2004) '"The new you"': class and transformation in lifestyle television', in S. Holmes and D. Jermyn (eds), *Understanding Reality Television*, London: Routledge, pp. 173–90.

Pham, M.-H.T. (2011) 'Blog ambition: fashion, feelings, and the political economy of the digital raced body', *Camera Obscura*, 26, 1: 1–36.

Pun, N. (2003) 'Subsumption or consumption? The phantom of consumer revolution in "globalizing China"', *Cultural Anthropology*, 18, 4: 469–92.

'Qiang kou xiao lajiao' [The Chongqing twins – Viviandan and MiuMiu] (2015) Online. Available: http://baike.baidu.com/view/1801107.htm (accessed 10 July 2015).

Rofel, L. (2007) *Desiring China: Experiments in Neoliberalism, Sexuality and Public Culture*, Durham: Duke University Press.

Rose, N. (1996) *Inventing Ourselves: Psychology, Power, and Personhood*, Cambridge: Cambridge University Press.

Rose, N. (1999) *Governing the Soul: The Shaping of the Private Self*, London: Free Association Books.

'Shipin: Hunan dianshitai wo shi da meiren Xiao Nini laoshi tuijian Dr. Lumen duo' [Video: Hunan Television Station, I am a great beauty, Teacher Xiao Nini recommends Dr Lumen flowers] (n.d.) Online. Available: http://v.youku.com/v_show/id_XNDIzMzAzNDIw.html (accessed 19 February 2015).

Sigley, G. (1996) 'Governing Chinese bodies: the significance of studies in the concept of governmentality for the analysis of government in China', *Economy and Society*, 25: 457–82.

Sigley, G. (2009) 'Suzhi, the body, and the fortunes of technoscientific reasoning in contemporary China', *Positions*, 17, 3: 537–66.

Song, G. and Lee, T.K. (2010) 'Consumption, class formation and sexuality: reading men's lifestyle magazines in China', *China Journal*, 64: 159–76.

Song, G. and Lee, T.K. (2012) '"New man" and "new lad" with Chinese characteristics? Cosmopolitanism, cultural hybridity and men's lifestyle magazines in China', *Asian Studies Review*, 36, 3: 345–67.

Sun, W. and Zhao, Y. (2009) 'Television culture with "Chinese characteristics": the politics of compassion and education', in G. Turner and J. Tay (eds), *Television Studies after TV: Understanding Television in the Post-Broadcast Era*, Abingdon: Routledge, pp. 96–104.

Wang, J. (2008) *Brand New China: Advertising, Media, and Commercial Culture*, Cambridge, MA: Harvard University Press.

Wang, X. (2003) 'A time to remember: the reinvention of the communist hero in post-communist China', *New Literary History*, 34, 1: 133–53.

Wang, Z. (2003) 'Gender, employment and women's resistance', in E. Perry and M. Selden (eds) *Chinese Society: Change, Conflict and Resistance*, London: Routledge-Curzon, pp. 158–82.

Wei Dan and Wei Qing (LadyAngel) (2015) *Qiangkou xiao lajiao* [Pungent Little Pepper] Online. Available: http://Qkxlj.blog.163.com (accessed 17 March 2015).

Woronov, T.E. (2009) 'Governing China's children: governmentality and "education for quality"', *Positions*, 17, 3: 567–89.

Xiao Nini (2012) *Houtian meinu yang chengji* [How to be a Beautiful Woman], Beijing: Jingji Kexue Chubanshe.

Xiao Nini (2015) Xiao Nini de xiangrikui xiaoban [Xiao Nini's sunflower class]. Online. Available: http://blog.sina.com.cn/nini1128066 (accessed 19 February 2015).

Xiaoman (2015) *Ai shenghuo, ai Xiaoman* [Love Life, Love Xiaoman]. Online. Available: http://blog.onlylady.com/xiaoman (accessed 30 January 2015).

XiaoP Laoshi (2013–2015) Hi! Wo shi Xiao P laoshi [Hi, I'm teacher XiaoP!]. Online. Available: http://weibo.com/perry28pp (accessed 19 February 2015).

Xu, G. and Feiner, S. (2007) 'Meinü jingji/China's beauty economy: buying looks, shifting value, and changing place', *Feminist Economics*, 13, 3–4: 307–23.

Xu, J.H. (2007) 'Brand-new lifestyle: consumer-oriented programmes on Chinese television', *Media, Culture and Society*, 29, 3: 363–76.

Yang, J. (2010) 'Nennu and shunu: gender, body politics and the beauty economy in China', *Signs*, 36, 2: 333–57.

Zhang, L. (2010) *In Search of Paradise: Middle-Class Living in a Chinese Metropolis*, Ithaca: Cornell University Press.

Zhang, L. and Ong, A. (eds) (2008) *Privatizing China: Socialism from Afar*, Ithaca: Cornell University Press.

'Zhubo Linda liangxiang 2012 Beijing guoji qiche zhanlan wei falali (Ferrari) zhantai' [Anchor Linda unveils 2012 Beijing International Automotive Exhibition of Ferrari] (2012) *Haibao.com*, 25 April. Online. Available: www.haibao.cn/article/199392.htm (accessed 19 February 2015).

Index

Page numbers in *italics* denote tables, those in **bold** denote figures.

For Product Safety Concerns and Information please contact our EU
representative GPSR@taylorandfrancis.com
Taylor & Francis Verlag GmbH, Kaufingerstraße 24, 80331 München, Germany

www.ingramcontent.com/pod-product-compliance
Ingram Content Group UK Ltd.
Pitfield, Milton Keynes, MK11 3LW, UK
UKHW022133190926
475702UK00013B/1778
9781138351486